Occasional Papers
of the
Crow Canyon Archaeological Center

William D. Lipe, *General Editor*
Ruth Slickman, *Copy Editor*
Roy Paul, *Production Editor*

No. 1

The Architecture of Social Integration in Prehistoric Pueblos

Edited by

William D. Lipe and Michelle Hegmon

1989

Members of the Board

Raymond T. Duncan, *Chairman*	C. Paul Johnson
Richard G. Ballantine	John O. Lohre
Albert L. Blum	Marianne O'Shaughnessy
Sara C. Duncan	Stuart M. Struever
Peggy V. Fossett	William R. Thurston
Alden C. Hayes	Edward B. Wasson

The Architecture of Social Integration in Prehistoric Pueblos

The Architecture of Social Integration in Prehistoric Pueblos

Edited by
William D. Lipe and Michelle Hegmon

OCCASIONAL PAPER No. 1
Crow Canyon Archaeological Center
Cortez, Colorado
1989

This book is printed on acid-free archival paper made from
60 percent recycled stock.

© 1989 Crow Canyon Archaeological Center

ISBN 0–9624640–0–7

Library of Congress Catalog Card Number: 89–081117

Table of Contents

List of Figures vii

List of Tables ix

Foreword by Ian M. Thompson xi

Acknowledgments xiii

Chapter 1 – Introduction
    Michelle Hegmon and William D. Lipe 1

Chapter 2 – Social Integration and Architecture
    Michelle Hegmon 5

Chapter 3 – Historical Perspectives on Architecture and Social Integration in the Prehistoric Pueblos
    William D. Lipe and Michelle Hegmon 15

Chapter 4 – Ritual Facilities and Social Integration in Nonranked Societies
    Michael A. Adler 35

Chapter 5 – Social Scale of Mesa Verde Anasazi Kivas
    William D. Lipe 53

Chapter 6 – Ritual and Nonritual Activities in Mesa Verde Region Pit Structures
    Mark D. Varien and Ricky R. Lightfoot 73

Chapter 7 – Unstuffing the Estufa: Ritual Floor Features in Anasazi Pit Structures and Pueblo Kivas
    Richard H. Wilshusen 89

Chapter 8 – Potluck in The Protokiva: Ceramics and Ceremonialism in Pueblo I Villages
    Eric Blinman 113

Chapter 9 – The Styles of Integration: Ceramic Style and Pueblo I Integrative Architecture in Southwestern Colorado
    Michelle Hegmon 125

Chapter 10 – Ritual, Exchange, and the Development of Regional Systems
    Stephen Plog 143

Chapter 11 – Changing Form and Function in Western Pueblo Ceremonial Architecture from A.D. 1000 to A.D. 1500
    E. Charles Adams 155

Chapter 12 – Kivas?
    Stephen H. Lekson 161

Chapter 13 – Comment on Social Integration and Anasazi Architecture
    T. J. Ferguson 169

Contributors 175

List of Figures

Chapter 1

    Figure 1: The Southwest. . . . . .Facing page 1

    Figure 2: The Pueblo area. 2

Chapter 4

    Figure 1: Low-level integrative facility size (in m^2) plotted against village population. 39

    Figure 2: Comparison of numbers of ritual and nonritual activities in all integrative facilities. 40

    Figure 3: Village population plotted against use-group population, low-level integrative facilities. 42

    Figure 4a: Use-group population plotted against integrative structure size (m^2), including all low-level integrative facilities. 43

    Figure 4b: Detail of Figure 4a, including only societies with two or more low-level integrative facilities and smaller than 80 m^2. 43

    Figure 5: Size of use-group plotted against size of integrative facilities, including all low- and high-level facilities. 44

    Figure 6: Size of use-group plotted against size of integrative facilities (m^2), including prehistoric Northern Anasazi kivas. 46

Chapter 5

    Figure 1: Prudden's "unit type pueblo" (after Prudden 1903: Figure 6). 54

    Figure 2: Plan map of Sand Canyon Pueblo (5MT765). 60

    Figure 3: Plan map of Goodman Point Pueblo (5MT604). 61

    Figure 4: Plan map of Green Lizard Site (5MT3901). 62

Chapter 6

    Figure 1: Plan map of architecture and excavation units at the Duckfoot site. . .74

    Figure 2: Intracommunity organization model proposed by the Dolores Archaeological Program (After Kane 1983). 76

    Figure 3: Inferred interhousehold organization at the time of initial construction and main occupation at Duckfoot. 77

    Figure 4: One possible interpretation of interhousehold organization immediately before abandonment. 77

    Figure 5: Front-to-back distribution of metates and manos from floor contexts only. 78

    Figure 6: Front-to-back distribution of complete ceramic vessels from floor contexts only. 78

    Figure 7: Front-to-back distribution of partial ceramic vessels, sherd containers, and modified sherds from floor contexts only. 78

    Figure 8: Front-to-back distribution of other floor artifacts. 79

Figure 9: Side-to-side distributions of metates and manos from floor contexts, grouped by inferred interhouseholds at abandonment. 80

Figure 10: Side-to-side distribution of complete ceramic vessels from floor contexts, grouped by inferred interhouseholds at abandonment. 80

Figure 11: Side-to-side distribution of artifacts from floor contexts, grouped by inferred interhouseholds at abandonment. 81

Figure 12: Front-to-back distribution of floor features. 82

Figure 13: Side-to-side distribution of floor features grouped by inferred interhouseholds at abandonment. 83

Figure 14: Map of the Duckfoot site architectural units showing burned (shaded) versus unburned structures. 84

Chapter 7

Figure 1: Typical pit structure plans, Basketmaker III to Pueblo V. 92

Figure 2: Pueblo I villages in the Dolores area, with enlargement of McPhee Village roomblocks. 93

Figure 3: Plan map of Pit Structure 201, Rio Vista Village (Site 5MT2182). . . .95

Figure 4: Zia altar. 96

Figure 5: Examples of Dolores pit structures with the three sipapu types defined by the DAP. 97

Figure 6: Plans and profiles of two central vaults in Dolores pit structures. . . . 101

Chapter 8

Figure 1: Plan of the roomblocks of McPhee Village. 114

Figure 2: Histogram of pit structure areas for the excavated pit structures of McPhee Village. 115

Figure 3: Cumulative frequency curves of cooking jar sherd rim radii for A.D. 840–880 and A.D. 880–900 refuse from McPhee Village. 119

Chapter 9

Figure 1: Design neatness examples. 132

Figure 2: Attributes used in information statistics. 132

Figure 3: Information statistics compared across categories. 136

Chapter 10

Figure 1: Representations of two different systems of interaction. 144

Chapter 13

Figure 1: Kroeber's schematic model of Zuni social structure. 170

Figure 2: Kroeber's hypothetical scheme of Puebloan social structure. 170

List of Tables

Chapter 4
    Table 1: Ethnographic data. 37

Chapter 5
    Table 1: Anasazi and Pueblo architectural data. 56

Chapter 7
    Table 1: Kruskal-Wallis one-way analysis of variance in pit structure floor area with groupings based on sipapu type 102

Chapter 8
    Table 1: Red ware frequencies in A.D. 860–900 refuse from McPhee Village. . 118
    Table 2: Cooking jar and decorated bowl frequencies in A.D. 840–900 refuse from McPhee Village. 119
    Table 3: Bowl sherd frequencies in A.D. 880–900 refuse from McPhee Village. 121
    Table 4: Red ware vessel form frequencies in A.D. 880–900 refuse from McPhee Village. 122

Chapter 9
    Table 1: Ceramic assemblages used in the analysis. 127
    Table 2: Information statistics and sample sizes. 134
    Table 3: Information statistics compared across categories. 135
    Table 3a: Average values of information statistics by category. 135
    Table 3b: Average values of information statistics by time period. 135
    Table 3c: Assemblage information statistics in relation to period means. . . . 135
    Table 4: Neatness scores by category. 136
    Table 5: Comparison of neatness scores. 136

Chapter 10
    Table 1: Average frequencies of red and orange wares per room and of Dogoszhi-style white wares on habitation sites with and without ceremonial structures. 149

x

Foreword

This is the inaugural volume of a new publication series, the Occasional Papers of the Crow Canyon Archaeological Center. Many of the papers included here were first presented in a symposium sponsored by the Crow Canyon Archaeological Center at the 1988 meeting of the Society for American Archaeology in Phoenix. Since that time a great deal of effort has been invested by the editors, the authors, and additional members of the Crow Canyon staff toward making this volume possible.

The Crow Canyon Archaeological Center is a private, not-for-profit institution headquartered on a permanent campus near Cortez, Colorado. The Center is committed to excellence in archaeological research and education. Research is conducted by a staff of veteran archaeologists assisted by lay participants from throughout the country. Although the Crow Canyon campus is surrounded by hundreds of prehistoric Puebloan sites, the Center's research is not only focused upon the archaeological resources of the immediate region, but also includes various commitments, such as hosting professional conferences, to compare its work with other research in the greater American Southwest and beyond.

Research at Crow Canyon relies upon a unique collaboration among thousands of people and among numerous institutions: The Center's lay participants—both students and adults—generous private foundations and individuals, research interns and volunteers, visiting graduate students, consulting scholars, the National Science Foundation, the Bureau of Land Management, the National Park Service, owners of private lands containing archaeological sites, a Board of Trustees with the commitment necessary to support experimentation and innovation, the Chairman's Council, Native American lecturers and participants, and a staff which long ago forgot the meaning of a forty-hour week.

It is to all of these contributing individuals and institutions that this volume is dedicated.

IAN M. THOMPSON
Executive Director
The Crow Canyon Archaeological Center
October, 1989

Acknowledgments

We want first to thank the authors who generously contributed chapters to this volume. We appreciate not only their prompt submission of manuscripts and quick responses to our editorial comments, but the enthusiasm and good humor with which they approached these tasks. We are pleased to have been able to facilitate what has been very much a cooperative publishing venture.

A camera-ready version of the volume was produced by computer at the Crow Canyon Center. This initial venture into desktop publishing ultimately required the help, tolerance, or cooperation of nearly everyone on the Crow Canyon staff, as well as many on the "outside." Notable for their contributions were Copy Editor Ruth Slickman and Production Editor Roy Paul. Both donated many hours of their own time to the work. We especially appreciate the patience and care with which they attended to the many changes we requested. Crow Canyon Executive Director Sandy Thompson provided encouragement when it was most needed.

Roy Paul selected the type faces, designed the page layouts, and formatted the entire volume on the computer. Lisa Shifrin of Washington State University did the majority of the drafting for the book, and Rhonda Conley of Triticum Press in Pullman, Washington, made photo-mechanical transfers (PMTs) of a number of the figures. The cover was designed by Nancy Leach of Graphic Interpretations in Durango, Colorado, and the book was printed by Arizona Lithographers, Incorporated, of Tucson, Arizona.

Gifts from George Feldman, Robert Seiffert, and Stefan Brecht helped make publication possible, as did assistance from Lewis Sullivan and Arizona Lithographers, Inc. We are most grateful for this support.

WILLIAM D. LIPE
　and
MICHELLE HEGMON

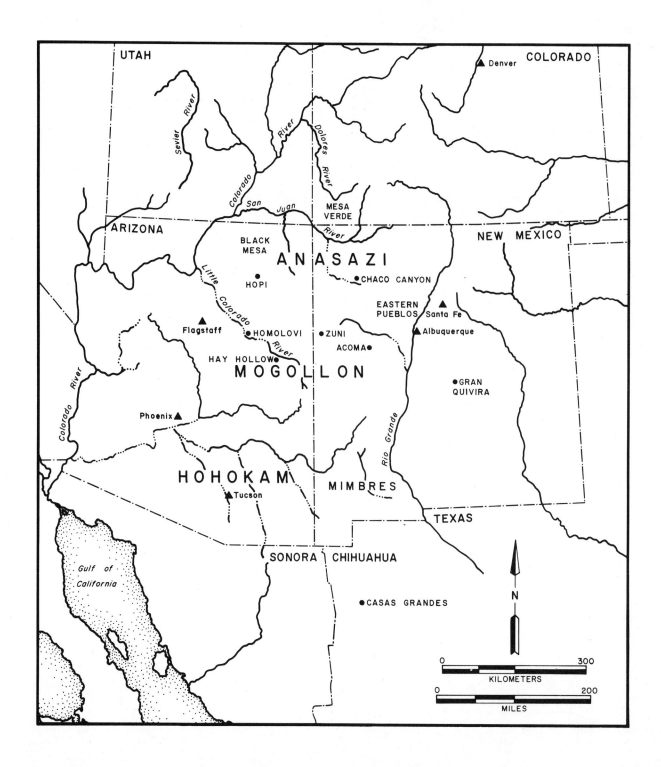

Figure 1: The Southwest

1
Introduction

Michelle Hegmon and William D. Lipe

For over 100 years, archaeologists working in the American Southwest (Figure 1) have looked to architecture in their studies of social integration in the prehistoric pueblos. Kivas in particular have been singled out for their role in integration, from the very earliest attempts to interpret prehistoric pueblos up to today. For example, Lewis Henry Morgan, in recounting his visit to Aztec Ruin in 1878, remarks that

> In the open court ... is another estuva [kiva] of great size.... These estuvas, which are used as places of council, and for the performance of their religious rites, are still found at all the present occupied pueblos in New Mexico (Morgan 1965[1881]:208-209).

Following this tradition, not only kivas but also protokivas (Morris 1939), Great Kivas (Plog 1974; Vivian and Reiter 1960), tri-walled structures (Vivian 1959), plazas (Adams, this volume), shrines (Rohn 1977:109-115) and other structures and features have been interpreted as important for ritual and other integrative activities. Debate over identifying and interpreting these structures—"When is a kiva?" (Smith 1952), "How are kivas used?" (Lekson 1988), "What is the function of tri-walled structures?" (Vivian 1959)—has also become an established tradition in Pueblo archaeology.

In this volume we continue in both traditions. The papers offer new perspectives and data on the roles that architectural features and facilities played in prehistoric pueblo integration. This first section (Chapters 1–3) provides a general introduction to the issues. It is followed by eight analytical papers that use a variety of methods and draw on data from several parts of the northern Southwest (Figure 2) to address the relationship between architecture and integration. The volume concludes with two sets of comments on the analytical papers.

The chapters in the first section provide a theoretical and historical perspective on architecture, integration, and kivas and serve as an introduction to the analytical papers that follow. In Chapter 2 Hegmon provides theoretical background to the relationship between architecture and social integration, with an emphasis on the role of ritual. She then examines the relationship in ethnographically known Pueblo societies. Lipe and Hegmon (Chapter 3) review various archaeological approaches to the study of architecture and integration including ethnographic analogy, functional classification of architectural space, community pattern analysis, and artifactual studies. They provide a historical and analytical perspective to each approach and discuss the contribution of the analytical papers in this light.

In section two (Chapters 4–11) the authors approach questions of architecture and integration by analyzing architectural form, both functionally and in relation to site structure, by discussing the form and distribution of floor features within structures and by looking at the distribution of artifact types and attributes in relation to types of structures. These analytical chapters are ordered chronologically and also with regard to the classes of data analyzed. The papers by Adler (Chapter 4) and Lipe (Chapter 5) both examine the relationship of public architecture to community structure. Adler takes the fairly unusual though eminently sensible approach of going beyond the Southwest to explore factors that affect the presence and use of integrative architecture. He bases his research on a survey of ethnographic literature from across the world, and then applies his findings to prehistoric and historic kivas. Lipe also takes a broad approach, though he stays in the Southwest and focuses on data from the Mesa Verde area. Using as his model a classic paper by Julian Steward (1937), Lipe examines room-to-kiva ratios from the Pueblo I through the ethnographic periods.

Varien and Lightfoot's paper (Chapter 6) begins a series of four chapters that focus on the northern San Juan region during the Pueblo I period. They present a detailed analysis of the Duckfoot Site, comparing artifacts, features, and abandonment mode among the four

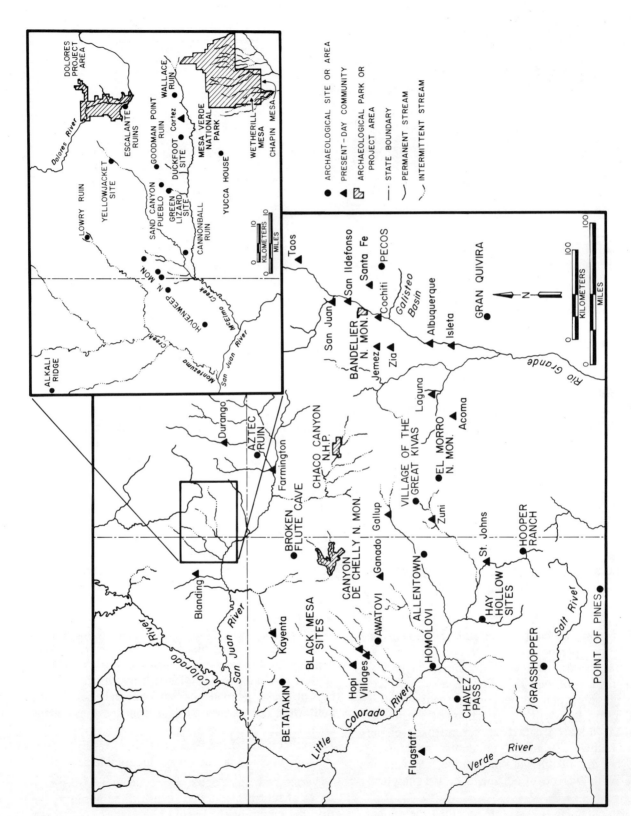

Figure 2: The Pueblo area.

pit structures and between the pit structures and surface rooms. Wilshusen (Chapter 7) also examines variation among pit structures, based principally on differences in sipapus and other ritual features. His most detailed analysis involves Dolores area Pueblo I pit structures, but he also looks at later pit structures/kivas and draws on ethnographic information. Blinman (Chapter 8) and Hegmon (Chapter 9) both use Wilshusen's feature analysis (along with information on size and other architectural associations) in their analyses of ceramics associated with different classes of Pueblo I pit structures. Blinman focuses on different wares and vessel forms, and Hegmon analyzes design style in black-on-white ceramics.

Plog (Chapter 10) also examines the association of ceramics with ritual architecture, though in another place and time. He looks at the association of the (possibly symbolic) Dogoszhi style and of imported red wares with kivas on Black Mesa. Adams (Chapter 11) discusses the latest prehistoric period in the Western Pueblo area and examines changes in kiva form and village layout in relation to the changing role of ritual, including the katsina cult, in cultural adaptation.

Finally, comments on the eight analytical chapters are offered in the concluding section. Lekson (Chapter 12), who has recently (1988) expressed his doubts that many prehistoric kivas functioned as specialized ceremonial structures, examines the analytical papers from this viewpoint. Because several of the authors had reacted to his 1988 paper (or to the version presented at the 1985 SAA meetings), he discusses the differing interpretations, backing off from some of his original points, clarifying and shoring up others. The debate continues. Ferguson (Chapter 13) uses a discussion of Zuni kivas and social integration as the starting point for considering some basic theoretical and methodological issues raised but not resolved by the papers in this volume. His concluding discussion outlines problems that need to be pursued in further research on this topic.

This volume developed out of the symposium "Architecture and Integrative Rituals: Anasazi Analyses," organized by Lipe and Hegmon and presented at the 53rd Annual Meeting of the Society for American Archaeology in Phoenix, Arizona. Eight papers by nine authors were presented at the symposium, and seven of these papers are included in the analytical section of this volume; all the papers have been revised since the SAA meeting, and several have been substantially expanded. Lekson and Ferguson served as symposium discussants, and their comments, revised in reaction to the revised analytical papers, are presented in the discussion section. The paper by Blinman and the introductory papers by Hegmon and by Lipe and Hegmon were prepared exclusively for this volume.

References

Lekson, Steve
1988   The Idea of the Kiva in Anasazi Archaeology. *The Kiva* 53:213-234.

Morgan, Lewis Henry
1965   *Houses and House-Life of the American Aborigines.* Reprinted by the University of Chicago Press, Chicago. Originally published 1881, as *Contributions to North American Ethnology, vol. 4.* U.S. Government Printing Office, Washington, D.C.

Morris, Earl
1939   *Archaeological Studies in the La Plata District, Southwestern Colorado and Northwestern New Mexico.* Carnegie Institution of Washington Publication No. 519. Washington, D.C.

Plog, Fred
1974   *The Study of Prehistoric Change.* Academic Press, New York.

Rohn, Arthur
1977   *Cultural Change and Continuity on Chapin Mesa.* The Regents Press of Kansas, Lawrence.

Smith, Watson
1952   *Excavations in Big Hawk Valley, Wupatki National Monument, Arizona.* Museum of Northern Arizona Bulletin No. 24. Flagstaff.

Steward, Julian
1937   Ecological Aspects of Southwestern Society. *Anthropos* 32:87-104.

Vivian, Gordon
1959   *The Hubbard Site and Other Tri-Wall Structures in New Mexico and Colorado.* National Park Service Archeological Research Series No. 5. Washington, D.C.

Vivian, Gordon and Paul Reiter
1960   *The Great Kivas of Chaco Canyon and Their Relationships.* Monographs of the School of American Research No. 22. Santa Fe.

2
Social Integration and Architecture

Michelle Hegmon

Architectural remains delineate prehistoric communities, and architectural spaces and boundaries—the built environment—help to create the social order that maintains living communities. This chapter examines the role of architecture in the social integration of non-hierarchical societies. Group rituals are essential to that integration, and architecture provides both shelter and symbolic content for the rituals. Social groups are often united or divided by the construction and use of shared structures. In ethnographically known Pueblo societies architecture is closely tied to ritual and ritual societies, though many social groupings are not differentiated architecturally. Pueblo architecture thus discourages extreme social segmentation and contributes to social integration.

To the archaeologist studying a site plan, architectural remains can outline the structure of the prehistoric community. The spaces occupied by the prehistoric inhabitants and the walls that constrained their movements are often clear, even with only sparse remains. Architecture constitutes the built environment; it is constructed by people in response to their needs and their conception of how both their community and the universe are ordered. Furthermore, once constructed, the built environment can contribute to maintaining and reinforcing social order, or if modified, the built environment can help to transform that order.

The most mundane and most grandiose architecture can be related to cultural conceptions of the universe. Bourdieu (1973) demonstrates how the two-room Berber house (the larger room is for humans, the smaller for livestock) in both its internal organization and relationship to the outside world is a microcosm of the same oppositions that govern the Berber universe. And in the same vein, though on a larger scale, the form of the medieval imperial Hindu city Vijayanagara is seen to embody "the principles and relationships that constituted the authority of the King" (Fritz 1986:53).

Architecture—particularly walls—can serve to constrain and restrict social relationships. The structure and placement of houses in Middle Virginia served to put visitors under scrutiny and protect occupants' privacy (Glassie 1975:120-121). Pre-nineteenth century houses were set far from the road, so a visitor's approach was long and easily observed, though once the door was opened the visitor was admitted directly into the family's main room. Later houses were less distant from the road, but open doors led only to a hallway; access to habitation rooms, especially bedrooms, was much more restricted.

The purpose of this chapter and of many papers in this volume is to explore how architecture can contribute to social order and integration. In societies in which order is imposed from above, and architecture reinforces the imperial ideology, the role of architecture in maintaining order is fairly clear-cut. However, in less hierarchical societies, including those that are the focus here, order depends more on integration and cooperation than on force. Architecture may help to define groups of individuals, but how does it contribute to the integration of those individuals into a social group or community? In order to approach this question, I begin by examining the nature of integration.

Integration and Ritual

Integration is the interdependence of units in a given organization. In relatively sedentary societies with non-coercive leadership (including, I would argue, most if not all Pueblo societies), integration is a particularly interesting and important problem. In sedentary societies people live and work together or in close proximity over extended periods. Therefore, conflicts and disagreements must be resolved; sedentary people, unlike mobile foragers, cannot avoid most problems simply by moving away (Lee and DeVore 1968:9; but see Silberbauer [1982:33] for a discussion of the serious implications of moving away by G/wi foragers). Fission is an option occasionally exercised by sedentary communities, but it represents a fairly drastic measure with long-term consequences (Whiteley 1988). Furthermore, recent formulations have emphasized that aggregated communities cannot be assumed to "arise naturally out of human sociability" (Johnson and Earle 1987:316), and these communities may be unstable in the absence of some kind of integrating mechanisms. Lacking leaders with the power to impose sanctions, maintain formal social control, or enforce decisions, such communities must achieve social integration by other means.

Social integration in sedentary societies with non-coercive leadership is achieved through a complex array of lines of cooperation and communication (see Braun and Plog 1982 for a recent summary). Households consisting of one or a few nuclear families are often the basic units of production and consumption. Hence, the basic social segments are quite small and have considerable economic independence. Kinship is usually the dominant principle in organizing social relations in these societies, and extended families and/or descent groups often play important roles in linking households and regulating social relationships among them. Integration of kin-based groups also is achieved through organizations such as age-grades, religious societies, or other sodalities that cross-cut groupings based on kinship and residence (Service 1971:102). Regional integration above the level of the local group is maintained through negotiated alliances or through extended kinship ties, such as the segmentary lineage system.

These organizations—households, extended families, descent groups, sodalities, alliances—provide the basis for social integration. However, an understanding of integration also requires an understanding of how organizations maintain order and how they extend their influence to other units. That is, why do people share their food with a distant third cousin? Why do they go to war to help the group across the valley?

Shared cultural norms may encourage cooperation. Some degree of order also is achieved through gift-giving and friendships, through informal controls such as gossip and witchcraft accusations, and through fear of retribution. However, an important and perhaps primary means of maintaining order in sedentary societies with non-coercive leadership is ritual, which links the ideological with the social.

A ritual is a relatively invariant and formal sequence of actions that is established by tradition (Rappaport 1979:175). Ritual is a form of communication that is neither unique to humans nor always religious—for example, etiquette is social ritual that depends on and reinforces social convention, but is not necessarily based on a religious ideology. However, religious rituals are uniquely human, and are a particularly important means of integration because they can endow ideological messages communicated in ritual with a degree of sanctity (Rappaport 1971a). Sanctification of the information communicated in ritual increases the likelihood that it will be considered truthful, and that it will be acted upon in a predictable and orderly manner (Rappaport 1971a:69). In fact, in societies lacking coercive leadership, sanctity can be seen as "a functional alternative to political power" (Rappaport 1971a:72). Religious rituals (including rituals that invoke traditions as well as those directly addressing supernatural beings) provide reasons to share with the third cousin: "Because it is traditional," or "It will please the ancestors," or "Because the gods said so."

Religious ritual promotes social integration in at least three general ways. First, participating in ritual and sharing the transcendent or numinous experiences it sometimes produces can reinforce social norms and promote social solidarity (Durkheim 1965 [1912]; Wallace 1966). Second, because ritually communicated information is sanctified, ritual can serve to sanctify and hence promote the acceptance of important social decisions such as the choice of a leader or mate, or entry into a war (Rappaport 1971a). Finally, in some cases ritual may help regulate aspects of the sociocultural system, including the distribution of food during lean months (Ford 1972) and the intensity and timing of various ecological relationships (Rappaport 1968).

Rituals can be conducted at various levels of social scale or inclusiveness, ranging from individuals and households to any of the organizations—descent groups, sodalities, regional alliances—that are part of the social structure of integration. Individual and household rituals are certainly important means of reinforcing tradition and social norms. However, rituals above the household level are essential to social integration, since such group rituals are an important means of sanctifying decisions or regulating systems at the community or regional level. In societies based on local group organization (relatively aggregated settlements consisting of from about 100 to 500 individuals) ceremonialism (group ritual) is pervasive and is also important for publicly defining local groups and their regional relationships (Johnson and Earle 1987:20, 199-200).

The Architecture of Integration

In societies that lack strong political institutions, group rituals involving more than one household are essential to social integration. To the extent that group rituals are conducted in a built environment, architecture takes on an important role in the ritual and hence in social integration. Furthermore, the social order can be reinforced in the spatial order defined by the architecture.

Architecture contributes to integration by defining boundaries and by symbolically reinforcing ideology and social norms. It is constructed in a historical and social context, and the intended uses of an architectural facility will ordinarily be considered in its design and construction. Thus the social context will, in a sense, have shaped the structure. In turn, the form of the structure will continue to shape the activities that take place within it and the perceptions of the participants. Therefore, the relationship between architecture and society is an active and dynamic one. The role of architecture in social integration can be conceived of in terms of both socio-spatial and symbolic components (McGuire and Schiffer 1983).

Members of a group must gather, often in a special place, in order to conduct group rituals. Architecture—including both buildings and bounded open spaces such as plazas—can provide that place. The size and form of the facility will set outside limits on the numbers of people who can participate, and on the kinds of activities that can be conducted. Scheduling of integrative activities may vary, depending on whether the space is completely enclosed or open to the elements. Degree of enclosure may also affect the separation of ritual space from other uses, and the extent to which unwanted participants or prying eyes can be excluded.

In most non-stratified societies, structures used for group ritual are built by the shared labor of those who will use them. Communal labor and special shared investments can create or reinforce social relationships. For example, among the Wogeo on an island off the coast of New Guinea, the *Niabwa* or men's house is built with communal labor, and its construction serves as a reconstruction or affirmation of the village social context. Each rafter signifies a plot of land, and the right to put up the rafter is tied to the right to use that land. Thus the Niabwa is a diagram for the parceling of land and the relationship of villagers' land rights and resource rights (Hogbin 1939).

Examples of both "public architecture" (Flannery 1972:38-39; 1976:334-335) and restricted ritual space abound in the literature on sedentary societies (see references in Adler, this volume). Some sort of public place or "dance ground" is characteristic even of small local groups with relatively non-complex political structures (Johnson and Earle 1987: Table 11). And in Mesoamerica the earliest public buildings are associated with early Formative villages, though cleared public spaces are known from earlier non-sedentary periods (Drennan 1976, 1983; Flannery 1976). Restricted ritual space is evident at the early Neolithic site of Çatal Hüyük in Turkey, where the location of shrines in relatively small rooms implies that access was limited to relatively few people at a time (Mellaart 1975:101).

The spatial and symbolic components of architecture are closely interconnected. Architectural structures and boundaries can physically express and reinforce some of the categories and distinctions recognized by a society. Architectural symbolism also derives from the specific historical associations built into the form and location of buildings, and from the symbolism of the various ritually-used features or paraphernalia associated with the structure.

The spatial order that is architecture embodies and thus "experientially and visibly" reinforces the social order basic to social integration (Kus 1982). Bourdieu (1973,1977) shows how the Berber house embodies basic cultural principles of opposition including male/female, culture/nature, and public/domestic, and he argues that a child growing up in that environment will assimilate these principles (1977:88). Similarly, the Karen (Thailand) house is seen as "a reflection, manifestation, and cause of the (socially constructed) reality" that embodies symbolic statements about male/female, chief/commoner relationships and helps to socialize the next generation (Hamilton 1987). The order need not always involve oppositions. Fritz (1987) argues that different forms of architectural symmetry in Chaco architecture convey relationships among social groups, including the indefinite repetition of structurally equivalent social units (translational symmetry), pairs of units such as moieties (mirror symmetry), and reciprocal relationships (rotational symmetry).

The ability of architecture to define and confine, include and exclude, makes the spatial arrangement of structures in a settlement a mnemonic or guide to expected social behaviors and social groupings. Bohannan (1965) suggests that this quality enables archaeologists and social anthropologists to employ a kind of proxemic analysis (e.g., Hall 1969) of architecture—that is, to use architectural arrangements as a mapping of what social groupings and spatial activity patterns were emphasized in a particular settlement. However, the social arrangements expressed when a complex of structures was built may change during the lifetime of the architecture. Parsons (1940) discusses how differential growth and shrinkage of unilineal kin groups in pueblos would soon modify a residential pattern that started with the kin groups occupying discrete blocks of rooms.

The bounding and defining qualities of architecture enable it to symbolize both groupings and divisions in a community, properties of social structure that group rituals must also reinforce. Thus, a ritually used architectural space may come to symbolize the group that controls access to it and uses it to conduct rituals that integrate and legitimize the group. Among the Melpa of the New Guinea Highlands "possession of a ceremonial ground is a matter of pride for group-segments and individual men. In fact, ceremonial grounds are closely connected with the fact of group segmentation" (Strathern 1971:40). Plazas, dance grounds and the like are also often the settings for ceremonials that allow different groups to display their numbers and prowess (Rappaport 1968:169), or that dramatize both the separateness and linkage of different social segments as they interact in a ritual performance.

Structures that house group rituals tend to be distinctive from ordinary habitations (Rapoport 1982:29-30) and to require construction investments that exceed utilitarian requirements (McGuire and Schiffer 1983:281). These expectations should be true even if the structure is not used exclusively for ritual. The distinctive characteristics reinforce, and perhaps help to sanctify, the ritual activities that the structures house. Rapoport (1982:40-41) documents the cues—whitewash, a bell tower, a pitched roof—that distinguish churches as special places in village communities.

Some architecture embodies symbolic meanings that reaffirm world view or contribute to ritual. Many dwellings, including Navajo hogans (Rapoport 1969b) and Pawnee lodges (Rapoport 1969a:50-52) symbolically represent a microcosm of the universe. Tukanoan community houses symbolically recreate the origin of the patrilineal group (Oliver 1987:164-165). Navajo ceremonial sweat lodges maintain a special link with the past because they are built using the traditional forked-stick construction method, which is no longer used for ordinary dwellings (Kluckhohn et al. 1971: 144, 318,320; Rapoport 1969b:74). And some structures are actually incorporated into ritual; for example, structures that house initiation rites symbolically become part of the ritual by providing "a cavity, which symbolizes the womb from which (a man) is reborn after initiation" (Oliver 1975:13).

Ritual structures also often house facilities and equipment necessary for the ritual. Storage of special ritual paraphernalia may be an important function of certain structures, and Flannery (1976) documents the importance of ritual paraphernalia in the interpretation of prehistoric structures. Of course, ritual material need not be stored in the same place that the ritual is conducted. Ritual features—including altars, shrines and other means of connecting this world with another—are important components of many ritual places. Ritual features clearly indicate the presence of ritual in a certain place, whether it is a domestic house or a specialized public building (Deal 1987).

As indicated by some of the examples discussed above, architecture and other forms of material culture are important media for the symbolic transmission of basic information. Language, actualized through speech and, in some societies, writing, clearly has a unique and perhaps primary role in symbolic communication. Language provides a highly flexible, precise, and rapid means of communication. But material culture, including architecture, can provide an important channel for transmitting certain kinds of information that may not be best communicated by language (see Wobst 1977). The large, permanent, three-dimensional nature of architecture makes it and the information it transmits a basic component of the physical environment. Furthermore, while speech is a transient event, architecture provides a medium that can transmit information continuously, and through both visual and tactile means. The permanence and continuity of materially and architecturally transmitted information may be particularly important in societies that lack writing (which is language expressed in material form, see Bourdieu 1977:89).

These characteristics of architecture make it a medium particularly well-suited to some special messages. The messages transmitted by material media often lack the precision and discursive qualities of verbal communication. But these lacks are not necessarily disadvantages. The non-discursive, sometimes vague messages cannot easily be disputed or falsified, and therefore may invoke a sense of timelessness similar to that of ultimate sacred propositions (Rappaport 1971b). The omnipresence of the architecture may contribute to the timelessness of the messages. Furthermore, information communicated through architecture is highly redundant, in that it is transmitted continuously and through at least two senses (vision and touch). Redundancy increases the predictability of the information while decreasing the amount of unique information that can be transmitted. Thus, redundancy can increase the accuracy of a message, and it is an important means of increasing the probability that the message will be received and accepted (see discussions of redundancy in Campbell 1982:72 and Pollock 1983:362-363).

As a medium of communication, architecture thus shares many qualities with ritual. The actions and key symbols of ritual are often refractory to verbal interpretation, but this does not lessen their importance (Rappaport 1979:199; Turner 1982:18). The complexity and uncertainty that are part of ritual contribute to its resilience (Lewis 1980:8-9). Furthermore, religious ritual serves to sanctify information and thus imparts a quality of "unquestionable truthfulness" to that information (Rappaport 1971a:69). Ritual involves the performance of a repetitive, invariant sequence of actions (Rappaport 1979: 175-176). Thus, ritually and architecturally transmitted messages share the quality of redundancy; that is, the information will be limited in quantity, but the message will be highly reliable.

The association of certain kinds of architecture and material culture—features, paraphernalia—with religious ritual is not surprising. As channels of information they share many properties. The concreteness and invariance of architecture and other forms of material culture should make them particularly suitable for conveying the same kinds of messages that religious ritual emphasizes—messages about basic values and conceptions of how the world is ordered.

Architecture and Integration in Historic Pueblo Societies

A kiva at Zuni is both an architectural structure (rectangular, and incorporated into the house block) and a social unit (a men's group, part of the Katsina Society). Clearly there is a relationship between social organization and architecture. However, the nature of the relationship and the role of architecture in social integration are highly complex and vary across the different pueblo societies. To conclude what has been to this point a general discussion of architecture and social integration, I will now examine how and to what extent the general principles developed above are supported by evidence from ethnographically known pueblo societies.

At risk of great oversimplification, social organization in historic pueblo societies can be described as a complex array of social categories and groupings. Integration is achieved because these groups and categories cross-cut one another; thus, the divisions created at one level are mediated at another.

Among the Western Pueblo, clans are the basic kinship units; but clans are cross-cut by other social units including, at Zuni, curing societies or fraternities, kiva groups, and gaming parties (Kroeber 1917:150-165, 183-188; see also Ferguson, this volume). Although there is overlap, and individuals often become members of kiva groups and priesthoods because of their clan affiliation, Kroeber (1917:183) argues that the institutions are separate and constitute "different planes of systematization (that) crosscut each other and thus preserve for the whole society an integrity that would be speedily lost if the planes merged and thereby inclined to encourage segregation and fission."

Moieties are the basic kinship units of the Eastern Pueblo, but Ortiz's (1979) description of the San Juan Tewa demonstrates how segmentation is discouraged both through checks and balances between the moieties and through the existence of other levels of organizations. The moieties (summer and winter) are temporally based, they rule during different times of the year and alternate in picking pueblo officials. Furthermore, the moieties are cross-cut by three levels of people paralleled by a tripartite spatial division of the world. The highest level, or Made People, consists of eight priesthoods that coordinate religious as well as subsistence and political activities. Six of these eight priesthoods draw their members from both moieties and "are a strongly cohesive force for San Juan society, because they mediate the sharp distinctions represented by the moiety societies" (Ortiz 1979:283).

Recent arguments have emphasized the inegalitarian and perhaps hierarchical nature of pueblo societies (Upham 1982; though see Ferguson 1981:342 and Ellis 1981:413-414 for opposing views). Clearly not every member of society has equal access to powerful information (Whiteley 1988:69), not every Tewa at San Juan can be a member of the Made People societies, and certain priests and other leaders have a great deal of influence and authority. But obtaining a position of influence and leadership (whether individual or group-based) depends on one's ability to convince others, and positions of leadership are generally not permanent but are rotated (e.g., Eggan 1950:91; Ortiz 1979:285-286). Further, no single status or group controls all the sacred information and ritual practices necessary for the successful operation and reproduction of the society. Thus, order cannot be imposed from above; it depends on some degree of consensus and cooperation, and on mechanisms that will promote integration.

In many respects, ritual is essential to integration in these societies. Pueblo ritual contributes to the continuance and proper balance of both universal forces and social relationships. Ortiz explains that the Tewa world is "not only a well-centered and well-bounded world, but also a well-ordered world, one informed by many explicit ideas for proper conduct even under constantly changing circumstances" (1979:287). Many of the social groupings that are the basis of the organizational structure are defined in terms of their ritual roles and reciprocal ritual obligations. Hopi clans are associated with certain ceremonies (Eggan 1950:90), and, according to Hopi mythology, certain clans were allowed to join a village on the basis of the ceremonies they could perform (Connelly 1979:543). Authority is often phrased in ritual terms (Eggan 1950:106), and community leaders are also often ritual leaders, or their leadership positions are ritually sanctified; several authors use the word "theocratic" to describe leadership systems, e.g., Ladd (1979:488) at Zuni and Lange (1979:373) at Cochiti. Ritual can also play a role in maintaining ecological and economic relationships, including maintaining pure strains of corn (Ford 1980) and regulating the redistribution of food (Ford 1972).

Pueblo rituals are conducted in all sorts of places—in households and at shrines far from the village, as well as in kivas and plazas. However, the pit shrines in kivas and plazas are the "most sacred of spots" (Parsons 1939:309), and kivas and plazas are the loci for most important group rituals or ceremonials (Whiteley 1988:62). Thus, the built environment plays an important role in pueblo ritual.

Archaeologists are arguing with increasing frequency that the prehistoric Anasazi structures they identify as kivas were not used exclusively for ritual (e.g., Cater and Chenault 1988). The same is apparently true for kivas and plazas in ethnographically known pueblo societies. Mindeleff suggested that the traditional kiva may have been used exclusively for ritual, but that the Tusayan kivas he observed in the late 19th Century also served as council houses and men's resorts and were "used as a workshop by the industrious and as a lounging place by the idle" (1891:130). Dozier (1970:140) confirms that kivas are "ceremonial structures which ... serve as theaters, dormitories for unmarried males, and men's workshops."

Furthermore, kivas are not the exclusive loci for ritual objects. Prayer sticks are used or planted in kivas, springs, mountain shrines, caves, and many other places (Parsons 1939:270). Many ritual objects and fetishes are seen as powerful and potentially dangerous, and therefore are often cached in caves away from the village (Parsons 1939:311). Altars and masks used in kiva ceremonials are often stored in individuals' houses (Parsons 1939:344) or in special storage rooms controlled by the social segment in charge of the particular ritual (Dozier 1965:45).

The construction and maintenance of kivas can be interpreted as contributing to social integration. Mindeleff (1891:118-130) describes the construction of a Tusayan kiva, and although he does not emphasize communal labor, he states that it was built by those who were to use it and that it was consecrated by a feast, dance, and naming ceremony. At Jemez Pueblo, the rebuilding of a kiva could both unite the community and affirm its social segments. "The entire community is expected to participate in the main job of raising the walls and laying the roof," though special details are prepared only by members of certain societies (Ellis 1952:149).

Kivas and at least some plazas have a strong symbolic component serving to reaffirm pueblo world view and traditional links with the past. They symbolize in a number of ways the origin myth of people's emergence from a lower world (Ortiz 1969:36-37). The cardinal directions (generally east, west, north, south, up, and down), and their symbolic associations are also represented or laid out in kivas (Hieb 1979:578; Parsons 1939:367). The very important middle (the place of emergence for the Hopi) is symbolically represented at many levels, e.g., by both the sipapu and the kiva (Hieb 1979:579). Similarly, the arrangement of plazas and roomblocks in Tewa villages expresses basic conceptions of the world as a series of concentric levels centered on the *nan sipu* or "earth navel" located in the plaza (Ortiz 1969:18-24; Swentzell 1988). Kivas may also maintain links with the past, because the basic architectural form (though variable in 20th Century Pueblos) apparently developed from the Basketmaker pit houses of antiquity (see Mindeleff's [1891:111-112] theory of survivals in religious architecture, and discussion in Lipe and Hegmon, this volume). Also, Ellis (1952:150) notes that traditional clothing had to be worn for the rededication of the Jemez kiva (though after some argument, blue jeans were permitted).

Although architectural symbolism is clearly documented, linkages between architecture and pueblo social units are often ambiguous. Both Hopi and Zuni clans are dispersed across the pueblo and not localized in certain areas or blocks (Kroeber 1917:103-109), though Adams (1983) found that Western Pueblo clan segments—that is, lineages—do tend to be localized, with doors providing relatively free access within the lineage's area. Both habitation areas and kivas often lack direct social correlates; Hawley definitively states that kivas should not be considered to be clan houses: "characteristically, clans do not have houses" (1950:26). She also documents the range of variability in the association of kivas with social units. The Zuni and Hopi have multiple kivas associated with katsina dance groups and to some extent tied to clans, though these social units are cross-cut by other organizations that do not necessarily have architectural correlates (Hawley 1950:295-296; see also Dozier 1965:43,46). Many Tewa villages have one or two moiety houses used by the moieties for meetings, some ceremonials, and storage of ceremonial paraphernalia. However, most Tewa villages (including San Ildefonso, Nambe, and San Juan) have only one large kiva, used by both moieties for katsina dances (Hawley 1950:289-290).

Conclusions

Many facets of architecture can be tied to social integration. Architectural structures reinforce social and cultural structures both spatially (by regulating movement and bounding social groups) and symbolically (by marking distinctions and by providing concrete associations with elements of history, myth, or world view). Ritual is one of the strongest links between architecture and social integration, especially in non-hierarchical societies. Ritual contributes to social integration by reinforcing cultural norms, by communicating and sanctifying important information, and by serving as a sort of systemic regulator. Architecture contributes by housing the ritual and symbolically reinforcing the ritual's message. As media of communication, architecture and ritual are similarly suited to convey the same kind of information about basic social values and world view.

A broad survey of ethnographic literature reveals examples of every sort of link between architecture and social integration. But the links found in pueblo ethnographies are more limited, at least at first glance. That is, symbolic and ritual meanings are pervasive in kivas and sometimes plazas, yet the association of social units with architectural units is often ambiguous. However, a second look suggests that this absence of clear architectural definition of social units can be a very important aspect of social integration. Pueblo societies are potentially highly segmentary, and social integration depends on the existence of social groupings that cross-cut other social segments. The shared use of kivas and plazas and the cross-cutting of kiva groups by other social units are important aspects of social integration in pueblo societies. Thus, the absence of architectural boundaries—that by affirming the distinctness of social groups, might encourage social segmentation—contributes to Pueblo social integration.

References

Adams, E. Charles
    1983   The Architectural Analogue to Hopi Social Organization and Room Use, and Implications for Prehistoric Northern Southwestern Culture. *American Antiquity* 48:44-61.

Bohannan, Paul
    1965   Introduction. In *Houses and House-Life of the American Aborigines,* by Lewis Henry Morgan. Reprinted by the University of Chicago Press, Chicago. Originally published in 1881 as *Contributions to North American Ethnology,* vol. 4. U.S. Government Printing Office, Washington, D.C.

Bourdieu, Pierre
    1973   The Berber House. In *Rules and Meaning,* edited by M. Douglas, pp. 98-110. Penguin, New York.

    1977   *Outline of a Theory of Practice.* Cambridge University Press, Cambridge, England. (Translated by Richard Nice).

Braun, David P. and Stephen Plog
    1982   Evolution of "Tribal" Social Networks: Theory and Prehistoric North American Evidence. *American Antiquity* 47:504-525.

Campbell, Jeremy
    1982   *Grammatical Man.* Simon and Schuster, Inc., New York.

Cater, John and Mark Chenault
    1988   Kiva Use Reinterpreted. *Southwestern Lore* 54(3):19-32.

Connelly, John C.
    1979   Hopi Social Organization. In *Southwest,* edited by A. Ortiz, pp. 539-553. Handbook of North American Indians, vol. 9, W. G. Sturtevant, general editor. Smithsonian Institution, Washington, D.C.

Deal, Michael
    1987   Ritual Space and Architecture in the Highland Maya Household. In *Mirror and Metaphor: Material and Social Constructions of Reality,* edited by D. W. Ingersoll, Jr. and G. Bronitsky, pp. 171-198. University Press of America, Landham, Maryland.

Dozier, Edward P.
    1965   Southwestern Social Units and Archaeology. *American Antiquity* 31(1):38-47.

    1970   *The Pueblo Indians of North America.* Holt, Rinehart and Winston, New York.

Drennan, Robert D.
    1976   Religion and Social Evolution in Formative Mesoamerica. In *The Early Mesoamerican Village,* edited by K. V. Flannery, pp. 345-368. Academic Press, New York.

    1983   Ritual and Ceremonial Development at the Early Village Level. In *The Cloud People: Divergent Evolution of the Zapotec and Mixtec Civilizations,* edited by K. V. Flannery and J. Marcus, pp. 46-50. Academic Press, New York.

Durkheim, Emile
    1965   *The Elementary Forms of the Religious Life.* Collier Books, New York. Originally published 1912.

Eggan, Fred R.
    1950   *Social Organization of the Western Pueblos.* University of Chicago Press, Chicago.

Ellis, Florence Hawley
    1952   Jemez Kiva Magic and its Relation to Features of Prehistoric Kivas. *Southwestern Journal of Anthropology* 8:147-163.

    1981   Discussion. In *The Protohistoric Period in the North American Southwest,* A.D. 1450–1700, edited by D. R. Wilcox and W. B. Masse, pp. 410-433. Arizona State University Anthropological Research Papers No. 24, Tempe.

Ferguson, T. J.
    1981   The Emergence of Modern Zuni Culture and Society: A Summary of Zuni Tribal History. In *The Protohistoric Period in the North American Southwest,* A.D. 1450–1700, edited by D. R. Wilcox and W. B. Masse, pp. 336-353. Arizona State University Anthropological Research Papers No. 24, Tempe.

Flannery, Kent V.
    1972   The Village as a Settlement Type in Mesoamerica and the Near East. In *Man, Settlement and Urbanism,* edited by P. J. Ucko, R. Tringham, and G. W. Dimbleby, pp. 23-53. Shenkman Publishing Co., Cambridge, Massachusetts.

    1976   Contextual Analysis of Ritual Paraphernalia from Formative Oaxaca. In *The Early Mesoamerican Village,* edited by K. V. Flannery, pp. 333-345. Academic Press, New York.

Ford, Richard I.
    1972   An Ecological Perspective on the Eastern Pueblos. In *New Perspectives on the Pueblos,* edited by A. Ortiz, pp. 1-18. University of New Mexico Press, Albuquerque.

    1980   The Color of Survival. *Discovery 1980:* 17-29. School of American Research, Santa Fe.

Fritz, John M.
    1986   Vijayanagara: Authority and Meaning of a South Indian Imperial Capital. *American Anthropologist* 88:44-55.

    1987   Chaco Canyon and Vijayanagara: Proposing Spatial Meaning in Two Societies. In *Mirror and Metaphor: Material and Social Constructions of Reality,* edited by D. W. Ingersoll, Jr. and G. Bronitsky, pp. 313-349. University Press of America, Landham, Maryland.

Glassie, Henry
    1975   *Folk Housing in Middle Virginia.* University of Tennessee Press, Knoxville.

Hall, Edward T.
    1969   *The Hidden Dimension.* Anchor Books, Doubleday and Co., Garden City, New York.

Hamilton, James W.
    1987   This Old House: A Karen Ideal. In *Mirror and Metaphor: Material and Social Constructions of Reality,* edited by D. W. Ingersoll, Jr. and G. Bronitsky, pp. 247-276. University Press of America, Landham, Maryland.

Hawley, Florence
    1950   Big Kivas, Little Kivas, and Moiety Houses in Historical Reconstruction. *Southwestern Journal of Anthropology* 6:286-302.

Hieb, Louis A.
    1979   Hopi World View. In *Southwest,* edited by A. Ortiz, pp. 577-580. Handbook of North American Indians, vol. 9, W. G. Sturtevant, general editor. Smithsonian Institution, Washington, D.C.

Hogbin, H. I.
    1939   Native Land Tenure in New Guinea. *Oceania* 10(2):113-165.

Johnson, Allen W. and Timothy Earle
    1987   *The Evolution of Human Societies.* Stanford University Press, Stanford, California.

Kluckhohn, Clyde, W. W. Hill, and Lucy Wales Kluckhohn
    1971   *Navajo Material Culture.* The Belknap Press of Harvard University, Cambridge, Massachusetts.

Kroeber, Alfred L.
    1917   *Zuni Kin and Clan.* Anthropological Papers of the American Museum of Natural History, vol. 18, Part II, pp. 39-204. New York.

Kus, Susan
    1982   Matters, Material and Ideal. In *Symbolic and Structural Archaeology,* edited by I. Hodder, pp. 47-62. Cambridge University Press, Cambridge, England.

Ladd, Edmund J.
    1979   Zuni Social and Political Organization. In *Southwest,* edited by A. Ortiz, pp. 482-498. Handbook of North American Indians, vol. 9, W. G. Sturtevant, general editor. Smithsonian Institution, Washington, D.C.

Lange, Charles H.
 1979 Cochiti Pueblo. In *Southwest,* edited by A. Ortiz, pp. 366-378. Handbook of North American Indians, vol. 9, W. G. Sturtevant, general editor. Smithsonian Institution, Washington, D.C.

Lee, Richard B. and Irving DeVore
 1968 *Man the Hunter.* Aldine, Chicago.

Lewis, Gilbert
 1980 *Day of Shining Red: An Essay in Understanding Ritual.* Cambridge University Press, Cambridge, England.

McGuire, Randall H. and Michael B. Schiffer
 1983 A Theory of Architectural Design. *Journal of Anthropological Archaeology* 2:277-303.

Mellaart, James
 1975 *The Neolithic of the Near East.* Charles Scribner's Sons, New York.

Mindeleff, Victor
 1891 *A Study of Pueblo Architecture, Tusayan and Cibola.* Eighth Annual Report of the Bureau of Ethnology to the Secretary of the Smithsonian Institution, 1886–87, pp. 13-228. Government Printing Office, Washington, D.C.

Oliver, Paul
 1975 *Shelter, Sign and Symbol.* Barrie and Jenkins, London.

 1987 *Dwellings: The House Across the World.* University of Texas Press, Austin.

Ortiz, Alfonso
 1969 *The Tewa World: Space, Time, Being and Becoming in a Pueblo Society.* University of Chicago Press, Chicago.

 1979 San Juan Pueblo. In *Southwest,* edited by A. Ortiz, pp. 278-295. Handbook of North American Indians, vol. 9, W. G. Sturtevant, general editor. Smithsonian Institution, Washington, D.C.

Parsons, Elsie Clews
 1939 *Pueblo Indian Religion.* University of Chicago Press, Chicago.

 1940 Relations between Ethnology and Archaeology in the Southwest. *American Antiquity* 5(3):214-220.

Pollock, Susan
 1983 Style and Information: An Analysis of Susiana Ceramics. *Journal of Anthropological Archaeology* 2:354-390.

Rapoport, Amos
 1969a *House Form and Culture.* Prentice Hall, Inc., Englewood Cliffs, N.J.

 1969b The Pueblo and the Hogan. In *Shelter and Society,* edited by P. Oliver, pp. 66-79. Frederick A. Praeger, Publishers, New York.

 1982 *The Meaning of the Built Environment: A Nonverbal Communication Approach.* Sage Publications, Beverly Hills, California.

Rappaport, Roy A.
 1968 *Pigs for the Ancestors: Ritual in the Ecology of a New Guinea People.* Yale University Press, New Haven, Connecticut.

 1971a Ritual, Sanctity, and Cybernetics. *American Anthropologist* 73:59-76.

 1971b The Sacred in Human Evolution. *Annual Review of Anthropology* 2:23-44.

 1979 *Ecology, Meaning, and Religion.* North Atlantic Books, Richmond, California.

Service, Elman R.
 1971 *Primitive Social Organization: An Evolutionary Perspective.* 2d ed. Random House, New York.

Silberbauer, George
 1982 Political Process in G/wi Bands. In *Politics and History in Band Society,* edited by E. Leacock and R. Lee, pp. 23-35. Cambridge University Press, Cambridge, England.

Strathern, Andrew
 1971 *The Rope of Moka.* Cambridge University Press, Cambridge, England.

Swentzell, Rina
 1988 Bupingeh: The Pueblo Plaza. *El Palacio,* 94(2):14-19.

Turner, Victor
 1982 Introduction. In *Celebration: A World of Art and Ritual,* edited by V. Turner, pp. 12-32. Smithsonian Institution Press, Washington, D.C.

Upham, Steadman
   1982   *Polities and Power.* Academic Press, New York.

Wallace, Anthony F. C.
   1966   *Religion: An Anthropological View.* Random House, New York.

Whiteley, Peter M.
   1988   *Deliberate Acts.* University of Arizona Press, Tucson.

3
Historical and Analytical Perspectives on Architecture and Social Integration in the Prehistoric Pueblos

William D. Lipe and Michelle Hegmon

Archaeologists working in prehistoric Southwestern pueblos have frequently used architectural evidence as the basis for inferences about social organization and social integration. The history and basic logic of several major approaches are reviewed: ethnographic analogy; assignment of functions or uses to architecturally defined spaces; and interpretation of community organization from analysis of differentiation and spatial patterning among structures. Because artifactual and architectural data are generally employed together, the chapter closes with a review of the use of artifacts in the study of social organization and integration in pueblo archaeology.

Below, we review the history of some of the analytic approaches widely used in studying social integration among the prehistoric pueblos. The emphasis is on architectural evidence, but since architecture is often interpreted with the aid of associated artifacts, and vice versa, it seems appropriate to include a section on approaches that emphasize how social integration can be studied with artifactual data. The review that follows is designed to help provide a historical context for the other papers in this volume. It is selectively biased toward work done in the northern part of the Pueblo Southwest, and especially in the San Juan drainage. It does not pretend to be a comprehensive or complete historical treatment of the several topics that it addresses. These topics include functional classification of architecturally defined spaces, community pattern analysis, inferences from properties of artifacts, and ethnographic analogy. Since ethnographic analogy is an issue in all the analytic approaches that are treated below, we begin with a brief discussion of this topic.

Ethnographic Analogy

Despite archaeologists' "chronic ambivalence" about ethnographic analogy (Wylie 1985:107), it remains a major source of behavioral interpretation of prehistoric cultural remains. Analogical interpretation in archaeology has frequently been uncritical and narrowly based, however—in the Southwest and elsewhere. The similarities between archaeological and historic Pueblo material culture and architecture were noted early, and they served to establish what often has been a facile and uncritical reading of the present into the past.

Much of the early systematic archaeological work in the Southwest was based on the assumption that all the prehistoric settlements there represented an undifferentiated Pueblo culture much like that known from history and ethnography. Taylor (1954) called this the "Cushing-Fewkes" period. Subsequent research documented substantial temporal and geographic variability in the archaeological record, and led to the development of cultural taxonomies (e.g., Colton 1939) that reflected variation in the formal aspects of architecture and material culture. Behavioral interpretations of prehistoric architecture and material culture did not begin to undergo explicit reassessment until somewhat later (e.g., Hawley 1950; Anderson 1969; Hill 1966, 1968, 1970a, 1970b). Only in the last few years have questions been raised about some of the major tenets of the analogical model of prehistoric Pueblo life—in particular, there have been serious challenges to the assumption that both the contact period and prehistoric Pueblos were classic tribal, egalitarian societies (e.g., Wilcox 1981; Upham 1982; Lightfoot 1984).

As Lekson has recently argued (1985, 1988), the interpretation of prehistoric Pueblo kivas by generations of Southwestern archaeologists exemplifies the largely unexamined analogies on which many behavioral interpretations of prehistoric Pueblos have been and often continue to be based. Indeed, the inference that prehistoric kivas functioned in the same way as historic ones was made by several influential early observers even without the aid of excavations. For example, in 1849, Lieutenant James H. Simpson wrote of Pueblo Pintado, the first Chacoan site he encountered:

> At different points about the premises were three circular apartments sunk in the ground, the walls being of masonry. These apartments the Pueblo Indians call estuffas [sic], or places where the people held their political and religious meetings [Simpson 1964:37].

Simpson had, within the previous two weeks, visited the *estufas* (kivas) of both Santo Domingo and Jemez in the company of Pueblo informants.

J. W. Powell also knew immediately what he was looking at when he viewed a depression adjacent to a small ruin in the Glen Canyon of the Colorado River, during his pioneering exploration of the Colorado River canyons in 1869. He remarks:

> In the space in the angle [formed by the masonry rooms], there is a deep excavation. From what we know of the people in the province of Tusayan, who are, doubtless, of the same race as the former inhabitants of these ruins, we conclude that this was a 'kiva' or underground chamber, in which their religious ceremonies were performed [Powell 1875:68].

So far as we can determine, Powell was the first to use the Hopi word *kiva* in print, instead of the Spanish *estufa*, a term that had gained popularity on the mistaken presumption that these Pueblo structures were sweatbaths (Mindeleff 1891:111). The ruin Powell visited was partially excavated in 1958 and 1959 during the Glen Canyon reservoir salvage project (Lipe 1960:114-135).

The early uncritical supposition that prehistoric Pueblo kivas all functioned like historic ones became "fossilized" in the early twentieth century when Southwestern archaeologists such as Edgar Hewett made the demonstration of continuities between historic and prehistoric Pueblos the cornerstone of a political battle to establish Pueblo land claims (Lekson 1988). As a result, if any formal similarities in architecture or features could be demonstrated between prehistoric structures and historic kivas, the former were to be called kivas also. Accompanying this kind of formal identification was the generally unstated implication that by analogy the prehistoric kivas housed the same kinds of activities and played the same functional roles in their prehistoric communities as historic period kivas in historic pueblo communities. In other words, the analogical question was posed in either-or terms. Either a prehistoric pit structure was a kiva in the same sense as a historic kiva, or it was interpreted as something else entirely—ordinarily as a domestic pit house, the primary residence of a household (Lekson 1988). Furthermore, the prevailing view of ethnographic kivas emphasized their role as specialized ceremonial structures (e.g., Kidder 1927:490) despite considerable ethnographic evidence that at least Western Pueblo kivas often housed a variety of activities only indirectly related to ceremonies. Although there have been notable exceptions (e.g., Brew 1946; Ambler and Olson 1977; Cater and Chenault 1988), Southwestern archaeologists have tended to accept the either-or form of the analogical question, and to assume that the prehistoric structures that they identify as kivas in fact functioned as specialized ceremonial spaces.

In an "attempt to be provocative rather than conclusive," Lekson (1988) suggests an alternative either-or interpretation: that Anasazi pit structures functioned primarily as domiciliary pit houses until the end of the Pueblo III period at about A.D. 1300, and that "true" kivas displaying the ethnographic pattern of activities and organizational functions emerged only in the Pueblo IV period. His presentation of this view at the 1985 Society for American Archaeology meetings (Lekson 1985) was one of the stimuli for the 1988 SAA session that included the initial versions of most of the papers in this volume.

The functional interpretation of prehistoric kivas and protokivas is a theme that connects all the papers in the volume. Collectively they represent a reassessment, using various lines of evidence and argument, of the analogical identification of prehistoric with historic Pueblo kivas—that is, of the inference that prehistoric kivas functioned in the same way that historic ones did. In the pages that follow this chapter, Adler (Chapter 4) surveys a cross-cultural sample to develop some generalizations about structures used for integrative ritual, thus establishing a basis for general, rather than specific, analogies. Lipe (Chapter 5) and Adams (Chapter 11) examine changes in architectural form and site structure as bases for recognizing changes in the ways kivas and protokivas served community integrative needs. Wilshusen (Chapter 7) traces continuities in feature types and their contexts in pit structures from the A.D. 600s to the ethnographic period. Varien and Lightfoot (Chapter 6) employ a detailed intrasite distributional analysis of both features and artifacts to show functional differences between protokivas and surface rooms in an early pueblo. Blinman, Hegmon, and Plog (Chapters 8–10) all use distributional analyses of artifact types and attributes across a number of sites to test the notion that socially integrative behaviors were differentially associated with Great Kivas, small kivas, or protokivas.

The papers in this volume thus use several lines of evidence and several types of investigation to address the problem of interpreting prehistoric pit structures. In combination, the approaches employed strengthen the assessment of analogies by "expanding the base of interpretation and elaborating the fit between source and subject" (Wylie 1985:101).

The overall result of the studies reported below is to show that either-or forms of the analog question are probably too simple. There are similarities and differences in form and function between prehistoric and historic protokivas and kivas, and the forms and functions of these structures changed substantially through time. Lekson's suggestion that kivas may commonly have had domiciliary functions through the Pueblo II and III periods is given tentative support, but it is also shown that the use of a pit structure to house ritual activities that integrated at least small multihousehold groups can be traced back to the Pueblo I period. In summary, a flexible use of ethnographic analogy, coupled with the examination of several lines of archaeological evidence, can shed new light on an old question and help reformulate it in a more productive way.

Functional Classifications of Architectural Spaces

A long-standing pursuit in Southwestern archaeology is the "functional" classification of architectural spaces into types such as "habitation room," "storage room," "ceremonial room," "kiva," "Great Kiva," "plaza," etc. For example, Fewkes' report (1909) on his work at Spruce-Tree House employed categories such as "plazas and courts," "secular rooms," and "kivas," under the heading "major antiquities." This approach depends on classifying architectural units on the basis of activities inferred to have taken place in them. Strictly speaking, such a classification would seem to be based on *use* rather than *function*, unless the organizational role of the structure in some larger configuration is emphasized. On the other hand, "functional classification" has long been used to refer to this procedure (Ciolek-Torrello 1985:41).

Such classifications depend on the inference of past activities from architectural characters, and/or from associated features or artifacts. Assigning a single "function" or use to an architectural space assumes that a general type of use—e.g., "habitation" was predominant. Archaeologists are increasingly becoming aware of the limitations of these simple monothetic classifications of architectural spaces. For example, gross architectural characteristics may indicate the primary *intended* use of a structure or space; features and importable artifacts may reflect its primary *actual* use during its lifetime, and portable items or remodeling evidence may represent its *last* use or may be thoroughly conditioned by the events surrounding the final *abandonment* of the space (Schiffer 1976, 1985, 1987; Ciolek-Torrello 1985). Furthermore, most architectural spaces probably housed numerous activities, and they may not have been limited to particular architectural types.

Although these issues all provide opportunities for productive and informative research, they are far from being well-understood at this point. Despite the limitations of functional classifications of architecture, the approach is time-honored in Southwestern archaeology, and hence has had a significant effect on how Southwesternists have used architectural evidence to make inferences about social integration, and especially about the character and role of religious ritual in the social integration of prehistoric pueblos.

In Southwestern archaeology there is a long history of inferring ritual and integrative uses for kivas and various other architectural forms, as noted above in the discussion of ethnographic analogy. The following comments survey some of the main kinds of evidence and logic used to make these assignments; a thorough historical treatment is not attempted. Once again, the functional interpretation of kivas occupies the bulk of the relevant literature and serves as a model of the approaches that have been used.

The earliest identifications and interpretations of prehistoric kivas were strongly conditioned by the expectation that prehistoric Pueblo cultures were generally similar to those observed historically and ethnographically. Since historic pueblos had kivas that were used for important ceremonies, late prehistoric pueblos would be expected to have these too. How were the prehistoric examples to be identified? Victor Mindeleff (1891:111) suggests a general interpretive principle:

> *General use of kivas.*—Wherever the remains of pueblo architecture occur among the plateaus of the southwest there appears ... throughout all changes of form ... the evidence of chambers of exceptional character ... distinguishable from the typical dwelling rooms by their size and position, and, generally, in ancient examples, by their circular form [V. Mindeleff 1891:111].

In other words, the architectural distinctiveness of one type of structure set it apart from another type; the formal difference presumably implied a functional difference (for a similar argument, see Smith 1952:162). It then took but a short jump to assign the expected "kiva" function to the prehistoric "chambers of exceptional character."

To the extent that an empirical demonstration was considered necessary, it took the form of showing that "ritual features" were associated with distinctive "kiva architecture." For example, Mindeleff examined surface evidence of a prehistoric circular kiva in the Hopi area, and noted a wall niche, which he identified as a *katchin kihu* or kachina house (V. Mindeleff 1891:117). Because this was a ritually important feature that he had observed in functioning Hopi kivas (V. Mindeleff 1891:121), he inferred that the prehistoric structure was also used for ceremonial purposes. Mindeleff (1891:117) went on to suggest that his observation provided a link between the rectangular kivas common in the historic Western Pueblo area and the earlier circular form, which was rare at Hopi, though common in the San Juan drainage.

Fewkes (1908) also used the presence of a ritual feature—the *sipapu*—to confirm the ceremonial function of circular kivas in the San Juan drainage. He was aware from his own ethnographic observations and his excavations at Awatovi (Fewkes 1898: 613), as well as from the work of V. Mindeleff (1891:117), that sipapus regularly occur in various forms in both historic and prehistoric Hopi kivas. Reporting on the excavations of kivas at Spruce Tree House in Mesa Verde National Park, he remarks about Kiva G:

> There is a small circular opening in the floor representing symbolically the entrance to the underworld, called by the Hopi the *sipapu*. ... The sipapu is the most revered place in the kiva, and about it are performed some of the most sacred rites. ... This is the first recognition in print of a *sipapu* in a circular kiva [Fewkes 1908:391].

In his seminal 1891 publication on Pueblo architecture, Victor Mindeleff had also suggested another interpretive principle—that of survivals—that proved influential in later functional interpretations of kiva, protokiva, and pit house architecture. Mindeleff thought that kiva construction would be likely to display

> ... survivals of early methods of arrangement that have long ago become extinct in the constantly improving art of housebuilding, but which are preserved through the well-known tendency of the survival of ancient practice in matters pertaining to the religious observances of a primitive people [V. Mindeleff 1891:111-112].

This established an expectation that, if they were indeed used for religious purposes, kivas should retain architectural characteristics of earlier residential structures (see also C. Mindeleff 1897:174). The notion of survivals in religious architecture provided a context in which documentation of the gradual appearance of the attributes of "kiva architecture" was implicitly seen as documenting a correspondingly gradual functional shift from residential pit house to specialized ceremonial chamber:

> The findings on Alkali Ridge, considered in conjunction with the work of others, notably Morris, Roberts, and Martin in the San Juan drainage, permit us now to present a more complete story than has ever before been possible of the steps by which the earth lodge of the early agriculturalists on the Colorado Plateau has been transformed into the sacred temple of their modern descendants [Brew 1946:203].

In this scenario, the problem became one of determining how much architectural change was required before a residential pit house could be considered a ceremonial kiva. Hence, a focus on the formal details of architecture (e.g., Lancaster and Pinkley 1952) was appropriate to pursuing the problem, in addition to being consistent with the prevailing taxonomic interests of the 1930s through early 1960s. The concept of the protokiva (Morris 1939:30-31;72) also helped resolve the issue of "When is a kiva?" (Smith 1952) by locating in the Pueblo I period a form architecturally and presumably functionally transitional between pit house and kiva. The circular San Juan kivas of the Pueblo II and III period were generally considered full-fledged ceremonial structures (Brew 1946:213), despite their substantial differences in size, shape, and position when compared with ethnographically described kivas (cf. Lekson 1988).

The "ethnographic model" of room function that developed from these nineteenth and early twentieth century studies posited that at least habitation, storage, and ceremonial structures should be present in prehistoric pueblos (Ciolek-Torrello 1985). This model has often led to the uncritical assignment of structures to these predetermined functional classes on the basis of a cursory analysis of gross architectural characteristics.

In the last several decades, archaeologists have attempted in a number of studies to examine this model critically by treating gross formal variation in architecture as a starting point for functional analysis. That is, variations in the size and form of structures are used as the primary indicators of functional differentiation, but the resulting classification is tested against variability in associated architectural details, features, artifacts, and/or ecofacts. The presumption is that robust functional patterning should be expressed in the covariation among some or all of these kinds of phenomena.

The best-known example of this approach is Hill's work at Broken K Pueblo in Arizona (Hill 1966, 1968, 1970a, 1970b). Hill (1970a) subdivided the population of excavated rooms at Broken K into three groups, on the basis of size and distinctive morphology. After showing that each group also displayed non-random associations of features such as mealing bins, hearths, and ventilators, he hypothesized that there were three functional room classes: habitation, storage, and ceremonial, as in the historic Western Pueblos. On the basis of activities reported to occur in these classes of rooms in Western Pueblo settlements, he developed a list of "test expectations" for archaeological associations of artifacts and ecofacts with these room classes. The archaeological record showed generally good agreement with the expectations, and he concluded that the functional room types at Broken K were similar to those at historic Western Pueblo villages. Although the statistical methods used to reach this conclusion can be criticized (cf. Ciolek-Torrello 1985), our interest here is in the basic logic of the approach.

Adams (1983) has recently assembled evidence to show that gross architectural variation in room size and location correlate well with functional differentiation among rooms in historic and protohistoric Western Pueblo settlements. Hence, he strengthens the ethnographic side of the "ethnographic model."

In a recent study of the social use of space at Turkey Creek Pueblo in east central Arizona, Lowell (1988) showed that a room's hearth type was a good predictor of its size and of other architectural and artifactual variables as well. On this basis, she argued that rooms with rectangular hearths were habitations; rooms with circular hearths were "miscellaneous activity" spaces; and rooms lacking hearths were used for storage. Additionally, two small clusters of rooms were inferred to be "kiva room groups" on the basis of their spatial association with the site's Great Kiva as well as their distinctive pattern of architectural, feature, and artifact characteristics. Lowell (1988) did not argue that these variables specifically indicated ritual activity, only that their pattern of co-occurrence was distinctive. She suggested that the two kiva room groups may have helped link the two main residential divisions of the settlement with the centrally-located Great Kiva, where village-wide integrative activities presumably were carried out.

The paper by Varien and Lightfoot (this volume) also uses gross variation in architectural form (pit structure, front surface room, back surface room) as the starting point for analysis, and uses the associations of features and artifacts to test a null hypothesis that there was no functional difference among the three types of structure. The artifacts and features do in fact vary strongly among the three structure types, and the null hypothesis is rejected. Functional interpretation of the associated artifact and feature assemblages employs a mix of general and specific analogies. The authors conclude that the data are consistent with use of the back rooms primarily for storage and of the front rooms for domestic activity, but that the pit structures show the greatest evidence of both domestic/residential and ritual activities.

Ciolek-Torrello (1978, 1985) used an inductive multivariate pattern-seeking approach to define functional room types by recurrent associations of various floor features and floor artifacts at Grasshopper Pueblo, a large Pueblo IV period site in Arizona. An R-mode factor analysis was used to define five (later reduced to four) factors representing groups of spatially associated variables (i.e., the artifacts and features as distributed across rooms), and these factors were interpreted as representing sets of related activities (e.g., manufacturing, food storage, food preparation, etc.). A Q-mode factor analysis was then used to group the rooms in terms of the pattern of occurrence of the same variables used in the R-mode analysis. The six room groups thus obtained were interpreted as functional types (e.g., limited activity rooms, habitation rooms, etc.). Each room type could be characterized in terms of the proportional representation of the activity sets that comprised the R-mode factors (Ciolek-Torrello 1985:54).

One result of the analysis was that no special class of "ceremonial structures" emerged. Variables that could be interpreted as indicating ritual activities tended to occur within one room type (Limited Activity) but only in about a third of these cases. These variables also were not confined to the three rooms in this class that had "kiva-like" benches (Ciolek-Torrello 1985: 53-55).

The value of this approach is that the resultant groupings are multivariate and polythetic, and hence can be based on a fuller use of the data than can monothetic approaches, which must by definition be based on only a few variables—usually gross architectural characters. The polythetic room types can each be characterized in terms of the relative strength of the several activity factors, rather than having to be considered as the exclusive province of a single kind of activity. Because floor artifacts and features were used in Ciolek-Torrello's analysis, the functional interpretations refer to the late or last uses of the rooms, rather than to intended uses, which might still be recoverable from variation in gross architectural features. The reliance on floor artifacts also makes the analysis subject to the difficulties of determining how site abandonment might have affected the patterns of use and discard which created most of the portions of the archaeological record that were analyzed (cf. Schiffer 1985, 1987). Ciolek-Torrello (1985) has attempted to control for these effects, but much remains to be understood about these assemblage formation processes.

There are other studies of prehistoric pueblos which have creatively addressed the question of functional room types (e.g., Dean 1969; Jorgenson 1975; DeGarmo 1976; Shafer 1982), and countless studies have used the concept in one form or another. The examples discussed above provide a sampling of the range of approaches that have been and continue to be used.

Regarding architectural indicators of social integration, the "functional type" discussions are dominated by the issue of interpreting "ordinary" or "regular-sized" kivas. Other potentially important structures, such as Great Kivas, plazas, shrines, tri-walls, and bi-walls, have received less attention. It seems generally to be assumed that plazas in prehistoric pueblos functioned much the same as they do in historic ones—some critical examination is obviously needed here. The multiple-walled buildings, which lack obvious ethnographic analogs, have been interpreted in a great variety of ways. Rohn (1977) proposes that these structures were involved in some way in rituals that helped integrate dispersed communities; Plog (1974) hypothesizes that they included storerooms, and were used in ritually-mediated food distribution; Vivian (1959) argues that they were domiciles of a "developing priestly class"; while Reyman (1986) suggests some were actually platform mounds, with the multiple chambers giving stability to the structure.

There seems to be general agreement that Great Kivas served as places of assembly for sizable groups, and that they must have housed activities that helped integrate several social segments, commonly from several settlements. Credible analyses that attempt to go beyond this very general kind of functional characterization are rare, though Lightfoot (1988) has recently analyzed the scale of work and cooperation required to build a Great Kiva. Fritz (1978, 1987) explored the layout and features of Chacoan Great Kivas as an expression of aspects of world view, while Plog (1974) discussed the possibilities that Great Kivas were involved in ritually-mediated redistribution. These leads remain largely unfollowed, however.

Community Pattern Analyses

Historically, and to some extent logically, related to the functional classification of architectural spaces are approaches that base inferences about prehistoric organization on the relative frequency and spatial position of structures in and among settlements. At intermediate levels of scale, this has been called "community pattern analysis" (Chang 1958:299) and at larger scale, it merges with settlement pattern studies (Willey 1953, 1956). Today, relational analysis of architectural units at an intrasite scale may often be referred to as part of "site structure analysis."

Spatial/configurational analyses of architecture have generally been used to identify and characterize the size and composition of social or socioeconomic groupings—e.g., households, residence units, communities, and the like. The starting point for this kind of analysis is a "functional" or use-based classification of architectural units. Inferences about the integration of communities or social segments have often depended on the frequency and spatial distribution of structures such as Great Kivas that were presumably used for ceremonies or other socially integrative activities (e.g., Longacre 1966; Lipe 1970).

This approach depends in part on an underlying assumption that humans use space efficiently, if not optimally. That is, it assumes that humans locate their activities to provide easy and regular access to important resources or social interactions. Which social activities and relationships they considered important can therefore be inferred from the spatial relationships among their architectural facilities and artifact assemblages, viewed as products of patterned behavior. Spatial inferences of this sort are of course strengthened when they serve as the basis for hypotheses which are then tested against other types of data, or alternatively, when proximity relationships are used as the tests, and the hypotheses are generated elsewhere.

Another assumption of the spatial/configurational approach is that the frequency and distributional regularity of integrative structures is inversely correlated with the scale or level of integration they are associated with. That is, if kivas are both common and regularly distributed, they must have been used by relatively small and redundant social segments. Great Kivas, on the other hand, are not only large but relatively rare—evidence that they served large numbers of people. This argument is stronger if it can also be shown that the Great Kiva in question was centrally located with respect to a number of habitations (i.e., that the structure was located so that it could be efficiently accessed by a relatively large population).

Inference of social organization from community pattern in the Pueblo Southwest was pioneered by Lewis H. Morgan in *Houses and House-Life of the American Aborigines* (Morgan 1965 [1881]). In this work, he used both archaeological and ethnographic data on domestic architecture, much of it from the Southwest, to support his ideas about the evolution of society that had been developed in *Ancient Society* (Morgan 1985 [1877]):

> House architecture, which connects itself with the form of the family and the plan of domestic life, affords a tolerably complete illustration of progress from savagery to civilization. Its growth can be traced from the hut of the savage, through the communal houses of the barbarians, to the house of the single family in civilized nations ... [Morgan 1975 (1877):6].

Documenting "communal houses" was important to Morgan because they reflected "gentile society," a key element of the stage of barbarism. Families related through the intermarriage of *gentes* (a gens was similar to a unilineal descent group) were expected to display "communism in living" through application of the "law of hospitality." They should "make common stock of . . . provisions [and erect] joint tenement houses large enough to accommodate several families" (Morgan 1965 [1881]: 63). He thought that structures such as the Iroquois longhouse and the historic pueblo clearly reflected gentile organization.

Though he was aware of "estufas" (Morgan 1965 [1881]:174) and the subdivision of both historic and prehistoric pueblos into discrete apartments (Morgan 1965 [1881]:154-155; 175), Morgan focused primarily on the size and degree of aggregation of the settlement as evidence of Pueblo social integration. He believed that even though families might have separate living quarters, the "law of hospitality" would require common stores or at least the free sharing of food and other goods (Morgan 1865[1881]:42-62). In order to further test his theories, Morgan proposed a program of archaeological and ethnographic research extending from the American Southwest through Mexico to Peru (Wilcox 1976:32-33) and Adolf Bandelier was soon commissioned by the Archaeological Institute of America to carry it out (Wilcox 1976:32-34). On the basis of his work in the Pueblo Southwest, Bandelier (1884, cited in Wilcox 1976) argued that Morgan's evolutionary theory could account for the archaeological presence of both small and large pueblo settlements. Early smallhouse settlements, occupied by perhaps one or two clans, gave way to the larger communal houses as part of the evolution of society from Upper-level Savagery to Lower-level Barbarism (Wilcox 1976:35). Cushing (1886, 1888; summarized in Wilcox 1975:35-36) also supported the theory with arguments that the "small houses" were each occupied by a single gens or clan, and that the large communal house or pueblos proper represented a gathering together of several clans.

This developmental sequence is reflected in aspects of the Pecos Classification (Kidder 1927) and has had profound, persistent, and often quite constraining effects on Southwestern archaeology. In addition to difficulties that derive from the improbable identification of small houses as clan residences (Parsons 1940; Aberle 1970), this sequence also led to a reluctance to accept contemporaneity among these different settlement types (cf. Wilcox 1976). Eventually, work at Chaco made it clear that even the Great Houses there were contemporary with nearby small houses (Kluckhohn 1939), while Brew (1946) documented the occurrence of large multiunit pueblos in the Pueblo I period, earlier than the small single-unit pueblos he excavated in the same area. The main point to be made here, however, is that the rudimentary early work of Morgan, Bandelier, and Cushing established the principle that the spatial configuration of architectural elements could serve as a basis for inferring aspects of social organization.

T. Mitchell Prudden (1903, 1914, 1918) elaborated this approach and provided empirical documentation for his inferences in the form of both excavation (1914, 1918) and survey (1903) maps and descriptions. On the basis of extensive reconnaissance in the San Juan drainage (Prudden 1903:234-239) he noted the recurrent association of an estufa or kiva, a small rectilinear block of contiguous surface rooms (usually located north of the kiva), and a burial or burial-and-trash mound (usually located south of the kiva). Adjacent rooms in the surface pueblo or "house" were often connected by doorways. This architectural complex he called the "unit type pueblo."

These small "units" frequently stood alone, but tended to occur "in community groups" (Prudden 1918:47). Not uncommonly, however, they were joined together into larger pueblos, though without losing their structural discreteness (Prudden 1903:234). These small house ruins were often spatially associated with "a larger and more commanding house," and also occurred close to "the great community houses" on Squaw, Bug, and Goodman Points (Prudden 1918:47).

Prudden interpreted unit type pueblos as the residential facilities of a basic social group:

> . . . if these simplest residences be recognized as marking family or clan units, as well as being structural units, the practices and traditions of the Pueblo people of today, which center in and are so largely determined by clan or other social relationships, make clear enough the impulse which led small groups of these earlier people, even in the near neighborhood of others, to maintain not only their separate houses, but also their separate ceremonial chambers and places of burial [Prudden 1914:34].

Prudden was aware that the prevailing theory of the time required that the small houses be the predecessors of the "communal" ones, but he ultimately decided (Prudden 1918) that this proposed sequence could be neither proved nor disproved on the basis of evidence at hand. He concluded, however, that

> there is evidently a close relationship between the larger and smaller forms, as well as between the artifacts which the excavations of both have disclosed. The motive for the different types of building seems, in part at least, to have been determined by the difference in site and some as yet undisclosed community requirements [Prudden 1918:49].

Considered in the abstract, Prudden's work established that the smallest commonly recurrent architectural unit was not a single structure, but a small spatial cluster of structures and other elements (e.g., the burial mound). This complex or "unit" was composed of a redundant set of functionally different elements, which showed consistent spatial/relational patterning within the unit. Functional interpretation of the unit as a whole led to the conclusion that it represented the space and facilities used by a basic social segment. These social segments were not isolates, but were parts of communities. The architectural and spatial expression of these communities might be a loose cluster of units, a cluster of units centered on a larger pueblo, or just a large pueblo. Most of the large pueblos themselves could be analyzed as being aggregates of the basic social/architectural units. That the structural integrity of the architectural unit was preserved within the larger aggregate indicated that the social integrity (and independence?) of the basic social segment was probably preserved also. The relationship between the small house units and the larger pueblos might be sequential, but did not have to be; site-specific environmental factors, or "community requirements" might result in both types being present concurrently.

Fewkes (1911:79-80; 1919:69-76) used the presumed sequence from small house to communal house in the San Juan drainage as the basis for a theory of organizational change that accounted for changes in the ratio of kivas to rooms from the prehistoric to the historic pueblos:

> ... we necessarily have in the growth of the community house the story of the social evolution of the Pueblo people. Clans or social units at first isolated later joined each other. ... The inevitable outcome would be a breaking down of clan priesthoods or clan religions and the formation of fraternities of priesthoods recruited from several clans. This in turn would lead to a corresponding reduction and enlargement of ceremonial rooms remaining. Two kivas suffice for the ceremonies of a majority of the Rio Grande pueblos; but Cliff Palace with a population of the same size had 23 ... [Fewkes 1919:75-76].

Community pattern analysis and, in particular, the changing ratios of kivas to rooms were employed by Steward (1937, 1955:151-172) as part of a theoretical study of how bands based on single lineages might have evolved into multilineage societies having non-localized clans. Steward reviewed the "unit type pueblos" of the San Juan area, and concluded that

> ... it is difficult to reconcile the division of the early villages into small house clusters with any other social unit than a unilateral lineage or band. Each house cluster is so large that it must have sheltered several families. But there would be no motive for unrelated families to band together instead of living in houses located at random. ... A rule of residence, however, would produce lineages whose houses would fit the archaeological facts. Archaeologists have frequently called these 'clan houses,' but this must not be understood to mean clan in the Hopi sense [Steward 1937:99].

Defensive needs, indigenous population growth, or movement of new groups into an area could cause multiple lineages to settle together. If these kin groups attempted to maintain real or fictive kinship ties and exogamy, clans would automatically result, and these would rapidly become nonlocalized. (Parsons [1940] discusses how difficult it would be for a growing kin group to maintain residential proximity, especially in an aggregated settlement). The development of clans is not inevitable, as illustrated by their weakness or absence in the Eastern Pueblos (Steward 1937:99).

Steward (1937) interpreted the unit pueblo kiva as an important element in the ceremonial integration of the localized lineage. Accepting the generally favored view that communal pueblos post-dated the small houses, he suggested that "the formerly separated small groups ... do not lose their social and ceremonial integrity" when they begin to amalgamate in the Pueblo II period. In Pueblo III and especially in Pueblo IV, however, the decreasing ratio of kivas to rooms is interpreted as the result of clan growth, perhaps by absorption of unrelated lineages, and eventually by the severing of the clan-kiva link (though he recognizes that vestiges of such a linkage remain ethnographically at Hopi). Steward does not specifically address the function of kivas in historic Pueblo villages, but it is implied that the reduction in kiva frequency and the severing of their ties with descent groups is part of a general process by which integration and political autonomy of the village is enhanced at the expense of kin groups.

Rohn (1965, 1971) used the spatial patterning of architectural elements to infer several levels of social integration at Mug House, in Mesa Verde National Park. Unlike previous workers, he specifically attempted to avoid inferring kinship-based groupings such as "clan" and "lineage" from the spatial arrangements of facilities that he observed. He argued that the archaeological patterns reflected not kinship patterns per se, but

> the durable remains of domestic cooperation. ... It is this sharing of material goods and the cooperation involved in satisfying the needs and wants of all the individuals concerned that may be reflected in archaeological remains. Thus the prehistorian may discern traces of groups that can be called socioeconomic, that is, their cohesion probably rests on sociological factors, but their recognition by the archaeologist depends on cooperative economic behavior [Rohn 1965:65].

Rohn (1965:65) used "the juxtaposition of rooms with different functions, building sequences, patterns of movement indicated by doorway locations, and the placement of hearths and other domestic features" to establish different levels of interaction and hence of inferred grouping. The smallest unit was the room suite, considered to be the facilities used by a household. Room suites were clusters of walled spaces that included at least one dwelling room, several storage rooms, a small outdoor work area, and sometimes a sleeping or work room. The functional classification of spaces depended on patterned differences among structures in size, location, and floor and wall features. Specific groupings of spaces into suites were based on proximity, interconnections inferred from doorway orientations, evidence that structures were built or remodeled together, and in some cases, on formal similarities in details of construction.

The second level of grouping was the "habitation unit," a term used by Bullard (1962) to refer to the association of a small number of surface rooms with a pit house or kiva. Rohn (1965:67) notes that this unit equates roughly to Prudden's "unit-type pueblo" and to Fewkes' (1909) "courtyard unit." Rohn did not correlate a specific kind of socioeconomic unit with this architectural/archaeological unit, but suggested that

> ... whatever sort of kin grouping occupied the old habitation units, it was undergoing modification during the Pueblo III occupation of Mug House, and has either passed out of existence since then, or has been modified further so it no longer affects site layout [Rohn 1965:68].

A third level of grouping was recognized on the basis of aligned doorless house walls that separated Mug House into two parts. Rohn (1965:69) suggests that this may reflect "some form of dual social division" but does not elaborate on this idea. A final level of social grouping is the community, which consists of Mug House, several nearby smaller sites, and facilities such as a water catchment that was probably used jointly by the residents of the several settlements that comprised the community.

Rohn's study of Chapin Mesa, which was completed as a dissertation in the early 1960s but not published until 1977, also includes some pioneering Southwestern applications of community pattern analysis. Rohn delineates communities on the basis of clusters of contemporaneous sites, most of which also display evidence of shared economic facilities (e.g., water catchment/distribution systems) and/or ceremonial facilities (e.g., a Great Kiva or bi-wall structure). Large sites, such as Cliff Palace, are interpreted as having provided some of the ceremonial facilities used by smaller outlying settlements that were part of the community.

Dean (1969, 1970) also analyzed the spatial patterning of functionally different structures in Pueblo III cliff dwellings to arrive at inferences about community organization and integration. Unlike the Mesa Verde sites studied by Rohn, the Tsegi Phase Kayenta cliff dwellings Dean studied displayed no intermediate level of grouping between the room cluster (household) and the settlement (village). Kivas were relatively rare, and there was a "lack of spatial or architectural relationships between kivas and subvillage residence units," i.e., specific room clusters (Dean 1970:165). From this, he inferred that kivas "must have been associated with some sort of nonlocalized social unit that included members of a number of households" (Dean 1970:165). The involvement of such dispersed groups in ritual would have strengthened village-level integration (Dean 1970:166), as it does in ethnographically known Western Pueblo communities.

Other architectural data, used in conjunction with tree-ring dates on structural beams, provided evidence of patterns of integration:

> Dendrochronological analyses show that tree-cutting at Betatakin was a communal rather than an individual or household activity [Dean 1969:80]. The construction of large community structures ... [also] required the coordinated efforts of large groups of people [Dean 1970:168].

Differences in patterns of integration between the two large cliff dwellings—Betatakin and Kiet Siel—were also noted. The stockpiling of timbers prior to construction, the pattern of its growth, and the homogeneity of its architecture indicated that Betatakin "was a unified 'community' throughout its history, whereas Kiet Siel was a frequently changing assemblage of historically unrelated households or fragments of other communities" (Dean 1970:168). The lack of Great Kivas or of formal spatial relationships among sites indicated to Dean that there were no strong structural relationships among villages. However, the Tsegi villages "were probably linked into a loosely defined 'community' by a network of informal ties based on trade, interpersonal relations, intermarriage, and contiguity" (Dean 1970:169).

In the analysis of Turkey Creek Pueblo discussed above, Lowell (1988) used wall construction events and patterns of redundant association among functionally different room types to infer the presence of both household and suprahousehold residential groups. Furthermore, the settlement could be divided into two main architectural blocks, both of which adjoined a Great Kiva and plaza. The two previously-discussed groups of "kiva rooms" were positioned so as to link each of the two main roomblocks with the Great Kiva. Lowell (1988) interpreted this configuration as indicating a possible dual division of the settlement as well as a village level of social integration.

As discussed above, artifactual data have generally been used to develop functional classifications of architectural spaces in pueblos, or to infer the activities that took place in these spaces. In the 1960s, Hill (1966, 1970) and Longacre (1964, 1966, 1970) launched an ambitious attempt to use the distributions of artifacts and ecofacts as direct indicators of the distribution and composition of social groups at prehistoric pueblos, in conjunction with spatial analysis of variation in architecture and features. The basic approach was to distinguish various blocks of rooms within the pueblos by the occurrence in them of distinctive constellations of variables that ranged from ceramic types and design elements to other artifact or feature types. The room clusters thus defined were then interpreted as the areas occupied by residence groups (Hill 1966) or localized descent groups (Longacre 1964). Comparison of organizational patterns at the Carter Ranch Pueblo (Longacre 1964, 1970) with those at the later Broken K Pueblo (Hill 1966, 1970) plus consideration of other settlement data from the region led to inferences about changes in modes of social integration (Longacre 1966; Hill 1966). Increasing aggregation of the population into larger villages, the appearance of Great Kivas, the decreasing ratio of kivas to rooms, increased size of residence groups, the tendency for architectural style to become more homogeneous, and the possibility that Broken K artifact distributions indicated some degree of localized production and exchange of goods all were taken to indicate an increasing scale and intensity of social integration, both within and between villages, perhaps in response to increasing climatic variability and subsistence risk (Longacre 1966; Hill 1966). This work has been challenged repeatedly on the basis of the adequacy of the statistical methods employed (Lischka 1975; Dumond 1977) and of the concepts used to model social organization and link it to archaeological variables (Allen and Richardson 1971; Stanislawski 1973, 1977). Hill and Longacre also do not appear to have taken sufficient account of the patterning introduced by processes of roomblock growth and remodeling (Wilcox 1988) and assemblage formation (Schiffer 1987:323-338). Nevertheless, the ambitious and imaginative nature of the work, and the attempt to apply new quantitative methods to the study of social organization, had a powerful and largely positive effect on a generation of archaeologists in the Southwest and elsewhere.

Southwestern archaeologists also have attempted to use differences in architectural scale or elaboration among buildings as an indicator of the degree of status differentiation or sociopolitical hierarchy in pueblo communities. As compared with the structures used by "ordinary" households or communities, the facilities of leaders and high status groups are expected to display more living and storage space per capita, higher investment in construction, and more ostentatious facades (Lightfoot and Feinman 1979; Lightfoot 1984; Lipe 1986; Kane 1986; Lipe and Kane 1986; Orcutt and Blinman 1987; Wilson 1989).

Recent Southwestern literature presents widely differing interpretations of the sociopolitical complexity of prehistoric Southwestern pueblo groups in the Pueblo III and IV periods (e.g., Upham 1982, 1985; Upham and Plog 1986; Plog 1983; Graves et al. 1982; Whittlesey 1984; Reid 1985). There is general agreement, however, that in the Pueblo II and early Pueblo III period, the "Chaco Phenomenon" (Cordell 1984:246-274; Judge 1979) exhibited a more complex social organization than either earlier or later Pueblo societies. Schelberg, for example, recognizes a three-tiered administrative hierarchy among settlements having Chacoan "Great Houses," and proposes a level of sociopolitical complexity "similar to that of the chiefdom" (Schelberg 1984). Much of the discussion of Chacoan social organization revolves around the social implications of the Great House architecture. These buildings differ markedly in scale, planning, labor investment, and ostentation from the smaller, more typical Anasazi settlements that are generally associated with them (Marshall et al. 1979; Lekson 1984; Powers 1984; Schelberg 1984; Toll 1985; Sebastian 1988). Although the evidence for actual social stratification appears weak (Johnson 1984) this was clearly "not an acephelous society" (Sebastian 1988:59). Sebastian (1988) argues that Chacoan Great House architecture was developed by emerging leaders in the tenth century A.D. as part of a competitive strategy to attract followers by sharing stored food in times of low agricultural production. The increasingly monumental Great Houses of the eleventh century, on the other hand, were part of a strategy by which leadership groups institutionalized their positions, perhaps by asserting control of the relationship between society and the supernatural world.

Another aspect of the Chacoan built environment with implications for social integration is the system of roads that evidently linked "Chacoan Outlier" sites with Chaco Canyon, and to some extent with one another, over an area nearly 200 km. in diameter (Marshall et al. 1979; Kincaid 1983; Powers et al. 1983; Betancourt et al. 1986; Nials et al. 1987). The roads provide the most convincing evidence that Chacoan social organization had a regional dimension. Evidence that thousands of building timbers were transported more than 75 km. from highland areas to Chaco Canyon (Betancourt et al. 1986) also convincingly documents the scale of Chacoan regional organization and a degree of work planning and control not found in earlier or later Anasazi developments.

Artifacts and Social Integration

Artifacts are used in the interpretation of almost all archaeological sites; in this sense, of course, any discussion of social organization and integration includes the study of artifacts. However, at least five general classes of artifactual evidence can be identified that are used more directly in research on social organization and integration in the Southwest. These are grave goods, ceramic vessel form and disposal pattern, ritual objects, style, and exchange. With the exception of grave goods, all are used in the analytical papers in this volume.

Mortuary analysis is often an excellent means of studying various aspects of prehistoric social organization. Although burial descriptions are standard in many Southwestern site reports, studies of burial treatment and grave goods in relation to social organization have been limited. The Pueblo III burials at the Rainbow Bridge Site 568 were interred with a relatively rich assemblage of artifacts. In her reanalysis of the material, Crotty (1983:60) argued that the "preferential treatment accorded senior women almost certainly denotes social organization based on tracing descent through the maternal line," and that differential treatment within age and sex categories indicates a degree of stratification not necessarily unlike that of the Western Pueblo clan system. Using mortuary data from Chaco Canyon, Akins (1986) argued that three levels of burials (differentiated on the basis of location as well as grave goods) indicate three levels of social rank. Mortuary data are also used in the debate over sociopolitical complexity in the Mogollon area. In her analysis of the large and well-preserved burial population of Grasshopper Pueblo, Whittlesey (1984, summarizing her 1978 dissertation) argues that differential mortuary treatment can be attributed to age and sex differences and to membership in religious societies such as those known from ethnographic pueblos. However, her conclusions are disputed by F. Plog (summarized in Upham and Plog 1986). He and other researchers working at Nuvakwewtaqa argue that the mortuary remains at that site, though badly disturbed, support their model of a society in which access to resources was restricted and controlled by a decision-making elite (Upham 1982; Upham and Plog 1986).

The use and disposal of certain sizes and forms of ceramic vessels can provide information about the context of use, including the size of the group and the occasion. Toll (1985) interprets the enormous quantity of ceramics in the trash mound at Pueblo Alto in Chaco Canyon as the remains deposited by large gatherings, possibly at harvest feasts. Turner and Lofgren (1966) use serving bowl and cooking jar sizes to estimate prehistoric household size, and they suggest that very large jars, common only after A.D. 900, were made for gatherings of more than one household and therefore were associated with the evolution of kivas. Blinman uses both lines of evidence here to support his model of prehistoric "potlucks." Bowl:jar ratios (there are relatively more bowls at sites with oversized pit structures) and cooking jar size (large cooking jars are not associated with oversized pit structures) suggest that food was prepared elsewhere and brought to gatherings at the oversized pit structures.

Archaeologists have long identified special or ritual objects in their collections. Despite the time-honored joke—if it looks weird and it's not obviously functional, it must be a ritual object—many researchers have used great care in their interpretations. Ellis (1967) in her study of *tcamahias,* and Vivian et al. (1978) in their study of wooden artifacts used very careful and detailed ethnographic analogy in their arguments. Vivian et al. concluded that the wooden artifacts were probably not altars but were used in some sort of public dramatization, and Ellis argued that at least some of the tcamahias were symbolic of the supernatural. Others emphasize the need for contextual information in interpretations of unusual objects (see Bradley 1988). The special nature of Chaco cylinder jars is suggested not only by their shape but also by their distribution—most were found in unique contexts in Pueblo Bonito (Neitzel 1985). Finally, archaeologists have noted certain attributes that may indicate the special, possibly ritual, roles of certain artifacts. These attributes include the labor invested in the production and painting and/or the symbolic meaning of certain wares and design styles (e.g., polychromes [Feinman et al. 1981] or fine hachure [Neitzel 1985; Windes 1984]). In this volume Varien and Lightfoot (Chapter 6) examine the distribution of possible special artifacts across the Duckfoot site, Wilshusen (Chapter 7) examines the marks left by the use of ritual objects (prayer sticks and altars like those known ethnographically from rituals), while Hegmon (Chapter 9) and Plog (Chapter 10) both consider the attributes of ceramics that might indicate a special role in ritual.

A historical review of style studies shows that researchers are developing increasingly detailed understandings of why people make and use style and how style relates to social organization. Early studies in the Southwest and elsewhere basically equated groups of similar traits—including ceramic style and technology as well as architectural forms—with cultures or ethnic affiliations. Kidder (1924:343), observing contractions in zones of architectural and ceramic similarity, concluded that Pueblo culture "passed through an early phase of wide territorial expansion marked by great uniformity of culture. It then drew in upon itself and enjoyed a period of efflorescence characterized by strong specialization in different branches." Colton used ceramics as primary evidence in his work to delineate *Prehistoric Culture Units and Their Relationships in Northern Arizona* (Colton 1939). For example, a phase—recognized in large part on the basis of ceramics—"is a concept of the culture of an Indian tribe during a short period of its history" (Colton 1953:68).

In the 1960s researchers began looking in more detail at stylistic similarities and differences (primarily in painted designs on ceramics), and thus were able to make more detailed inferences about social organization. In the tradition of the New Archaeology these researchers rejected the equation of traits with culture. However, their explanation of stylistic variation was little changed from earlier decades, except that style was equated with interaction instead of culture—"the smaller and more closely tied the social aggregate, the more details of design would be shared" (Longacre 1970:28). Clusters of design elements were used to identify uxorilocal residence units (if women were the potters) within a community, and at Carter Ranch these units were associated with kivas (Hill 1970b; Longacre 1970). Studies of stylistic similarity and homogeneity were also used to study interaction between communities (Leone 1968; Tuggle 1970).

Following soon after were other studies that found fault with nearly every aspect of the early attempts at "ceramic sociology," including the assumption that styles were passed from mother to daughter (Stanislawski 1973), the statistical methods used (Plog 1978a, 1978b), and lack of control of factors such as ceramic exchange that could affect the distribution of styles (Plog 1980a, 1980b). However, the initial studies and the criticisms that followed prompted further research that focused on two general classes of questions. First, why do people paint their pottery and create these different styles? Second, what are the variables of style most appropriate for study?

The first question represented a fairly radical theoretical change from the earlier studies. Drawing from the information exchange theory of Wobst (1977) researchers considered style to have a function as a means of transmitting information (Plog 1980a). That is, prehistoric people did not just passively accept the style of those around them; rather, they actively used style to convey information about their social position and group affiliation. Thus, style could actually be used to establish social networks and increase social integration. Braun and Plog (1982:514-515) interpreted the development of regional stylistic traditions, increasing stylistic similarity between communities, and increasing community homogeneity as evidence for "increasing supralocal cooperation and social integration" indicative of the development of regional tribal social networks. Graves (1982) found that Plog's model of style change based on the information exchange theory did not fully explain design style variation in White Mountain Red Ware; however, Graves also posited an active role for style in symbolizing group affiliation in exchange networks. Hegmon (1986) argued that increases in stylistic diversity on Black Mesa indicated an increase in information exchange, and thus a strengthening of the socially integrative network. She uses similar reasoning in her paper in this volume (Chapter 9), where she argues that the relatively great stylistic diversity in ceramics associated with oversized pit structures can be attributed to information exchange at gatherings of socially distant persons.

As style came to be used to address more and more detailed questions about prehistoric social organization, more attention was given to methods for classifying and analyzing style. The studies are voluminous, and here we give only examples at either end of the spectrum. Some researchers advocate a hierarchical attribute-based approach that can be systematically applied to sherds (Plog 1980a; Redman 1978; Hantman et al. 1984). This approach is used in the paper by Hegmon. In contrast, Washburn (1977; Washburn and Matson 1985) advocates the analysis of design structure, particularly symmetry, which often can only be analyzed on whole vessels, but is argued to be more culturally sensitive than separate elements. Another approach, explicitly focused on social processes, is the production step measure of Feinman et al. (1981). This measure does not analyze design style as such, but it provides a means of quantifying the effort entailed in making different kinds of ceramics and thus identifying more highly valued (generally more elaborate) ceramics. In this volume neither Plog nor Hegmon use the production step measure, but they do attempt to identify special ritual-associated ceramics based on design attributes (the Dogozshi style, and design formality and neatness).

Finally, in what we regard as a very encouraging development, researchers have begun to agree that there are many correct answers to both the above questions. That is, people make and use style for different reasons, some more active than others; and many kinds of stylistic analyses can be used to answer a variety of questions. Plog (1989) found that some patterns of stylistic variation could be best explained as the product of rote learning (isochrestic variation [see Sackett 1985; Wiessner 1985:161]) while other patterns indicate more active use of stylistic symbols in information exchange. Kintigh (1985) suggested that some stylistic attributes might be produced by intentional symbolism and others (possibly more subtle attributes) produced by shared learning contexts. F. Plog (1983) argued that some attributes (including ceramic technology and corrugation styles) distinguish small localities while others (types and wares as well as architectural styles) distinguish provinces and sometimes social alliances that drew relatively autonomous villages "into a larger, overarching social and economic organization" (1983:323; see also Cordell and Plog 1979; Upham 1982). Hegmon's paper in this volume examines different aspects of style (design diversity, formality, and neatness) as indications of both information exchange and ritual use of ceramics.

Exchange and style are closely interrelated in studies of social organization. Not only must exchange be understood or controlled for in stylistic analyses, but both are part of the same general social processes. That is, both play a role in social interaction; style can be seen as information exchange, and material exchange can help to disseminate stylistic information. Beginning with the pioneering work of Shepard (1942, 1965) Southwestern archaeologists have studied the material properties of artifacts to determine where they were produced (or at least to identify groups of artifacts that appear to have been produced in the same place) and thus to investigate patterns of prehistoric exchange and their relationship to social organization and economy. Not all such studies find evidence for exchange, however. In their analysis of obsidian in New Mexico, Findlow and Bolognese (1982) concluded that much of the archaeological distribution could be explained by direct access procurement rather than exchange. Analyses of Salado Polychromes (widespread in 14th Century Mogollon sites) indicate that the style and manufacturing technology were shared over a large area, but the vessels themselves were not widely exchanged; instead, evidence indicates they were locally produced (Crown and Bishop 1987; Danson and Wallace 1956).

In two areas widely separated by time and space, evidence of exchange demonstrated that communities were not as isolated as some had thought. Shepard (1942, 1965) and later Warren's (1969) work with Pueblo IV Rio Grande Glaze Wares demonstrated a high degree of productive specialization, exchange, and economic interdependence between villages. Chipped stone and ceramic evidence similarly demonstrated inter- and intraregional exchange in central and northern Arizona (Plog 1980b; 1986). Braun and Plog (1982) suggest that an increase in exchange intensity (greater volume, shorter distance), in conjunction with the development of zones of stylistic similarity, indicates an increase in regional integration. In Chapter 10 of this volume, Plog draws from these studies of exchange and finds that imported red and orange wares are strongly associated with sites with ceremonial structures. Blinman (Chapter 8) similarly finds an association of imported red wares and sites with oversized pit structures.

Finally, the exchange and movement of goods have also been used in interpretations of political organization and arguments for prehistoric social complexity. A large proportion of ceramics in Chaco Canyon during the Classic Bonito Phase were tempered with sanidine basalt from the Chuska area approximately 80 km. west of Chaco Canyon. "The co-occurrence of Chuska ceramics in Chaco Canyon and Chaco sites in the Chuska Valley suggests that there may have been some Chaco-based organization of, or control over, ceramic manufacture in the Chuska Valley" (Toll et al. 1980). Upham and others (Upham et al. 1981; Upham 1982) argue that certain relatively labor-intensive ceramic wares (determined according to the production step measure) were centrally produced and tend to be found only on larger sites, suggesting restricted access to the material and control by a managerial elite. They suggest that this ceramic exchange may have symbolized political alliances in the fourteenth and fifteenth centuries (Upham 1982:157). However, at least for the Jeddito Alliance, evidence for centrally controlled production is questionable, since clay composition analysis shows that Jeddito Yellow Wares (in the Hopi Mesas area) were produced at several villages, and there is no evidence of centrally controlled resources within the villages (Bishop et al. 1988).

Artifacts are powerful evidence in studies of social integration and other topics. The studies in this volume demonstrate this power and also demonstrate the importance of interpreting the artifacts in context. Study of vessel form, exchange, and style are all closely linked, as is shown in the papers by Blinman, Hegmon and Plog. Furthermore, interpretations of artifacts and the architectural contexts where they are found are closely linked, as is shown most directly by Varien and Lightfoot and generally by all the papers in this volume.

References

Aberle, David
   1970   Comments. In *Reconstructing Prehistoric Pueblo Societies,* edited by William A. Longacre, pp. 214-223. University of New Mexico Press, Albuquerque.

Adams, E. Charles
   1983   The Architectural Analogue to Hopi Social Organization and Room Use, and Implications for Prehistoric Northern Southwestern Culture. *American Antiquity* 48(1):44-61.

Akins, Nancy J.
   1986   *A Biocultural Approach to Human Burials from Chaco Canyon, New Mexico.* Reports of the Chaco Center No. 9. National Park Service, Santa Fe.

Allen, William L. and James B. Richardson III
   1971   The Reconstruction of Kinship from Archaeological Data: The Concepts, the Methods, and the Possibility. *American Antiquity* 36(1):41-53.

Ambler, J. Richard and Alan P. Olson
1977   *Salvage Archaeology in the Cow Springs Area.* Museum of Northern Arizona Technical Series No. 15. Flagstaff, Arizona.

Anderson, Keith M.
1969   Ethnographic Analogy and Archaeological Interpretation. *Science* 163:133-138.

Bandelier, Adolf
1884   *Reports by A. F. Bandelier on His Investigations in New Mexico During the Years 1883-84.* Archaeological Institute of America, Fifth Annual Report:55-98. Boston. (Cited in Wilcox 1976)

Betancourt, Julio L., Jeffrey S. Dean, and Herbert M. Hull
1986   Prehistoric Long-Distance Transport of Construction Beams, Chaco Canyon, New Mexico. *American Antiquity* 51(2):370-375.

Bishop, Roland L., Veletta Canouts, Suzanne P. DeAtley, Alfred Qoyawayama, and C. W. Aikins
1988   The Formation of Ceramic Analytical Groups: Hopi Pottery Production and Exchange, A.C. 1300–1600. *Journal of Field Archaeology* 15:317-337.

Bradley, Bruce
1988   Unusual Vessel Forms from Sand Canyon Pueblo, Colorado. *Pottery Southwest* 15(2):1-2.

Braun, David P. and Stephen Plog
1982   Evolution of "Tribal" Social Networks: Theory and Prehistoric North American Evidence. *American Antiquity* 47:504-525.

Brew, John Otis
1946   *The Archaeology of Alkali Ridge, Southeastern Utah.* Papers of the Peabody Museum of American Archaeology and Ethnology No. 21. Harvard University, Cambridge, Massachusetts.

Cater, John and Mark Chenault
1988   Kiva Use Reinterpreted. *Southwestern Lore* 54(3):19-32.

Chang, Kwang-Chih
1958   Study of the Neolithic Social Grouping: Examples from the New World. *American Anthropologist* 60:298-334.

Ciolek-Torrello, Richard
1978   *A Statistical Analysis of Activity Organization: Grasshopper Pueblo, Arizona.* Unpublished Ph.D. dissertation, Department of Anthropology, University of Arizona, Tucson.

1985   A Typology of Room Function at Grasshopper Pueblo, Arizona. *Journal of Field Archaeology* 12:41-63.

Colton, Harold S.
1939   *Prehistoric Culture Units and Their Relationships in Northern Arizona.* Museum of Northern Arizona Bulletin No. 17. Flagstaff.

1953   *Potsherds.* Museum of Northern Arizona Bulletin No. 25. Flagstaff.

Cordell, Linda S., and Fred Plog
1979   Escaping the Confines of Normative Thought: A Re-evaluation of Puebloan Prehistory. *American Antiquity* 44:405-429.

Cordell, Linda S.
1984   *Prehistory of the Southwest.* Academic Press, Orlando, Florida.

Crotty, Helen K.
1983   *Honoring the Dead: Anasazi Ceramics from the Rainbow Bridge-Monument Valley Expedition.* Museum of Cultural History, Monograph Series No. 23. University of California at Los Angeles.

Crown, Patricia L. and Ronald L. Bishop
1987   The Manufacture of Salado Polychrome. *Pottery Southwest 14(4):1-3.*

Cushing, Frank H.
1886   *A Study of Pueblo Pottery as Illustrative of Zuni Culture Growth.* Fourth Annual Report of the Bureau of Ethnology to the Secretary of the Smithsonian Institution 1883–1884: pp. 467-521. Government Printing Office, Washington, D.C.

1888   *Preliminary Notes on Origin, Working Hypothesis, and Primary Researches of the Hemenway Southwestern Archaeological Expedition.* Congres International des Americanistes, Berlin. (cited in Wilcox 1976)

Danson, E. B., and R. M. Wallace
1956   A Petrographic Study of Gila Polychrome. *American Antiquity* 22:180-182.

Dean, Jeffrey
1969   *Chronological Analysis of Tsegi Phase Sites in Northeastern Arizona.* Papers of the Laboratory of Tree-Ring Research No. 3. University of Arizona, Tucson.

1970   Aspects of Tsegi Phase Social Organization: A Trial Reconstruction. In *Reconstructing Prehistoric Pueblo Societies,* edited by William A.

Longacre, pp. 140-174. University of New Mexico Press, Albuquerque.

DeGarmo, Glen D.
1975 *Coyote Creek, Site 01: A Methodological Study of a Prehistoric Pueblo Population.* Unpublished Ph.D. dissertation, Department of Anthropology, University of California at Los Angeles.

1977 Identification of Prehistoric Intrasettlement Exchange. In *Exchange Systems in Prehistory,* edited by Timothy K. Earle and Jonathan Ericson, pp. 153-170. Academic Press, New York.

Dumond, Don
1977 Science in Archaeology: The Saints Go Marching In. *American Antiquity* 42(3):330-348.

Ellis, Florence Hawley
1967 Use and Significance of the Tcamahia. *El Palacio* 74:35-43.

Feinman, Gary M., Steadman Upham, and Kent G. Lightfoot
1981 The Production Step Measure: An Ordinal Index of Labor Input in Ceramic Manufacture. *American Antiquity* 46:871-882.

Fewkes, J. Walter
1898 *Archeological Expedition to Arizona in 1895.* Seventeenth Annual Report of the Bureau of American Ethnology to the Secretary of the Smithsonian Institution 1895–1896: pp. 519-744. Government Printing Office, Washington, D.C.

1908 Ventilators in Ceremonial Rooms of Prehistoric Cliff-Dwellings. *American Anthropologist,* n.s., 10:387-398.

1909 *Antiquities of the Mesa Verde National Park: Spruce-Tree House.* Bureau of American Ethnology Bulletin 41. Government Printing Office, Washington, D.C.

Findlow, Frank J., and Marissa Bolognese
1982 Regional Modeling of Obsidian Procurement in the American Southwest. In *Contexts for Prehistoric Exchange,* edited by J. E. Ericson and T. K. Earle, pp. 53-81. Academic Press, New York.

Fritz, John
1978 Paleopsychology Today: Ideational Systems and Human Adaptation in Prehistory. In *Social Archeology: Beyond Subsistence and Dating,* edited by Charles L. Redman et al., pp. 37-59. Academic Press, New York.

1987 Chaco Canyon and Vijayanagara: Proposing Spatial Meaning in Two Societies. In *Mirror and Metaphor: Material and Social Constructions of Reality,* edited by D. W. Ingersoll, Jr. and G. Bronitsky, pp. 313-349. University Press of America, Landham, Maryland.

Graves, Michael W.
1982 Breaking Down Ceramic Variation: Testing Models of White Mountain Redware Design Style Development. *Journal of Anthropological Archaeology* 1:305-354.

Graves, Michael W., William A. Longacre, and Sally J. Holbrook
1982 Aggregation and Abandonment at Grasshopper Pueblo. *Journal of Field Archaeology* 9:193-206.

Hantman, Jeffrey L., Kent G. Lightfoot, Steadman Upham, Fred Plog, Stephen Plog, and Bruce Donaldson
1984 Cibola Whitewares: A Regional Perspective. In *Regional Analysis of Prehistoric Ceramic Variation: Contemporary Studies of the Cibola Whitewares,* edited by A. P. Sullivan and J. L. Hantman, pp. 17-35. Anthropological Research Papers No. 31. Arizona State University, Tempe.

Hawley, Florence
1950 Big Kivas, Little Kivas, and Moiety Houses in Historical Reconstruction. *Southwestern Journal of Anthropology* 6:286-302.

Hegmon, Michelle
1986 Information Exchange and Integration on Black Mesa, Arizona, A.D. 931–1150. In *Spatial Organization and Exchange: Archaeological Survey on Northern Black Mesa,* edited by S. Plog, pp. 256-281. Southern Illinois University Press, Carbondale.

Hill, James N.
1966 A Prehistoric Community in Eastern Arizona. *Southwestern Journal of Anthropology* 22(1):9-30.

1968 Broken K Pueblo: Patterns of Form and Function. In *New Perspectives in Archeology,* edited by Sally R. Binford and Lewis R. Binford, pp. 103-142. Aldine Publishing Co., Chicago.

1970a Prehistoric Social Organization in the American Southwest: Theory and Method. In *Reconstructing Prehistoric Pueblo Societies,* edited by William A. Longacre, pp. 11-58. University of New Mexico Press, Albuquerque.

1970b   *Broken K Pueblo: Prehistoric Social Organization in the American Southwest.* Anthropological Papers of the University of Arizona No. 18. Tucson.

Johnson, Gregory A.
1989   Dynamics of Southwestern Prehistory: Far Outside–Looking In. In *Dynamics of Southwestern Prehistory,* edited by Linda S. Cordell and George J. Gumerman. Smithsonian Institution Press, Washington, D.C., in press.

Jorgenson, Julia
1975   A Room Use Analysis of Table Rock Pueblo, Arizona. *Journal of Anthropological Research* 31:149-161.

Judge, W. James
1979   The Development of a Complex Cultural Ecosystem in the Chaco Basin, New Mexico. In *Proceedings of the First Conference on Scientific Research in the National Parks,* edited by R. M. Linn, vol. 2, pp. 901-906. U.S. National Park Service Transactions and Proceedings Series No. 5. Washington, D.C.

Kane, Allen E.
1986   Social Organization and Cultural Process in Dolores Anasazi Communities, A.D. 600–900. In *Dolores Archaeological Program: Final Synthetic Report,* compiled by David A. Breternitz, Christine K. Robinson, and Timothy G. Gross, pp. 633-661. Bureau of Reclamation, Engineering and Research Center, Denver, Colorado.

Kidder, Alfred V.
1924   *An Introduction to the Study of Southwestern Archaeology.* Yale University Press, New Haven.

1927   Southwestern Archaeological Conference. *Science* 66(1716):489-491.

Kincaid, Chris (editor)
1983   *Chaco Roads Project, Phase I: A Reappraisal of Prehistoric Roads in the San Juan Basin, 1983.* Bureau of Land Management, Albuquerque.

Kintigh, Keith W.
1985   Social Structure, the Structure of Style, and Stylistic Patterns in Cibola Pottery. In *Decoding Prehistoric Ceramics,* edited by B. Nelson, pp. 35-74. Southern Illinois University Press, Carbondale.

Kluckhohn, Clyde
1939   Discussion. In *Preliminary Report on the 1937 Excavations, Bc 50-51, Chaco Canyon, New Mexico,* edited by Clyde Kluckhohn and Paul Reiter, pp. 151-190. University of New Mexico Bulletin, Anthropological Series, vol.3, No. 2. Albuquerque, New Mexico.

Lancaster, James A. and Jean M. Pinkley
1952   Excavation at Site 16 of Three Pueblo II Mesa-Top Ruins, in *Archeological Excavations in Mesa Verde National Park, Colorado, 1950,* by James A. Lancaster, Jean M. Pinkley, Philip F. Van Cleave, and Don Watson, pp. 23-86. Archeological Research Series No. 2. National Park Service, Washington, D.C.

Lekson, Steve
1984   *Great Pueblo Architecture of Chaco Canyon, New Mexico.* Publications in Archeology No. 18B, National Park Service, Albuquerque, New Mexico. (Reprinted 1986 by the University of New Mexico Press, Albuquerque)

1985   The Idea of the Kiva in Anasazi Archaeology. Paper presented at the 50th Annual Meeting of the Society for American Archaeology, Denver, Colorado.

1988   The Idea of the Kiva in Anasazi Archaeology. *The Kiva* 53(3):213-234.

Leone, Mark
1968   Neolithic Economic Autonomy and Social Distance. *Science* 162:1150-1151.

Lightfoot, Kent G.
1984   *Prehistoric Political Dynamics: A Case Study from the American Southwest.* Northern Illinois University Press, DeKalb.

Lightfoot, Kent G. and Gary M. Feinman
1982   Social Differentiation and Leadership Development in Early Pithouse Villages in the Mogollon Region of the American Southwest. *American Antiquity* 47(1): 64-86.

Lightfoot, Ricky R.
1988   Roofing an Early Anasazi Great Kiva: Analysis of an Archaeological Model. *The Kiva* 53(3):253-272.

Lipe, William D.
1960   *1958 Excavations, Glen Canyon Area.* University of Utah Anthropological Papers No. 44. Salt Lake City, Utah.

1986   Modeling Dolores Area Cultural Dynamics. In *Dolores Archaeological Program: Final Synthetic Re-*

port, compiled by David A. Breternitz, Christine K. Robinson, and G. Timothy Gross, pp. 439-467. Bureau of Reclamation, Engineering and Research Center, Denver, Colorado.

Lipe, William D. and Allen E. Kane
1986 Evaluation of the Models with Dolores Area Data. In *Dolores Archaeological Program: Final Synthetic Report,* compiled by David A. Breternitz, Christine K. Robinson, and G. Timothy Gross, pp. 703-707. Bureau of Reclamation, Engineering and Research Center, Denver, Colorado.

Lischka, Joseph J.
1975 Broken K Revisited: A Short Discussion of Factor Analysis. *American Antiquity* 40:220-227.

Longacre, William A.
1964 Archaeology as Anthropology: A Case Study. *Science* 144:1454-1455.

1966 Changing Patterns of Social Integration: A Prehistoric Example from the American Southwest. *American Anthropologist* 68(1):94-102.

1970 *Archaeology as Anthropology: A Case Study.* Anthropological Papers of the University of Arizona No. 17. Tucson.

Lowell, Julie
1988 The Social Use of Space at Turkey Creek Pueblo: An Architectural Analysis. *The Kiva* 53(2):85-100.

Marshall, Michael, John R. Stein, Richard W. Loose, and Judith Novotny
1979 *Anasazi Communities of the San Juan Basin.* Public Service Company of New Mexico and the State Historic Preservation Bureau, Santa Fe.

Mindeleff, Cosmos
1897 *Cliff Ruins of Canyon de Chelly, Arizona.* Sixteenth Annual Report of the Bureau of American Ethnology to the Secretary of the Smithsonian Institution 1894–1895: pp. 73-198. Government Printing Office, Washington, D.C.

Mindeleff, Victor
1891 *A Study of Pueblo Architecture, Tusayan and Cibola.* Eighth Annual Report of the Bureau of Ethnology to the Secretary of the Smithsonian Institution, 1886–1887: pp. 13-228. Government Printing Office, Washington, D.C.

Morgan, Lewis Henry
1965 *Houses and House-Life of the American Aborigines.* Reprinted by The University of Chicago Press (originally published in 1881 as Contributions to North American Ethnology, vol. 4. Government Printing Office, Washington, D.C.).

1985 *Ancient Society.* University of Arizona Press, Tucson (originally published 1877).

Morris, Earl H.
1939 *Archaeological Studies in the La Plata District, Southwestern Colorado and Northwestern New Mexico.* Carnegie Institution of Washington Publication No. 519. Washington, D.C.

Neitzel, Jill
1985 Regional Styles and Organizational Hierarchies: The View from Chaco. Paper presented at the 50th Annual Meeting of the Society for American Archaeology, Denver.

Nials, Fred, John Stein, and John Roney
1987 *Chacoan Roads in the Southern Periphery: Results of Phase II of the BLM Chaco Roads Project.* Cultural Resources Series No. 1. Bureau of Land Management, Albuquerque, New Mexico.

Orcutt, Janet D. and Eric Blinman
1987 Leadership and the Development of Social Complexity: A Case Study from the Dolores Area of the American Southwest. Manuscript in possession of the authors, Santa Fe, New Mexico.

Ortiz, Alfonso
1969 *The Tewa World: Space, Time, Being and Becoming in a Pueblo Society.* University of Chicago Press, Chicago.

Parsons, Elsie Clews
1940 Relations Between Ethnology and Archaeology in the Southwest. *American Antiquity* 5(3):214-220.

Plog, Fred
1974 *The Study of Prehistoric Change.* Academic Press, New York.

1983 Political and Economic Alliances on the Colorado Plateaus, A.D. 600–1450. In *Advances in New World Archaeology* No. 2, edited by F. Wendorf and A. E. Close, pp. 289-330. Academic Press, New York.

Plog, Stephen
1978 Social Interaction and Stylistic Similarity: A Reanalysis. In *Advances in Archaeological Method and Theory,* vol. 1, edited by M. B. Schiffer, pp. 143-182. Academic Press, New York.

1980a *Stylistic Variation in Prehistoric Ceramics: Design Analysis in the American Southwest.* Cambridge University Press, Cambridge, England.

1980b Village Autonomy in the American Southwest: An Evaluation of the Evidence. In *Models and Methods in Regional Exchange,* edited by R. E. Fry, pp. 135-146. SAA Papers No. 1. Society for American Archaeology, Washington, D.C.

1986 Change in Regional Trade Networks. In *Spatial Organization and Exchange: Archaeological Survey on Northern Black Mesa,* edited by S. Plog, pp. 282-309. Southern Illinois University Press, Carbondale.

1989 Sociopolitical Implications of Southwestern Stylistic Variation. In *The Use of Style in Archaeology,* edited by M. Conkey and C. Hastorf. Cambridge University Press, Cambridge, England, in press.

Powell, John Wesley
1875 *Explorations of the Colorado River of the West and Its Tributaries. Explored in 1869, 1870, 1871, and 1872, Under the Direction of the Secretary of the Smithsonian Institution.* Government Printing Office, Washington, D.C.

Powers, Robert P.
1984 Regional Interaction in the San Juan Basin: The Chacoan Outlier System. In *Recent Research on Chaco Prehistory,* edited by W. James Judge and John Schelberg, pp. 23-36. Reports of the Chaco Center No. 8. Division of Cultural Research, National Park Service, Albuquerque, New Mexico.

Powers, Robert P., William B. Gillespie, and Stephen H. Lekson
1983 *The Outlier Survey: A Regional View of Settlement in the San Juan Basin.* Reports of the Chaco Center No. 3. Division of Cultural Research, National Park Service, Albuquerque, New Mexico.

Prudden, T. Mitchell
1903 The Prehistoric Ruins of the San Juan Watershed in Utah, Arizona, Colorado, and New Mexico. *American Anthropologist,* n.s., 5(2):224-288.

1914 The Circular Kivas of Small Ruins in the San Juan Watershed. *American Anthropologist,* n.s., 16(1):33-58.

1918 *A Further Study of the Prehistoric Small House Ruins in the San Juan Watershed.* Memoirs of the American Anthropological Association, vol. 5, No. 1.

Redman, Charles L.
1978 Multivariate Artifact Analysis: A Basis for Multidimensional Interpretations. In *Social Archaeology: Beyond Subsistence and Dating,* edited by C. L. Redman et al., pp. 349-372. Academic Press, New York.

Reid, J. Jefferson
1985 Measuring Social Complexity in the American Southwest. In *Status, Structure, and Stratification: Current Archaeological Reconstructions,* edited by Marc Thompson, Maria Teresa Garcia, and Francois J. Kense, pp. 167-173. Proceedings of the Sixteenth Annual Chacmool Conference. The Archaeological Association of the University of Calgary, Calgary, Alberta.

Reyman, Jonathan
1986 A Reevaluation of Bi-Wall and Tri-Wall Structures in the Anasazi Area. In *Contributions to the Archaeology and Ethnohistory of Greater Mesoamerica,* edited by William J. Folan, pp. 293-334. Southern Illinois University Press, Carbondale.

Rohn, Arthur
1977 *Cultural Change and Continuity on Chapin Mesa.* The Regents Press of Kansas, Lawrence, Kansas.

Sackett, James R.
1985 Style and Ethnicity in the Kalahari: A Reply to Wiessner. *American Antiquity* 50:154-159.

Schiffer, Michael B.
1976 *Behavioral Archeology.* Academic Press, New York.

1985 Is There a "Pompeii Premise" in Archaeology? *Journal of Anthropological Research* 41(1):18-41.

1987 *Formation Processes of the Archaeological Record.* University of New Mexico Press, Albuquerque.

Sebastian, Lynne
1988 *Leadership, Power, and Productive Potential: A Political Model of the Chaco System.* Unpublished Ph.D. dissertation, Department of Anthropology, University of New Mexico, Albuquerque.

Schelberg, John D.
1984 Analogy, Complexity, and Regionally-based Perspectives. In *Recent Research on Chaco Prehistory,* edited by W. James Judge and John D. Schelberg, pp. 5-21. Reports of the Chaco Center No. 8. National Park Service, Albuquerque, New Mexico.

Shafer, Harry
  1982 Classic Mimbres Phase Households and Room Use Patterns. *The Kiva* 48(1-2):17-37.

Shepard, Anna O.
  1942 *Rio Grande Glaze Paint Ware*. Contributions to American Anthropology and History, vol. 7, No. 39. Carnegie Institution of Washington, Washington, D.C.

  1965 Rio Grande Glaze-Paint Pottery: A Test of Petrographic Analysis. In *Ceramics and Man*, edited by F. R. Matson, pp. 62-87. Viking Fund Publications in Anthropology No. 41. Aldine, Chicago.

Simpson, James H.
  1964 *Navajo Expedition: Journal of a Military Reconnaissance from Santa Fe, New Mexico, to the Navajo Country, Made in 1849*, Frank McNitt, editor. University of Oklahoma Press, Norman.

Smith, Watson
  1952 *Excavations in Big Hawk Valley, Wupatki National Monument, Arizona*. Museum of Northern Arizona Bulletin No. 24. Flagstaff, Arizona.

Stanislawski, Michael B.
  1973 Review of *Archaeology as Anthropology: A Case Study*, by William A. Longacre. *American Antiquity* 38:117-121.

  1977 Ethnoarchaeology of Hopi Pottery Making: Styles of Learning. In *Experimental Archeology*, edited by Daniel Ingersoll, John E. Yellen, and William MacDonald, pp. 378-408. Columbia University Press, New York.

Steward, Julian H.
  1937 Ecological Aspects of Southwestern Society. *Anthropos* 32:87-104.

Swentzell, Rina
  1988 *Bupingeh:* The Pueblo Plaza. *El Palacio* 94(2):14-19.

Taylor, Walter
  1954 Southwestern Archeology, Its History and Theory. *American Anthropologist* 56(4) Part 1:561-575.

Toll, H. Wolcott
  1985 *Pottery, Production, Public Architecture, and the Chaco Anasazi System*. Ph.D. dissertation, University of Colorado. University Microfilms, Ann Arbor, Michigan.

Toll, H. Wollcott, Thomas C. Windes, and Peter J. McKenna
  1980 Late Ceramic Patterns in Chaco Canyon: The Pragmatics of Modeling Ceramic Exchange. In *Models and Methods in Regional Exchange,* edited by R. E. Fry, pp. 95-118. SAA Papers No. 1. Society for American Archaeology, Washington, D.C.

Tuggle, H. David
  1970 *Prehistoric Community Relations in East-Central Arizona*. Ph.D. dissertation, University of Arizona. University Microfilms, Ann Arbor, Michigan.

Turner, Christy G., II, and Laurel Lofgren
  1966 Household Size of Prehistoric Western Pueblo Indians. *Southwestern Journal of Anthropology* 22:117-132.

Upham, Steadman
  1982 *Polities and Power: An Economic and Political History of the Western Pueblo*. Academic Press, New York.

  1985 Interpretations of Prehistoric Complexity in the Central and Northern Southwest. In *Status, Structure, and Stratification: Current Archaeological Reconstructions,* edited by Marc Thompson, Maria Teresa Garcia, and Francois J. Kense, pp. 175-180. Proceedings of the Sixteenth Annual Chacmool Conference. The Archaeological Association of the University of Calgary, Calgary, Alberta.

Upham, Steadman and Fred Plog
  1986 The Interpretation of Prehistoric Political Complexity in the Central and Northern Southwest: Toward a Mending of the Models. *Journal of Field Archaeology* 13:223-238.

Upham, Steadman, Kent G. Lightfoot, and Gary M. Feinman
  1981 Explaining Socially Determined Ceramic Distributions in the Prehistoric Plateau Southwest. *American Antiquity* 46:822-833.

Vivian, Gordon
  1959 *The Hubbard Site and Other Tri-Wall Structures in New Mexico and Colorado*. National Park Service Archeological Research Series No. 5. Washington, D.C.

Vivian, Gordon and Paul Reiter
  1960 *The Great Kivas of Chaco Canyon and Their Relationships*. Monographs of the School of American Research No. 22. Santa Fe, New Mexico.

Vivian, R. Gwinn, Dulce N. Dodgen, and Gayle H. Hartmann
1978   *Wooden Ritual Artifacts from Chaco Canyon, New Mexico: The Chetro Ketl Collection.* Anthropological Papers of the University of Arizona No. 32. Tucson.

Warren, Helene
1969   Tonque, One Pueblo's Glaze Pottery Industry Dominated Middle Rio Grande Commerce. *El Palacio* 76:36-42.

Washburn, Dorothy K.
1977   *A Symmetry Analysis of Upper Gila Area Ceramic Design.* Papers of the Peabody Museum of Archaeology and Ethnology, vol. 68. Harvard University, Cambridge.

Washburn, Dorothy K., and R. G. Matson
1985   Use of Multidimensional Scaling to Display Sensitivity of Symmetry Analysis of Patterned Design to Spatial and Chronological Change: Examples from Anasazi Prehistory. In *Decoding Prehistoric Ceramics,* edited by B. A. Nelson, pp. 75-101. University of Southern Illinois Press, Carbondale.

Whittlesey, Stephanie M.
1984   Uses and Abuses of Mogollon Mortuary Data. In *Recent Research in Mogollon Archaeology,* edited by S. Upham, F. Plog, D. G. Batcho, and B. E. Kauffman, pp. 276-284. Occasional Papers No. 10, New Mexico State University, Las Cruces.

Wiessner, Polly
1985   Style or Isochrestic Variation? A Reply to Sackett. *American Antiquity* 50:160-166.

Wilcox, David R.
1976   How the Pueblos Came to Be the Way They Are: The Problem Today. Paper presented in partial fulfilment of the preliminary exam, Department of Anthropology, University of Arizona, Tucson.

1981   Changing Perspectives on the Protohistoric Pueblos, A.D. 1450-1700, in *The Protohistoric Period in the North American Southwest, A.D. 1450–1700,* edited by David R. Wilcox and Bruce Masse, pp. 378-409. Arizona State University Anthropological Research Papers No. 24. Tempe, Arizona.

1988   Developmental Cycles at Broken K Pueblo. Paper presented at the 21st Chacmool Conference, "Households and Communities," Department of Archaeology, University of Calgary, Alberta, Canada.

Willey, Gordon R.
1953   *Prehistoric Settlement Patterns in the Viru Valley, Peru.* Bureau of American Ethnology Bulletin 155. Washington, D.C.

Willey, Gordon R., editor
1956   *Prehistoric Settlement Patterns in the New World.* Viking Fund Publications in Anthropology No. 23. Wenner-Gren Foundation for Anthropological Research, Inc., New York.

Wilson, Peter J.
1989   *The Domestication of the Human Species.* Yale University Press, New Haven, Connecticut.

Windes, Thomas C.
1984   A View of the Cibola Whitewares from Chaco Canyon. In *Regional Analysis of Prehistoric Ceramic Variation: Contemporary Studies of the Cibola Whitewares,* edited by A. P. Sullivan and J. L. Hantman, pp. 94-119. Anthropological Research Papers No. 31. Arizona State University, Tempe.

Wobst, H. Martin
1977   Stylistic Behavior and Information Exchange. In *Papers for the Director: Research Essays in Honor of James B. Griffin,* edited by C. E. Cleland, pp. 317-342. Anthropological Papers No. 67. Museum of Anthropology, University of Michigan, Ann Arbor.

Wylie, Alison
1985   The Reaction Against Analogy. In *Advances in Archaeological Method and Theory,* vol. 8, edited by Michael B. Schiffer, pp. 63-111. Academic Press, New York.

4
Ritual Facilities and Social Integration in Nonranked Societies

Michael A. Adler

Archaeological investigators of Anasazi architecture generally assume that kivas served primarily as a context for ritual activity above the household level. This paper approaches that assumption through a cross-cultural survey of socially integrative architecture among nonstratified societies. Questions considered are: (1) Is the presence or absence of an integrative facility dependent upon the scale or population of the host community? (2) What range of activities is carried out in the facility? (3) What portion of the society has access to the integrative facility? Aspects of social organizational theory are found to be helpful in interpreting the generalized observations on integrative facilities. Finally, the resulting insights are applied to data on prehistoric and historic kivas.

Introduction

Debate over the function and variability of prehistoric Anasazi kivas has been a major topic in Southwestern archaeology since the first subterranean round rooms were described (Fewkes 1896; Mindeleff 1891). Throughout the kiva debate, the primary data used for explanatory approaches to kiva function have been drawn from ethnographic reports of historic Eastern and Western Pueblo groups (e.g., Cater and Chenault 1988; Davis and Winkler 1975; Hawley 1950). However, it is evident that our continuing dependence upon ethnographic and archaeological data from the southwestern United States has limited our understanding of kiva function, including the possible use of kivas as socially integrative facilities. I propose that our interpretation of the evolution and function of Anasazi and Pueblo kivas should be informed by a broader understanding of the organizational role played by socially integrative facilities in other societies.

The first part of this paper attempts to develop this broader perspective through an ethnographic survey of integrative facilities utilized by nonranked societies. As used here, a socially integrative facility is a structure or prepared space socially acknowledged as a context for integration of individuals above the family level. The theory of scalar stress (Johnson 1978, 1982, 1983, 1988), which addresses various human responses to the stresses of controlling information and decision-making, is used here to help explain structural and functional variability observed in ethnographic examples of integrative facility use. Results of this approach suggest that within relatively small, politically nonstratified communities, integrative facilities remain generalized in use. That is, they commonly serve as a context for both secular and ritual activities. However, as the size of the interacting community increases, certain socially integrative facilities tend to be constructed and used almost exclusively for ritual activities.

The final part of this paper relates these observations on integrative structure use to data on prehistoric and historic kivas in the southwestern United States. It is proposed that prior to A.D. 1300, small prehistoric kivas of the northern San Juan region served as loci for both secular and sacred socially integrative activities. However, prehistoric Great Kivas and historic Pueblo kivas appear to be more similar to specialized ritual facilities.

The Ethnographic Sample

Twenty-eight cultures were included in this study (Table 1). The cultures are located in four geographical areas, namely North America (n = 7), South America (n = 8), New Guinea/Oceania (n = 10), and Africa (n = 3). This does not pretend to be a representative sample of sedentary and semisedentary small-scale societies, but serves as the basis for a preliminary study to which more societies can be added. Because this body of ethnographic data was collected to aid our understanding of prehistoric and historic kivas, all societies included in this initial ethnographic survey lie outside the Eastern and Western Pueblo regions. Data from the Human Relations Area Files (HRAF) served as a starting point for the collection of ethnographic data, and subsequent research incorporated ethnographic literature not included in the HRAF.

Several criteria were used to select the cultures included in this survey, and to assemble the relevant criteria. First, the societies are nonhierarchical in sociopolitical structure: that is, they are "tribal" (For recent syntheses of tribal societies see Braun and Plog 1982; Feinman and Neitzel 1984; Johnson and Earle 1987). As defined here, tribal or nonranked societies exhibit sustained political autonomy at or below the community level, though communities do sporadically integrate into larger intercommunity groups for defense, ritual or other purposes.

Second, these groups are sedentary for at least part of each year. Since my objective is to examine the mechanisms of ritual and secular integration above the family level and below the level of the politically integrated region, only groups inhabiting sedentary communities for at least part of every year were included in this study. Following the lead of other comparative studies of community organization (Murdock 1949; Murdock and Wilson 1972), a community is the maximum number of people who reside together and have regular, face-to-face interaction.

Third, population estimates had to be available. Because the size of the largest community in each society is a significant variable here, a number of estimates were sought for each society. Ethnographic data on community population were sometimes quite variable. When there was a great deal of variance in population estimates, the most commonly cited figure for the largest community was used. This has probably resulted in conservative estimates for the size of the largest communities in each society.

Finally, when the above criteria were met, data on the presence, size and use of socially integrative facilities were sought. An integrative facility is a structure or prepared space socially acknowledged as a context for daily or episodic integration of individuals above the family level. Examples are dance houses, sudatories, clan houses, plaza structures and men's houses. I use the term "socially integrative facility" rather than "ritually integrative facility" because, as I stress later, we should pay attention to the degree to which nonritual activities occur in those spaces also used for ritual integration.

I also define two types of integrative facilities in this paper. Because different integrative facilities are used by various communities and parts of communities, I use the term "low-level facility" in describing those facilities that serve to integrate only a portion of a community. In contrast, high-level facilities are utilized for social activities involving groups from multiple low-level facilities. High-level facilities can integrate groups from one community or from a number of separate communities.

Variability in Tribal Integrative Facilities

In order to understand the organizational role of socially integrative facilities, the relationship of facility size and use to group size is investigated. The study is aimed at answering two major questions. First, how is the size of the local community related to the presence and size of integrative facilities? Second, why is there a wide range of activities associated with some facilities but not with others?

Presence of Integrative Facilities

Based upon this sample, community size does not seem to dictate presence or absence of socially integrative facilities. Of the 28 groups investigated, 22 utilized a structurally separate communal building. Integrative facilities are present in communities of all sizes (Figure 1, Table 1), from those with several families (Tareumiut and Yuman) to those with hundreds of families (Arapesh). As a generalization, communities that are sedentary for even a few months contain integrative facilities. These facilities serve as important foci to organize and disseminate material resources and information.

The several exceptions to this generalization are also informative. Where separate integrative facilities are not present in a community, plazas, dance areas or temporary plazas are often utilized for integrative activities above the family level. The Tallensi, Timbira, and Yanomamo all use plazas as integrative spaces, but lack structures that serve as integrative facilities. Though this paper does not include plazas in subsequent comparisons, plaza areas should certainly be considered integrative facilities. Johnson and Earle (1987:table 11) note that dance grounds are characteristic of local groups, further supporting the broad presence of integrative facilities on the community level.

Societies in which the entire community resides in a single longhouse also seem to fall outside the general pattern, since they have no separate structures that

Table 1: Ethnographic Data.

	Village Population	Mean Number Integrative Facilities	Use Group Size	Domestic Facility Size (m²)	Integrative Facility Size (m²)
Arapesh	250	1	250	30	220M
Arapesh-x	—		500+	—	250+
Baktaman	250	8	30	34	46
Bororo	200	1	200	72L	190M
Buka	250?		?	?	M?
Dogon	210	7	30	37	36
Elema	500	3	150	35	186M
Elema-x	—		300	—	280
Etoro	75	1	75	140L	70L*
Fang	250	5	50	20	60
Gt. Basin	75	3	25	37	41
Jivaro	300	1	300?	300L	L*
Kiwai	250	2	100?	300L	300?M
Maidu	175	7	25	70	33
Maidu-x	—		350	—	90
Mandan	320	8	40	70	51
Mandan-x	—		600	—	180
Maring	100		?	?	M
Mundurucu	200	1	200	68L	200M
Nambiquara	50?	1	50?	40	P
New Ireland	220	7	30	30	50
N. Pomo	150	6	25	14	30
N. Pomo-x	—		300	—	170
Orokaiva	150	6	25	25	30
Orokaiva-x	—		300	—	140
Sherente	200		?	?	M
Tallensi	300		?	?	D
Tapirape	200	1	200	90L	180M
Tareumiut	100	5	20	23	37
Timbira	200		?	20	P
Wogeo	100	1	100	32	45M
Yanomamo	150		?	80?	P
Yuman	150	4	35	24	54
Yurok	200	9	22	14	40
Yurok-x	—		400	—	170?

? = Significant uncertainty in estimate
P = Plaza used for integrative activity – no separate structures present
M = Men's house and integrative facility
D = Dance ground used as area for integrative activity
L = Longhouse domestic facilities
L* = Etoro and Jivaro longhouses have a partitioned area for male use only
x = High-level socially integrative facility – integrates low-level use groups

serve as socially integrative facilities. However, ethnographic accounts of these groups often describe sections of the longhouse that are set aside as meeting places, dance areas, or men's sections. In these cases, the space used for social integration has been incorporated into the groups' living quarters. The Etoro, Jivaro and Nambiquara utilize this type of communal housing (Table 1).

Integrative Structure Use

There are indications in the data that some facilities are meant to be used by entire communities (high-level facilities), and other facilities (low-level) serve smaller portions of a community. In view of the range of variation in socially integrative facilities, it is logical to ask whether certain activities are related to the various types.

A listing of the activities carried out in each facility would be too massive an undertaking. Instead, I focus on two categories, ritual and nonritual. The reason for using them is obvious, since one of the driving questions behind this collection of papers is to what extent kivas were utilized for ritual and/or domestic activities. By tabulating the presence or absence of five ritual and five nonritual activities for each facility, broader patterns of facility use can be applied to our current kiva dilemma.

Nonritual activities include cooking, informal visiting, eating daily meals, sleeping and craft production. Ritual activities include meetings of societies and sodalities, initiation rites, group-sponsored activities (such as dances), multivillage ceremonial activities, and storage of ritual items. For example, the Mandan medicine lodge is used for only one secular activity (eating) and three ritual activities (moiety meetings, initiation rites, and multivillage ceremonial activities).

These two categories of activities are certainly not mutually exclusive. For example, eating and cooking often occur in a ritual context. They were added to the nonritual side of the graph only when it was clear that these two activities occurred in the facility on a daily basis.

When we look at the overall trends in facility use (Figure 2), most low-level integrative structures (n = 17) fall into the class I call "generalized-use facilities." By generalized use, I mean that the structures are used as often for day-to-day domestic activities as they are for ritual activities. In fact, ritually integrative activities generally occur a *minority* of the time these more general-use integrative facilities are in use.

Within this sample, relatively few structures (n = 7) are used primarily for integrative ritual. It is significant that all facilities primarily housing ritual activities are high-level integrative facilities. It is also notable that high-level facilities are not the only contexts for ritual activity. Ritual also takes place in generalized-use, low-level facilities (Figure 2). However, high-level facilities are conspicuous for their lack of use in nonritual activities. We will return to this point later.

A strong relationship is also evident between facility use and the number of facilities present in the settlement (Figure 2, Table 1). The dominant pattern throughout this sample is that multiple low-level facilities are found in each community. A portion of the community uses them for both nonritual and ritual activities, so they are considered general-use integrative facilities. In contrast, high-level facilities serve larger groups than low-level facilities and are a context for the integration of groups from multiple low-level facilities. In some cases high-level facilities integrate groups from more than one community. The range of activities in high-level facilities is relegated almost exclusively to ritual activities.

There are cases that do not fit the simple dichotomy of high-level and low-level facilities. Several societies in this study have a single integrative facility per settlement used as a men's house (Arapesh, Bororo, Etoro, Jivaro, Mundurucu, Tapirape, Wogeo in Table 1), and these facilities appear to double as both low- and high-level facilities. However, when ethnographic descriptions are available, many of these community structures are described as internally "partitioned." That is, different moiety or clan groups are associated with architecturally or socially demarcated areas within the single structure. So, in an organizational sense, it may be that we can treat these singular integrative facilities as multiple low-level facilities housed under a single roof. Added support for this interpretation comes from the fact that when they are present in these cultures (five of seven cases), domiciliary long houses are generally internally partitioned, and each longhouse houses several family groups (Table 1).

The Theoretical Approach

To help explain some of the variability in these data, I have drawn upon a body of anthropological theory that addresses the social organization of information and decision-making in human societies (Carneiro 1967; Ember 1963; Flannery 1972; Moore 1983), focusing most heavily upon the work of Gregory Johnson (1978, 1982, 1983). Johnson has studied common patterns in organizational structure as they relate to overall population size, social group size and social hierarchy. He proposes that all human groups face common organizational problems related to the stresses of controlling information and making decisions. The size of consensual decision-making organizations is limited by humans' capacities to process information. Groups

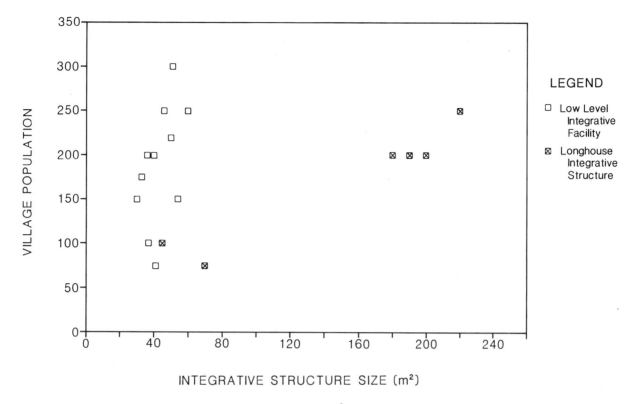

Figure 1: Low-level integrative facility size (in m²), plotted against village population.

comprised of about two to six participants or subgroups are the most efficient for decision-making. But, as the number of individuals or decision-making units seeking consensus exceeds this crucial limit of six, the difficulty in arriving at a final decision increases exponentially in relation to group size. This difficulty is what Johnson (1982:394) terms scalar stress.

Scalar Stress

Johnson has used data from hunter-gatherer groups (1982) and pastoral nomad groups (1983) to argue that there are three major, but not mutually exclusive, choices available for groups plagued by scalar stress. First, groups can fission into smaller entities. Second, groups can utilize a nonconsensual decision-making hierarchy: that is, they can follow the dictates of a leader. Finally, they can organize into a sequential hierarchy, whereby groups of fairly equal size exist without an institutionalized decision-making hierarchy.

Sequential hierarchies generally mitigate scalar stress by increasing the operational size of the units that must agree upon a decision. An example of such a change is seen in !Kung San camps. During the rainy season, when groups are dispersed, the !Kung nuclear family is the basic decision-making unit, which Johnson calls the "basal unit." However, when families aggregate at water holes during the dry season, the larger extended family becomes the basal unit. Because each basal unit participates in decision-making at the camp level, an increase in basal unit size during the dry season population aggregations decreases the potential of scalar stress. When the size of the basal unit increases, fewer total basal units have to participate in the decision-making process (Johnson 1982:397).

Integrative Facilities and Scalar Stress

Scalar stress theory is well-suited to the present study of socially integrative facilities. One of the defining attributes of nonranked societies is that the process of decision-making involves relatively more group-based consensus than that seen in ranked societies. In my application of the scalar stress theory to the present data, I assume that socially integrative activities, including ritual, often play an important role in the process of decision-making and information control within tribal societies. This does not mean that socially integrative activities serve as the only context within which decisions are made, or that all activities in socially integrative facilities involve decision-making. Instead, I assume that they serve as one of several potential contexts for information exchange and decision-making. As such, an investigation of the uses and sizes of integrative facilities provides a suitable context

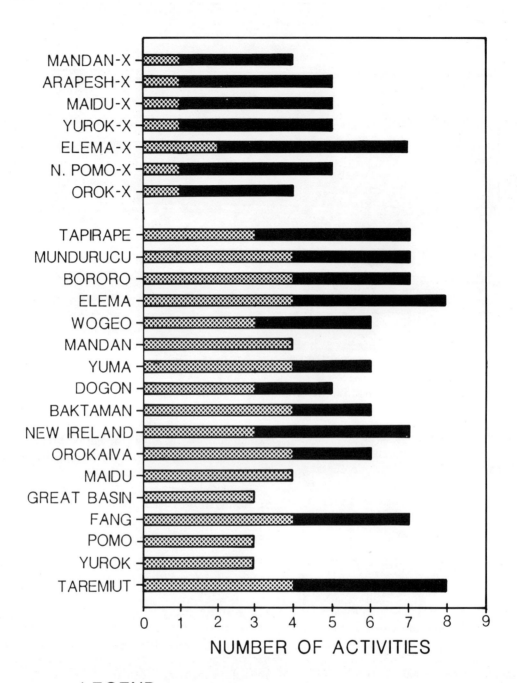

Figure 2: Comparison of reported numbers of ritual and nonritual activities in both high-level and low-level integrative facilities. An X following the group name signifies a high-level integrative facility.

within which to study social responses to the constraints of scalar stress.

Basal Units and Low-Level Facilities

Let us return to our discussion of the data with scalar stress in mind. If socially integrative facilities are common in nonranked societies, the first question should concern the relationship between community and integrative facility size.

According to Johnson, basal unit size should increase as the size of the population aggregation increases. If this is so, and if we assume that integrative facilities are used by basal units, increases in basal unit size should result in an increase in the size of integrative structures. That is, as the scale of the sequentially hierarchical system increases, the integrative structure should expand to accommodate the larger organizational basal unit.

When we compare the size of low-level integrative facilities with the size of the largest community, the expected positive relationship between increased settlement size and increased facility size is only weakly borne out (Figure 1). This is consistent with Johnson's finding that overall community size is not a good indicator of scalar stress (Johnson 1982:392). This is because decision-making basal units often operate below the community level.

Stronger relationships exist between community size, the size of the low-level integrative facility, and the population of the group most intimately associated with its use (Figures 3, 4a and 4b). This group, here called the use-group, was derived by dividing the population of the largest community by the average number of integrative facilities in the community. As community size increases, there is an associated increase in the size of groups using an integrative facility (Figure 3). As might be expected, the size of the integrative facility increases as the use-group increases in size. This relationship between use-group size and integrative structure size holds fairly well for those societies with low-level facilities (Figure 4a), as well as with the subset of these societies with more than one low-level facility per settlement (Figure 4b). Again, these comparisons do not include high-level integrative facilities.

Thus, there is a positive relationship between community and use-group size. This follows Johnson's argument that the size of decision-making groups should increase as possible scalar stress increases. Though each individual group may experience more scalar stress, the overall potential stress within the community decreases. This is because an increase in the size of decision-making units results in a decrease in the number of such groups in the community. As might be expected, the concomitant increase in the size of low-level integrative facilities (Figure 4a and 4b) is necessary to accommodate the increased size of the use-groups.

High-Level Facilities and Social Integration

Although scalar stress theory predicts an increase in basal unit size as community size increases, Johnson notes that an upper size-limit probably exists for basal units. However, even within this limited data set there are integrative facilities serving several hundred individuals. Use-groups of this size are far larger than those associated with low-level integrative facilities, and are well beyond the size limit of effective basal unit size postulated by Johnson. The lack of fit between the size of high-level integrative facilities and their associated use-groups is obvious in comparison to the low-level integrative facilities (Figure 5).

If scalar stress places limits on effective information-processing and decision-making, then how do large integrative facilities function efficiently in the face of potentially great scalar stress? One solution to this quandary may be related to the variation in facility use. It was noted above that the range of *nonritual* activities in the facilities narrows as the size of the use-group increases. Looking once again to theories of human information-processing, there are good reasons to associate greater ritual specialization with large aggregations. Rappaport (1968, 1979), Turner (1969), and others have proposed that ritual creates a context in which a great deal of information can be disseminated efficiently to large numbers of participants. This is because ritual activity reduces some of the ambiguity inherent in information exchange and decision-making, making the information communicated much more distinct to those present. To reduce the variability and "streamline" the messages being encoded, ritual involves what Rappaport (1979:192) calls a "liturgical order."

Liturgical order refers to the relatively invariant sequence of acts and utterances found in ritual. For example, as a ritual, a Catholic mass is organized to include exceptional liturgical order. The mass has an established agenda and is notable for its fixed formality. So, in an organizational sense, a liturgical order in any activity introduces significant redundancy into the information being exchanged. This redundancy facilitates more effective communication within the social context, since there is less room for innovation and error (Rappaport 1979:178). As might be expected, effective communication becomes increasingly important as the number of participants (communicators) in a social gathering grows.

I would propose that the ritual specialization of some socially integrative facilities represents another facet of

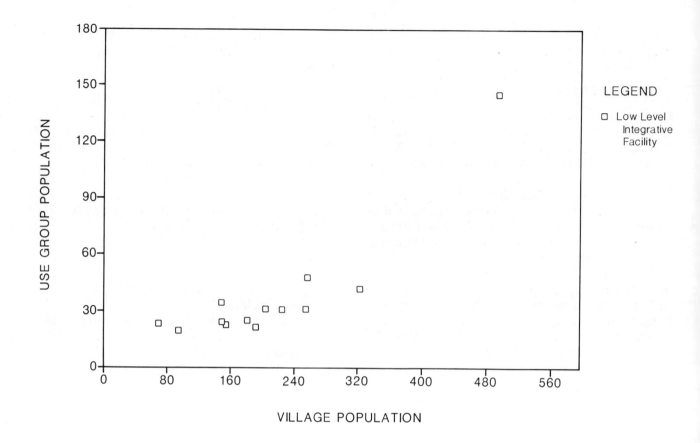

Figure 3: Village population plotted against average use-group population, low-level integrative facilities only. Note positive relationship between village size and use-group size.

the "liturgical order." By restricting access and use, ritual specialization of integrative facilities creates a space in which sacred activity is the only, or at least the major, activity associated with its integrative function. By codifying ways of doing things, ritual can more clearly delineate what information and activity the public can expect at the facility.

As an example, among the Elema of New Guinea (Williams 1940), the largest *eravo* (men's house) is utilized for all settlement-wide and multivillage rituals. Several characteristics mark the large eravo as special. None of the smaller *baupo eravo,* or men's houses, are allowed within the plaza surrounding the great eravo. Women are not allowed to live within close proximity of the facility. This ordering of the integrative space dictates a new, narrower range of possible activities and information available in that context. This helps delineate the range of socially pertinent information disseminated within the ritually specialized context.

High-level facilities generally serve as fine examples of ritually integrative structures. That is, use of high-level facilities is usually restricted to ritual activities or use by sanctioned individuals. It is significant that this narrowing of activities and information is not accomplished through an absolute increase in ritual activities, but through a decrease in the secular activi-

ties associated with them (Figure 2). While more generalized integrative structures are used for a wide range of ritual and secular activities, ritually specialized spaces are characterized by a decrease in the quotidian. This specialization sets the facility apart as qualitatively different from the generalized facilities.

Ritually Integrative Facilities Revisited

When they are found in the ethnographic record, specialized ritually integrative facilities share some interesting characteristics. First, these facilities are used more sporadically than general-use integrative facilities. Integrative rituals occur periodically in specialized facilities, but the facilities are usually dormant, often watched over by a custodian. Examples include the Yurok dance house, the Mandan medicine lodge, and the Baktaman cult house. In contrast, general-use integrative facilities are often used daily.

Second, when ritually specialized facilities are not being used for large-scale integrative rituals, regular use of the facility is generally restricted to small, exclusive groups of sanctioned individuals. For example, Ilahita Arapesh spirit houses are used exclusively by males who have undergone several levels of sacred initiation (Tuzin 1976,1980). This specialized men's

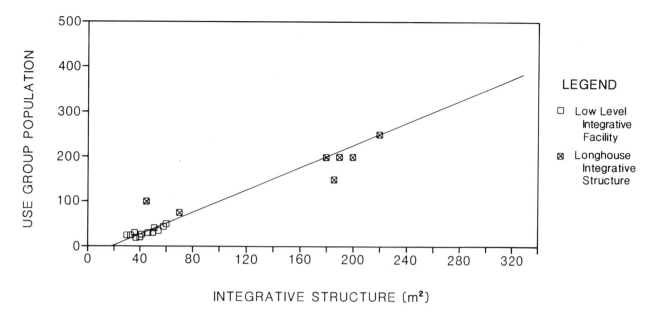

Figure 4a: Use-group population plotted against integrative structure size (m^2), including all low-level integrative facilities.

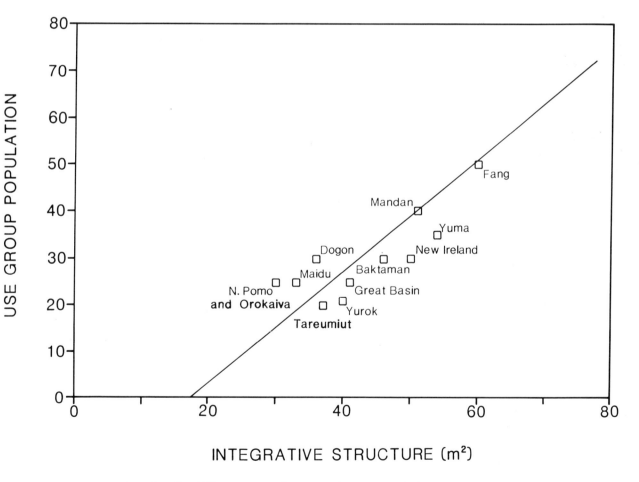

Figure 4b: Detail of Figure 4a, including only those societies with two or more low-level integrative facilities per settlement, and smaller than 80 m^2.

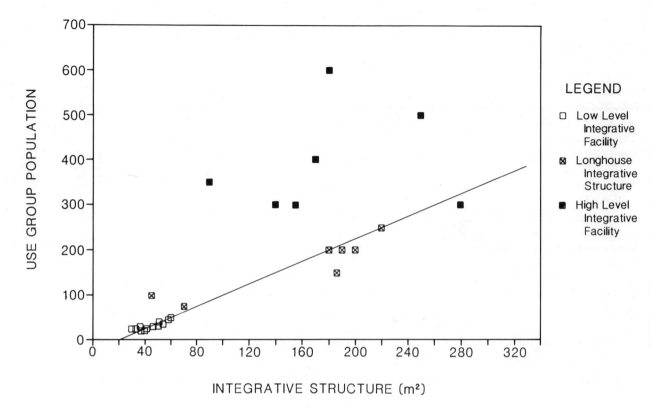

Figure 5: Size of use-group plotted against size of integrative facility (m^2), including all low-level and high-level facilities. Note the lack of fit for the high-level facilities (solid squares), indicating less average floor space per person compared to that for low-level facilities.

house is used regularly for meetings, cooking and consumption of ritually sanctioned foods, and most importantly, the storage of secret ceremonial paraphernalia. These spirit houses are located in a ceremonial hamlet, and access is restricted to initiated men who can enter only those plazas and structures associated with their initiate grade.

Finally, as mentioned above, ritually specialized facilities are associated with exceptionally large use-groups, often including the members of several interacting but separate communities. As noted, not all of the use-group will have regular access to the facility, however. Nearly all the seven examples of ritually specialized facilities included in the study were associated with a large community or group of integrated communities containing at least 300 individuals. This population estimate does not represent a minimum community size above which we will necessarily find ritually specialized contexts for social integration. However, it does indicate that such facilities are often associated with large population aggregations and increased population densities.

Kivas in Broader Organizational Perspective

One of the major stresses faced by interacting individuals or groups is how to organize themselves while retaining adaptive flexibility. Johnson shows quite elegantly that many aspects of social structure can be explained as means for reducing the stresses inherent in information-processing and decision-making. Johnson has touched briefly on ways in which ritual, or in his words, "generalized feather-waving" (1982:405-6), may reduce the communication load in large aggregations. The present study posits an explicit relationship between integrative facilities, ritual, and their combined potential to reduce scalar stress in nonranked, relatively sedentary societies. Though there are clear regularities in the ethnographic data on integrative facilities, the approach used here does not provide a formula for determining the function of all purported integrative facilities, including kivas. Instead, the results of this study can be used to suggest some relationships between kivas and systems of Anasazi social integration and ritual activity.

Kivas and Community Size

First, the ethnographic cases show that in relatively small communities, with populations no greater than 150–175 individuals, generalized use of integrative facilities is the dominant pattern. These shared spaces are often used by several families and are the loci of secular as well as ritual activities. Our own body of literature on Anasazi archaeology is replete with examples of small villages and communities, particularly those labeled "unit type pueblos" by Prudden (1903, 1914). Judge (1988) proposes that between A.D. 700–1300 the average habitation site in the San Juan Basin contained between 6.9–10.9 rooms. Sites of this size probably housed one to two extended families or similar groups. This average site size is consistent with other estimates from the same period across the northern Southwest (Adler 1988; Fetterman and Honeycutt 1987; Lipe 1970; Neily 1983).

Rohn (1977) has argued (I think correctly) that these small Anasazi settlements were probably part of dispersed communities that interacted on a regular basis. But even if these Anasazi communities included several interacting settlements, they would still fall within the population range (less than 175 people) of those ethnographic cases exhibiting generalized use of integrative facilities. From an organizational perspective, kivas associated with these small sites may well have housed a variety of ritual and nonritual activities.

The average size of Anasazi integrative facilities also supports the argument that they had a generalized function. Focusing on pre–A.D. 1300 kivas from the Mesa Verde area, these presumed integrative facilities average about 13 m^2 (Lipe, this volume), well within the size range of the generalized facilities included in this study (Figure 6). Rohn (1971, 1977) has proposed that 12–15 people were associated with the use of each kiva. Even if Rohn's estimate is doubled, the average kiva use-group would fall well within the normal range associated with ethnographic examples of low-level integrative facilities.

If the regularities observed for the ethnographic examples of generalized integrative facility are representative, prehistoric kivas should contain evidence of secular as well as ritual activities. In the Mesa Verde region, kivas and early Pueblo pit structures often exhibit evidence of cooking, food preparation, weaving, pottery production, and tool making (Bradley 1986, 1987; Gillespie 1976; Luebben 1982, 1983; O'Bryan 1950; Rohn 1971; Wilshusen 1986, 1988). Cater and Chenault (1988) have recently argued that, contrary to some interpretations, kivas were more important as contexts for nonritual activities than previously thought. Similarly, Lekson (1988) has argued that, prior to A.D. 1300, kivas were used almost entirely as domestic facilities.

Large Kivas and Anasazi Community Integration

A substantial percentage of Anasazi communities appear to have population levels which would benefit from use of socially integrative structures. In fact, the prehistoric Southwest had many examples of high population densities and large population aggregations. Some of these aggregations, such as Shabik'eschee Village in Chaco Canyon, occurred as early as A.D. 600, and may have contained 75 or more individuals (Wills and Windes 1989). Later Anasazi settlements with populations in the hundreds are well-represented in the northern San Juan from A.D. 700 through A.D. 1300. In light of the probable scalar stress inherent in such dense population aggregations, it is likely that high-level, ritually specialized integrative facilities existed in large Anasazi communities. The most probable candidate for such facilities would be the class of large structures commonly known as Great Kivas.

Prehistorically, Great Kivas are generally associated with either large aggregated habitation sites or with clusters of contemporaneous habitations. In other words, these large structures appear to have been associated with high population densities (but see Orcutt et al. 1987). Though specific population estimates are not available, Great Kivas served communities many times the size of the common unit pueblo, or even of most community clusters comprised of a few unit pueblos.

Examples of excavated Great Kivas are not numerous in the northern Southwest. The average diameter of 10 Great Kivas built between A.D. 900–1150 is 15.9 meters (s.d. = 2.5 m), based upon examples from Aztec Ruin (Morris 1921), Lowry Ruin (Martin 1936) and Chaco Canyon (Lekson 1984). This average diameter would result in 199 m^2 of floor area for these massive structures. Thus, Great Kivas fall within the size range of the specialized ritual facilities seen in the ethnographic record (Figure 6). As with the ethnographic examples of specialized ritual facilities and generalized facilities, there is a significant gap in overall size between the smaller kivas and the Great Kivas. Given the limited number of excavated Great Kivas, facility use is difficult to interpret. However, it is clear from excavated examples that there is an increase in the number and kind of specialized internal features in Great Kivas. These features include caches of unique items, opposing formalized floor vaults or foot drums, and multiple sipapus. Thus, Great Kivas are quantitatively larger than the smaller, Prudden-unit kiva, and they also exhibit standardized, qualitative differences which mark them as a separate class of integrative facility (see Wilshusen, Chapter 7, this volume).

There is no firm evidence of regular use of Great Kivas for secular activities, but in light of the very small excavated sample the negative evidence is inconclusive. However, based upon this study, I would predict that if Great Kivas did serve as high-level integrative facilities, their use for nonritual activities would have been limited. It is to be hoped that future excavations will address the question of specialized use for Great Kivas.

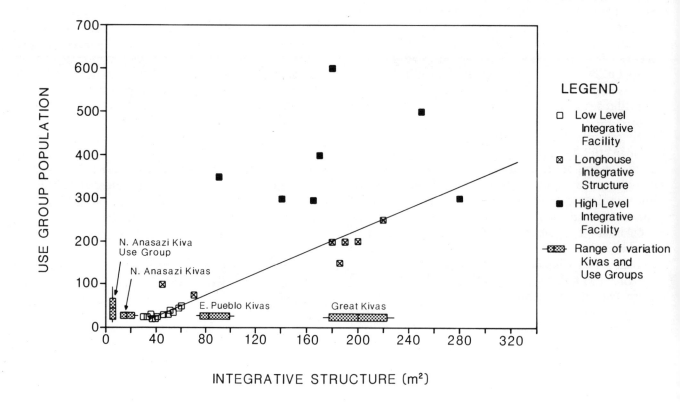

Figure 6: Size of use-group population plotted against size of integrative structure (m²), including data on prehistoric Northern Anasazi kivas. Use-group size not plotted for prehistoric Anasazi Great Kivas or for historic Eastern Pueblo kivas.

Eastern Pueblo Groups and Historic Kiva Use

Finally, if we include observations from the historic Rio Grande Pueblos (Figure 6), it is evident that the relationships between Eastern Pueblo population size, integrative structure size, and access limitations parallel the nonpueblo ethnographic patterns. The estimated average population for 18 Eastern Pueblo villages in 1948 was 570 individuals per settlement (Dohm 1988). Though there is substantial variance around this mean (s.d. = 391), these settlements are still large in comparison to most of the ethnographic cases used here.

The average kiva size in the Eastern Rio Grande Pueblo is 81 m² (s.d. = 39 m²), several times the average size of the prehistoric Anasazi kiva. Based upon the expectations derived from scalar stress theory, this great increase in floor area is related to an increase in basal unit size. Indeed, the high room-to-kiva ratio (>120:1) reported by Lipe (this volume) for Eastern Pueblo villages indicates a large use-group for each kiva. Assuming a conservative estimate of five rooms per household for the Eastern Pueblo (but see Dohm 1988), an average Eastern Pueblo kiva use-group of 24 households would be much larger than the one- to two-household use-group proposed for the smaller Anasazi kivas.

Based upon the ethnographic data on integrative structures serving communities of this size, it is not unreasonable to expect Eastern Pueblo settlements to contain, or have access to, ritually more specialized integrative facilities. Along these lines, we should expect not only a limitation on the number of people permitted regular access to these facilities, but a decrease in the range of nonritual activities carried out in these larger spaces.

Because of ritual restrictions, anthropologists do not know the entire range of specific activities that occur in the Eastern Pueblo kivas (Hawley 1950; Parsons 1939). However, evidence indicates that regular public access to the kivas is restricted, and kiva use is confined predominantly to ritual activities and to public performances associated with religious ceremonies.

Ortiz (1969:37) reports that at San Juan Pueblo there was selective membership in the ritual organizations associated with the kivas. Though the entire community was invited into the kiva for certain portions of initiation rites and social dances, the general populace did not have access to the facilities. In addition, secret moiety rooms located off the main kiva were never entered by members of the opposite moiety. Ritually recruited individuals known as *Towa e* were chosen to repair and clean the kivas, and were charged with opening and heating the facilities prior to any ritual (Ortiz 1969:72).

Parsons' (1939) discussions of various Eastern Pueblo ceremonies describe a range of activities that occurred in the kivas. Parsons (1939:437) notes that eating, sleeping, and craft activities were permitted in them, but mainly during retreats. Retreats often lasted four, and sometimes seven days, during which time participants lived in the kivas. The rest of the time they served as a context for meetings and public performances associated with society-sponsored ceremonies.

Hawley (1950) argues that there are two distinct types of kivas used by Puebloan cultures, namely big kivas and little kivas. Only one or two big kivas are found in each village. Big kivas differ from little kivas in that big kivas are "community buildings used only for affairs open to the village as a whole" (1950:287). Little kivas are restricted to use by smaller groups within the village. In Tiwa settlements, such as Isleta, the big kiva is a sacred community structure, and Isletans believe their lives are planted within its walls (1950:288).

The various aspects of the Eastern Pueblo kiva, including its large size, large associated use-group, and lack of use for nonritual domestic activities, fits the expectations of this model. The scalar stress inherent in large Eastern Pueblo villages would create substantial organizational hurdles. By ritually circumscribing the contexts within which large-scale social integration and interaction occurred, Eastern Pueblo communities reduced organizational stress.

Summary

Though we have seen the variation present in ethnographic examples of socially integrative facilities, there are informative commonalities. Among those groups with relatively small communities, integrative facilities tend to be generalized in use and are often utilized by both sexes for secular as well as ritual activities. In such a context, it is expected that decision-making and information flow would remain more generalized. Small groups are able to function with less stress in decision-making and information processing, and require less of the ordering that ritual brings to the realm of social action. This is not to say that small groups lack ritual, but rather that relatively fewer responses to scalar stress may be required, ritual being only one potential avenue to alleviate scalar stress.

A generalized integrative context for the dissemination of information is apparently efficient for small, dispersed populations. However, the effectiveness of generalized integrative contexts may be reduced as the interacting community grows. Streamlining or specializing the ritual realm is one means of increasing the effectiveness of information exchange and decision-making in larger integrated communities. Integrative facilities can be made more specialized by restricting regular public access, decreasing the amount of nonritual activity associated with their use, and restricting the occasions on which they are used.

From the vantage point of organizational theory, it is apparent that systemic parallels to kivas and kiva function exist in different shapes, sizes, and contexts throughout many of the world's societies. The purpose of this paper has been to outline these systemic parallels and adopt a theoretical approach that treats prehistoric Anasazi kivas as integrative facilities linked inexorably to a social organizational context. This approach will allow archaeologists to break out of the present cycle of interpreting kivas based solely upon Southwestern ethnography and archaeological data. The upshot is that we can come to better understand both those social processes and practices which the Puebloan peoples share with the world's cultures, as well as those practices which may be unique to the past and present native cultures of the American Southwest.

Acknowledgments

Portions of this research were supported by National Science Foundation Dissertation Improvement Grant No. 8707021 and by the Crow Canyon Archaeological Center. My thanks to Jeanne Athos-Adler, Bruce Bradley, Michelle Hegmon, William Lipe, Gary Feinman, Izumi Shimada, John Speth, Mark Varien, and Richard Wilshusen for comments, suggestions and encouragement. I wish I could have done justice to all their assistance. As always, any errors are solely my responsibility.

Appendix 1: Sample cases used

Culture Groups	References	Culture Groups	References
North America		Timbira	Nimendaju (1946)
Maidu	Kroeber (1925)		HRAF file SO8
	Bean (1978)	Yanomamo	Chagnon (1968)
Mandan	Will and Spinden (1906)		Johnson and Earle (1987)
	Lowie (1917)		HRAF file SQ18
	HRAF file NQ17		
Owens Valley Paiute	Liljeblad and Fowler (1986)	*Africa*	
N. Pomo	Kroeber (1925)	Dogon	Griaule and Dieterlen (1954)
	Bean (1978)		Tait (1950)
	Loeb (1926)		HRAF file FA8
	HRAF file NS18	Fang	Balandier (1955)
Tareumiut	Burch (1978)		Fernandez (1982)
	Lantis (1947)		HRAF file FH9
Gila River Yuma	Spier (1933)	Tallensi	Fortes (1945)
	HRAF file NT15		HRAF file FE11
Yurok	Kroeber (1925)		
	HRAF file NS31	*New Guinea/Oceania*	
		Arapesh	Tuzin (1976, 1980)
South America		Baktaman	Barth (1975)
Bororo	Cook (1907)	Buka	HRAF file ON6
	Levi-Strauss (1963)	Elema	Williams (1940)
	HRAF file SP8	Etoro	Kelly (1974)
Jivaro	Nimendaju (1943)	Kiwai	Landtman (1927)
	Steward (1948)	New Ireland	Powdermaker (1933)
Mundurucu	Murphy and Murphy (1974)		HRAF file OM10
	HRAF file SQ13	Orokaiva	Williams (1930)
Nambiquara	Gross (1979)		HRAF file OJ23
	Levi-Strauss (1945)	Tsembaga Maring	Rappaport (1968)
	Price (1987)	Wogeo	Hogbin (1935)
	HRAF file SP17		HRAF file OJ27
Sherente	Nimendaju (1942)		
	Steward (1948)		
Tapirape	Lowie (1949)		
	HRAF file SP22		

References

Adler, Michael
1988 *Archaeological Survey and Testing in the Sand Canyon/Goodman Point Locality, 1987 Field Season.* Crow Canyon Archaeological Center, Cortez, Colorado. Submitted to the Bureau of Land Management, San Juan Resource Area Office, Durango, Colorado.

Balandier, Georges
1955 *Sociologie Actuelle de l'Afrique Noire.* Presse Universaire de France, Paris. Translated by D. Crawford, HRAF file FH9.

Barth, Frederick
1975 *Ritual and Knowledge Among the Baktaman of New Guinea.* Yale University Press, New Haven.

Bean, Lowell J.
1978 Social Organization. In *California,* edited by R. Heizer and W.C. Sturtevant, pp. 673-682. Handbook of North American Indians, vol. 5, William G. Sturtevant, general editor. Smithsonian Institution, Washington, D.C.

Bradley, Bruce
1986 *1985 Annual Report of Test Excavations at Sand Canyon Pueblo (5MT765).* Crow Canyon Archaeological Center, Cortez, Colorado. Submitted to the Bureau of Land Management, San Juan Resource Area Office, Durango, Colorado, under ARPA Permit No. C-39466a.

1987 *Annual Report of Excavations at Sand Canyon Pueblo (5MT765), Crow Canyon Archaeological Center, Cortez, Colorado. 1986 Field Season.* Submitted to the Bureau of Land Management, San

Juan Resource Area Office, Durango, Colorado, under ARPA Permit No. C-39466a.

Braun, David and Stephen Plog
1982 Evolution of "Tribal" Social Networks: Theory and Prehistoric Evidence. *American Antiquity* 47:504-525.

Burch, E. S.
1978 Traditional Eskimo Societies in Northwest Alaska. *Senri Ethnological Studies 4:253-304*. National Museum of Ethnology, Osaka, Japan.

Carneiro, Robert L.
1967 On the Relationship Between Size of Population and Complexity of Social Organization. *Southwestern Journal of Anthropology* 23:234-243.

Cater, John D. and Mark L. Chenault
1988 Kiva Use Reinterpreted. *Southwestern Lore* 54(3):19-32.

Chagnon, Napoleon
1968 *Yanomamo: The Fierce People*. Holt, Rinehart and Winston, New York.

Cook, William Azel
1907 The Bororo Indians of Matto Grosso, Brazil. *Smithsonian Miscellaneous Collections* 50:48-62.

Davis, Emma Lou and James Winkler
1975 Ceremonial Rooms as Kiva Alternatives: SOC-45 and SDV-3. In *Collected Papers in Honor of Florence Hawley Ellis*, edited by T. R. Frisbie, pp. 47-59. Papers of the Archaeological Society of New Mexico No. 2. Albuquerque.

Dohm, Karen
1988 Effects of Population Nucleation on House Size for Pueblos in the American Southwest. Ms. in possession of the author, Smithsonian Institution, Washington, D.C.

Ember, M.
1963 The Relationship Between Economic and Political Development in Non-industrialized Societies. *Ethnology* 2:228-248.

Feinman, Gary and Jill Nietzel
1984 Too Many Types: An Overview of Sedentary Pre-state Societies in the Americas. In *Advances in Archaeological Method and Theory*, vol. 7, edited by Michael Schiffer, pp. 39-102. Academic Press, New York.

Fernandez, James
1982 *Bwiti: an Ethnography of the Religious Imagination in Africa*. Princeton University Press, Princeton.

Fetterman, Jerry and Linda Honeycutt
1987 *The Mockingbird Mesa Survey, Southwestern Colorado*. Cultural Resource Series No. 22. Bureau of Land Management, Denver, Colorado.

Fewkes, Jesse W.
1896 The Prehistoric Culture of Tusayan. *American Anthropologist* 9:151-174.

Flannery, Kent V.
1972 *The Cultural Evolution of Societies*. Annual Review of Ecology and Systematics 3:399-426.

Fortes, Meyer
1945 *The Dynamics of Clanship among the Tallensi*. Oxford University Press, London.

Freeman, J. D.
1955 *Report on the Iban of Sarawak*. Iban Social Organization, vol. 1. Government Printing Office, Kuching, Sarawak.

Gillespie, William
1976 *Culture Change at the Ute Mountain Site: A Study of the Pithouse-Pueblo Transition in the Mesa Verde Region*. Unpublished M.A. thesis, Department of Anthropology, University of Colorado, Boulder.

Griaule, Marcel and G. Dieterlen
1954 The Dogon. In *African Worlds,* edited by Daryll Forde, pp. 83-110. Oxford University Press, London.

Gross, Daniel
1979 Central Brazilian Social Organization. In *Brazil: Anthropological Perspectives: Essays in Honor of Charles Wagley,* edited by M. L. Margolis and W.E. Carter, pp. 321-343. Columbia University Press, New York.

Hawley, Florence
1950 Big Kivas, Little Kivas, and Moiety Houses in Historical Reconstruction. *Southwestern Journal of Anthropology* 6:286-302.

Heizer, Robert F. and A.B. Elsasser
1980 *The Natural World of the California Indians*. University of California Press, Berkeley.

Hogbin, H.I.
1935　Native Culture of Wogeo. *Oceania* 5:308-337.

Johnson, Allen W. and Timothy Earle
1987　*The Evolution of Human Societies: From Foraging Groups to Agrarian State.* Stanford University Press, Stanford.

Johnson, Gregory A.
1978　Information and the Development of Decision-making Organizations. In *Social Archaeology: Beyond Subsistence and Dating*, edited by Charles L. Redman et al., pp. 87-112. Academic Press, New York.

1982　Organizational Structure and Scalar Stress. In *Theory and Explanation in Archaeology: The Southampton Conference*, edited by C. Renfrew, M. Rowlands and B. Segraves, pp. 389-421. Academic Press, New York.

1983　Decision-making and Pastoral Nomad Group Size. *Human Ecology* 11 (2):175-199.

1988　Dynamics of Southwestern Prehistory: Far Outside–Looking In. In *Dynamics of Southwestern Prehistory*, edited by Linda Cordell and George Gumerman. Smithsonian Institution Press, Washington D.C., in press.

Judge, James
1988　Chaco Canyon—San Juan Basin. In *Dynamics of Southwestern Prehistory*, edited by Linda Cordell and George Gumerman. Smithsonian Institution Press, Washington D.C., in press

Kelly, Raymond
1974　*Etoro Social Structure: A Study in Structural Contradiction.* University of Michigan Press, Ann Arbor.

Kroeber, Alfred L.
1925　*Handbook of the Indians of California.* Bureau of American Ethnology Bulletin 78. Washington, D.C.

Landtman, Gunnar
1927　*The Kiwai Papuans of British New Guinea.* Macmillan and Co, London.

Lantis, Margaret
1947　*Alaskan Eskimo Ceremonialism.* Monographs of the American Ethnological Society. University of Washington Press, Seattle.

Lekson, Stephen H.
1984　*Great Pueblo Architecture of Chaco Canyon, New Mexico.* Publications in Archeology No.18B. National Park Service, Albuquerque, N.M.

1988　The Idea of the Kiva in Anasazi Archaeology. *The Kiva* 53:213-234.

Levi-Strauss, Claude
1945　The Social and Psychological Aspects of Chieftainship in a Primitive Tribe. *Transactions of the New York Academy of Sciences*, Series 2, 7:16-32.

1972　*Triste Tropiques.* Translated by J. Russell. Atheneum, New York.

Liljeblad, Sven and Catherine S. Fowler
1986　The Owens Valley Pauite. In *Great Basin*, edited by Warren D'Azevedo. Handbook of North American Indians, vol. 11, William Sturtevant, general editor. Smithsonian Institution, Washington, D.C.

Lipe, William D.
1970　Anasazi Communities in the Red Rock Plateau, Southeastern Utah. In *Reconstructing Prehistoric Pueblo Societies*, edited by William Longacre, pp. 84-139. University of New Mexico Press, Albuquerque.

Loeb, Edwin M.
1926　*Pomo Folkways.* University of California Publications in American Archaeology and Ethnology, vol. 19, No. 2. Berkeley.

Lowie, Robert H.
1913　*Societies of the Crow, Hidatsa and Mandan Indians.* Anthropological Papers of the American Museum of Natural History, vol. 11, No. 3. New York.

1949　Social and Political Organization of the Tropical Forest and Marginal Tribes. In *The Comparative Ethnology of South American Indians*, edited by J. H. Steward, pp. 313-350. Handbook of South American Indians, vol. 5. Bureau of American Ethnology Bulletin 143, Washington, D.C.

Luebben, Ralph
1982　Two Pueblo III Kiva Complexes Associated with Subterranean Rooms, Southwestern Colorado. *The Kiva* 48:63-81.

1983　The Grinnell Site: A Small Ceremonial Center Near Yucca House, Colorado. *Journal of Intermountain Archaeology* 2:1-26.

Martin, Paul S.
　1936　*Lowry Ruin in Southwestern Colorado.* Anthropological Series, vol. 23. Field Museum of Natural History, Chicago.

Mindeleff, Victor
　1891　A Study of Pueblo Architecture. *Eighth Annual Report of the Bureau of Ethnology,* pp. 13-228. Government Printing Office, Washington, D.C.

Moore, James A.
　1983　The Trouble With Know-it-alls: Information as a Social and Ecological Resource, in *Archaeological Hammers and Theories,* edited by James A. Moore and Arthur Keene, pp. 173-191. Academic Press, New York.

Morris, Earl H.
　1921　*The House of the Great Kiva at Aztec Ruin.* Anthropological Papers of the American Museum of Natural History, vol. 26, No. 5. New York.

Murdock, George P.
　1949　*Social Structure.* Macmillan Co., New York.

Murdock, George P. and Suzanne F. Wilson
　1972　Settlement Patterns and Community Organization. *Ethnology* 11:254-295.

Murphy, Yolanda and Robert F. Murphy
　1974　*Women of the Forest.* Columbia University Press, New York.

Neily, Robert B.
　1983　*The Prehistoric Community on the Colorado Plateau: An Approach to the Study of Change and Survival in the Northern San Juan Area of the American Southwest.* Unpublished Ph.D. dissertation, Department of Anthropology, Southern Illinois University, Carbondale.

Nimendaju, Curt
　1942　*The Serente.* Translated by Robert H. Lowie. Publications of the Frederick Webb Hodge Anniversary Publications Fund, Los Angeles.

　1948　*The Eastern Timbira.* Translated and edited by Robert H. Lowie. University of California Publications in American Archaeology and Ethnology No. 41. Berkeley.

O'Bryan, Deric
　1950　*Excavations in Mesa Verde National Park 1947-1948.* Gila Pueblo Medallion Papers No. 39, Globe, Arizona.

Orcutt, Janet, Eric Blinman and Timothy Kohler
　1987　Explanations of Population Aggregation in the Mesa Verde Region Prior to A.D. 900. Paper presented at the Southwest Symposium, session on "Elites and Regional Systems." Tempe, Arizona.

Ortiz, Alfonso
　1969　*The Tewa World.* University of Chicago Press, Chicago.

Parsons, Elsie (Clews)
　1939　*Pueblo Indian Religion.* University of Chicago Press, Chicago.

Powdermaker, Hortense
　1933　*Life in Lesu: The Study of a Melanesian Society in New Ireland.* W.W. Horton Publishing, New York.

Price, David
　1987　Nambiquara Geopolitical Organization. *Man,* n.s., 22:1-24.

Prudden, T. Mitchell
　1903　The Prehistoric Ruins of the San Juan Watershed in Utah, Arizona, Colorado and New Mexico. *American Anthropologist,* n.s., 5:224-286.

　1914　The Circular Kivas of Small Ruins in the San Juan Watershed. *American Anthropologist,* n.s., 16:33-58.

　1918　*A Further Study of Prehistoric Small House Ruins in the San Juan Watershed.* Memoirs of the American Anthropological Association No. 5.

Rappaport, Roy A.
　1968　*Pigs for the Ancestors: Ritual in the Ecology of a New Guinea People.* Yale University Press, New Haven.

　1979　*Ecology, Meaning and Religion.* North Atlantic Books, Berkeley.

Rohn, Arthur
　1971　*Mug House, Mesa Verde National Park,* Colorado. Archeological Research Series No. 7-D. National Park Service, Washington, D.C.

　1977　*Cultural Change and Continuity on Chapin Mesa.* Regents Press of Kansas, Lawrence, Kansas.

Spier, Leslie
　1933　*Yuman Tribes of the Gila River.* University of Chicago Press, Chicago.

Steward, Julian H. (editor)
1948 *Tropical Forest Tribes*. Handbook of South American Indians, vol. 3. Bureau of American Ethnology Bulletin 143. Washington, D.C.

Tait, David
1950 An Analytical Commentary on the Social Structure of the Dogon. *Africa* 20(3):175-199.

Turner, Victor
1969 *The Ritual Process*. Aldine Publishing, Chicago.

Tuzin, Donald F.
1976 *The Ilahita Arapesh: Dimensions of Unity*. University of California Press, Berkeley.

1980 *The Voice of the Tambaran*. University of California Press, Berkeley.

Will, G. F. and Spinden, H.J.
1906 The Mandans. *Papers of the Peabody Museum of American Archaeology and Ethnology,* vol. 3, No. 4. Harvard University, Cambridge.

Williams, F. E.
1930 *Orokaiva Society*. Oxford University Press, London.

1940 *Drama of Orokolo: the Social and Ceremonial Life of the Elema*. Oxford University Press, London.

Wills, W. H. and Thomas C. Windes
1989 Evidence for Population Aggregation and Dispersal During the Basketmaker III Period in Chaco Canyon, New Mexico. *American Antiquity* 54 (2):347-369.

Wilshusen, Richard H.
1986 The Relationship Between Abandonment Mode and Ritual Use in Pueblo I Anasazi Protokivas. *Journal of Field Archaeology* 13:245-254.

1988 Sipapus, Ceremonial Vaults and Foot Drums (or a Resounding Argument for Protokivas). In *Dolores Archaeological Program: Supporting Studies: Additive and Reductive Technologies,* compiled by Eric Blinman, Carl J. Phagan, and Richard H. Wilshusen, pp. 649-671. Bureau of Reclamation, Engineering and Research, Denver, Colorado.

5
Social Scale of Mesa Verde Anasazi Kivas

William D. Lipe

Pueblo I to III Mesa Verde settlements typically have one protokiva or kiva for each block of six to nine rooms, a pattern indicative of kiva use by a relatively small and common social segment such as an extended family or minimal lineage. These ordinary small Pueblo I protokivas and Pueblo II and III kivas were probably used for both ritual and domestic activities.

Chacoan outliers in the Mesa Verde area have fewer and larger kivas, and a less regular patterning of kivas to room blocks. Kivas at Chacoan sites may have functioned at a larger scale of social integration than at Mesa Verde settlements.

At roughly A.D. 1300, approximately coincident with the abandonment of the Mesa Verde area, most Puebloans shifted from a Mesa Verde-like pattern of many small kivas to one of large plaza-oriented sites with only a few relatively large kivas. Following Steward (1937) and Adams (this volume), this suggests a larger integrative scale for kiva use, and stronger village-level organization. Continuities in kiva architecture and ritual features suggest that aspects of the religious ideology associated with earlier kivas were incorporated into the new organization.

Introduction

The model for this paper is Julian Steward's classic 1937 article entitled "Ecological Aspects of Southwestern Society." In that paper, Steward used the ratio of rooms to kivas as a measure of the scale of social integration in both prehistoric and historic Pueblo communities. He noted that from the Pueblo I through the Pueblo III periods in the San Juan drainage, the ratio of surface rooms to kivas is quite low—around five or six rooms for each kiva. Drawing on work by Prudden (1903, 1914, 1918), Fewkes (1911), and Roberts (1930, 1931, 1932, 1933), Steward suggested that the small "units," each consisting of a kiva and a few spatially associated "houses," retained their "social and ceremonial integrity" even after the "growth of communal houses" (large pueblos) in the Pueblo II period (Steward 1937:96-97). In other words, the large pueblos appear to consist of a number of the smaller unit pueblos joined together. Not until the Pueblo IV period did the ratio of rooms to kivas increase dramatically, as "political autonomy passed from the localized lineage to a wider group—the Pueblo village" (Steward 1937:102). It was also in the early Pueblo IV period that the construction of large pueblos around plazas became common in the Rio Grande through Western Pueblo areas, although Steward did not discuss this (but see Adams' comments in Chapter 11, this volume).

Following Prudden's and Steward's lead, others have pursued similar or related approaches to using architectural characteristics and spatial relationships as indicators of prehistoric Anasazi social organization (e.g., Eggan 1950; Hawley 1950; Rohn 1965, 1971, 1977; Dean 1970; Wilcox 1976; Powers et al. 1983; McKenna and Truell 1986; Lekson 1984, 1985, 1988; Adams, this volume). My purpose is to evaluate Steward's model after 50 years' more fieldwork, with primary emphasis on the spatial patterning of kivas and surface rooms in the central Mesa Verde Anasazi area, from the Pueblo I through Pueblo III periods, or from about A.D. 750 to 1300. I also review selected evidence from the Pueblo IV and historic periods in both the Eastern Pueblo (Rio Grande) and Western Pueblo (Zuni and Hopi) areas.

My Mesa Verde area data are drawn from published reports on excavated sites in the core portion of that culture area—that is, north of the San Juan Valley and extending from Mesa Verde in the east to the Montezuma Creek drainage in the west. This core area centers on the McElmo and Montezuma Creek drainages and includes the Montezuma Valley near Cortez and the Dolores Valley near the town of Dolores (Chapter 1, Figures 1 and 2). Primarily because of time limitations on my research, the San Juan Valley proper and the La Plata Valley are not included. The area had exceptionally good dry-farming potential and dense populations, numbering in the few tens of persons per km^2 at some times and places (cf. Schlanger 1985). My primary research questions about this area in the Pueblo I–III periods are (1) "What was the approximate size of the social group that used a kiva?" and (2) "Were there changes in the size of this group through time?" My secondary questions are (3) "Were Mesa Verde Anasazi kivas used to help integrate social groups?" and (4) "If they were, what were the integrative mechanisms?" Other possible integrative facilities—e.g., Great Kivas, tri-wall structures, and plazas—are briefly discussed in relation to specific points, but are not treated here in a systematic way.

In order to use kiva and surface room data to infer the scale of social groups who used kivas, I made several assumptions. The first is that the size of the kiva had a more or less regular relationship to the size of the group that used it, or at least to the number of people who could physically be together in it at the same time. The same assumption holds for the sizes of surface rooms. In the paper, these assumptions are used primarily in discussing *relative* sizes of social groups.

Second, I assume that spatial propinquity counts for something in social interaction. That is, structures located immediately adjacent to one another are more likely to have been used by the same group than are structures located far apart, or separated from one another by other structures. This is the assumption that I believe Prudden made in 1903 when he defined the "unit type pueblo" by the recurring spatial association of a kiva, a small block of rooms, and a burial mound (Figure 1). He noted that these clusters occurred by themselves, but also formed the basic building blocks or "units" in larger Mesa Verde area pueblos. Roberts (1939a) showed how this pattern, common in the Pueblo II and III periods, developed during Pueblo I out of Basketmaker III antecedents. Morris (1939) called the Pueblo I pit structures "protokivas," in part because they occupied the same position in the site structure as kivas in the later Pueblo II and III settlements. Working in the Mimbres area, Anyon and LeBlanc (1980) also found that a single kiva or "large room" was spatially associated with many of the roomblocks that comprised Classic period Mimbres villages. They argued that each of these structures probably housed integrative activities for its roomblock group, while plaza activities helped integrate the entire community.

In prehistoric pueblos, a regular spatial association between a protokiva or kiva and a small block of rooms made it possible for Steward (1937), Lekson (1988), and others to use room-to-kiva ratios as a proxy for the size of the local group integrated by a kiva. If kivas had clustered in one part of a settlement or had been distributed in a less regular way, the inference would not have been as straightforward. Close association with a particular roomblock, of course, does not preclude the possibility that a kiva was used by a non-localized group such as a sodality. But on the basis of analogy with historic Western Pueblos (Eggan 1950) I infer that kiva use by sodalities that draw their membership from across the community does not produce the regular, modular type of kiva distribution commonly seen in Mesa Verde Anasazi settlements. Instead, historic Western Pueblo sodality kivas tend to be spaced irregularly in relation to surface roomblocks, and in some cases the kivas themselves are clustered in one or a few parts of the settlement (cf. maps in Stubbs 1950 and Mindeleff 1891). At the Pueblo IV period site of Awatovi, the kivas excavated in the Western Mound were also clustered (Smith 1972).

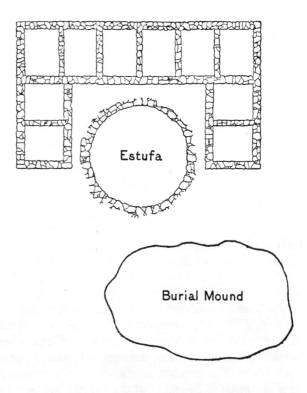

Figure 1: Prudden's "unit type pueblo" (after Prudden 1903:Figure 6).

A final assumption bears more on the secondary, or "type of integration" aspect of the paper than on the main, or "social scale" aspect. This assumption is that the marked and consistent *formal* differences between kivas and the associated surface rooms are likely to have been rooted in some consistent *functional* or *cognitive* differences. In other words, Mesa Verde kivas did not just happen to be round, deep, roof-entered, and located south of the surface rooms as a result of normal variation in dwelling room construction. These formal differences are likely to signal some consistent differences in the activities that went on in these different types of structures, and perhaps in the meanings that the Anasazi attributed to them.

Lekson has recently questioned this assumption, or at least the version of it that always views kivas as specialized ceremonial chambers, and rooms as purely domestic (Lekson 1985, 1988). By raising these questions, Lekson has caused us to take a fresh look at the issues. I agree with most of his conclusions, except when he seems to imply that evidence of domestic activities in a kiva or protokiva precludes its having been used for integrative religious or social rituals. I think there is evidence that both domestic and ritual activities frequently took place in Mesa Verde kivas and protokivas (see also Cater and Chenault 1988 and Varien and Lightfoot, Chapter 6, this volume). Recognizing evidence of either or both kinds of activities and understanding their relationships to types and scales of integration are the central research questions regarding Anasazi kiva use.

The results of my survey of the social scale of Mesa Verde kivas are presented in Table 1. Basically, these data support Steward's model by showing that the "unit pueblo" pattern was well-established in the Mesa Verde area by late Pueblo I and continued in generally similar form through the Pueblo III period until the abandonment of the area in the late A.D. 1200s. An abundance of new field data and better chronologies have become available in the last 50 years, permitting recognition of some interesting variations on this general pattern. In addition to data from the Mesa Verde area in the Pueblo I to Pueblo III periods, I added some from Pueblo IV and from the historic Pueblos in the Rio Grande and the Western Pueblo area, just to show that Steward is still right about these periods as well. The pre–A.D. 1300 northern San Juan pattern of many small kivas incorporated in architectural "units" contrasts strongly with the Pueblo IV and Historic Pueblo pattern. Furthermore, the historic Western Pueblo sodality kiva pattern contrasts with that of the historic Eastern Pueblos, which are dominated by the larger moiety kivas. Overall, the post–A.D. 1300 kivas are larger in both the Eastern and Western Pueblo areas, and are dramatically less common relative to surface rooms, than in the Mesa Verde area from Pueblo I through Pueblo III.

Pueblo I Period, Mesa Verde Area

The first data set in Table 1 is from the late A.D. 800s (late Pueblo I) and is derived from recent work on the Dolores Archaeological Project (cf. Breternitz et al. 1986) and at the Duckfoot Site in southwestern Colorado (cf. Varien and Lightfoot, this volume). The 52 late Pueblo I pit structures/protokivas that were measured had a mean floor area of about 25 m^2. The large standard deviation (Table 1) is due to the presence at some Dolores area sites of occasional "oversized" pit structures, as discussed below (see also Wilshusen, Chapter 7, this volume). Typically, each pit structure (except for some of the "oversized" ones) was located just south of a small group of seven to eight rooms, which had an average total area between two and three times that of the pit structure. Several room suites, each consisting of a large front living room and two back storage rooms, can ordinarily be recognized in this group of rooms. Several such groups of rooms-with-a-protokiva are often joined side by side into a roomblock.

Dolores Project researchers inferred that each surface room suite (one front and two back rooms) was controlled by a single household, probably composed of four or five people. Each group of two or three contiguous surface room suites was occupied by an "interhousehold group"—perhaps an extended family or minimal lineage. The households in this group shared the use of the pit structure/protokiva (Kane 1983, 1984). The pit structure, which lacked direct access to long-term storage facilities, was not inferred to have been either a specialized ceremonial chamber or a separate habitation, but to have been used by the interhousehold group for both domestic and ritual activities (Kane 1984, 1986a and b; Lipe and Kohler 1984). Evidence for both types of activity are commonly found in the pit structures (Varien and Lightfoot, this volume). Features interpreted as ritual or symbolic include simple and complex sipapus, floor vaults, and certain sand-filled pits, as discussed by Wilshusen (1986, and in this volume).

Schlanger (1985) argues that, in the average "interhousehold cluster," the disparity between total front room floor area and usable pit structure floor area was too great to have permitted the pit structure to be a common sleeping area for the several households that shared it. (In pit structures, usable floor space is considerably smaller than total floor space because of the presence of a large firepit, a wingwall, often an ashpit, and numerous other floor features.) Consequently, the pit structure is not likely to have been the primary residence for the entire interhousehold group, or even

Table 1: Anasazi and Pueblo Architectural Data.

Anasazi and Pueblo Samples	KIVAS				ROOMS			ROOMS TO KIVAS		
	Total Floor Area (m^2)	No.	Mean Floor Area (m^2)	s.d.	Total Floor Area (m^2)	No.	Mean Floor Area (m^2)	Ratio of Rooms to Kivas (counts)	Ratio of Room Area:Kiva Area	Room Space Per Kiva (m^2)
M.V. Anasazi: 850–900 (P I)	1,295	52	24.9	10.6	3,264 (est)	119	8.3	7.6 (est)	2.5 (est)	62.8 (est)
M.V. Anasazi: 1000–1150 (P II)	466	35	13.3	5.0	1,329	228	5.8	6.5	2.9	38.0
"Chaco Outliers" 1050–1150	186	9	20.6	6.4	1,185	137	8.7	15.2	6.4	131.6
M.V. Anasazi: 1150–1300 (P III)	688	56	12.3	3.4	2,596	506	5.1	9.0	3.8	46.4
Hopi: 1300–1600 (P IV)	639	31	20.6	7.2	?	?	?	26.7	??	
Hopi: 19th Century	474	15	31.6	4.3	?	?	?	?	?	?
Hopi and Acoma: 1948	1,089	24	45.4	15.8	23,100	968+	?	40 +	21.2	962.5
Eastern Pueblos: 1300–1600	?	37±	?	?	?	2,600±	?	70±	?	?
Eastern Pueblos: 1948	2,197	27	81.4	38.8	115,843	3,257+	?	120+	52.7	4,290.5

Notes on sources for Table 1.

Mesa Verde Anasazi, A.D. 850–900. Data on pit structure floor areas is from 48 Dolores Archaeological Project pit structures measured by Richard Wilshusen (personal communication 1988), and from four Duckfoot Site pit structures measured by Mark Varien and Ricky Lightfoot (personal communication 1988). Data on surface room areas and ratios of room counts to pit structures are from Dolores Archaeological Project data summarized by Wilshusen (1985). This latter sample overlaps with, but is not identical to, the sample from which the Dolores Project pit structure floor area measurements were obtained. This is because not all the surface rooms associated with the 48 pit structures were excavated or yielded suitable floor area measurements; nor were floor area measurements obtainable from all the pit structures associated with the surface room sample.

Mesa Verde Anasazi, A.D. 1000–1150. All data are from published site maps; kiva and surface room floor area measurements were made by electronic planimeter. Sites and components used in this analysis were: Alkali Ridge Site 3, Site 5 (late component), Site 7 (Pueblo II component), Site 9, Site 11 (late component), Site 12 (early component), Site 12 (late component) (Brew 1946); Badger House, Mancos Phase component (Hayes and Lancaster 1975); Big Juniper House, Component D (Swannack 1969); Dominguez Ruin (Reed 1979); Ewing Site, Units 1–6 (Hill 1985); Mesa Verde Site 1 (O'Bryan 1950); Mesa Verde Site 16, Unit Pueblos No. 1 and 2 (Lancaster and Pinkley 1954); Mesa Verde Site 102, Pueblo II component (O'Bryan 1950); Mesa Verde Site 866 (excluding protokiva) (Lister 1966); Mesa Verde Site 875, First and Second Villages (Lister 1965); Mesa Verde Site 1086 (Lister 1967); Mesa Verde Site 1088, early and late components (Lister and Smith 1968); Mesa Verde Site 1104 (Lister and Breternitz 1968); Mesa Verde Site 1914 (Hewett 1968); Mustoe Site, Pueblo II component (Gould 1982); Wood Rat Knoll (roomblock and Kiva 2 only) (Nickens 1977).

Mesa Verde Area "Chaco Outliers," A.D. 1050–1150: All data are from published site maps; kiva and surface room floor area measurements were made by electronic planimeter. Sites and components used in this analysis were: Escalante Ruin (excluding Kiva B) (Hallasi 1979); Lowry Ruin, fourth addition (Martin 1936), and Wallace Ruin, Chacoan occupation (Bradley 1988b). My choice of Martin's fourth addition as representing the maximum size of Lowry Ruin in "Chacoan" times is based on my reading of the architectural and ceramic evidence he presents (Martin 1936). Also, tree-ring dates from Lowry (Robinson and Harrill 1974; Ahlstrom et al. 1985) indicate that most of the building at Lowry took place in the very late A.D. 1000s and early 1100s, a period when most of the Chacoan sites north of the San Juan appear to have been built.

Mesa Verde Area Anasazi, A.D. 1150–1300. All data are from published site maps; kiva and surface room floor area measurements were made by electronic planimeter. Sites and components used in this analysis were: Alkali Ridge, Site 1 (Unit 1) and Site 6 (Brew 1946); Badger House, Mesa Verde Phase occupation (Hayes and Lancaster 1975); Beartooth Pueblo (Martin 1930); Cannonball Ruin, South Pueblo (Morley 1908); Green Lizard Site, West Unit (Huber and Bloomer 1988); Grinnell Site (Luebben 1983); Herren Farm Ruin, Unit III (Martin 1929); Hoy House (Nickens 1981); Mancos Canyon Site 4 (Reed 1958); Mesa Verde Site 34 (excluding Kiva II) (O'Bryan 1950); Mesa Verde Site 499, Second Village, Stage 3 (Lister 1964); Mesa Verde Site 1926 (Birkedal 1968); Mug House, Component C (Rohn 1971); Mustoe Site, Pueblo III component (Gould 1982); Nancy Patterson Village, Pueblo III Household Unit (Thompson et al. 1986); Sand Canyon Pueblo, 100, 200, 300, 500, and 1200 blocks (Bradley 1986, 1987, 1988a); Spruce Tree House (Fewkes 1909); Sun Point Pueblo (Lancaster and Van Cleave 1954).

Hopi, A.D. 1300–1600. Kiva floor areas are those published by Smith (1972:105) from excavated kivas at Awatovi and Kawaika-a in northeastern Arizona. The room-to-kiva ratio is based on Smith's (1971, 1972) reports of work in the Western Mound at Awatovi. A large, roughly cross-shaped excavation was to have been seasonally used as the group's primary residence in the winter. As can be seen in Table 1, however, the differences between total surface room and pit structure floor areas are not so great as to preclude further argument, though I do think Schlanger is right. Also, the lack of direct access from the pit structure to the surface storage rooms indicates that the pit structure probably was not the primary residence for an additional household, but that it was shared by the households based in the surface roomsuites. In any case, the typical Pueblo I pit structure/protokiva appears to have been a standard element in the set of facilities used by a relatively small-scale group consisting of several co-residential, economically cooperative households, probably related as an extended family or minimal lineage.

Wilshusen (1985, 1986, and in this volume) and Kane (1986 a and b) have also made a convincing case that *some* Pueblo I pit structures were loci for ritual activity that served groups larger or more influential than the ordinary extended family. Such pit structures tend to be larger than ca. 25 m^2, and some are much larger—up to ca. 60 m^2. This size variation accounts for the large standard deviation for Pueblo I pit structure floor areas in Table 1. These larger pit structures are located in village-sized settlements rather than in hamlets, and they have more elaborate ritual features and less evidence of domestic economic activities than the smaller "ordinary" pit structures. However, their overall floor plan is generally just a larger version of the typical late Pueblo I pit structure, though relatively more space is devoted to ritual features. A few of these pit structures that have elaborate ritual features are only average in size, but most are "oversized." Wilshusen (1986 and in this volume), Orcutt and Blinman (1988), Kane (1986 a and b) and Lipe et al. (1988) have interpreted these pit structures as being the loci for activities that promoted social control and effective group decision-making under conditions of increased population density and settlement size.

Inferences of social scale remain fuzzy, but it is assumed that ritual activities associated with these "special" pit structures affected a considerably larger group than would be true for a "standard" pit structure. The special ritual features in the former type of facility may have helped provide ideological validation for claims of influence and authority made by particular individuals, families or associations. The generally larger size of these structures would also have permitted larger groups to use them, though not at the scale of an entire village population (or even of a large roomblock). For instance, these pit structures may have been used for integrative activities such as hosting members of other residential or kin groups, or people from other villages, at ceremonies or feasts. Blinman (Orcutt and Blinman 1988; Blinman 1988 and Chapter 8 in this volume) presents ceramic evidence for a "potluck" type of feasting at "U-shaped roomblocks" in the large villages. The largest and most ritually specialized pit structures excavated in the Dolores area occur with this distinctive type of roomblock at McPhee Village (Kane and Robinson 1988), the area's largest late Pueblo I community.

The "oversized" pit structures discussed above are not to be confused with Great Kivas, which also occur in Dolores area Pueblo I settlements (cf. Lightfoot 1988; Lightfoot et al. 1988). These structures are much rarer and larger than the oversized pit structures and do

---

Notes on Sources for Table 1 (continued).

carried out in the Western Mound, and all kivas and rooms encountered were excavated (Smith 1971:Figures 3 and 4). Three kivas and approximately 80 rooms that were occupied late in the history of the mound were excavated (Smith 1971:Figure 4; Smith 1972). This places them early in the Pueblo IV period. Altogether, 24 kivas were excavated at Awatovi (Smith 1972), as well as "several hundred" rooms (Smith 1972:7). Judging by the amount of area excavated and the fact that the "sequentially numbered" rooms at Awatovi reached at least No. 908 (Smith 1972:66), the ratio of approximately 27 rooms per kiva derived from the Western Mound data is probably quite conservative.

Hopi, 19th Century. Kiva floor areas were calculated from linear measurements of 15 kivas made at the Hopi villages by Stephen and reported by Mindeleff (1891:136).

Hopi and Acoma, 1948. Data are from planimeter measurements by Nick Scoales of maps in Stubbs (1950), based on 1948 aerial photos. Hopi settlements measured were Walpi, Mishongnovi, Shipaulovi, and Shongopavi. Precise room counts cannot be made from Stubbs' maps because some sections of these pueblos are multiple-storied, and the floor plans of upper and lower stories may differ. Also, not all room walls extend through the roof level, even in upper stories or single story sections. The room counts that are given were made by Dohm (1987), based only on the room walls that showed at roof level. Consequently, these are counts of minimum numbers of rooms; the actual counts must be somewhat higher.

Eastern Pueblos, A.D. 1300–1600. The data for the room-to-kiva ratio are from Steward (1937), who obtained them from surface counts made by Hewett at five sites on the Jemez Plateau (Hewett 1906; the sites are Tshirege, Tsankawi, Otowi, Yapashi, and Kotyiti). The ratio derived from these sites appears to be consistent, in a general way, with data from the Galisteo Basin (Nelson 1914), Gran Quivira (Hayes et al. 1981) and other large Pueblo IV sites in the Eastern Pueblo area, as reported in Stuart and Gauthier (1981).

Eastern Pueblos, 1948. Data are from planimeter measurements made by Karen Dohm and by Nick Scoales of maps in Stubbs (1950), based on 1948 aerial photos (also see Dohm 1987). Settlements measured were Santa Clara, San Ildefonso, Nambe, Santo Domingo, Isleta, Zia, Jemez, San Felipe, Taos, Picuris, and Santa Ana. As in the Hopi and Acoma data derived from Stubbs (1950), precise room counts could not be made. The counts given are of minimum numbers of rooms. The actual counts must be somewhat higher.

not show a clear spatial association with specific roomblocks; they may even be spatially separate from habitation sites. Their floor plans and features are quite different from those of the oversized pit structures. It seems likely that Great Kivas housed different kinds of activities and functioned at a larger scale of integration than the oversized pit structures.

Pueblo II Period, Mesa Verde Area

Apart from these two kinds of larger and more problematic pit structures, the typical late Pueblo I configuration conforms quite well to Prudden's modular or "unit type pueblo" construct, even though he based his observations on Pueblo II and III settlements (cf. Roberts 1939a). The Pueblo II and III patterns are also generally similar to those of the Pueblo I period (Table 1). Probably there is continuity of both population and culture in the study area during the 400 to 500 years in question. The paucity of data from the A.D. 900s may cast some doubt on this assumption, however. Hayes (1964) reports that sites of the Ackmen Phase, which should include the A.D. 900s, are the most numerous of any phase on Wetherill Mesa, but elsewhere in the central Mesa Verde area, few sites dating to the tenth century have been identified, excavated, or reported. Whether this is a result of low population during this period or of sampling bias is not clear at this point, though I suspect the former. If so, some of the changes in architecture and site layout between Pueblo I and II could be associated with new immigration into the area in the A.D. 1000s. In any case, I was unable to compile an adequate data set from the central Mesa Verde area for the 900s, so in Table 1, my Pueblo II data are from sites dating A.D. 1000 to 1150.

The data that do exist, however, indicate to me a rapid shift at about A.D. 900 from the square Pueblo I protokiva with wingwalls and numerous floor pits to the round Pueblo II kiva with a relatively uncluttered floor. More or less round structures, with some "transitional" characteristics such as vestigial wingwalls, occur in the very late A.D. 800s or early 900s in the Mesa Verde area—e.g., Pit Structure 32 at Grass Mesa in the Dolores area (Lipe et al. 1988), and Structure 2 at the Ute Canyon Site in Mancos Canyon (Gillespie 1976). The period around A.D. 900 was one of rapid depopulation of the Dolores area, and substantial population shifts seem to have occurred elsewhere in the Mesa Verde area at about this time, as well as a movement away from large villages and large roomblocks to smaller settlements and settlement units. Speculatively, in this turbulent period a rapid selection for different modes of integrative symbolism, ritual activities, or domestic activities may be somehow reflected in the architectural change from protokiva to kiva. On the other hand, there is also a clear continuity through this time in specific ritual features, in the underground character of the kiva and in the orientation, size, and spatial structure of the pit structure and surface room unit. In the Mesa Verde area, the period A.D. 900–1050 is one where truly "more work needs to be done."

Compared with the square Pueblo I protokivas, the Pueblo II post–A.D. 1050 pit structures referenced in Table 1 are uniformly round in plan and usually have well-developed benches, pilasters, and a southern recess at bench level. In other words, they display the classic characteristics of Mesa Verde kivas. Both the surface rooms and the kivas have smaller floor areas than in Pueblo I (5.8 m^2 vs. 8.3 m^2 for rooms, and 13.3 m^2 vs. 24.9 m^2 for kivas—see Table 1), though the ratio of total room area to total kiva area is similar. The amount of room space per pit structure is substantially less in Pueblo II, however (38.0 m^2 vs. 62.8 m^2). Some of the difference may be due to poor archaeological visibility of surface rooms in the Pueblo II period—these sometimes were made of jacal, which may have little archaeological expression. Furthermore, if Pueblo II rooms were made of masonry, they often were robbed of stones by later inhabitants of nearby settlements. Also, a number of fairly early reports were consulted, and it may be that a unit's total habitation area was less likely to be documented prior to the development of "settlement archaeology."

The decrease in mean pit structure floor size between Pueblo I and II may be related to "uncluttering" the floors. Unlike Pueblo I protokivas, Pueblo II kivas lack wingwalls and have relatively few floor pits and other features, though they do tend to have rather large banquettes and southern recesses. These areas, which are not present in Pueblo I protokivas, were not included in the Pueblo II kiva floor area measurements because they generally do not appear to have been suitable sitting or sleeping places. On the other hand, they would have been useful for getting equipment and supplies off the floor and temporarily out of the way. Recent excavations at Sand Canyon Pueblo by the Crow Canyon Archaeological Center have demonstrated that pottery vessels, stone axes, bone awls, and other portable items were often kept on these banquettes (Bradley 1986, 1987, 1988a).

As in the Pueblo I protokivas, many of the Pueblo II kivas have probable ritual features, such as sipapus and floor vaults, that do not occur in the surface rooms. My impressions are that evidence could be assembled to support the same interpretation made for the Pueblo I structures—that the Pueblo II kiva was the locus for religious rituals which primarily served to help integrate a small group of co-residential households. Whether the change in kiva shape, size, and floor features is related to more specialization for religious ritual, or to the exclusion of some people (e.g., women [Gillespie 1976]), or to neither of these changes, is not clear. I think that Pueblo II kivas may well have functioned like Pueblo I protokivas—that they continued to be loci for both domestic and ritual activities by several households that had other, more separate facilities in the roomblock, including long-term storage facilities (cf. Cater and Chenault 1988). What is needed for the Pueblo II and III periods is detailed comparative studies of associated surface rooms and kivas that combine analyses of architectural, feature, and assemblage evidence. Varien and Lightfoot's analysis (this volume) deals only with the Pueblo I period, but shows what can be accomplished with a systematic treatment of these kinds of data.

Typical Pueblo I protokivas and Pueblo II kivas appear to have functioned primarily to integrate small social groups, on the order of several households. Did any of the Pueblo II kivas operate at a larger social scale, as claimed for some Pueblo I pit structures? I can't answer that at this point, but I did note while doing the survey that the largest Pueblo II kivas (in the size range of 20 to 30 m^2) tended to be isolated, or at least not in normal propinquity to a specific small block of surface rooms; they also appear to have more elaborate floor features. These might perhaps be analogous to the oversized pit structures of the Pueblo I Dolores Valley villages. This possibility needs to be investigated by larger-scale, more detailed studies of settlement structure and the distribution of features than have been done to date.

I also had no Pueblo II data from settlements as large as the late Pueblo I villages in the Dolores area. Such settlements may exist, but they are not well-represented in the literature reporting on excavations. There were clusters of hamlet-sized settlements which undoubtedly comprised communities (Rohn 1977; Hill 1985), but they are not aggregated tightly enough to be obvious villages. A lower degree of aggregation may have lessened the need for tight social control and for group decision-making—functions that in the late Pueblo I period may have promoted the intensification of religious ritual and the development of integrative facilities with elaborate ritual features. Also in the late Pueblo II period, "Chacoan great houses" may have provided facilities that focused larger-scale integrative activities.

The third data set in Table 1 is called "Chaco Outliers" (Powers et al. 1983) and includes data from only three sites in the study area—Escalante Ruin (Hallasi 1979); Wallace Ruin (Bradley 1974, 1988b); and Lowry Ruin (Martin 1936). Though contemporary with the other late Pueblo II sites, these Chacoan sites are architecturally distinctive. They contrast with nearby contemporaneous settlements in having a compact, pre-planned layout, multiple stories, much more substantially built masonry walls, kivas included within the roomblock, larger kivas, larger rooms, and a higher ratio of rooms to kivas. A Chacoan-style Great Kiva is present at Lowry Ruin, and Great Kivas also appear to be associated with several unexcavated Chacoan outliers in the study area (e.g., Yucca House, Casa Negra, and the Ansel Hall site).

In the San Juan Basin to the south of the study area, the contrasts between Chacoan great houses (Lekson 1984; Powers et al. 1983) and surrounding sites are even more pronounced. The great houses generally incorporate formal plaza areas, have few but relatively large kivas, and have a room-to-kiva ratio that varies widely from one great house to the next. The great houses do not appear to be simple aggregates of room suite-kiva units, although parts of some sites perhaps show this pattern (cf. Lekson 1984). At Chaco Canyon and elsewhere in the San Juan Basin, the contemporaneous small sites associated with the great houses have kiva sizes and room-to-kiva ratios resembling those of late Pueblo II sites in the Mesa Verde area (McKenna and Truell 1986; Powers et al. 1983). In fact, my impression is that the overall distribution of Chaco outliers is rather well-correlated with the overall distribution of Anasazi settlements having formally distinctive small kivas located in unit type pueblos.

I think that many or most of the Chacoan great house kivas in the San Juan Basin and in the Mesa Verde area played a different, and probably larger-scale, integrative role than kivas in the associated small sites. It is also difficult to make a case, on the basis of spatial patterning, that most great house kivas are parts of a unit-pueblo-like facility used by an extended family or other small-scale social segment within the great house.

The three southwest Colorado Chacoan outliers included in Table 1 differ less profoundly from their surrounding settlements than do the great houses in the San Juan Basin. Nevertheless, these three Colorado Chacoan sites have larger kivas, larger rooms, a higher ratio of rooms to kivas, and a much greater ratio of room space to kiva space than contemporaneous non-Chacoan sites in the area. These differences suggest to me that the Chacoan kivas functioned at a larger social scale than the kivas of typical late Pueblo II Mesa Verde area settlements.

Pueblo III Period, Mesa Verde Area

The fourth data set in Table 1 is from Mesa Verde sites dated to the A.D. 1150–1300 period (Pueblo III). The hamlet-sized settlements so common in the Pueblo II period persist in the study area, but in addition there are a number of very large, village-sized settlements that include from one hundred to several hundred surface

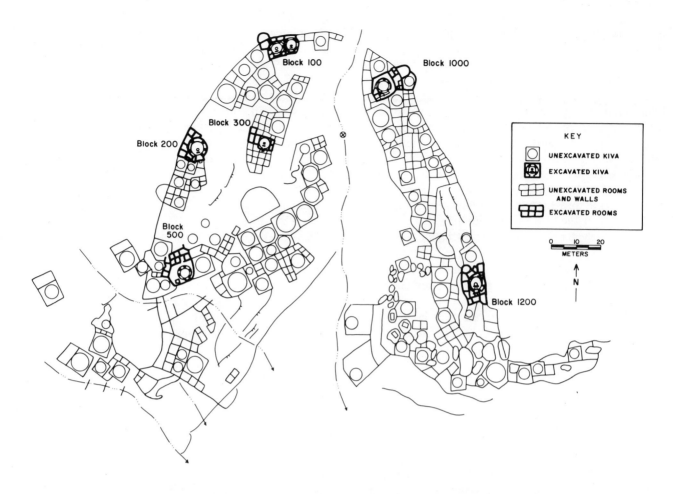

Figure 2: Plan map of Sand Canyon Pueblo (5MT765). Excavated areas shown in heavy lines; other wall lines based on surface mapping.

rooms and numerous kivas (Rohn 1983). Some of these are as large or larger than the major late Pueblo I villages such as McPhee. Among the largest Pueblo III settlements in the study area are the Yellowjacket Site (Lange et al. 1986); Sand Canyon Pueblo (Figure 2) (Bradley 1986, 1987, 1988a); Goodman Point Ruin (Figure 3) (Fewkes 1919); the Lancaster or Clawson Ruins (Martin 1929); the Bug Mesa or Monument Ruins (Leh 1942), the Mud Springs or Toltec Ruin (Holmes 1878; Fewkes 1919), and the large cliff dwellings, such as Long House (Cattanach 1980) and Cliff Palace (Fewkes 1911). Little excavation has been done in the open sites; an exception is Sand Canyon Pueblo, where the Crow Canyon Archaeological Center is carrying out an excavation program (Adams 1985; Bradley 1986, 1987, 1988a).

The indices employed in Table 1 do not suggest a departure from the prevailing unit pueblo pattern during the Pueblo III period in the central Mesa Verde area. Also, Rohn's detailed analysis of Mug House (1965, 1971) at Mesa Verde National Park showed that "kiva groups" existed and were relatively small at this site late in the 1200s. In the study area as a whole, Pueblo III kivas and rooms are slightly smaller than those in Pueblo II, though this may be due to the crowding of structures in the cliff dwellings that were common in this period. The ratios of rooms to kivas, and of room area to kiva area, rise somewhat when compared with Mesa Verde Pueblo II, and room space per kiva increases slightly.

The relatively low standard deviation for Pueblo III kiva sizes stems from the rarity of either very large or very small kivas in the data set. Thus, oversized kivas comparable to the large Pueblo I protokivas discussed above have not been found, even at the larger sites. As noted above, however, there has been little excavation at the very large open sites.

Great Kivas appear to be rare during the Pueblo III period in the central Mesa Verde area, although large walled courtyard spaces at Long House (Cattanach 1980) and Fire Temple (Fewkes 1921; Cassidy 1960) in Mesa Verde National Park have floor vaults and other features often associated with Great Kivas (Vivian and Reiter 1960). Circular Great Kiva depressions also

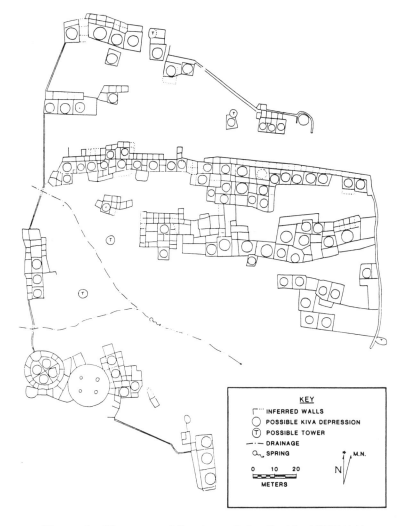

Figure 3: Plan map of Goodman Point Pueblo (5MT604). Wall lines based on surface mapping.

occur at the Goodman Point and Yellowjacket Sites, but it is conceivable that these belong to a late Pueblo II occupation, rather than to the post–A.D. 1150 component that appears to account for the greatest intensity of occupation at these two sites.

Other Pueblo III structures that may have served as public architecture with integrative functions are D-shaped bi-walled structures, including "Sun Temple" (Fewkes 1916; Rohn 1977), located close to Cliff Palace at Mesa Verde National Park, and a similar but unexcavated structure at Sand Canyon Pueblo.

Also present in some probable Pueblo III contexts (e.g., at the Mud Springs Ruins complex) are circular-plan tri-wall structures (Holmes 1878; Vivian 1959) which may have served in some ways as integrative facilities. However, some if not all may date to the early A.D. 1100s rather than to the Pueblo III period as defined here (Lekson 1983; Kane 1986a:384-385).

Pueblo IV type formal rectilinear plazas enclosed on three or four sides by roomblocks do not appear in Pueblo III (or earlier) sites in the study area. Several of the large, late, open pueblos do have informally bounded open areas that may have served as small plazas (e.g., Sand Canyon Pueblo—see Figure 2). At some Pueblo III sites in the study area (e.g., Yellowjacket, Goodman Point [Figure 3], Lancaster Ruin), the numerous roomblocks run east–west and are arranged in parallel series. The spaces between the rows of roomblocks may have functioned as plazas, as they do in some of the similarly-arranged historic Hopi villages (cf. Stubbs 1950).

Recent excavations by the Crow Canyon Archaeological Center promise to shed some light on integrative facilities and modes of integration in the thirteenth century, just prior to the abandonment of the Mesa Verde area. Recent work at the Green Lizard Site (Figure 4) (Huber and Bloomer 1988) has demonstrated that Prudden units are alive and well in the A.D. 1200s in the study area (also see Gould 1982; Lister 1964; O'Bryan 1950). Near the Green Lizard site is the much larger

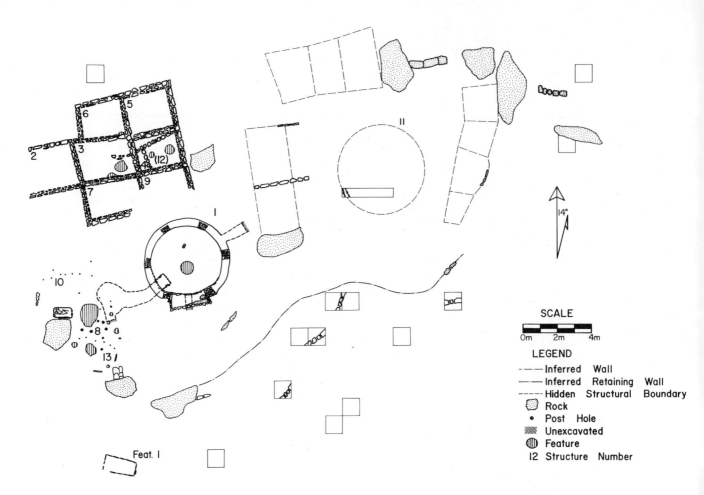

Figure 4: Plan map of the Green Lizard Site (5MT3901). Western portion has been excavated.

Sand Canyon Pueblo (Figure 2), which appears to date between approximately A.D. 1240 and 1280, and may actually have been occupied only between 1250 and 1280. This site is enclosed by a wall and has at least 90 kivas, 300 to 400 rooms, 17 towers, and a D-shaped bi- or tri-walled structure similar to Sun Temple. There is also at least one informal plaza on the western side of the site. The multiplicity of kivas contrasts strongly with the pattern displayed by large villages during the Pueblo IV period in both the Eastern and Western Pueblo areas. This feature of site structure appears to link Sand Canyon Pueblo with the earlier pattern of aggregated unit modules displayed by other large Pueblo I through Pueblo III settlements in the study area, rather than with the general Pueblo IV pattern.

However, only three of the six blocks of kivas and rooms excavated so far at Sand Canyon Pueblo (Bradley 1986, 1987, 1988a) conform closely to a unit type pueblo model, in the sense of exhibiting a well-defined cluster of both large and small rooms associated with a specific kiva. The three other excavated kiva-and-room groups have yielded architectural configurations and feature data that do not fit this model as well. For example, in the "100 Block" (Bradley 1986, 1987), kiva space is very high in relation to room space, and it is difficult to make a case that any of the small associated surface rooms were habitation or living rooms; they appear more likely to have been storage rooms associated with the kivas.

A glance at the Sand Canyon site map (Figure 2) also indicates some other departures from the segmental configuration expected under the "aggregated-unit pueblo" model. In particular, the concentration of large kivas on the west side of the site is striking, as is the scarcity of surface rooms associated with them. Caution should be used in extrapolating surface depression diameter to kiva size, however. Recent excavations by Bradley in a large depression in the "1000 Block" in the northeast part of Sand Canyon Pueblo have shown that the size of the mapped depression there relates to the size of the courtyard area into which an average-size kiva is set.

Nonetheless, the spatial patterning of architecture elements at Sand Canyon Pueblo suggests that these large "west side" kivas may not have been part of standard habitation units used by a few households. In other words, it seems possible that some may have been used by groups who did not reside in the immediately adjacent rooms. Ceremonial associations or other sodality type groups who drew membership from several residential units may have used them. Another possibility is that some kivas at Sand Canyon were used by groups that lived in the smaller settlements, such as Green Lizard, that were dispersed around Sand Canyon Pueblo.

The D-shaped tri-wall structure and the informal plazas at the site must also have played roles in social integration. Sand Canyon is much larger than other excavated late thirteenth-century Mesa Verde sites reported in the literature (including Cliff Palace). It may also have been a central site in a dispersed community of Prudden-unit habitations such as Green Lizard. As in the Pueblo I case discussed earlier, an increased need for social control and orderly decision-making in a context of increased community size and population density could have resulted in the "promotion" of some kivas to use in larger scale social integration.

Pueblo IV and Historic Period

The "unit type pueblo" pattern, one of small kivas closely associated with specific small blocks of habitation and storage rooms, continued in the Mesa Verde area until the very late A.D. 1200s, when this region was abandoned along with the other remaining populated portions of the Four Corners area. The unit pueblo pattern was also present over much of the remainder of the Pueblo area, but it did not survive long, if at all, after A.D. 1300, even in areas that continued to be populated. Instead, it was rapidly replaced by a pattern of larger settlements with few kivas. These Pueblo IV period settlements generally were oriented around plazas (see Adams, this volume).

In the Rio Grande or Eastern Pueblo area, some sites dating to the middle or late A.D. 1200s appear to be single or aggregated unit type pueblos, with room-to-kiva ratios in approximately the same range as in the Mesa Verde area (Stubbs and Stallings 1953; Timothy A. Kohler, personal communication). Whether these sites were built by migrants from the Mesa Verde area is not clear, and the pattern does not appear to have a great deal of time depth in the area. At about A.D. 1300 the room-to-kiva ratio increased greatly in the Eastern Pueblo area (see Table 1), concurrent with the formation of much larger pueblos that were laid out around plazas. Early in Pueblo IV, there was some use of an oval settlement plan (cf. Hayes et al. 1981; Hewett 1938), but this gave way to rectilinear plans, often with multiple plazas (e.g., Hewitt 1906; Nelson 1914). I did not have time to measure the floor areas of Pueblo IV kivas and rooms in the Rio Grande area, but my impressions are that the kivas are generally rather small, and certainly not as large as the typical moiety kivas dominant in nineteenth and twentieth century Rio Grande villages (Table 1; Stubbs 1950). Many Pueblo IV sites also appear to have a few small kivas rather than two large ones—i.e., more like historic period Taos than historic period Santa Clara (Stubbs 1950). Most reports on the larger Pueblo IV sites either date to the early twentieth century and do not provide very detailed internal site chronologies, or they present only surface mappings of rooms and kivas. Consequently, it is difficult to tell how many rooms and kivas were actually in use at a given time. The room-to-kiva ratios are so markedly different from the Pueblo I–III Mesa Verde ones, however, that these problems do not affect the contrast that can be drawn between these two sets of data.

In the Zuni portion of the Western Pueblo area, the small kiva-and-unit pueblo pattern was established well before the Pueblo III period (Woodbury 1979; Zier 1976; Roberts 1931, 1932, 1939b). In this area, the shift to large plaza-oriented sites and a radical decrease in the numbers of kivas relative to rooms also occurred about A.D. 1300 (Woodbury 1979; Kintigh 1985).

Moving farther west, it is my impression that in the Tusayan and Kayenta areas, prior to A.D. 1300, the small kiva-and-unit pueblo pattern was present but more variable in expression than in the central Mesa Verde area or the upper San Juan drainage as a whole. Pueblo II and III period Tusayan and Kayenta area kiva architecture also tends to be less formal and distinctive than in the Mesa Verde area. The Kayenta area appears to have been abandoned by the very late A.D. 1200s, contemporaneous with the final abandonment of the Mesa Verde area. Populations in the Tusayan (Hopi) area swelled at about the same time, and large, plaza-oriented villages with few kivas had largely replaced earlier settlement forms by A.D. 1300 (Adams, this volume). Adams traces the development of this community pattern to antecedents in the Upper Little Colorado-Mogollon Rim area in the mid- to late 1200s.

To the southeast, in the Mimbres area of New Mexico, Anyon and LeBlanc (1980) date the appearance of plaza-oriented pueblos to the Classic Mimbres period, which they place at A.D. 1000–1150. They also note that subterranean kivas and "large rooms," to which they assign a ritual/integrative function, appear during this same period. There apparently is no more than one of these structures per roomblock, and some roomblocks have none.

Thus, the Mimbres area displays a pattern of large villages oriented around plazas, with a low ratio of kivas to rooms, well before these settlement characteristics become common in Pueblo sites farther north. The principal exceptions are some of the Chacoan great houses of the period A.D. 1050–1150 in the San Juan Basin. Chacoan plazas, however, are located to the south or in "front" (Reed 1956) of a single roomblock, rather than between or surrounded by roomblocks, as is the case with Mimbres, Little Colorado, and Pueblo IV Anasazi settlements. Hence, Chacoan site layout continues to follow the basic Anasazi settlement plan that was dominant from Pueblo I through Pueblo III (Reed 1956). Functionally, however, the appearance of plazas in either type of settlement layout probably indicates an investment in ceremonies or other public activities that helped integrate people at the community or supra-community level.

Summary and Conclusions

Although some Pueblo I–III Mesa Verde protokivas and kivas may have served relatively large social units, most appear to be associated with quite small-scale ones, probably at the level of a few co-residential and economically cooperative households. Unlike nearly all surface rooms, Mesa Verde protokivas and kivas commonly have architectural and floor features that can be interpreted as serving ritual and symbolic ends, probably in the context of a religious ideology. Here I would include not only sipapus and floor vaults but the subterranean or pseudo-subterranean character and the roof entries of the kivas themselves. The myth of original emergence from an underworld or underworlds is universal and important in historic Pueblo mythology (Dozier 1970: 203–204). It seems likely that this myth is also quite old and prehistorically widespread. I do not find it surprising that the material symbols of this central myth underwent some changes in form and in architectural contexts during nearly 1500 years of prehistory and history. What is striking is how much continuity in form has been maintained through time (see Wilshusen, this volume). It is also understandable that these symbols came to be incorporated into the social context in somewhat different ways at different times. They may have served primarily small-scale groups before A.D. 1300, and primarily larger groups after that date.

From Pueblo I through Pueblo III the maintenance of powerful religious symbols and rituals by an extended family or other small co-residential unit may have helped make this unit not only economically but also ideologically self-sufficient. Socioeconomic organization based on the strength of these relatively small units may have promoted the well-documented flexibility of northern Anasazi settlement and adaptation.

In the drier western part of the Mesa Verde area outside the Mesa Verde-McElmo core area, the basic unit of Anasazi settlement appears to have been even smaller—the individual household rather than the kiva group (Jennings 1963; Lipe 1970: Matson, Lipe and Haase 1988), so there is nothing intrinsic or inevitable about unit pueblos. Even the extended family is a potentially fissionable unit that requires some mechanism of integration (cf. Johnson and Earle 1987). The small protokiva or kiva appears to have played an important integrative role for groups of this scale in the more productive and densely-settled portions of the Mesa Verde area during the Pueblo I through Pueblo III periods.

It appears likely that at least some Pueblo I–III period Mesa Verde kivas served groups larger than, or at least different from, an interhousehold unit. Sodality organizations such as medicine or dance societies could have been housed in such structures. Alternatively, an interhousehold group that wished to increase its influence over community or intercommunity affairs might have used a larger, more elaborate kiva in conjunction with ceremonious hosting of key individuals from other groups. Use of religious as well as social rituals in these contexts would have provided supernatural sanction for such efforts.

In addition to housing some types of religious rituals, the Pueblo I–III Mesa Verde kiva also must have contributed to social integration through its role as a jointly constructed and jointly used facility for certain domestic/economic activities shared among households. It may also have been a place where visitors from other interhousehold units or from other communities could be given hospitality, and where such guests and their hosts could exchange gifts of food or other materials (also see papers by Blinman and by Plog, this volume).

The small kiva/unit pueblo/modular aggregate pattern was very common in the Mesa Verde area and over large parts of the Anasazi area prior to about A.D. 1300, and was present in sites ranging from small hamlets to villages of several hundred rooms. At about A.D. 1300, as the abandonment of the Mesa Verde area and the rest of the northern San Juan region was completed, there was a rapid shift to larger, plaza-oriented villages with few kivas throughout the remaining populated portion of the Anasazi area. After A.D. 1300 the use of kiva architecture, and presumably its associated symbols and symbolic features, appears to have become restricted to groups that functioned at a community level of social integration, or at least at a level above the extended family or minimal lineage.

This shift may have been the result of the rapid spread and adoption of institutions that originated outside the Anasazi area, such as pan-community sodalities like the Katsina cult (Adams, this volume), or more formalized leadership patterns, or both. Alternatively, patterns of this sort may have been present but only weakly developed in earlier Anasazi societies, but were strongly selected for during the tumultuous times of the very late A.D. 1200s and early 1300s. As noted above, there is some architectural and site-structure evidence suggesting such patterns may have been present in the Mesa Verde area before A.D. 1300. To date, this evidence is better for the Pueblo I and II periods than for Pueblo III. This, plus the synchrony of change from Eastern through Western Pueblo areas at A.D. 1300, tends to favor a "rapid spread and adoption" hypothesis such as the one put forward by Adams (this volume).

In either scenario we still must account for the loss of the small kiva/unit pueblo pattern, which had lasted for 500 years and had been functional in a variety of environments and in small and large settlements. As Steward (1937) and Eggan (1950) recognized, the conditions that selected against the small-scale kiva pattern and favored a restricted larger-scale use of kivas and their symbolic paraphernalia must have been the demographic disruption, movement, and coalescence that affected the Anasazi world in the middle and late A.D. 1200s.

The Pueblo III to Pueblo IV shift in the social scale of kiva use appears to represent a shift in the scale and composition of the most important social "survival vehicle" (Adams 1981) in Anasazi society. Before A.D. 1300, the Anasazi tended to emphasize a small, and hence mobile, group of cooperating households as the most important social unit. They built facilities and features that directly symbolized the integration of those units and provided the medium for rituals and other social activities to express and reinforce that integration. Although there were also integrative mechanisms for linking these small units into larger communities, they appear to have been relatively weak; in any case, the culture history of the Mesa Verde and other Anasazi areas reveals repeated cycles of the aggregation and subsequent dispersal of communities that range in form from loose clusters of hamlets to densely packed villages, such as McPhee (Pueblo I) or Sand Canyon (Pueblo III).

After A.D. 1300 the village community of several hundred persons appears to have become a stronger and ritually more reinforced social unit, though one still subject to occasional fission along kinship or factional lines. The association of kivas with sodalities or moieties meant that the symbolic properties of these structures were being controlled by groups having membership drawn from a number of residential/kinship units scattered throughout the community (Eggan 1950; Dean 1970). Furthermore, as Adams (this volume) points out, the formalization of a central plaza or plazas provided a locale for community ceremonies. In the Eastern Tewa pueblos, the plaza is also the location of the *nansipu* or "earth navel" that marks the center of the cosmos for each village, and is an important orienting point for Tewa world view (Ortiz 1969, 1972; Swentzell 1985, 1988). If the village moves, the nansipu, or center, moves with it. Thus, "sacred space can be recreated again and again without exhausting its reality" (Ortiz 1972:142). Prior to A.D. 1300, sacred space may have moved with the interhousehold group rather than with the village.

Acknowledgments

I wish to dedicate this paper to Jesse D. Jennings, who gave me my first opportunity to work on Anasazi kivas, and from whom I learned much of what I know about how to do archaeological fieldwork, and how to look for patterns in archaeological data.

The research for this paper was supported in part by National Science Foundation Grant No. 8706532 to the Crow Canyon Archaeological Center. I especially wish to acknowledge the many hours of careful work that Nick Scoales put into making planimeter measurements from site report maps. I am also grateful to Richard Wilshusen, Mark Varien, Ricky Lightfoot, and Karen Dohm for sharing their data with me. Michelle Hegmon and David Breternitz made many helpful comments on earlier drafts of the paper. I of course take responsibility for any errors of omission, commission, or interpretation that the paper contains.

References

Adams, E. Charles
    1985   *Annual Report of Test Excavations at 5MT765, Sand Canyon Pueblo, and Archaeological Survey in T36N, R18W, Sections 12 and 24, and T36N, R16W, Sections 29 and 30.* Crow Canyon Campus of the Center for American Archeology, Cortez, Colorado. Submitted to the Bureau of Land Management, San Juan Resource Area, Durango, Colorado.

Adams, Richard N.
    1981   The Dynamics of Societal Diversity: Notes from Nicaragua for a Sociology of Survival. *American Ethnologist* 8(1):1-20.

Anyon, Roger and Steven A. LeBlanc
    1980   The Architectural Evolution of Mogollon-Mimbres Communal Structures. *The Kiva* 45(3):253-277

Birkedal, Terje
    1968   Site 1926, An Isolated Pueblo III Kiva Near Long House, Wetherill Mesa. In *Contributions to Mesa Verde Archaeology: V. Emergency Archaeology in Mesa Verde National Park, Colorado, 1948–1966,* edited by Robert H. Lister, pp. 95-100.

Blinman, Eric
   1988   *The Interpretation of Ceramic Variability: A Case Study from the Dolores Anasazi.* Unpublished Ph.D. dissertation, Department of Anthropology, Washington State University, Pullman, Washington.

Bradley, Bruce A.
   1974   Preliminary Report of Excavations at the Wallace Ruin. *Southwestern Lore* 40(3 and 4):63-71.

   1986   *1985 Annual Report of Test Excavations at Sand Canyon Pueblo (5MT765).* Crow Canyon Archaeological Center, Cortez, Colorado. Submitted to the Bureau of Land Management, San Juan Resource Area Office, Durango, Colorado.

   1987   *Annual Report of Excavations at Sand Canyon Pueblo (5MT765), 1986 Field Season.* Crow Canyon Archaeological Center, Cortez, Colorado. Submitted to the Bureau of Land Management, San Juan Resource Area Office, Durango, Colorado.

   1988a   *Annual Report on the Excavations at Sand Canyon Pueblo, 1987 Field Season.* Crow Canyon Archaeological Center, Cortez, Colorado. Submitted to the Bureau of Land Management, San Juan Resource Area Office, Durango, Colorado.

   1988b   Wallace Ruin Interim Report. *Southwestern Lore* 54(2):8-33.

Breternitz, David A., Christine K. Robinson, and E. Timothy Gross, compilers
   1986   *Dolores Archaeological Program: Final Synthetic Report.* Bureau of Reclamation, Engineering and Research Center, Denver, Colorado.

Brew, John O.
   1946   *Archaeology of Alkali Ridge, Southeastern Utah.* Papers of the Peabody Museum of American Archaeology and Ethnology, vol. 21. Harvard University, Cambridge, Massachusetts.

Cassidy, Francis
   1960   Fire Temple, Mesa Verde National Park. In *The Great Kivas of Chaco Canyon and Their Relationships,* by Gordon Vivian and Paul Reiter, pp. 73-81. Monographs of the School of American Research No. 22. Santa Fe, New Mexico.

Cater, John D. and Mark L. Chenault
   1988   Kiva Use Reinterpreted. *Southwestern Lore* 54(3):19-32.

Cattanach, George S., Jr.
   1980   *Long House, Mesa Verde National Park, Colorado.* National Park Service Publications in Archeology No. 7H. Washington, D.C.

Dean, Jeffrey S.
   1970   Aspects of Tsegi Phase Social Organization: A Trial Reconstruction. In *Reconstructing Prehistoric Pueblo Societies,* edited by William A. Longacre, pp. 140-174. University of New Mexico Press, Albuquerque.

Dohm, Karen
   1987   Effect of Population Nucleation on House Size for Pueblos in the American Southwest. Unpublished manuscript in the possession of the author, Dept. of Anthropology, Smithsonian Institution, Washington, D.C.

Dozier, Edward P.
   1970   *The Pueblo Indians of North America.* Holt, Rinehart, and Winston, New York.

Eggan, Fred
   1950   *Social Organization of the Western Pueblos.* University of Chicago Press, Chicago.

Fewkes, J. W.
   1909   *Antiquities of the Mesa Verde National Park: Spruce Tree House.* Bureau of American Ethnology Bulletin 41. Smithsonian Institution, Washington, D.C.

   1911   *Antiquities of the Mesa Verde National Park: Cliff Palace.* Bureau of American Ethnology Bulletin 51. Smithsonian Institution, Washington, D.C.

   1916   *Excavation and Repair of Sun Temple, Mesa Verde National Park.* U.S. Government Printing Office, Washington, D.C.

   1919   *Prehistoric Villages, Castles, and Towers of Southwestern Colorado.* Bureau of American Ethnology Bulletin 70. Washington, D.C.

   1921   Field Work on the Mesa Verde National Park. In *Explorations and Fieldwork of the Smithsonian Institution in 1920.* Smithsonian Miscellaneous Collections, vol. 72(6).

Gillespie, William
   1976   *Culture Change at the Ute Canyon Site: A Study of the Pithouse–Kiva Transition in the Mesa Verde Region.* Unpublished Master's thesis, Department of Anthropology, University of Colorado, Boulder.

Gould, Ron
  1982 *The Mustoe Site.* Unpublished Ph.D. dissertation, Department of Anthropology, University of Texas, Austin.

Hallasi, Judith
  1979 Archaeological Excavation at the Escalante Site, Dolores, Colorado, 1975 and 1976. In *The Archaeology and Stabilization of the Dominguez and Escalante Ruins,* by Alan D. Reed et al., pp. 197-245. Bureau of Land Management, Colorado, Cultural Resources Series No. 7. Denver.

Hawley, Florence
  1950 Big Kivas, Little Kivas, and Moiety Houses in Historical Reconstruction. *Southwestern Journal of Anthropology* 6:286-302.

Hayes, Alden
  1964 *The Archeological Survey of Wetherill Mesa, Mesa Verde National Park.* National Park Service Archeological Research Series 7A. National Park Service, Washington, D.C.

Hayes, Alden C. and James A. Lancaster
  1975 *Badger House Community, Mesa Verde National Park.* National Park Service Publications in Archeology No. 7E. Washington, D.C.

Hayes, Alden C., Jon Young, and A. H. Warren
  1981 *Excavation of Mound 7, Gran Quivira National Monument, New Mexico.* National Park Service Publications in Archeology No. 16. Washington, D.C.

Hewett, Arthur F., Jr.
  1968 The Salvage Excavation of Site 1914, Navajo Hill. In *Contributions to Mesa Verde Archaeology: V. Emergency Archaeology in Mesa Verde National Park, Colorado, 1948–1966,* edited by Robert H. Lister, pp. 37-44. University of Colorado Studies, Series in Anthropology No. 15. Boulder, Colorado.

Hewett, Edgar L.
  1906 *Antiquities of the Jemez Plateau, New Mexico.* Bureau of American Ethnology Bulletin 32. Washington, D.C.

  1938 *The Pajarito Plateau and Its Ancient People.* University of New Mexico and School of American Research. Albuquerque, New Mexico.

Hill, David V.
  1985 Pottery Making at the Ewing Site. *Southwestern Lore* 51(1):19-31.

Hill, James N.
  1966 A Prehistoric Community in Eastern Arizona. *Southwestern Journal of Anthropology* 22(1):9-30.

Holmes, William H.
  1878 Report on the Ancient Ruins of Southwestern Colorado, Examined During the Summers of 1875 and 1876. In *Tenth Annual Report of the U.S. Geological and Geographical Survey of the Territories for 1876,* pp. 383-408. Washington, D.C.

Huber, Edgar K and William W. Bloomer
  1988 *Annual Report of Investigations at Green Lizard (5MT3901), Montezuma County, Colorado.* Crow Canyon Archaeological Center, Cortez, Colorado. Submitted to the Bureau of Land Management, San Juan Resource Area, Durango, Colorado.

Jennings, Jesse D.
  1963 Anthropology and the World of Science. *University of Utah Bulletin* 54(18). Salt Lake City.

Johnson, Allen W. and Timothy Earle
  1987 *The Evolution of Human Societies.* Stanford University Press, Stanford, California.

Kane, Allen E.
  1983 Introduction to Field Investigations and Analysis. In *Dolores Archaeological Program: Field Investigations and Analysis—1978,* prepared under the supervision of David A. Breternitz, pp. 1-37. Bureau of Reclamation, Engineering and Research Center, Denver.

  1984 The Prehistory of the Dolores Project Area. In *Dolores Archaeological Program: Synthetic Report 1978—1981,* prepared under the supervision of David A. Breternitz, pp. 21-51. Bureau of Reclamation, Engineering and Research Center, Denver.

  1986a Prehistory of the Dolores River Valley. In *Dolores Archaeological Program: Final Synthetic Report,* compiled by David A. Breternitz et al., pp. 353-435. Bureau of Reclamation, Engineering and Research Center, Denver.

  1986b Social Organization and Cultural Process in Dolores Anasazi Communities, A.D. 600–900. In *Dolores Archaeological Program: Final Synthetic Report,* compiled by David A. Breternitz et al., pp.

633-661. Bureau of Reclamation, Engineering and Research Center, Denver.

Kane, Allen E. and Christine K. Robinson (compilers)
1988 *Dolores Archaeological Program: Anasazi Communities at Dolores: McPhee Village*. Bureau of Reclamation, Engineering and Research Center, Denver.

Kintigh, Keith W.
1985 *Settlement, Subsistence, and Society in Late Zuni Prehistory*. Anthropological Papers of the University of Arizona No. 44. Tucson, Arizona.

Lancaster, James A. and Jean M. Pinkley
1954 Excavation at Site 16 of Three Pueblo II Mesa-Top Ruins. In *Archeological Excavations in Mesa Verde National Park, Colorado, 1950*, by James A. Lancaster et al., pp. 23-86. National Park Service Archeological Research Series No. 2. Washington, D.C.

Lancaster, James A. and Philip F. Van Cleave
1954 Excavation of Sun Point Pueblo. In *Archeological Excavations in Mesa Verde National Park, Colorado, 1950*, by James A. Lancaster et al., pp. 87-111. National Park Service Archeological Research Series No. 2. Washington, D.C.

Lange, Frederick, Nancy Mahaney, Joe Ben Wheat, and Mark L. Chenault
1986 *Yellow Jacket: A Four Corners Anasazi Ceremonial Center*. Johnson Books, Boulder, Colorado.

Leh, Leonard
1942 A Preliminary Report on the Monument Ruins in San Juan County, Utah. *University of Colorado Studies, Series C, Studies in the Social Sciences* 1(3):261-295.

Lekson, Stephen H.
1983 Dating the Hubbard Tri-wall and Other Tri-wall Structures. *Southwestern Lore* 49(4):15-23.

1984 *Great Pueblo Architecture of Chaco Canyon, New Mexico*. National Park Service Publications in Archeology No. 18B. National Park Service, Washington, D.C.

1985 The Idea of the Kiva in Anasazi Archaeology. Paper Presented at the 50th Annual Meeting of the Society for American Archaeology, Denver, Colorado.

1988 The Idea of the Kiva in Anasazi Archaeology. *The Kiva* 53(3):213-234.

Lightfoot, Ricky R.
1988 Roofing an Anasazi Great Kiva: Analysis of an Architectural Model. *The Kiva* 53(3):253-272.

Lightfoot, Ricky R., Alice Emerson, and Eric Blinman
1988 Excavations in Area 5. In *Dolores Archaeological Program: Anasazi Communities at Dolores: Grass Mesa Village (5MT23)*, compiled by William D. Lipe et al., pp. 561-766. Bureau of Reclamation, Engineering and Research Center, Denver.

Lipe, William D.
1970 Anasazi Communities in the Red Rock Plateau. In *Reconstructing Prehistoric Pueblo Societies*, edited by William Longacre, pp. 84-139. University of New Mexico Press, Albuquerque.

Lipe, William D. and Bruce A. Bradley
1988 Prehistoric Pueblo Organization, Sand Canyon Locality, Southwestern Colorado. Crow Canyon Archaeological Center, Cortez, Colorado. Research proposal submitted to the National Science Foundation.

Lipe, William D. and Timothy A. Kohler
1984 Method and Technique: Prehistory. In *Dolores Archaeological Program: Synthetic Report 1978–1981*, prepared under the supervision of David A. Breternitz, pp. 9-20. U.S. Bureau of Reclamation, Engineering and Research Center, Denver.

Lipe, William D., Timothy A. Kohler, Mark D. Varien, James N. Morris, and Ricky R. Lightfoot
1988 Synthesis. In *Dolores Archaeological Program: Anasazi Communities at Dolores: Grass Mesa Village (5MT23)*, compiled by W. D. Lipe et al., pp. 1213-1276. Bureau of Reclamation, Engineering and Research Center, Denver.

Lister, Robert H.
1964 *Contributions to Mesa Verde Archaeology: I. Site 499, Mesa Verde National Park, Colorado*. University of Colorado Studies, Series in Anthropology No. 9. Boulder, Colorado.

1965 *Contributions to Mesa Verde Archaeology: II. Site 875, Mesa Verde National Park, Colorado*. University of Colorado Studies, Series in Anthropology No. 11. Boulder, Colorado.

1966 *Contributions to Mesa Verde Archaeology: III. Site 866, and the Cultural Sequence at Four Villages in the Far View Group, Mesa Verde National Park, Colorado.* University of Colorado Studies, Series in Anthropology No. 12. Boulder, Colorado.

1967 *Contributions to Mesa Verde Archaeology: IV. Site 1086, an Isolated Above-Ground Kiva in Mesa Verde National Park, Colorado.* University of Colorado Studies, Series in Anthropology No. 13. Boulder, Colorado.

Lister, Robert H. (assembler and editor)
1968 *Contributions to Mesa Verde Archaeology: V. Emergency Archaeology in Mesa Verde National Park, Colorado, 1948–1966.* University of Colorado Studies, Series in Anthropology No. 15. Boulder, Colorado.

Lister, Robert H. and David A. Breternitz
1968 The Salvage Excavation of Site 1104, Wetherill Mesa. In *Contributions to Mesa Verde Archaeology: V. Emergency Archaeology in Mesa Verde National Park, Colorado, 1948–1966,* edited by Robert H. Lister, pp. 69-88. University of Colorado Studies, Series in Anthropology No. 15. Boulder, Colorado.

Lister, Robert H. and Jack E. Smith
1968 Salvage Excavations at Site 1088, Morfield Canyon. In *Contributions to Mesa Verde Archaeology: V. Emergency Archaeology in Mesa Verde National Park, Colorado, 1948–1966,* edited by Robert H. Lister, pp. 5-32. University of Colorado Studies, Series in Anthropology No. 15. Boulder, Colorado.

Luebben, Ralph
1983 The Grinnell Site. *Journal of Intermountain Archeology* 2(2):1-26.

Martin, Paul S.
1929 The 1928 Archaeological Expedition of the State Historical Society of Colorado. *The Colorado Magazine* 6(1):1-35.

1930 The 1929 Archaeological Expedition of the State Historical Society of Colorado in Co-operation with the Smithsonian Institution. *The Colorado Magazine* 7(1):1-40.

Martin, Paul S. (with reports by Laurence Roys and Gerhardt von Bonin)
1936 *Lowry Ruin in Southwestern Colorado.* Field Museum of Natural History, Anthropological Series, vol. 23(1). Chicago.

Matson, R. G., William D. Lipe, and William R. Haase
1988 Adaptational Continuities and Occupational Discontinuities: the Cedar Mesa Anasazi. *Journal of Field Archaeology* 15(3):245-264.

McKenna, Peter J. and Marcia L. Truell
1986 *Small Site Architecture of Chaco Canyon, New Mexico.* National Park Service Publications in Archeology No. 18D. National Park Service, Santa Fe, New Mexico.

Mindeleff, Victor
1891 *A Study of Pueblo Architecture: Tusayan and Cibola.* Annual Report of the Bureau of Ethnology No. 8, pp. 13-228. Smithsonian Institution, Washington, D.C.

Morley, Sylvanus G.
1908 The Excavation of the Cannonball Ruins in Southwestern Colorado. *American Anthropologist,* n.s., 10:596-610.

Morris, Earl
1939 *Archaeological Studies in the La Plata District, Southwestern Colorado and Northwestern New Mexico.* Carnegie Institution of Washington Publication No. 519. Washington, D.C.

Nelson, Nels C.
1914 *Pueblo Ruins of the Galisteo Basin, New Mexico.* Anthropological Papers of the American Museum of Natural History, vol. 15(1). New York City.

Nickens, Paul
1977 *Wood Rat Knoll: A Multicomponent Site in Butler Wash, Southeastern Utah.* Department of Anthropology, University of Denver.

1981 *Pueblo III Communities in Transition: Environment and Adaptation in Johnson Canyon.* Memoirs of the Colorado Archaeological Society No. 2. Boulder, Colorado.

O'Bryan, Deric
1950 *Excavations in Mesa Verde National Park, 1947–1948.* Medallion Papers No. 34. Gila Pueblo, Globe, Arizona.

Orcutt, Jan and Eric Blinman
1988 Leadership and the Development of Social Complexity: A Case Study from the Dolores Area of the American Southwest. Manuscript in possession of the senior author, National Park Service, Santa Fe, New Mexico.

Ortiz, Alfonso
    1969   *The Tewa World: Space, Time, Being, and Becoming in a Pueblo Society.* University of Chicago Press, Chicago.

    1972   Ritual Drama and Pueblo World View. In *New Perspectives on the Pueblos,* edited by Alfonso Ortiz, pp. 135-161. University of New Mexico Press, Albuquerque.

Powers, Robert P., William B. Gillespie, and Stephen H. Lekson
    1983   *The Outlier Survey: A Regional View of Settlement in the San Juan Basin.* Reports of the Chaco Center No. 3. Division of Research, National Park Service, Albuquerque.

Prudden, T. Mitchell
    1903   The Prehistoric Ruins of the San Juan Watershed in Utah, Arizona, Colorado and New Mexico. *American Anthropologist,* n.s., 5(2):224-288.

    1914   The Circular Kivas of Small Ruins in the San Juan Watershed. *American Anthropologist,* n.s., 16:33-58.

    1918   *A Further Study of Prehistoric Small House Ruins in the San Juan Watershed.* Memoirs of the American Anthropological Association No. 5(l).

Reed, Alan D.
    1979   The Dominguez Ruin: A McElmo Phase Pueblo in Southwestern Colorado. In *The Archaeology and Stabilization of the Dominguez and Escalante Ruins,* by Alan Reed et al., Part 1, pp. 1-196. Bureau of Land Management, Colorado, Cultural Resources Series No. 7. Denver.

Reed, Erik
    1956   Types of Village Plan Layouts in the Southwest. In *Prehistoric Settlement Patterns in the New World,* edited by Gordon R. Willey, pp. 11-17. Viking Fund Publications in Anthropology No. 23. New York.

    1958   *Excavations in Mancos Canyon, Colorado.* University of Utah Anthropological Papers No. 35. Salt Lake City.

Roberts, Frank H. H.
    1930   *Early Pueblo Ruins in the Piedra District, Southwestern Colorado.* Bureau of American Ethnology Bulletin 96. Washington, D.C.

    1931   *The Ruins at Kiatuthlanna, Eastern Arizona.* Bureau of American Ethnology Bulletin 100. Washington, D.C.

    1932   *The Village of the Great Kivas on the Zuni Reservation.* Bureau of American Ethnology Bulletin 111. Washington, D.C.

    1933   Some Early Pueblo Remains in Eastern Arizona. *Smithsonian Institution Exploration and Fieldwork in 1932:* 65-68.

    1939a   The Development of a Unit-Type Dwelling. In *So Live the Works of Men,* edited by Donald D. Brand and Fred E. Harvey, pp. 311-323. University of New Mexico Press, Albuquerque.

    1939b   *Archaeological Remains in the Whitewater District, Eastern Arizona. Part I. House Types.* Bureau of American Ethnology Bulletin 121. Washington, D.C.

Robinson, William J. and Bruce G. Harrill
    1974   *Tree-Ring Dates from Colorado V: Mesa Verde Area.* Laboratory of Tree-Ring Research, University of Arizona, Tucson.

Rohn, Arthur
    1965   Postulation of Socio-economic Groups from Archaeological Evidence. In *Contributions of the Wetherill Mesa Archeological Project,* assembled by Douglas Osborne, pp. 65-69. Society for American Archaeology Memoir No. 19.

    1971   *Mug House, Mesa Verde National Park, Colorado.* National Park Service Archeological Series No. 7D. Washington, D.C.

    1977   *Cultural Change and Continuity on Chapin Mesa.* The Regents Press of Kansas. Lawrence, Kansas.

    1983   Budding Urban Settlements in the Northern San Juan. In *Proceedings of the Anasazi Symposium, 1981,* edited by Jack E. Smith, pp. 175-180. Mesa Verde Museum Association, Mesa Verde National Park, Colorado.

Schlanger, Sarah
    1985   *Prehistoric Population Dynamics in the Dolores Area, Southwestern Colorado.* Unpublished Ph.D. dissertation, Department of Anthropology, Washington State University, Pullman.

Smith, Watson
- 1971 *Painted Ceramics of the Western Mound at Awatovi*. Papers of the Peabody Museum of Archaeology and Ethnology No. 38. Harvard University, Cambridge, Massachusetts.

- 1972 *Prehistoric Kivas of Antelope Mesa, Northeastern Arizona*. Papers of the Peabody Museum of Archaeology and Ethnology, vol. 39(1). Harvard University, Cambridge.

Steward, Julian
- 1937 Ecological Aspects of Southwestern Society. *Anthropos* 32:87-104.

Stuart, David E. and Rory P. Gauthier
- 1981 *Prehistoric New Mexico: Background for Survey*. Historic Preservation Division, Office of Cultural Affairs, State of New Mexico. Santa Fe, New Mexico.

Stubbs, Stanley A.
- 1950 *Birds-Eye View of the Pueblos*. University of Oklahoma Press, Norman.

Stubbs, Stanley A. and W. S. Stallings, Jr.
- 1953 *The Excavation of Pindi Pueblo, New Mexico*. Monographs of the School of American Research and the Laboratory of Anthropology No. 18. Santa Fe, New Mexico.

Swannack, Jervis D., Jr.
- 1969 *Big Juniper House, Mesa Verde National Park*. National Park Service Archeological Research Series No. 7-C. Washington, D.C.

Swentzell, Rina
- 1985 An Understated Sacredness. *MASS*, Fall issue, 1985. School of Architecture and Planning, University of New Mexico.

- 1988 Bupingeh: The Pueblo Plaza. *El Palacio* 94(2):14-19.

Thompson, Charmaine, Shane A. Baker, James R. Allison, and Kenneth L. Wintch
- 1986 *The Nancy Patterson Village Archaeological Research Project, Field Year 1985, Preliminary Report No. 3*. Brigham Young University, Museum of Peoples and Cultures, Technical Series No. 86-27. Provo, Utah.

Vivian, R. Gordon
- 1959 *The Hubbard Site and Other Tri-wall Structures in New Mexico and Colorado*. National Park Service Archeological Research Series No. 5. Washington, D.C.

Vivian, R. Gordon and Paul Reiter
- 1960 *The Great Kivas of Chaco Canyon and Their Relationships*. Monographs of the School of American Research No. 22. Santa Fe, New Mexico.

Wilcox, David
- 1976 How the Pueblos Came to Be As They Are: The Problem Today. Unpublished preliminary examination paper, Department of Anthropology, University of Arizona, Tucson.

Wilshusen, Richard
- 1985 Architectural Trends in Prehistoric Anasazi Sites at Dolores, Colorado, A.D. 600–1200. *Dolores Archaeological Program Technical Reports* DAP-274. Prepared for Cultural Resources Mitigation Program: Dolores Project, Bureau of Reclamation, Upper Colorado Region, Salt Lake City, Utah. Contract No. 8-07-40-S0562.

- 1986 The Relationship Between Abandonment Mode and Ritual Use in Pueblo I Anasazi Protokivas. *Journal of Field Archaeology* 13:245-254.

Woodbury, Richard B.
- 1979 Zuni Prehistory and History to 1850. In *Southwest*, edited by Alfonso Ortiz, pp. 467–473. Handbook of North American Indians, vol. 9, William C. Sturtevant, general editor. Smithsonian Institution, Washington, D.C.

Zier, Christian J.
- 1976 *Excavations Near Zuni, New Mexico: 1973*. MNA Research Paper No. 2. Musuem of Northern Arizona, Flagstaff.

6
Ritual and Nonritual Activities in Mesa Verde Region Pit Structures

Mark D. Varien and Ricky R. Lightfoot

> *Excavation data from the Duckfoot Site, a ninth century hamlet in southwestern Colorado, are used to investigate how early Pueblo pit structures were used. The distribution of floor artifacts and features across the site is used to infer activities associated with pit structures and surface rooms, taking into account modes of abandonment and assemblage formation. Architectural suites consisting of a pit structure and associated surface "front" and "back" rooms are also compared. Unlike the surface rooms, the pit structures have evidence of ritual use, as well as ritual modes of abandonment. They do not appear to have been specialized for ritual use, however, because domestic features and artifacts are also abundant in them. There is strong evidence for multiple-household shared use of pit structures, and also for considerable variation from one pit structure to the next in the activities represented.*

Introduction

To begin our study of pit structure use we quote Earl Morris, who introduced the term "protokiva" to the archaeological literature:

> Although the underground chamber was for some time maintained as the principal domiciliary unit of each residential cluster, the above-ground rooms gradually assumed the function of the family living quarters, and the subterranean chamber became invested with ceremonial character. This change was completed somewhere between the norms of Pueblo I and II [Morris 1939:36].

Morris was essentially addressing the same question we are asking today: How does pit structure use change when surface habitation rooms become a part of the architectural configuration of the site? A "protokiva," for Morris, was a pit structure that bridged the gap between a pit house and a kiva, primarily in terms of architectural style and to a lesser degree in terms of structure use (Morris 1939:30, 34, 36). "Protokiva" is not a popular term today, because it raises the problem of teleological reasoning; the interpretation of pit structure use is limited and biased if we assume a priori that pit houses changed into kivas. In this paper we are concerned with the same type of structures that Morris labeled "protokivas," late Pueblo I pit structures on sites in the Mesa Verde region where surface rooms interpreted as habitations are also present. We will drop the term "protokiva," however, for the more generic label, "pit structure." The *use* of these pit structures remains a problem to resolve, and ritual use is but one interpretation considered. "Ritual activity," as it is used in this paper, refers to religious ceremony conducted by a group.

To examine pit structure use we focus on an extremely well-preserved, well-dated, and thoroughly excavated site, the Duckfoot Site (Lightfoot 1985, 1987; Lightfoot and Van West 1986; Lightfoot and Varien 1988). The Duckfoot Site (Figure 1) is a relatively small late Pueblo I habitation in the Mesa Verde region, occupied by four to seven households. Comparisons are made between Duckfoot pit structures and surface rooms, using architectural data, floor artifact and feature assemblages, and abandonment mode. Pit structure and room use patterns appear to be distinct, based on these comparisons. The same data sets are used to compare pit structures to each other. Variation between pit structures suggests they may have been used differently as well.

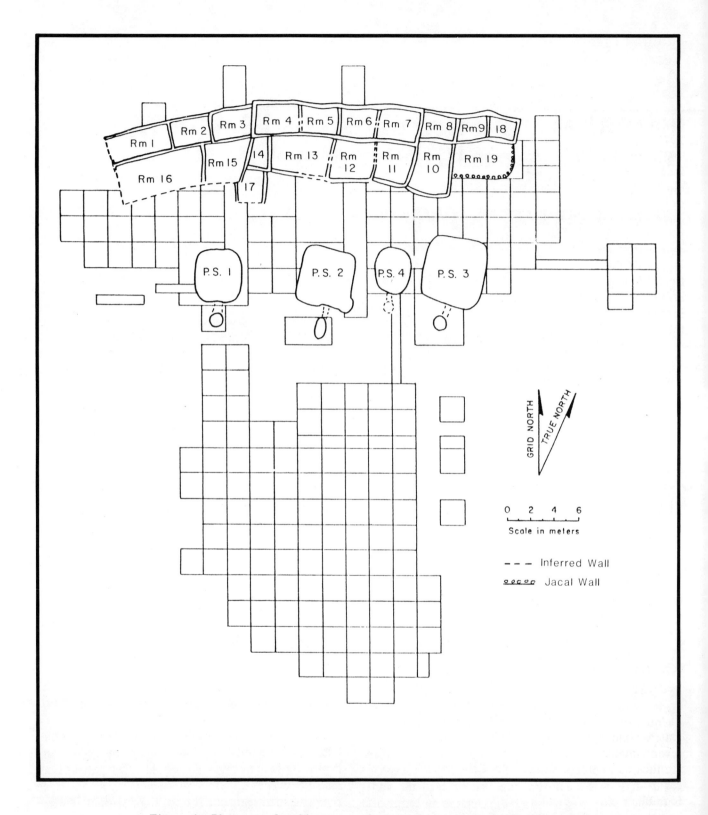

Figure 1: Plan map of architecture and excavation units at the Duckfoot site.

Pueblo I Communities in the Mesa Verde Region

Anasazi population in the Mesa Verde region was both dense and aggregated by the late Pueblo I period (Morris 1939; Martin 1939; Brew 1946; Hayes and Lancaster 1975; Brisbin et al. 1988; Lipe et al. 1988; Wilshusen 1985a, 1986a; Kane 1986; Orcutt 1987). Many sites include several roomblocks of over 50 rooms, spatially clustered into large communities (Orcutt 1987). Variation in pit structure size is an important aspect of these Pueblo I sites. Excluding Great Kivas, pit structure size recorded by the Dolores Archaeological Program ranges from under 10 m^2 to oversized pit structures as large as 64 m^2 (Kane 1986; Wilshusen 1985a). This tremendous size variation suggests that pit structures may have varied greatly, both in their range of uses and in the size of the social groups who used and maintained them.

Duckfoot (Figure 1) is a relatively small site located 12 km northwest of Mesa Verde. Architectural units at Duckfoot include 19 surface rooms and four small- to moderate-sized pit structures (Lightfoot 1985, 1987; Lightfoot and Van West 1986; Lightfoot and Varien 1988). Site reconnaissance indicates that Duckfoot is part of a larger dispersed community that includes one large settlement with a probable oversized pit structure (Lightfoot 1985).

Several factors make Duckfoot an excellent site at which to examine the question of pit structure use. The entire site has been excavated, and preservation was excellent due to burning and the absence of looting and plowing. Burned roof fall covered most pit structure and front room floors, sealing the contents and minimizing postabandonment scavenging, mixing, and contamination. Tree-ring dates are plentiful, and indicate initial construction in the mid- to late A.D. 850s, with the last remodeling in the early A.D. 870s.

An Architectural Model of Household Organization

Pueblo I site layout in the Anasazi region is repetitively patterned from site to site. Roomblocks containing a row of smaller rooms fronted by a row of larger rooms are located on the north end of the site, an associated group of pit structures is found to the south of the roomblock, and south of the pit structures is the midden. Social organization models developed by the Dolores Archaeological Program are based largely on this repeated architectural pattern (Figure 2). Surface room suites consisting of a front room and one or two back rooms are interpreted as having been occupied by a household. Two or more households sharing the use of a pit structure formed an interhousehold group. The sum of adjacent interhouseholds composed the roomblock group, and a cluster of roomblock groups formed a community (Kane 1986).

Initial construction at Duckfoot (Figure 3) included three pit structures (1, 2, and 3), eight front rooms (16, 15, 14, 13, 12, 11, 10, and 19), and ten back rooms (1, 2, 3, 4, 5, 6, 7, 8, 9, and 18). Following the Dolores model, the roomblock contains seven household units. Evidence from wall junctures and differences in building techniques can be used to divide the roomblock into three interhousehold suites. Residents of Rooms 15 and 16 would have stored food in Rooms 1, 2, and 3, and formed an interhousehold group that shared Pit Structure 1. Similarly, residents of Rooms 11, 12, and 13 would have used Rooms 4, 5, 6, and 7 for storage, and shared Pit Structure 2. Rooms 10 and 19 are living rooms associated with storage Rooms 8, 9, and 18, and Pit Structure 3 was shared by this interhousehold group.

Architectural evidence also indicates that the pueblo was remodeled during its occupation, and several rooms apparently changed in the way they were used. Remodeling removed hearths from Rooms 10 and 15, and these rooms appear to have changed from habitations to work areas or specialized storage facilities. Pit Structure 4, a small (9 m^2) pit structure, was added, possibly replacing Pit Structure 2 (Figure 4). These architectural changes are interpreted as indicating changes in household organization, or at least in the spatial organization of households, prior to abandonment. Remodeling resulted in fewer front rooms with cooking and heating facilities, and a large pit structure was possibly replaced by a smaller one; these changes may indicate a decrease in site population. While our architectural model of organization at the time of construction indicates each pit structure was shared by two or more households, it is possible that by the time of abandonment some of the pit structures were used only by a single household. Evaluation of the organizational pattern at abandonment has only begun, but a possible reconstruction is as follows: (1) two households were centered in Rooms 13 and 16, and they shared the use of Room 15 and Pit Structure 1; (2) two households were centered in Rooms 11 and 12, and they shared Pit Structure 4; and (3) one household was living in Room 19, using remodeled Room 10 and Pit Structure 3. The abandonment-organization model presented here and in Figure 4 is only one of several possibilities, but these structure groupings are used for artifact comparisons in the remainder of this paper.

Structure Use

Floor artifacts, features, and abandonment mode are analyzed to examine the types of activities that took

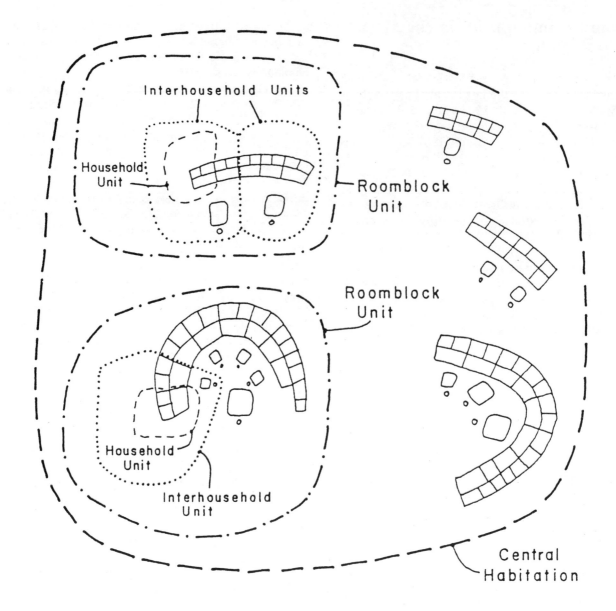

Figure 2: Intracommunity organization model proposed by the Dolores Archaeological Program (After Kane 1983).

place within structures. These data sets are compared in two ways. First, front-to-back comparisons attempt to differentiate the nature of use of pit structures, front rooms, and back rooms. These comparisons deal with the fundamental problem of pit structure and surface room use at sites that contain both pit structures and pueblos (cf. Gilman 1987; Gillespie 1976; Morris 1939). Pueblo I pit structure use cannot be understood by looking at pit structures as if they were isolated units. Instead, we evaluate pit structures in a comparative framework that includes the other architectural units of the site. Second, side-to-side comparisons search for similarities and differences between structures, or groups of structures, of the same type. Often archaeologists lump structures of one type (e.g., pit structures) into a functional category (e.g., pit houses or kivas) and then talk about the categories as if they represent a single type of use (e.g., domestic or ritual). It is unlikely that all pit structures were used in the same manner, and determining the range of variation in artifacts, features, and abandonment mode is an important step toward a better understanding of pit structure use.

Front-to-back comparisons at Duckfoot reveal that some activities are common to both front rooms and pit structures. Pit structures, however, contain evidence for activities not present in the front rooms. Side-to-side comparisons demonstrate that variation is present between units of the the same type. Standard household and interhousehold artifact and feature assemblages are not present.

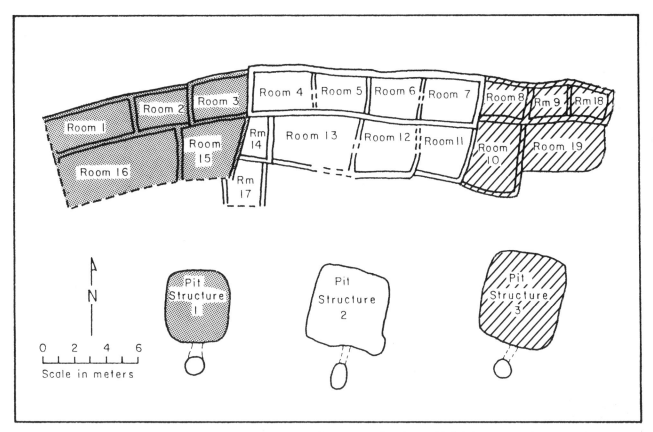

Figure 3: Inferred interhousehold organization at the time of initial construction and main occupation at Duckfoot.

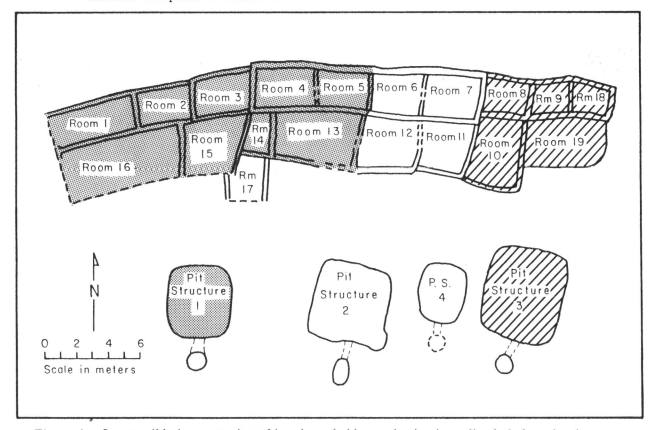

Figure 4: One possible interpretation of interhousehold organization immediately before abandonment.

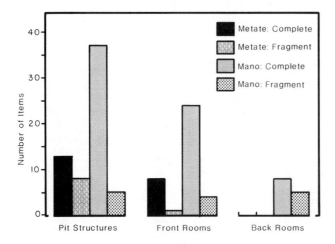

Figure 5: Front-to-back distribution of metates and manos from floor contexts only.

Artifacts

Floor artifact assemblages are conditioned primarily by use immediately before abandonment, and probably do not reflect structure use for the entire period of occupation. Metates are the one artifact type that might be an exception, and reflect long-term use of space, as they are heavy (up to 45 kg) and not easily transported. Because manos and other tools are less cumbersome, they may have been moved in and out of structures as needed. The distribution of metates and manos is examined as an indicator of mealing activities (Figure 5). Both pit structures and front rooms contained numerous metates and manos, with the highest numbers in the pit structures. Back rooms contained only manos and mano fragments. Mealing therefore occurred in both pit structures and front rooms. Back rooms may have been used for tool storage, but they were not the location of mealing activities.

The distribution of ceramic vessels and tools on structure floors is examined as an indicator of a variety of activities such as cooking, food preparation, and storage. Floor-associated ceramic artifacts include complete vessels (jars, ollas, bowls, a seed jar, and a dipper), specialized ceramic forms (miniatures, effigies, and pipes), partial vessels, sherd containers, and modified sherds. Individual sherds were also present on structure floors, but are not considered in this analysis. Pit structures had the largest number of ceramic items, including the majority of complete vessels and all but one of the specialized forms (Figure 6). Front rooms had fewer whole vessels, but contained numerous partial vessels, some sherd containers, and a few modified sherds (Figure 7). Partial vessels are large portions of broken vessels. Sherd containers are usually smaller than partial vessels and are characterized by having been shaped and/or reused as shallow containers. Mod-

ified sherds are small sherds that have been altered by use or shaping after breakage. Back room ceramic artifacts include three complete vessels in Room 2 and a single sherd container in Room 18.

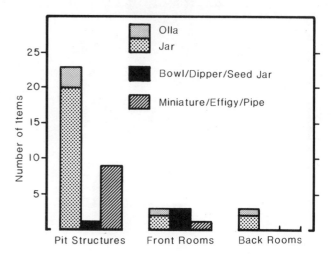

Figure 6: Front-to-back distribution of complete ceramic vessels from floor contexts only.

The remaining floor artifacts include a variety of items (Figure 8). Pit structures contained the largest number of items and the greatest diversity of types; front rooms had less diversity and fewer items; back rooms contained the fewest artifacts. Peckingstones were the most common tool in both pit structures and front rooms (one inferred use for peckingstones is for

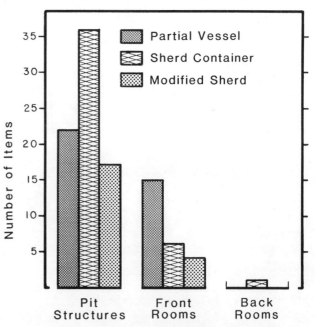

Figure 7: Front-to-back distribution of partial ceramic vessels, sherd containers, and modified sherds from floor contexts only.

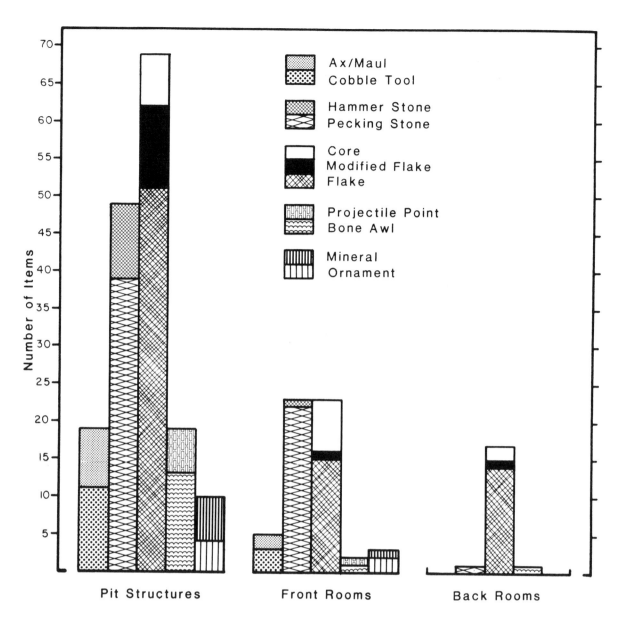

Figure 8: Front-to-back distribution of other floor artifacts.

refurbishing the grinding surfaces of manos and metates). Numerous artifact types, including axes, projectile points, bone awls, ornaments, and minerals, were found almost exclusively in pit structures.

While the quantity and diversity of artifacts distinguishes pit structure, front room, and back room assemblages from each other, substantial variation also exists when side-to-side comparisons are made of structures of the same type. Metates and manos were found in all pit structures, but the numbers in each structure vary (Figure 9). Complete sets of mealing tools were recovered from four front rooms: 16, 13, 12, and 19.

Side-to-side variation is best illustrated by the distribution of complete vessels (Figure 10). Pit Structure 1 contained the most ceramic material: 13 jars, 2 ollas, and 1 seed jar. Complete vessels ranged from from 1 to 4 in the remaining pit structures. Specialized forms were rare (1) in Pit Structure 1 but numerous (5) in Pit Structure 3.

The remaining tools compared side-to-side (Figure 11) show similar patterns. While many items of a particular type were present in each structure, the mix of types and the number of items vary. Peckingstones, for example, range from one peckingstone in Pit Structure 3 to 26 found in Pit Structure 2.

Summarizing the artifact assemblage data, we can say that (1) evidence of domestic activities, especially mealing and cooking, was present in the front rooms and the pit structures; (2) the number, density, and diversity of artifacts was greatest in the pit structures,

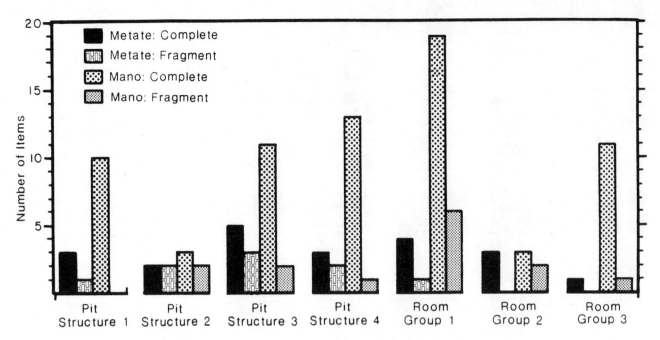

Figure 9: Side-to-side distribution of metates and manos from floor contexts, grouped by inferred interhouseholds at the time of abandonment (as shown in Figure 4).

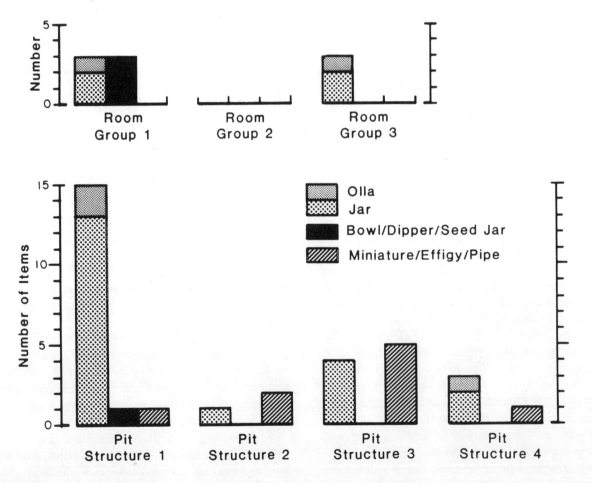

Figure 10: Side-to-side distribution of complete ceramic vessels from floor contexts, grouped by inferred interhouseholds at the time of abandonment (as shown in Figure 4).

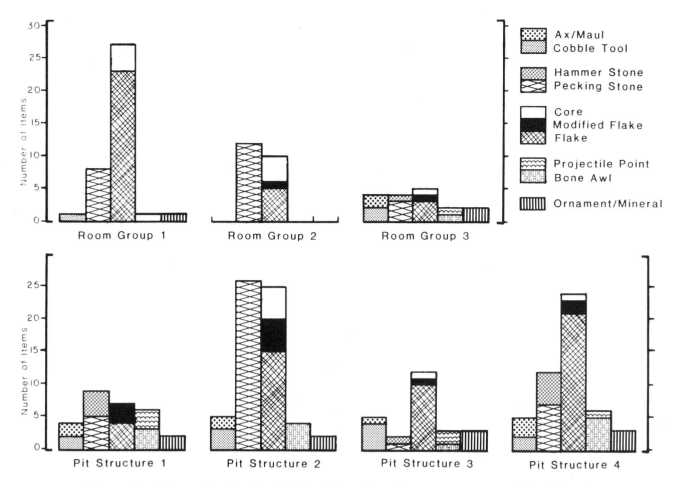

Figure 11: Side-to-side distribution of artifacts from floor contexts, grouped by inferred interhouseholds at the time of abandonment (as shown in Figure 4).

suggesting intensive use immediately prior to abandonment; (3) back rooms contained few items, suggesting they were not the location of domestic activities and may have been used primarily for food storage; and (4) the quantities and types of artifacts varied greatly from structure to structure, making it difficult to define a standard household or interhousehold tool kit. The variation may indicate that structure function was complementary and that functionally redundant facilities for each household did not exist.

Feature Assemblages

Because features are more stationary than artifacts they are better indicators of long-term structure use. Comparisons between the features found in back rooms, front rooms, and pit structures indicate that each class of facilities has a distinctive array of feature types. Side-to-side variation is also noted, especially when pit structure feature assemblages are compared to each other.

Features are rare in back rooms, more common in front rooms, and most abundant in pit structures (Figure 12). All front rooms at Duckfoot have hearths, although two had been capped or truncated by other features and were not in use at the time of abandonment. Short-term storage features such as bins, bell-shaped pits, and large pits are numerous in front rooms. Short-term storage features are absent in pit structures, though the wingwalls divide off a portion of the structure that may serve the same purpose.

The presence of cylindrical sand-filled pits most clearly distinguishes pit structures from surface rooms, as these features were found only in the pit structures (Figure 12). Sipapus are one type of cylindrical sand-filled pit found on the axis of symmetry north of the hearth. In addition to location and fill, sipapus are often recognized by associated small holes that are also filled with sand. Sand-filled pits and sipapus with associated small holes apparently relate to an activity taking place in pit structures that does not occur in surface rooms. Wilshusen (1985b, and this volume), working with feature assemblages in Dolores area pit structures, interprets sand-filled pits as sockets for altars, and sipapus with associated small holes as features used for ritual activities.

Cylindrical sand-filled pits also illustrate the variation in feature assemblages in a side-to-side comparison

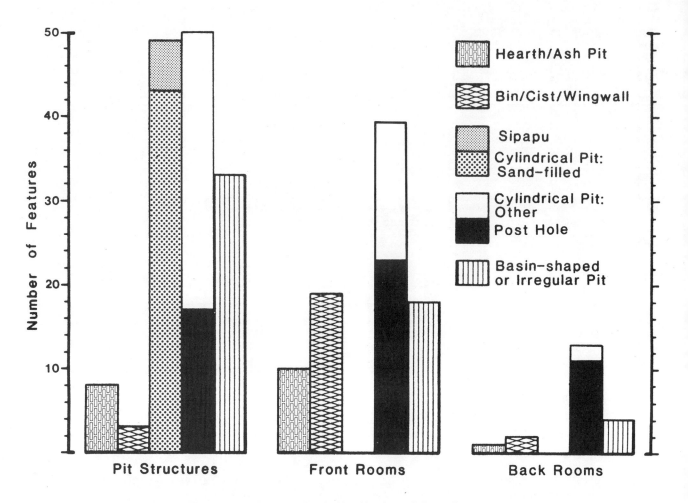

Figure 12: Front-to-back distribution of floor features.

of pit structures (Figure 13). Two sipapus (one capped and the other in use) are the only sand-filled pits in Pit Structure 1. Pit Structure 2 has 6 sand-filled pits, Pit Structure 4 has 12, and Pit Structure 3 has the most, with 25. Feature assemblages, like artifact assemblages, are not duplicated from structure to structure.

Mode of Abandonment

The last category used to compare architectural units at Duckfoot is the abandonment mode (Figure 14). Except for Room 3, the back rooms did not burn. All front rooms, except Room 15, burned, and Pit Structures 1, 3, and 4 also burned. Pit Structure 2 did not burn, but the unburned roof was intentionally destroyed. Unburned roof fall covered the Pit Structure 2 floor, and postholes in the northeast and northwest corners were deliberately filled, capped, and covered with piles of clean sand.

All four pit structures contained human remains on the floor. Two adults were found in Pit Structure 1; one of these covered the hearth. An adult articulated torso with the arms and legs missing was northwest of the hearth in Pit Structure 2. The remains of a single adult in Pit Structure 3 lay along the axis of symmetry, with the head near the sipapu and the knees over the rim of the hearth. Pit Structure 4 contained the remains of a child, a juvenile, and an adult. The head and shoulders of the adult covered the hearth, and the juvenile and child were north and northeast of the hearth, respectively.

The interments are interpreted as burials associated with the deliberate destruction of all four pit structures, and not as individuals trapped by an accidental, catastrophic event. Pit structures in the Dolores project area also show evidence of deliberate destruction and use as tombs (Wilshusen 1986b; Stodder 1987:357).

Summary and Conclusions

Artifacts, features, and abandonment mode have been examined in an attempt to determine how pit structure use changed when enclosed surface habitation rooms appeared on sites. These comparisons illustrate the differences between and within sets of architectural units.

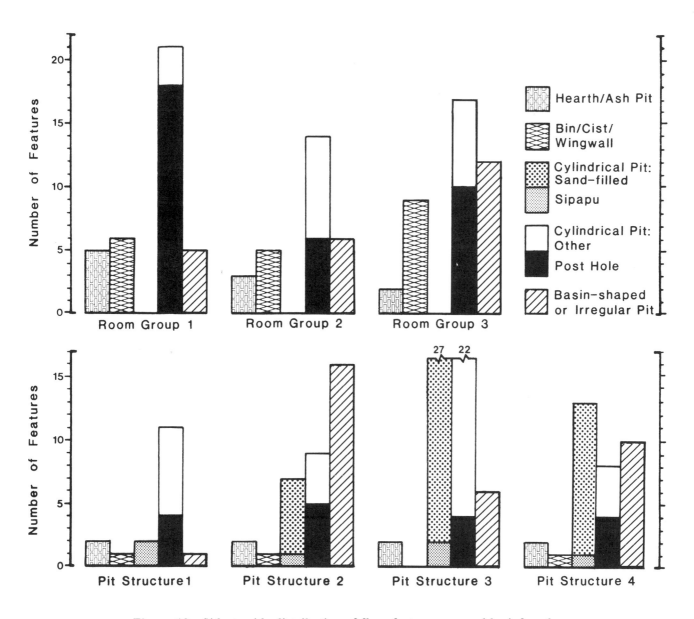

Figure 13: Side-to-side distribution of floor features grouped by inferred interhouseholds at the time of abandonment (as shown in Figure 4).

Four contrasting models are proposed to guide our summary of the Duckfoot data:

(1). Pit structures were the main habitations, and front rooms did not function as habitations. Therefore the pit structure, rather than the surface room suite, represents the locus of the household.

(2). Both pit structures and front rooms represent habitations, but they were used during different seasons. Gilman (1987) interpreted pit structures as specialized for use as winter habitations, while Powell (1983) has interpreted small sites with pit structures as sites occupied during the summer season.

(3). Pit structures represent shared use by households who had their primary residence in the surface roomblock. Pit structure use was domestic, and pit structures were integrative only insofar as they were shared by multiple households.

(4). Pit structures were becoming specialized for ritual activity, and this ritual use distinguished pit structures from surface habitation rooms, which were purely domestic.

The question of whether the pit structures or the front rooms represent habitations is addressed first. Pit structures contain hearths, mealing activity areas, and ceramics for food preparation, consumption, and storage. Front surface rooms lack the robust feature and artifact assemblages found in pit structures, but domestic use for extended periods of time is indicated by hearths, short-term storage facilities, mealing tool kits, and ceramic artifacts for cooking and eating. Most impor-

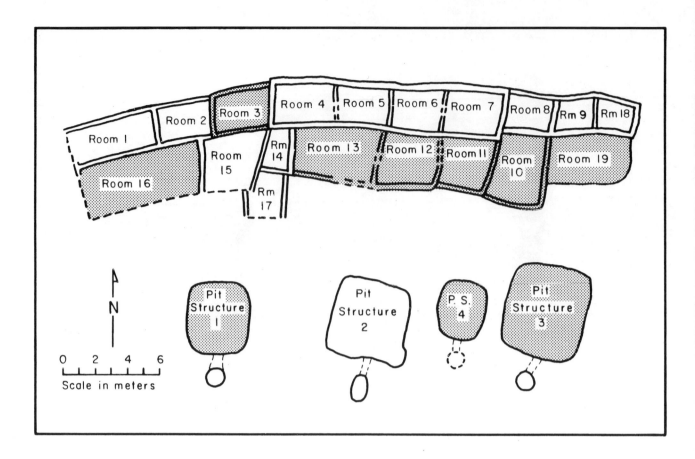

Figure 14: Map of the Duckfoot site architectural units showing burned (shaded) versus unburned structures.

tantly, storage rooms were entered from the front rooms; in this way, access to and knowledge of stored food resources was restricted and controlled by the occupants of the front rooms. Households, as defined by the surface room suites, are interpretable as habitations where basic activities of storage and consumption occurred (cf. Wilk and Rathje 1982). Control of storage may indicate that these households also organized production activities (e.g., farming and acquisition of resources).

The second model, which proposes the seasonal use of different structure types, suggests some interesting possibilities. If pit structures were in use during the season of abandonment this might produce the larger pit structure assemblages. However, strictly biseasonal use should result in the abandonment of one set of facilities. If this were the case we would expect portable artifacts to be absent from either the front rooms or the pit structures. The presence of portable tools in all Duckfoot front rooms and in each of the pit structures indicates that strict biseasonal use of these different structure types is unlikely. Seasonality might affect structure use in ways other than strict biseasonal occupation and abandonment. The highest site population may have occurred in the winter when mobility was restricted and subsistence was dependent on stored food (Gilman 1987). Larger momentary site population in the winter might have produced more intense use of all the architectural facilities on the site.

Third, do pit structures represent shared domestic use? It has been noted that floor artifacts indicate that Duckfoot pit structures contained ample evidence of domestic activity. Larger, more diverse tool kits in pit structures might result from shared use. Remodeling sequences, abandonment sequences, and the effects of occupation duration on floor assemblages need to be better understood before this hypothesis can be accepted or rejected. Currently, the best case for shared use is two households with habitations in Rooms 16 and 13 (Lightfoot 1988) that combine to use Pit Structure 1. Two similar sets of ceramic vessels and containers were found in the east and west halves of Pit Structure 1, and this distribution may represent evidence for shared use. Architectural data suggest that construction of architectural facilities was organized by the interhousehold group (Wilshusen 1984, 1988), which may indicate that production was organized at the level of the interhousehold rather than the household.

Regarding the final model of pit structure use, we can say that Duckfoot pit structures were not used exclusively for ritual activity. However, ritual activity, like all prehistoric behavior, is difficult to assess. Just as an incomplete understanding of site formation limits our ability to interpret how artifact assemblages relate to the daily use of the structure, we lack the middle-range theory that links ritual behavior to the formation of the archaeological record. What is a ritual artifact? Ornaments, pipes, effigy vessels, miniature vessels, minerals, and curated projectile point types are all present almost exclusively in the pit structures, but it is unclear if these artifacts and their locations constitute evidence for ritual use of pit structures.

Features and abandonment mode are not subject to the range of site formation processes that affects artifacts, and may offer our best data set for recognizing ritual behavior. When pit structures and surface rooms are compared, feature assemblages and abandonment mode display striking contrasts. One explanation for the differences observed between pit structure and surface rooms is that ritual activity was present in the pit structures but not in the rooms. The presence of sand-filled pits, including sipapus with small holes, and the use of the pit structures as burial chambers may reflect ritual use of pit structures. Seasonality of use and ritual use may be mutually reinforcing. If larger populations were present during the winter, the need for ritual integrative behavior might be greater as well. Also, winter would be the season when the most time would be available for ritual activity.

Sipapus in each of the pit structures may indicate the presence of an interhousehold shrine. Evidence for ritual activity to integrate the entire hamlet may be present as well, and limited to a single structure. Pit Structure 3 is the largest pit structure on the site, it has the greatest number of sand-filled pits, and it lacks wing walls. Wing walls have been interpreted as associated with domestic use by creating a facility for short-term storage. Disappearance of this feature creates a larger main chamber, and this has been cited as an architectural change that marks the transition from pit house to kiva (Lancaster et al. 1954:55). Pit Structure 3 may have been used both as a domestic pit house and, as needed, for ritual activity that integrated the entire site.

The final point we would like to make concerns the variation between artifact and feature assemblages when structures are compared side to side. This variation indicates that a standard household or interhousehold assemblage is not present at Duckfoot. Households and interhouseholds may have been the basic social units for the functions of production, storage, and consumption, but activities that resulted in artifact deposition and feature construction may have cross-cut architectural boundaries. Household and interhousehold assemblages may have complemented each other functionally rather than representing functionally distinct entities repeated across the site.

We have tried to demonstrate some of the variation in pit structure assemblages and suggest ways that the variation might be patterned. We have shown the distribution of domestic activities, presented the evidence for shared use, and suggested that ritual activity was greater in the pit structures than in other areas of the site. As work continues with data from the Duckfoot site, as well as data from other areas in the Anasazi region, we hope that the accumulated studies will further refine our understanding of pit structure use.

References

Brew, John O.
1946 *Archaeology of Alkali Ridge, Southeastern Utah.* Papers of the Peabody Museum of American Archaeology and Ethnology, vol. 21. Harvard University, Cambridge.

Brisbin, Joel M., Allen E. Kane, and James N. Morris
1988 Excavations at McPhee Pueblo (Site 5MT4475), a Pueblo I and Early Pueblo II Multicomponent Village. *Dolores Archaeological Program: Anasazi Communities at Dolores: McPhee Village,* compiled by A. E. Kane and C. K. Robinson, pp. 63-403. Bureau of Reclamation, Engineering and Research Center, Denver.

Gillespie, William B.
1976 *Culture Change at the Ute Canyon Site: A Study of the Pithouse-Kiva Transition in the Mesa Verde Region.* Unpublished Master's thesis, Department of Anthropology, University of Colorado, Boulder.

Gilman, Patricia A.
1987 Architecture as Artifact: Pit Structures and Pueblos in the American Southwest. *American Antiquity* 52(3):538-564.

Hayes, Alden C., and James A. Lancaster
1975 *Badger House Community, Mesa Verde National Park, Colorado.* Publications in Archeology No. 7E. National Park Service, Washington, D.C.

Kane, Allen E.
1983 *Fieldwork and Systematics.* Dolores Archaeological Program Technical Reports DAP-058. Final report submitted to Bureau of Reclamation, Upper Colorado Region, Salt Lake City, Utah, in compliance with Contract No. 8-07-40-S0562.

1986 Prehistory of the Dolores River Valley. In *Dolores Archaeological Program: Final Synthetic Report,* compiled by David A. Breternitz, Christine K. Robinson, and G. Timothy Gross, pp. 353-438. Bureau of Reclamation, Engineering and Research Center, Denver.

Lancaster, James A., Jean M. Pinkley, Philip F. Van Cleave, and Don Watson
1954 *Archeological Excavations in Mesa Verde National Park, Colorado, 1950.* Archeological Research Series No. 2. National Park Service, Washington, D.C.

Lightfoot, Ricky R.
1985 *Report of 1984 Investigations Conducted Under State Permit 84-15.* Report submitted to the Office of the State Archaeologist, Colorado Historical Society, Denver. Crow Canyon Archaeological Center, Cortez, Colorado.

1987 *Annual Report of Investigations at the Duckfoot Site (5MT3868), Montezuma County, Colorado.* Report submitted to the State Archaeologist, Colorado Historical Society, Denver. Crow Canyon Archaeological Center, Cortez, Colorado.

1988 Refitting Studies at the Duckfoot Site, An Early Anasazi Pueblo. Paper presented at the 53rd Annual Meeting of the Society for American Archaeology, Phoenix, Arizona.

Lightfoot, Ricky R., and Carla Van West
1986 *Excavation and Testing Conducted on Private Land Under State Permit 85-22.* Report submitted to the Office of the State Archaeologist, Colorado Historical Society, Denver. Crow Canyon Archaeological Center, Cortez, Colorado.

Lightfoot, Ricky R., and Mark D. Varien
1988 *Report of 1987 Investigations at the Duckfoot Site (5MT3868), Montezuma County, Colorado.* Report submitted to the Office of the State Archaeologist, Colorado Historical Society, Denver. Crow Canyon Archaeological Center, Cortez, Colorado.

Lipe, William D., Timothy A. Kohler, Mark D. Varien, James N. Morris, and Ricky R. Lightfoot
1988 Synthesis. In *Dolores Archaelogical Program: Anasazi Communities at Dolores: Grass Mesa Village,* compiled by W. D. Lipe, J. N. Morris, and T. A. Kohler, pp. 1213-1276. Bureau of Reclamation, Engineering and Research Center, Denver.

Martin, Paul S.
1939 *Modified Basket Maker Sites: Ackmen-Lowry Area, Southwestern Colorado, 1938.* Anthropological Series, Field Museum of Natural History, vol. 23, No. 3. Chicago.

Morris, Earl H.
1939 *Archaeological Studies in the La Plata District, Southwestern Colorado and Northwestern New Mexico.* Carnegie Institution of Washington, Publication 519. Washington, D.C.

Orcutt, Janet D.
1987 Changes in Aggregation and Spacing, A.D. 600-1175. In *Dolores Archaeological Program: Supporting Studies: Settlement and Environment,* compiled by Kenneth Lee Petersen and Janet D. Orcutt, pp. 617-648. Bureau of Reclamation, Engineering and Research Center, Denver.

Powell, Shirley L.
1983 *Mobility and Adaptation: The Anasazi of Black Mesa, Arizona.* Southern Illinois University Press, Carbondale.

Schiffer, Michael B.
1987 *Formation Processes of the Archaeological Record.* University of New Mexico Press, Albuquerque.

Stodder, Ann L. W.
1987 Physical Anthropology. In *Dolores Archaeological Program: Supporting Studies: Settlement and Environment,* compiled by Kenneth Lee Petersen and Janet D. Orcutt, pp. 339-506. Bureau of Reclamation, Engineering and Research Center, Denver.

Wilk, Richard, and William Rathje
1982 Household Archaeology. *American Behavioral Scientist* 25(6):617-639.

Wilshusen, Richard H.
1984 Engineering the Pithouse to Pueblo Transition. Paper presented at the 49th Annual Meeting of the Society for American Archaeology, Portland, Oregon.

1985a Architectural Trends in Prehistoric Anasazi Sites at Dolores, Colorado, A.D. 600–1200. *Dolores Archaeological Program Technical Reports* DAP-274. Final report submitted to the U.S. Bureau of Reclamation, Upper Colorado Region, Salt Lake City, Contract No. 8-07-40-S0562.

1985b Sipapus, Ceremonial Vaults, and Foot Drums (or a Resounding Argument for Protokivas). *Dolores Archaeological Program Technical Reports* DAP-278. Final report submitted to the U.S. Bureau of

Reclamation, Upper Colorado Region, Salt Lake City, Contract No. 8-07-40-SO562

1986a Excavations at Rio Vista Village (Site 5MT2182), a Multicomponent Pueblo I Village. In *Dolores Archaeological Program: Anasazi Communities at Dolores: Middle Canyon Area,* compiled by A. E. Kane and C. K. Robinson, pp. 209-658. Bureau of Reclamation, Engineering and Research Center, Denver.

1986b The Relationship between Abandonment Mode and Ritual Use in Pueblo I Anasazi Protokivas. *Journal of Field Archaeology* 13:245-254.

1988 Comment on "Architecture as Artifact: Pit Structures and Pueblos in the American Southwest," by Patricia A. Gilman. *American Antiquity,* in press.

7
Unstuffing the Estufa: Ritual Floor Features in Anasazi Pit Structures and Pueblo Kivas

Richard H. Wilshusen

> *Originally thought to be sweat baths (estufas) by the Spaniards, kivas have been defined by archaeologists as pueblo structures specially constructed for ceremonial purposes. The actual use of prehistoric kivas is rarely discussed by archaeologists because prehistoric evidence of ceremonial or ritual activity is perceived as uninterpretable or uncommon. As a consequence, archaeological classifications of kivas are based largely on architectural form, rather than on interior features. Based on changes in architectural form, kivas do not appear in the archaeological record until Pueblo II or III. However, an examination of Pueblo I pit structures reveals that ritual features commonly associated with historically documented kivas can be identified in certain pit structures that date to A.D. 850–880. The distribution of these ritual features may offer as much or more information about the use of Anasazi ceremonial structures as pit structure size, shape, or construction.*

Show me your classification system and I will tell you how far you have come in the perceptions of your research problems. [Kubiena 1948 cited in Buol et al. 1973]

Introduction

Southwestern archaeologists in the 1980s are reconfronting a problem first faced by archaeologists at the turn of the century: how to classify those structures originally called *estufas* (Nordenskiold 1893) or *kivas* (Mindeleff 1891). After excavating literally hundreds of these structures we have a classification of kivas based largely on differences in architectural size and shape and roof construction, but with little regard for differences in content. We talk about Mesa Verde kivas, Chaco kivas, protokivas, square kivas, *kihus,* Great Kivas, tri-wall structures, bi-wall structures, ceremonial rooms, and round rooms, but we still have little idea whether architecturally different classes of structures represent different uses. We presume that Great Kivas are more important or that they integrated larger numbers of people because they have larger floor areas (cf. Lightfoot 1984:72-73), but otherwise we are barely able to discuss why these differences in size and shape have any social meaning.

Archaeologists can partially remedy the kiva classification problem by focusing less on geographical differences in architectural form and more on differences in pan-Anasazi ritual features within archaeologically contemporaneous structures which may be kivas. In many cases it is possible to identify ritual features such as sipapus and altars on pit structure floors, and these features can be as useful in understanding prehistoric lifeways as so-called "economic" features, such as hearths or in situ metates.

Lekson (1988) has recently argued that kivas were defined too early in the archaeological sequence of Southwestern development, and that the idea of the kiva as a center for community rituals is probably inappropriate before Pueblo IV. I take an opposite tack and argue that our idea of a kiva is muddled precisely because we define prehistoric kivas too late in the archaeological sequence. If a kiva is primarily a ceremonial room, then one can argue that there are such structures as early as Pueblo I.

To see how we have arrived at our present state of affairs we must "unstuff the estufa." Just as Mindeleff (1891:111) recognized that the Spanish characterization of these structures as estufas, or sweat lodges, was incorrectly borrowed from other indigenous groups with which the Spanish were more familiar, so we must understand the history of how we, as archaeologists, have stuffed the estufa. By the early 1930s archaeologists had accepted two key assumptions which restricted their view, and continue to restrict ours, of what a prehistoric kiva could look like.

The first assumption is that the cultural evolution of pueblo society was gradual and progressive. By the first Pecos Conference it was generally accepted that Pueblo III was the "classic" or "great" period of Anasazi development—the first period of large pueblo communities with well-developed arts, architecture, and social organization (Kidder 1927:490). Kidder recognized that a large and important class of proto-Mesa Verde ruins existed, but also emphasized that these ruins, and presumably the societies which built them, were less highly developed (Kidder 1962 [1924]:207). Though protoforms of kivas (Morris 1939) and large villages (Brew 1946) were recognized for the Pueblo I period, the gradual change in pit structure design between Pueblo II and III (Lancaster and Pinkley 1954:53-59) and a proposed shift between Pueblo II and III from small to large communities (Kidder 1927:490; McGregor 1965:222-223,243), reinforced the assumption that these "conservative" Pueblo peoples were as slow to develop the idea of ceremonial structures as they were to establish real pueblos.

A second assumption is that all historic kivas functioned equally as centers of community ritual performance. Thus, if prehistoric and historic kivas were functionally equivalent (Fewkes 1898:611-614; Mindeleff 1891:111-112), all prehistoric kivas must have equal roles in the ritual affairs of a community. It was understood that Great Kivas were something of an exception, but even native informants noted that kivas devoted wholly to ceremony had existed in better times in the past (Mindeleff 1891:130). So, with the exception of Great Kivas, all kivas were assumed to be equal.

We will not be able to unstuff the estufa unless we confront these assumptions, and recognize how they are erroneous.

Before developing a two-pronged attack on the stuffed estufa I should state my own assumptions/biases. I start with Dozier's definition of a kiva: a generally all-purpose ceremonial structure used by various ceremonial organizations for rites that affect a whole community, or at least a large segment of it (1965:44). Dozier defines what I call "community kivas." I recognize as well a second general class of kivas, "corporate kivas," which serve as special activity areas and ritual chambers for particular corporate groups. Corporate groups are essentially co-residential, with common socioeconomic interests; a community is made up of various competing corporate groups (cf. Hayden and Cannon 1982). Ritual performance in corporate kivas affects a subset of the community; in contrast, community kivas house integrative activities which affect the whole community. It is conceivable that a community kiva might be controlled by a particular corporate group, but its scale of service in ritual performance is at the community level. Much of the present confusion over kivas is due to our failure to distinguish between the functions of corporate and community kivas. Community kivas can be distinguished in both prehistoric and historic contexts, and the first recognizable community kivas date to Pueblo I, or much earlier than is generally accepted.

In this discussion I focus primarily on the contents of potential community kivas and do not spend much time describing their shape, depth, or construction. This is not to say that architectural patterns are to be discounted; it simply emphasizes the importance of the variety and patterns of ritual features in any future classification of kivas. I accept the model that ritual may have provided a means to organize people in early villages in the absence of any powerful or formal authorities (cf. Rapapport 1968, 1971). One of the signs of increased dependence on ritual as a mechanism for organizing increased numbers of people is the appearance of specialized ceremonial structures (Adler, this volume). I argue that the two classes of kivas, community and corporate, must be distinguished by their interior features as well as by their exterior architecture.

Gradual Change and Anasazi Kivas

To challenge the idea of gradual change it is first necessary to review the historical development of current ideas about pit structure and pueblo change. The data I present are intended to complement the recent historical essay on "the idea of the kiva" by Lekson (1988), but I come to different conclusions than those reached by Lekson.

The Problem of Pit Structure Change

Most Southwestern archaeologists accept that pit structures have served two distinct functions over the last 1500 years. Early Anasazi pit structures served as seasonal or semi-permanent domiciles (e.g., Cordell 1984:218-219; Gilman 1987; Morris and Burgh 1954) and are commonly called "pit houses" or simply "houses." Similarly, most archaeologists accept the assertion that most pit structures associated with the historic pueblos are all-purpose ceremonial structures, or kivas (e.g., Kessell 1987; Kidder 1962). It is clear in the historic accounts that the structures called "kivas" were not houses.

> They use kivas, of which some pueblos have more, others less. They are sometimes nine in one pueblo, as at Pecos, and one in others, as at Nambe. Some of them are underground, and others are above ground with walls like a little house, and of them all, some are round while others are rectangular.... These kivas are the chapter, or council, rooms, and the Indians meet in them, sometimes to discuss matters of their government for the coming year, their planting, arrangements for work to be done, or to elect new community officials, or to rehearse their dances, or sometimes for other things [Fray Dominguez 1777, cited in Kessell 1987:299].

One might think that the question of the transition from pit house to kiva would have been one of the first addressed by Southwestern archaeologists, but actually it was not asked until several decades after the general acceptance of prehistoric, as well as historic, kivas. It is important to recognize this fact to understand the present classificatory muddle of pit structures, pit houses, and various kiva types.

Early anthropologists such as Mindeleff (1891:111) and Fewkes (1898:612-614; 1909:20) recognized the importance and antiquity of kivas in pueblo life long before the possibility of pit houses was seriously considered. By the time Fewkes was excavating at Mesa Verde (i.e., 1907) it was a given that kivas were a key indicator of Pueblo culture. If early Pueblo culture was to be found in the cliff dwellings of Mesa Verde, then kivas would be found there also. As Lekson has noted (1988:222), this was definition by fiat.

There were many questions asked about these early kivas, but even in these discussions the assumed ceremonial use of these Pueblo III pit structures was clear. For example, Hewett assumed that an upright slab (i.e., the deflector) between the ventilator and the hearth was an altar, and that the ventilator was also a strictly ceremonial feature (Kidder 1958:257-258), until Fewkes showed that both features were related to ventilation (Fewkes 1908).

There was not much discussion of sipapus (the small opening in the pit structure floor between the hearth and the wall opposite the deflector), other than to note that similar symbolic openings to the underworld were an expected feature in modern Hopi kivas (Fewkes 1909:18). If there was a need to confirm this feature in other potential kivas, one simply referred the reader to Fewkes (e.g., Morley 1908:603; Prudden 1914:48).

As more and more Southwestern ruins were surveyed and excavated in the 1910s and 1920s, two things became clear. First, the types of prehistoric ceremonial chambers were not restricted to the two kiva types, circular and quadrilateral, proposed by Fewkes (1908). There were Great Kivas (Morris 1921), Chaco style kivas (Pepper 1920), Mesa Verde style kivas (Fewkes 1909), Kayenta kivas (Kidder and Guernsey 1919), rectangular kivas (Hodge 1923), towers (Fewkes 1919), and kihus (Fewkes 1911). Second, though prehistoric pit houses had been documented (e.g., Hough 1920), and it was recognized that pit houses were "perhaps prototypes of the Pueblo kivas" (Kidder 1962 [1924]:230), it was not until Roberts' excavation of Shabik'eshchee (1929) that the connection between Basketmaker III pit houses and later kivas could be discussed in detail.

Since the 1930s archaeologists have worked out the specifics of the architectural changes associated with the shift from Basketmaker III pit houses to what were argued to be highly standardized Pueblo III ceremonial rooms, or kivas; but the generalizations about kivas that could be made at or soon after the first Pecos Conference (i.e., 1927) have changed very little: (1) kivas were ceremonial structures, but also represented a survival of a domiciliary architectural form (Roberts 1929:81-90), (2) kivas "varied ... greatly in form and interior arrangements, and ... the types shaded into each other so imperceptibly that no valid distinctions as to essential function could be drawn" (Kidder 1927:490), and (3) if one had a pueblo, one also must have a kiva (Hewett 1930:210).

I do not wish to devalue the post-1930s work of archaeologists sorting out the details of the shift from pit house to kiva, I simply recognize that excellent work such as that by Morris (1939), Brew (1946), and Lancaster and Pinkley (1954) was necessarily constrained by the old assumption that Pueblo III kivas were equivalent to historic kivas. Since there were clear-cut pit houses as late as the end of Basketmaker III (A.D. 750), the transition to kivas must have occurred between A.D. 750 and 1100.

Based on changes in architectural form, the A.D. 750–900 period pit structures were protokivas and the A.D. 900–1100 structures were early forms of kivas. This preserved the old concept of Pueblo III kivas as "classic" forms and allowed a period of gradual change between the classic pit house and the classic kiva. The gradual change in pit structure architecture between Basketmaker III and Pueblo III (Figure 1) fits well with this model (Lancaster and Pinkley 1954:53-61).

The only problem is that this model depended heavily on architectural features such as pit structure shape, depth, roof support, and wall construction to define the function of the structures as analogous to modern kivas. Other than Fewkes' original assertion that these round structures were kivas, there was little evidence gathered to support the argument that they had been used primarily for ceremony. The woes of those archaeologists who

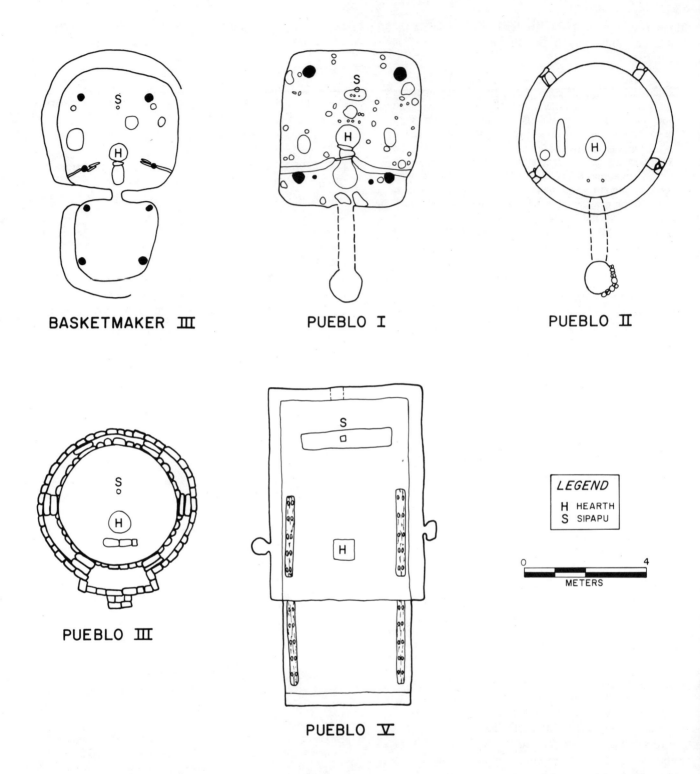

Figure 1: Typical pit structure plans, Basketmaker III to Pueblo V (adapted from Brisbin and Varien 1986: Figure 3.4; Kleidon 1988:Figure 4.33; Lancaster and Pinkley 1954:Plate 34; and Mindeleff 1891:Figure 22).

had to define prehistoric kivas on aspects other than architecture illustrated that the old question, "when is a kiva?" still was unanswered (Smith 1952). Why should pit structures be ceremonial just because of shape or location in the pueblo? What if they were only round rooms (Lekson 1984:50) or pit houses (Lekson 1988:226)? Maybe the change from pit house to kiva was even more gradual than the normative model prescribes. Or, as I will suggest later, maybe it was more sudden.

The Problem of Pueblo Change

Early Southwestern archaeologists supported the statement that true kivas did not occur until Pueblo II or III by the "fact" that only at this time were large pueblos of masonry surface rooms regularly associated with pit structures (i.e., kivas). It could be argued that the surface dwellings were only gradually used to replace the domiciliary function of the pit house, and this consequently allowed increasingly specialized religious use of pit structure space (e.g., Brew 1946:207). In fact, archaeologists were hesitant to define a pit structure as a kiva if it lacked an associated pueblo, even if the pit structure had all the morphological features of a "kiva" and was in a time period when "kivas" were accepted features.

With the normative model, the development of proper-looking masonry pueblos occurred in lock-step with the development of classic Mesa Verde and Chaco kiva forms. Kivas as community ceremonial centers are reasonably associated with aggregation. One can expect increased social tension and increased organizational problems in village settings. Ritual is a powerful means of governing the activities of large numbers of people in the absence of powerful authorities (Rappaport 1971:184; also Adler this volume; Gross 1979; Haviland 1987; Johnson 1982), so as pueblos get larger and more complex, the less surprising it is to have a structure devoted to the ceremonial integration of the community (i.e., a kiva).

Archaeologists were aware of contradictions to the above normative model. For example, they were aware that early Pueblo I villages had up to 300 rooms, but they argued that the arrangement of these villages "is probably the ancestor of the unit type of pueblo which developed shortly later and which then had *a definite kiva* associated with it" (McGregor 1965:242, emphasis added). In short, the Pueblo I villages which were as large or larger than the "classic" villages of Pueblo III were no more than a bunch of small unit pueblos and not equivalent to a Pueblo III village. In syntheses of Southwestern prehistory, Pueblo I surface architecture is typically illustrated by sites no bigger, and sometimes smaller, than the later Pueblo II unit pueblos (e.g.,

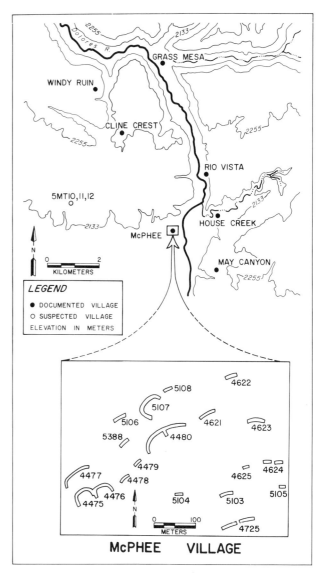

Figure 2: Pueblo I villages in the Dolores area, with an enlargement of the McPhee Village roomblocks (adapted from Kane 1986:Figure 14.1; and Kane 1988:Figure 1.1).

Cassells 1983:Figure 7-25; Gladwin 1957:172; McGregor 1965:Figure106).

Yet, there was evidence of gradual and orderly change between Pueblo I and III which could be used to argue that Pueblo III kivas were *not* equivalent in integrative function to later kivas. Julian Steward (1937) used comparisons of the ratios of pit structures to surface rooms at sites of different time periods to assess whether the round pit structures of Pueblo II and III were indeed analogous to modern kivas.

Pit Structure and Pueblo Change Considered Together

Steward showed that kiva-to-room ratios increased from approximately 1:6 to 1:97 (1937:Table 1) from

Pueblo I to historic times. He argued that this change could be best explained by the Pueblo II and III kivas functioning not so much as village-based kivas which integrated multiple lineages, but as "lineage dwellings." Only as large population aggregates, or villages, became more common did Steward expect the organization of labor and of lineages to change into a form more like that of modern Pueblos and to produce truly "modern" multi-lineage kiva groups. Based on his data, Steward concluded that this occurred by at least A.D. 1300.

Steward's study and updates by Lekson (1988) and Lipe (Chapter 5, this volume) make clear many contradictions in the traditional recognition of kivas. If one defines a kiva as the architectural correlate of a village-integrating ceremonial association (cf. Dozier 1965:44; Lekson 1988:224-225), then Steward's 1:11 ratio for Pueblo III appears to deny the possibility of kivas at Mesa Verde. Certainly in modern pueblos there are not separate associations for every eleven rooms, or approximately every three to four households. In fact, Steward represented the Pueblo V data as kiva to household (rather than room) ratios, apparently to make the contrast between Pueblo III and V less striking.

Lekson (1988) has examined a much larger data base than Steward and argues, citing numerical relationships of pit structures and rooms, that it is inappropriate in most cases to define kivas before Pueblo IV. So, almost a hundred years after the first definition of a prehistoric kiva, and sixty years after archaeologists first discussed a model of gradual change from pit house to kiva, we have a proposal that the recognition of Pueblo III kivas was flawed because it pushed change at too fast a rate, and that Pueblo III kivas are really pit houses.

We have been misled by exterior appearances and by a built-in assumption that Anasazi were conservative folk, who were slow to change. If the development of kivas is related to the development of village-integrating ceremonial associations, then I propose that we should look for the earliest kivas in the earliest Southwestern villages. In the next section I present evidence that there are highly specialized ritual pit structures in Pueblo I villages that appear to have functioned as community kivas.

Pueblo I Villages and Pit Structures with Ritual Features

Pueblo I Villages

Upon first inspection most Pueblo I villages are unimpressive. They are problematic on surveys because they are usually no more than low mounds. They are difficult to see as villages because they were single-storied, discontinuous roomblocks which stretched across 20 or more hectares. Yet, if one examines plan maps of those Pueblo I villages that have been intensively and extensively excavated, the villages are strikingly large and well-organized. In the following discussion, a village is defined as an aggregated settlement of (approximately) 30 or more households. The focus is on the San Juan region, simply because the work that has been done on the Pueblo I period has been focused in this area.

There have been three main periods of investigation of Pueblo I villages: The first consisted of a group of classic studies from the 1920s to the 1930s, which overturned Kidder's original conception (1962 [1924]:229-234) of a simple pre-Pueblo stage (e.g., Brew 1946; Martin and Rinaldo 1939; Morris 1939); the second came in the 1960s when Hayes and Lancaster attempted to define an entire Pueblo I community (1975); and the most recent and probably most intensive investigation has been the Dolores Archaeological Program's (DAP) work at two multi-roomblock villages, McPhee and Grass Mesa (Kane and Robinson 1988; Lipe et al. 1988). This discussion of Pueblo I villages and ceremonial structures focuses on the Dolores, and especially the McPhee Village, research.

Based on the dating results (Breternitz et al. 1986:Table 1.1) and on a much-improved understanding of structure use-life in this setting (e.g., Ahlstrom 1985; Schlanger 1985; Varien 1984), it can be argued that the largest phase of construction in McPhee Village dates between A.D. 860–880 and represents a population of approximately 640–850 people (Kane 1988:38). This is but one of at least seven contemporaneous villages within a 10 km stretch of the Dolores Valley (Figure 2), so we are looking at a potential momentary population of at least 2000–4000 people. Population densities of 30 or more people per sq km are reasonable for the valley and surrounding agricultural land (Schlanger 1985:Table 5.2).

With the aggregation of population into these villages it is reasonable to expect the generation of new sequential social hierarchies, such as village-wide ritual societies, or a simultaneous hierarchy characterized by a more coercive leadership to manage the organizational problems of such a setting (Johnson 1982). Kane (1989) and Orcutt and Blinman (1987) have all shown that there is little evidence of coercive leadership for Pueblo I at Dolores, so it is reasonable to expect an intensification of existing modes of information exchange and integration, such as community ritual. Ceremonial organizations can serve to maintain order among relatively larger aggregates of people without necessitating formally defined authorities.

Adler (this volume) has demonstrated that specialized ritual structures are often associated with larger population aggregates (i.e., 300–400 individuals or more). Since at least five of the seven Dolores villages had approximately 300 or more people, it is possible that there were specialized ceremonial structures, or early community kivas, in some of the Dolores villages. Just as one does not expect airplanes at the beginning of this century to look like airplanes today, it is reasonable to expect that the early Anasazi ceremonial structures do not have exteriors which mark them as "kivas." One must look at the features within to recognize them as community ceremonial structures.

Ritual Features in Pueblo I Pit Structures

It has long been recognized that artifacts such as altars (Vivian et al. 1978), prayer sticks (Morris 1980:131,133; Roberts 1932:60-61), and other items of Pueblo ritual (e.g., Hayes and Lancaster 1975:87-93) are found in Anasazi sites. However, because many of these artifacts were constructed of wood, they are rarely preserved; they are even more unusual in use-association contexts.

Though artifacts are highly movable and rarely abandoned in situ (Schiffer 1976), floor features are often excellent markers of activity areas. I have documented elsewhere that feature evidence of prayer sticks, altars, and sipapus is regularly associated with certain pit structures in northern Anasazi villages by the mid–800s (Wilshusen 1986a,1988a). I repeat the basic elements of the argument for the use of altars and prayer sticks in this section, and discuss sipapus in the last part of the paper.

ALTARS

A number of researchers have recorded Pueblo I pit structures that are literally riddled with small-diameter, cylindrically-shaped floor features, usually filled with clean sand (e.g., Bullard 1962:172; Gillespie 1975:76; Morris 1939:61). In early discussions of these features, archaeologists interpreted them as pot-rests or storage areas for small items, but in several places researchers noted that they might be small, paired postholes for frameworks such as looms or altars (Brew 1946:155; Lancaster and Pinkley 1954:50; Martin and Rinaldo 1939:370). I have argued that these features are common in certain pit structures which date to A.D. 850–880 (Wilshusen 1988a:32), that they indeed appear to be paired, and reasonably could have supported a rigid framework of some sort. However, they do not appear to be substantial enough to have been a part of a loom (cf. Kent 1957:482-489; Smith 1972:121-122), and they are not positioned to suggest a partition.

In two cases at Dolores, paired posts were found on the east sides of intentionally burned pit structures. In both cases there were at least six complete bowls, jars,

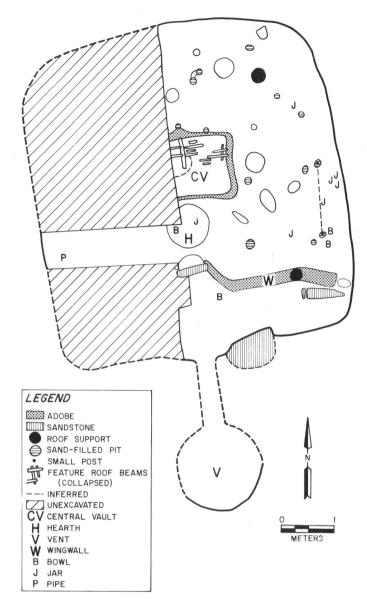

Figure 3: Plan map of Pit Structure 201, Rio Vista Village (Site 5MT2182). Note the arrangement of sand-filled pits and the cluster of ceramic vessels in the southeast corner of the structure (adapted from Wilshusen 1986b:Figure 3.118).

and dippers, and one miniature vessel in the area of the two posts. In the case of Pit Structure 10 at Grass Mesa Village (5MT23), with an apparent construction date of A.D. 867 (Lightfoot et al. 1988), there was a considerable quantity of corn in several baskets amidst the ceramic vessels. In Pit Structure 201 at Rio Vista Village (5MT2182), apparently constructed in A.D. 866 (Wilshusen 1986b), at least two ceramic vessels contained cornmeal (Figure 3). In both cases the paired posts and groupings of vessels appear to represent altars with associated offerings.

In modern pueblos, altars serve as a backdrop for ritual performances and for offerings such as medicine

Figure 4: Zia altar (adapted from Stevenson 1894:Plate 28).

or prayer-meal bowls, ears of corn, and prayer sticks (Figure 4). Altars are only set up for ceremonies and are taken down at their conclusion. Specific ceremonies may require that altars be set up facing specific directions. Historically documented altars are anchored in sand ridges or are inserted into slots or holes in the floor (Vivian et al. 1978:38-41).

> [An altar] frame consists of two vertical slats set on the floor near the ends of the sand ridge and joined near the top by a horizontal cross-piece. A variation on this frame altar consists of several spaced horizontal slats or rods tied between the uprights. These rods form a framework upon which to tie decorated slats and slabs of wood, painted altar cloths, idols, and similar items [Vivian et al., 1978:38].

Altars are an integral part of ceremonies at Jemez, the Keresan pueblos, Zuni, the Hopi pueblos, and possibly Isleta (Vivian et al. 1978:38). Well-made, painted wooden altar pieces have been found in Anasazi sites in Chaco Canyon in contexts dating to approximately A.D. 1100.

The Dolores pit structures with these potential altar features were purposefully set on fire at abandonment (Wilshusen 1986a:247;1988b:13-16). Any vegetal construction such as an altar would have had little chance to survive the blaze, so evidence for altars at Dolores is necessarily circumstantial. Yet, several lines of evidence support the interpretation of these features as anchor holes for the posts of an altar framework. Positive evidence consists of the repeated paired arrangement of these features and the two cases in which paired posts in such features are associated with bowls or baskets of corn. The negative evidence adds to this argument. Despite multiple occurrences in Pueblo I pit structures, these features do not occur in surface structures. The features are usually filled with sand or floored over, so it has been difficult to associate them with any expected domestic activity. All these aspects suggest a temporary, and possibly special, one-time use of the features—such as an altar emplacement. If several groups shared use of the structure, or if different ceremonies were performed at different times of the year, then one might expect a multitude of pits such as these.

If we consider each paired set of cylindrically-shaped features as evidence of a single altar emplacement, then there are commonly 15 to 38 altar set-ups in those pit structures that I later argue are specialized ritual structures in the Dolores Pueblo I villages. Assuming that only one altar is set up for any particular ceremony, and that this altar is moved twice during the ceremony, we would expect only three "set-ups." The numerous emplacements thus represent either a greater scale of altar movement or a greater intensity of use than one might expect in a pit house.

PRAYER STICK IMPRESSIONS

A second type of ritual feature often found in pit structures with altar emplacements is what was termed a "cluster of small holes" or "stick impressions" by DAP excavators. These impressions range from 3 to 15 cm in depth and from 0.5 to 3.5 cm in width. They typically occur in clusters of three to more than 50 separate impressions. In the Dolores area there are several different types of insects that burrow into the ground (e.g., cicadas) and thus also create small "features" in a pit structure floor. In cross-section, the clusters of small holes are easily separated by form and fill from noncultural disturbances such as insect burrows. The cultural features are detected only at floor level, are rounded or pointed at their base and usually filled with sand. Their form often suggests the imprint that would be left if a small, pointed stick were thrust into the ground. Because of their small size and because they are often filled with sand and covered by remodelings of pit structure floors, these features are often difficult to detect, and it is possible they are more common than has been documented. In the DAP excavations, clusters of small holes were documented in 25 separate pit structures dated between approximately A.D. 725 and A.D. 900, and in all but one case they were in and around the feature that was interpreted as the sipapu.

Based on the locations of the clusters of small holes, and their shape and construction, I have argued that they are best interpreted as locations where prayer sticks were planted. Prayer sticks are prerequisite for many, if not all, ceremonies at the Zuni, Hopi, Keresan, and some of the Tiwan and Tewan pueblos (Parsons 1939: 270). Prayer sticks are used in a variety of ways; in the case of shrines, such as sipapus, they are deposited in or "planted" around the shrine (Parsons 1939:309). As the entryway to the other world, the

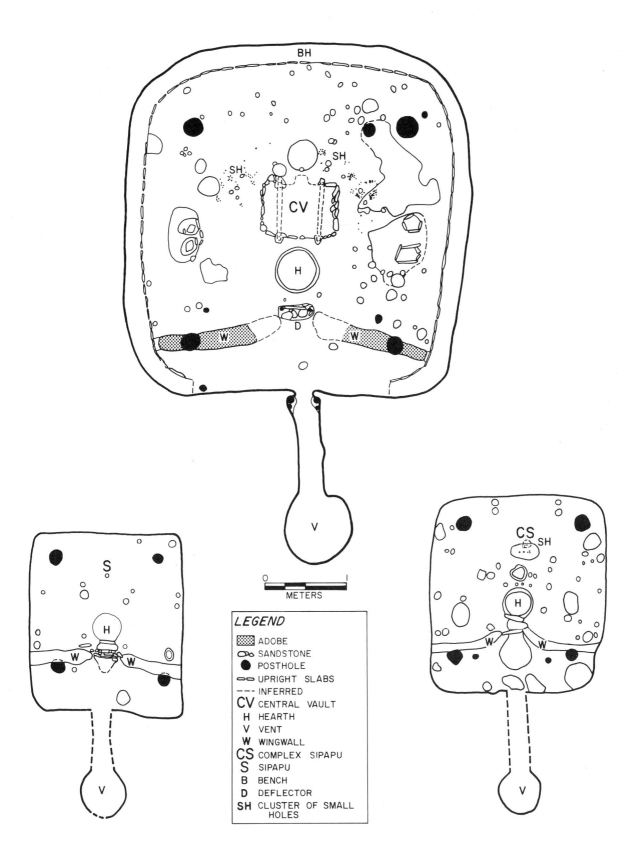

Figure 5: Examples of Dolores pit structures with the three sipapu types defined by the DAP (adapted from Brisbin et al. 1988:Figure 2.73; and Kleidon 1988:Figures 4.33 and 4.38).

sipapu serves as a suitable repository for prayer sticks, prayer feathers, and other offerings such as turquoise, shell, or other special objects (Parsons 1939:274-277).

THE SIGNIFICANCE OF RITUAL FEATURES

Altar emplacements, prayer stick groupings, and sipapus are merely the most obvious ritual features found in certain Dolores pit structures that date to the mid–A.D. 800s. In the past, archaeologists have been reasonably cautious about interpreting these features. The interpretive arguments I have offered are based on multiple lines of evidence and the elimination of alternative arguments; this would not have been possible without the large DAP sample of excavated Pueblo I pit structures. I do not expect these arguments to convince all readers; however, it is necessary to accept that whatever these features are, they are not aesthetic frills or minor aspects of the use of Pueblo I pit structures. For example, in Pit Structure 3 at McPhee Pueblo the three ritual feature types mentioned above account for 80 percent of the 91 floor pits associated with Surface 2 (see Figure 5). If one discounts the nine roof support posts and three irregularly shaped pits, the features related to ritual use of the structure account for 92 percent of the floor features. I do not agree with Lekson (1988:227) when he states that "[a]rguments about sipapus, floor vaults, and benches probably *obscure larger patterns* in a well-intended quest to document an architectural development, from pit house to kiva, that I contend is a myth" (emphasis added). Instead, the interpretation of these features is *central* to understanding whether specialized structures for community rituals actually date to much earlier in the Anasazi record than one in favor of gradual change might propose.

Lekson has proposed that pre-Pueblo IV Great Kivas are the best analogues to modern Pueblo ceremonial structures (1988:230). Great Kivas are clearly important community structures and the closest thing we have to monumental architecture in Basketmaker III and Pueblo I (cf. Lightfoot 1988); but they are not the focus of this discussion of possible early kivas for several reasons. First, there are very few excavated early Great Kivas, and it is difficult to make clear generalizations about their function and position within a community. Second, in the few cases where we have chronological and spatial relationships for Pueblo I communities with Great Kivas, it appears that they are not necessarily coincident with the largest Pueblo I villages (Orcutt et al. 1988). For example, the Great Kivas at the large Pueblo I sites of Grass Mesa (Lightfoot 1988) and Site 1676 (Hayes and Lancaster 1975) predate the main occupations at these sites. In these cases it appears that Pueblo I Great Kivas may be the architectural correlates of ceremonial associations that integrate dispersed communities or regions, and thus a continuation of a pattern first evident with Basketmaker Great Kivas (e.g., Roberts 1929:73-81).

If Great Kivas are not regularly associated with the largest Pueblo I village occupations, does this mean that these villages did not require community-wide coordination, or that village-wide ritual associations were so ephemeral that they left little evidence in the archaeological record? I have tried to show that Pueblo I villages were large and complicated communities, and that it is reasonable to expect some form of sequential ritual organization in these communities. In addition, I have noted that many features in certain Pueblo I pit structures can be interpreted to indicate ritual use of the structures. By assuming that the gradual change in pit structure architecture from Pueblo I to Pueblo III is a "mirror" of an equally slow change in ritual organization, I think we have missed an important shift in structure function from domestic to ritual. To be able to recognize possible specialized ritual pit structures or community kivas in Pueblo I villages, we must also recognize that all kivas are not equal.

Are All Kivas Created Equal?

A second assumption, the premise that all kivas—both modern and prehistoric—are created equal, has probably generated more problems for archaeologists than the assumption of gradual and progressive change. The premise is bound up in an egalitarian view of the pueblos, common long before archaeologists became common Southwestern fixtures. Some of the oldest views of the pueblos are as villages governed by a religiously-based democracy (e.g., Donaldson 1893:10,17). Though not all early students of Southwestern prehistory agreed with the premise of a classless Southwestern society (e.g., Cushing 1888), Kidder probably was more in the mainstream when he stated that "[few] races have gone as far toward civilization as did the Pueblos while still retaining the essential democracy of primitive life" (1962 [1924]:343).

The kiva played a most important role in the governance of this presumed egalitarian society. With the exception of Great Kivas (see Lightfoot 1984:12,72-73 for a review of Great Kivas as administrative centers), it has been assumed that all contemporaneous kivas are equal. This is an oversimplification, and aspects other than pit structure size can be used to isolate potential village, or community, kivas. In much of the following discussion I focus on a key kiva feature, the sipapu.

Sipapu is the Hopi word for the "pit shrine which is theoretically the most sacred of spots, for to it the people are 'tied'" (Parsons 1939:309). A sipapu is an earth navel; it represents the center or middle of the cosmos (Ortiz 1972:142). In his quest to define Kayenta kivas, Watson Smith stated that "[a sipapu] is a feature whose presence, if positively established, should serve beyond question to identify a room as a kiva, since its ceremonial significance is such that it could not occur in a purely secular room" (Smith 1952:160). One of the first identifications of a prehistoric kiva was based on the presence of a feature interpreted as a sipapu (Fewkes 1898:612-613).

The importance of the sipapu in the definition of kivas is not surprising, yet at first glance it does not seem a useful criterion in separating kivas from earlier pit houses. This is because Basketmaker pit structures, which clearly were used as houses, also have features interpreted as sipapus (e.g., Morris 1980:28-31; Brisbin and Varien 1986:140-146). However, when one reads Fewkes' description of the first excavated prehistoric sipapu, or Mindeleff's early descriptions of some sipapus in Hopi villages, they do not sound like the features we regularly call sipapus in the archaeological record in the northern Southwest. I offer the case that early archaeologists recognized at least two types of sipapus, and that different types of sipapus help distinguish community kivas from corporate kivas.

Because most early archaeologists assumed that all non-Great Kivas were functionally equivalent, this distinction was lost early in archaeology's history; by the early 1900s only one type of sipapu was recognized. Changes in the sipapu may be an important means to recognize changes in certain pit structures that specialize them for community ritual performances. To recognize these distinctions it is necessary to examine the history of the idea of the sipapu.

Differences in Sipapus and Kivas

The first good description of a sipapu in the general ethnological literature is in Mindeleff's summary of Tusayan architecture.

> In the main floor of the kiva there is a cavity about a foot deep and 8 or 10 inches across, which is usually covered with a short, thick slab of cottonwood, whose upper surface is level with the floor. Through the middle of this short plank and immediately over the cavity a hole of 2 or 2.5 inches in diameter is bored. This hole is tapered, and is accurately fitted with a movable wooden plug, the top of which is flush with the surface of the plank. The plank and cavity usually occupy a position in the main floor near the end of the kiva. This feature is the sipapuh, the place of the gods, and the most sacred portion of the ceremonial chamber. Around this spot the fetishes are set during a festival . . . (1891:121-122).

It is important to note that this sipapu was in a *mungkiva,* or the chief kiva of the village. It is the kiva frequented by the village chief and the chief talker or councilor. As Mindeleff notes, the chief kiva is usually the largest one in a village and the one in which more elaborate ceremonies are observed (Mindeleff 1891:134). Two other sipapus with plank roofs are noted by Mindeleff, but only one of these is identified, and it is in the chief kiva of another village (1891:130).

If we were to encounter a sipapu such as those just described in an archaeological context, we would likely find only a square or rectangular pit feature. If the structure was abandoned in a special manner—for example, if it was burned, then we might find a portion of the burned plank—but only if we were careful in the excavation of the burned roof fall, and the plank was preserved.

Mindeleff illustrates a second type of sipapu, which would look much more like those we encounter as archaeologists working in the northern Southwest. Mindeleff remarks that in this sipapu "the plug is let into an orifice in one of the paving stones . . . instead of into a cottonwood plank" (1891:126).

There is a third possibility mentioned by Mindeleff: there are kivas which lack a sipapu (1891:130). These kivas have a diminished role in the ceremonial life of the village.

Though early archaeologists such as Fewkes recognized that roofed sipapus existed in both modern and late prehistoric Hopi sites, the features that Fewkes excavated in Pueblo III Mesa Verde sites were like the second type of Hopi sipapu, the hole cut into the stone floor. Tracing the history of Southwestern archaeology, it is apparent that this sipapu, one not roofed with a wooden plank, became an expected feature of prehistoric kivas (Fewkes 1909:18; Fewkes 1911:58-59; Kidder and Guernsey 1919:50,60; Morley 1908:602-603; Morris 1919:169; Prudden 1914:47-48). The presence of a feature interpreted as a sipapu was often cited as "an important link" between the ancient and modern Pueblo people (e.g., Prudden 1914:48); and when there were questions about sipapus, the typical response was to cite Fewkes' original interpretation of this feature type at Spruce Tree House.

It was not until the 1920s that archaeologists commonly recognized a class of potentially roofed features called "rectangular vaults" (Judd 1922:115-116; Morris 1921:130-132). At times, rectangular vaults occurred in the location of the sipapu, or to the north of the hearth in alignment with the hearth and ventilator (e.g., Roberts 1931:98). It was common for pit structures with intact rectangular vaults to be destroyed by fire (e.g., Judd 1922:115-116; Morris 1921:128; Roberts 1931:98), so there was rarely an opportunity to find an intact roof over the feature (see Judd 1959:116 for an exception). Roberts (1932:59) suggested that the shelf-like features at each end of a vault would have allowed a plank to be set over the deeper portion of the pit without breaking the floor line. He argued that these roofed features might be analogous to Acoma and Hopi foot drums; yet ultimately he discounted the idea that the vault features served as both sipapus and floor drums, as they did at Acoma and the Hopi mesas (1932:60). I presume that Roberts dismissed the prehistoric vaults as sipapus because they were not correctly positioned (i.e., most vaults were located in a lateral position rather than aligned with the hearth and ventilator) and because, in at least three cases, he had "regular" or small pit sipapus in pit structures with vaults (Roberts 1931:97-98; 1932:53,87). Yet the idea of a modern plank-covered sipapu as an analogue to the vault features was sufficiently intriguing that Roberts mentioned it again before the end of the report (1932:89).

Meanwhile, ethnologists continued to document roofed sipapus in modern pueblos. Leslie White illustrated such a sipapu in the head "estufa" of Acoma and noted that a sipapu with a plank roof was exclusive to the *cacique*'s, or chief's, kiva (1932:31,41). By 1939 Parsons was able to summarize the evidence for roofed sipapus, or what are also called foot drums, at Hopi, Isleta, Acoma, and Zuni; and she mentions archaeological examples of roofed sipapus (e.g., the vault in Kiva A at Village of the Great Kivas [1939:382]).

Though some archaeologists continued to recognize the possibility of roofed sipapus (Bullard 1962:167; Smiley 1952:39; Smith 1972:120-121), it could not be argued until the Dolores Project that: (1) what have been called floor vaults or rectangular vaults in the archaeological literature are comparable in many cases to wooden-roofed sipapus; (2) roofed sipapus, or floor vaults, date to at least A.D. 860 and are found throughout the northern Southwest; and (3) a roofed sipapu may be expected in the most important kivas in some modern pueblo communities, and may also have occurred in the most important kivas dating as early as A.D. 860.

I have presented the Dolores data pertinent to this argument elsewhere (Wilshusen 1986a, 1988a), but let me briefly recount it here.

The Variety of Sipapus in Pueblo I Dolores Pit Structures

There are three basic sipapu types in Pueblo I pit structures at Dolores (Figure 5). These types have been termed "simple sipapu", "complex sipapu," and "central vault" or "lateral vault."

Simple sipapus are commonly seen in Basketmaker III pit houses dating to the A.D. 600s (Bullard 1962:166-167), and are regularly found in pit structures in the Mesa Verde region until abandonment in the late 1200s (Lancaster and Pinkley 1954:60). By convention, sipapus are small (less than 10 cm in diameter), usually well-made cylindrical pit features located in the northern portion of a pit structure in a north-south line with the ventilator or antechamber and hearth. As mentioned earlier, simple sipapus in the DAP sample are often distinguished by a secondary feature, a cluster of small holes which appear to be the result of "planting" pointed wooden sticks in and around the hole interpreted as the sipapu. Prayer sticks are regularly planted at shrines such as sipapus (Parsons 1939:309). Based on the DAP evidence the clusters of small stick impressions are best interpreted as a result of this kind of activity (Wilshusen 1988a; Brisbin 1986). In 25 of 50 cases at Dolores, there are stick impressions in and around features interpreted as sipapus.

By A.D. 725–760 a second sipapu type is sometimes found in place of the simple sipapu. A complex sipapu is defined as a large (mean dimensions of 43 by 29 cm), shallow (mean depth of 19 cm), sand-filled basin consistently pock-marked with numerous impressions of sticks or cut by small cylindrical features similar in size and shape to simple sipapus. There are 14 examples of complex sipapus at Dolores, 10 dating to A.D. 850–880. Perhaps this feature is more widespread than presently recognized throughout the Southwest (e.g., Brew 1946:166-167; Daifuku 1961:26-28; O'Bryan 1950:41-43; Reed et al. 1985:57), but the feature's subtle construction makes it difficult to recognize in published site reports, so its temporal or spatial distribution is not yet delineated outside the Dolores area.

By A.D. 860 another sipapu type appeared at Dolores in addition to simple and complex sipapus. This is the roofed sipapu, or what archaeologists have also called a vault. At Dolores the most common and earliest form of this feature is the central vault. The 16 examples of this type known from the Dolores Project are all in pit structures in the large villages dating to the A.D. 860s and 870s. Central vaults are subrectangular pit features located immediately to the north of the hearth. Based on the DAP sample, the average dimensions are a length of 133 cm, width of 98 cm, and a depth of 37 cm. In at least nine of the DAP cases there is good evidence that the features had a wood and plaster roof level with the pit structure floor. The central vault roofs consisted of two to three main beams set into shelves or excavated "arms" on the periphery of the feature, a number of smaller cross-members that rested on the main beams, and a plaster cap at floor level (Figure 6). In four of the remaining DAP cases, if a roof was associated with the central vault it had been razed, and the feature filled with sand or sandy loam. The final three central vaults are defined as such on their position and shape, but were so disturbed by post-abandonment activities that it is difficult to determine if the features were roofed. After almost one hundred years of archaeological work in the northern Southwest we do not like to think that there are still unknown feature types. In the case of the DAP

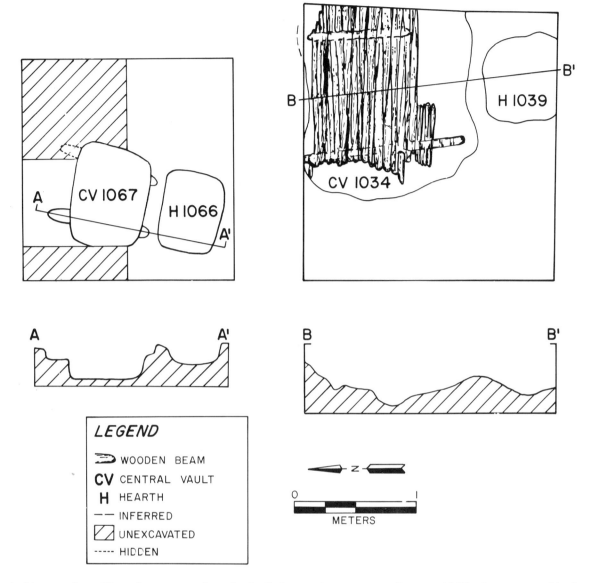

Figure 6: Plans and profiles of two central vaults in Dolores pit structures: Feature 1067, pit structure 51, Grass Mesa Village (Site 5MT23) and Feature 1034, Pit Structure 106, Rio Vista Village (Site 5MT2182) (adapted from Wilshusen 1986a:Figures 4 and 6).

central vaults there were two problems which confounded our ability to recognize them as a new feature type. The first problem was simply defining the morphology of the features. For example, we did not recognize that they were roofed because, in almost all cases, the pit structure roof had been purposefully burned, and it was difficult to distinguish the feature's roof from the collapsed pit structure roof. However, there was stratigraphic evidence of a surface in the burned roof fall within the feature, and the excavation of several well-preserved central vault roofs provided an explanation for these collapsed surfaces within the feature fill.

The second major problem was to understand the feature's function. What function could a roofed pit to the north of the hearth possibly have? It might have functioned as a storage pit, but there was no reason to have a permanently roofed storage chamber in the middle of the structure. Several other aspects of the feature made any explanation of its function difficult. In several cases the feature was surrounded by the clusters of small holes which were expected with shrines such as sipapus. In other instances the feature had been purposefully filled so full of clay or other "clean" fill that the fill preserved impressions of the feature's roof. This suggested that either the feature had been filled and then roofed, which made no sense at all, or that there had been a hole or other means of access through the roof.

The north-south alignment of the features, the fact that some were surrounded by the clusters of stick impressions, the inference that some had holes in their roofs, and the lack of a clear-cut simple or complex sipapu in pit structures with these features all reinforced the interpretation of them as early roofed sipapus.

In three cases at Dolores it is demonstrated that the central vault could be replaced by lateral vaults, and vice versa. In two pit structures the central vaults had been filled in, and in at least one case the feature roof was clearly intact. In both structures it appears that roofed lateral vaults had replaced the filled-in central vaults. In the third structure two lateral vaults had apparently been replaced by a single central vault. As I argue in the next section, the possibility existed for pit structures to have either centrally placed or lateral vaults through at least Pueblo III or IV.

Once three possible sipapu types were recognized in the pit structures of the Dolores Pueblo I villages, a series of other patterns became clear. An examination of 44 pit structures in three contemporaneous Dolores villages (McPhee, Rio Vista, and Grass Mesa) showed a significant association between sipapu type and the way a pit structure was abandoned. It became apparent that when pit structures contained only simple sipapus the inhabitants simply walked away at the time of abandonment, and the roofs collapsed over time. Pit structures with complex sipapus had paired burials on their floor, and the pit structure roofs were collapsed on top of the burials. Pit structures with roofed sipapus or central vaults were almost always burned (Wilshusen 1986a).

The different sipapu types also are associated with pit structures having significantly different floor areas (Table 1). Central vaults typically occur in structures with the largest floor areas (mean of 34.2 m^2), and complex and simple sipapus are normally associated with much smaller pit structures (mean floor areas of 21.0 m^2 and 22.5 m^2 respectively). The above test is based on the same sample of contemporaneous pit structures used in the tests of association between sipapus and abandonment mode discussed above (cf. Wilshusen 1986a:Table 1).

If there are three sipapu types at Dolores, why did earlier investigators of Pueblo I sites not discover these same types? Again, we must return to the two assumptions that guided investigators in their assessment of early kivas. It was assumed that change was gradual; thus, a feature such as a vault, normally associated with later Great Kivas, seemed incongruous in a Pueblo I pit structure. Excavators did not deny the presence of such features (a number of examples are noted in the section on vaults), but the presence of such features was regarded as exceptional. In addition, the normal abandonment mode for pit structures with intact vaults, not only at Dolores but throughout much of the Southwest, is deliberate destruction by fire. This made the detection of the wooden roofs over vaults more difficult. Dolores excavators had the "luxury" of being able to excavate several contemporaneous villages and could focus on patterned differences in the construction, use, and abandonment of many pit structures.

Secondly, it has been assumed that all kivas are equal. This does not appear to be the case at Dolores, nor for much of Pueblo prehistory, nor for the historic Hopi kivas (e.g., Whiteley 1987:63) which served as the original analogue for prehistoric kivas. With the recognition of three different kinds of sipapus, it is possible to propose that in some Pueblo I villages there were at least two levels of ritual organization, one at the local residence level and another at the community level.

Community Kivas, Corporate Kivas, and Ritual Organization

Kivas are said to be controlled by clans or kiva groups among the Western pueblos and by village associations among the Eastern Pueblos (Eggan 1950:299-300; 1983:723-728). There are typically more households per kiva among an Eastern Pueblo such as Santo Domingo than among a Western Pueblo such as Old Oraibi. The ritual organizations of both Eastern and Western Pueblos are full of oppositions and cross-cutting alli-

Table 1: Kruskal-Wallis one-way analysis of variance in pit structure floor area with groupings based on sipapu type (simple sipapu, complex sipapu, and roofed sipapu).

Ritual Feature Association	Pit Structure Floor Area			
	N	Mean	s.d.	Median
simple sipapu	14	22.5	6.41	21.6
complex sipapu	9	21.0	7.23	19.9
central vault	15	34.2	15.36	28.6

H_0 There is no difference in floor area between pit structures with different types of sipapus.

H_1 There are differences in floor area between pit structures with different types of sipapus.

$H = 8.72$, df = 2, $p < 0.02$*

Therefore reject H_0 in favor of H_1.

The Kruskal-Wallis test is used since the distributions do not approximate normality. For comparison's sake, ANOVA results for this data set are: $F = 5.71$, $p < 0.01$.

* Siegel 1956: Table C.

ances, but in the simplest terms kivas can be defined as functioning either at the corporate group (i.e. lineage, clan, or kiva group) or at the community level. Kivas in the Eastern pueblos usually are organized around community-defined moieties and function as community kivas; the moieties have an important role in community social, economic, political, and ritual affairs. Among the Western pueblos the idea of a community kiva has been more difficult to define. Recent discussions of Acoma (Garcia-Mason 1979:463) and Hopi social organization (Whiteley 1987:61-64) have renewed earlier views (e.g., White 1932) that kiva groups can be ranked in relative importance and that particular kivas serve as centers of community decision-making. It should be noted that, though a single chief kiva may be recognized for a Hopi village, this definition is not static or universal among the inhabitants of a village (e.g., a comparison of Mindeleff's listing of chief kivas [1891:136-137] for various Hopi villages with that of Stephen's [1936:1177-1178] shows two contradictions).

Prehistoric kivas appear to have similar ranking in village-level society. I propose at least two levels of prehistoric kiva organization in the northern Southwest for Pueblo I through IV. A corporate group kiva integrated either a distinct residential or social group, usually of no more than two to eight households. It may have served as a common place for special economic activities, as well as a place for group rituals. In contrast, a community kiva was the center of community ritual, with the term "community" referring in this case to a village community. A village normally had at least 20–30 households. Communities consisted of groups of people who interacted regularly for social, economic, and political purposes.

I propose that vault features probably marked community kivas and that pit structures with simple sipapus or complex sipapus had less importance in community ritual and decision-making, and are best interpreted as corporate kivas.

The pit structures discussed by Varien and Lightfoot (Chapter 6, this volume) are examples of early corporate group kivas. These structures are not equivalent to present-day Hopi "clan kivas"; they are too numerous, and in many cases the construction of particular Pueblo I pit structures can be associated with the construction of particular surface room suites. I refer the reader to Varien and Lightfoot's discussion of these structures and their many non-ritual uses. My focus is restricted here to recognizing prehistoric community kivas.

A cautionary note is probably appropriate at this time. I do not consider the presence of a roofed sipapu—whether it is a central vault or a pair of lateral vaults—to be a sure sign that a structure was used for community ritual. Any definition of community ritual structures will be polythetic. The emphasis in this paper is simply that certain features, such as roofed sipapus and altars, occur in community kivas in modern pueblos and that these types of features may mark community kivas in early pueblo villages.

Several lines of evidence support the suggestion that Dolores pit structures with vault features can potentially be interpreted as community ritual structures. Those with central vaults consistently have greater numbers of altar emplacements than pit structures with other forms of sipapus. This is reasonably related to the scale or intensity of ritual use, and presumably a structure which serves multiple groups or a more important group will get more use. As demonstrated earlier, the average size of these pit structures is significantly greater than other contemporaneous pit structures in the same community. It should be recalled that the chief kivas noted in Mindeleff's description (1891) are usually the largest kiva in a village, have a roofed sipapu, and are the site of the most elaborate, or special, ceremonies. Orcutt and Blinman (1987) and Blinman (1988:317-327) show that McPhee Village roomblocks having pit structures with central or lateral vaults have significantly higher numbers of nonlocal ceramics; there is also evidence of increased consumption, but not increased preparation, of food. One activity common to many community-based ceremonial gatherings is the exchange of food (Ford 1972; Toll 1985; Wilshusen, 1986 observations in Amazonian villages).

A roofed sipapu is nothing more than a symbol, and symbols can be used in different ways to achieve the same result. In the case of Dolores it appears that there were two distinct types of ritual organization, if we use patterned relationships of ritual symbols as a guide. At McPhee Village there are only four known pit structures with vaults out of a sample of 26 contemporaneous pit structures. If we interpret the four McPhee structures with vaults as community kivas, there are approximately 17–25 households per community kiva in this situation. This averages out to about 50–70 rooms to one community kiva, a perfectly respectable ratio even for Pueblo V kivas (cf. Steward 1937:Table 1). Three of the four structures with vaults have floor areas almost twice as large as the average for Dolores pit structures. In contrast, in Areas 1–5 at Grass Mesa Village, 9 of 15 contemporaneous pit structures have central vaults. Though three of the Grass Mesa structures are twice as large as an average structure, none of these can be clearly isolated as one which functioned as a community kiva. It appears that the ritual organization at Grass Mesa was a more sequential hierarchy in which all corporate groups had equal access to the symbols of ritual performance. Under careful scrutiny certain pit structures at Grass Mesa may be judged as community ritual structures, based on additional criteria, but it is difficult to create two classes of kivas at Grass Mesa based on differences in floor features.

A key difference in the vault features between McPhee and Grass Mesa Villages may be that there are only central vaults in Grass Mesa Village, and in three of four cases at McPhee lateral vaults replace or are replaced by central vaults. If the interpretation of vaults as roofed sipapus is correct, then the idea of lateral vaults—or two sipapus—in the same structure is a radical change. Two points of emergence make sense only if there are two different groups controlling the use of the same structure. Dual divisions have relevance only on the village or community level (Dozier 1965:41) and may serve as devices to regulate rivalry and opposition between many different groups (Eggan 1950:302). By creating sanctioned divisions and dividing responsibilities in a society it may be possible to channel opposition that might, if unchecked, result in *ad hoc* factions which could split the community. Thus, the creation of a sacred symbol of dual division within a village may coincide with the first use of a kiva for community ceremony.

Admittedly the Dolores experiment with community kivas was short-lived; pit structures with floor vaults are restricted to the largest villages dating to A.D. 850–880. Yet the evidence supports an interpretation that these pit structures had special roles in the ritual governance of the community. The numerous ritual features, the apparent role in community feasting, the size and placement of these structures—all support the idea that the community kiva may have occurred at the earliest pueblo villages. In short, the change to community kivas may have been sudden, rather than gradual. The rapidity of the change may have contributed to its short-lived appearance in Pueblo I, but structures that probably functioned as community kivas recurred in other village settings until both villages and community kivas became regular features in Pueblo IV times. One of the ritual features most commonly associated with potential community kivas between Pueblo I and V is the roofed sipapu, or vault. The final section of this paper examines the continuity of this feature type, starting with the earliest examples and continuing through to A.D. 1890.

Roofed Sipapus or Floor Vaults, Basketmaker III to Pueblo V

The earliest verified example of a roofed central vault I am aware of is in an over-sized late Basketmaker pit structure recently excavated at Site 5MT8837, 3.5 miles west of Pleasant View, southwest Colorado (Kuckelman 1988). This vault, as well as a possible one in Pit House 7 at Broken Flute Cave (Morris 1980:28-31), shows that the vault form of sipapu may have existed as a powerful symbol as early as the A.D. 600s. However, the first central vault that occurs in a possible community ritual structure in a village setting is in Pit House B at Site 13, Alkali Ridge (Brew 1946:162-165). With a floor area of approximately 61 m^2, Pit House B is the largest pit structure in this village of over 300 rooms. In addition to what appears to be a central vault (Pit F), there are a number of other nondomestic features (e.g., Pits G, Q, and N and at least eight possible altar anchors). Pit House B and two other pit structures with possible central vaults date to the first half of the ninth century (Daifuku 1961:23-26; O'Bryan 1950:38-40), and were all burned at abandonment.

In the mid- to late ninth century there are at least 16 examples of the central vaults documented at Dolores (see Wilshusen 1988a:14-26 for summary and references) and other possible examples at Mesa Verde (Hayes and Lancaster 1975:58-59), Allantown (Roberts 1939:32), and Ute Mountain Reservation (Gillespie 1975:33-34). Potential community ceremonial structures at Dolores have already been discussed. Structure 2 at the Ute Canyon Site (Site 5MTUMR2347) was judged by Gillespie to be "the first clearly ceremonial structure at the Ute Mountain Locality. It appears to have had a community-wide or intercommunity integrative function, probably serving the whole Ute Canyon Locality as well as the pit houses and surface rooms in the immediate community" (1976:65). Protokiva D at Site 1676 (Mesa Verde) is not as large, nor does it have the many possible altar holes of Structure 2 at the Ute Canyon Site, but it still has what appears to be a central vault. It may not be coincidental that it is beside a Great Kiva, which was abandoned shortly before the construction of Protokiva D, and that its construction dates to the time of Badger House Community's greatest population. Of these 20 examples of central vaults, all but three are in pit structures that were burned. This is a significant association; many of the pit structures without central vaults have other abandonment modes (Wilshusen 1986a).

Examples of vault features in the tenth century are less common, but large, extensively excavated Pueblo II villages are also rarely reported. The possible vault features I have encountered for this period are at Mesa Verde (O'Bryan 1950:34-35), Allantown (Roberts 1939:106-107), Zion National Park (Schroeder 1955:29-30), and the Ganado area (Olson 1971:21-22). It should be noted that pit structures with vaults also occurred at this time in the Mogollon region (Bluhm 1957:18; Breternitz 1959:13; Wheat 1955:56-62). The Mogollon cases are interesting because they are found in pit structures associated with pit house villages, not pueblo villages. Wheat (1955:61-62) and Bluhm (1957:27) both argue that the structures with vaults are not domestic structures, but are instead specialized ritual structures, or early community kivas.

By the late eleventh century pit structures with vault features were very common, but then again there are more excavated villages for this time period. The near-total lack of sipapus (i.e., what is called a "simple" sipapu in this discussion) in late Pueblo II Great Kivas (Vivian and Reiter 1960:82) and Chacoan round rooms (Lekson 1984:54; McKenna and Truell 1986:211-212; McLellan 1969:94) has long been noted. Yet at the same time the vault feature is practically omnipresent in Great Kivas, the larger Chacoan kivas, and some of the larger kivas at the small sites. Based on the arguments I have already proposed for the DAP examples, I would suggest that the lateral vaults in the Chacoan structures are roofed sipapus and that many of these structures functioned as community kivas. Certainly the idea that Great Kivas served as administrative/ceremonial centers for these communities is not new (Lekson et al. 1988:108; Lightfoot 1984:72-73; Plog 1974:122-127). Explanations of the role of community ritual structures call for them to control either the redistribution of communally stored goods or the maintenance of a ceremonial round which controlled large feasts. Lekson (1984:54) has remarked on the frequency with which vault features in eleventh-century Chacoan pit structures have been dismantled or filled with sand. If we consider that the role of community kiva was not static, then it is reasonable to find these features dismantled. It would be surprising if there were *not* a number of different community kivas in the life history of a community. Certainly the transfer of a community sipapu from one kiva to another is noted by Stephen for the Hopi (1936:1174).

Pit structures with lateral or central vaults are also found in so-called Chacoan outliers in the northern San Juan (Eddy 1977:39; Martin et al. 1936:42-45,46-51; Morris 1921:119-120,130-133; Vivian and Reiter 1960:77) and Zuni (Roberts 1931:98, 1932:58-60,88-91) regions in the eleventh century. The Chaco phenomenon, both in the Chaco Canyon region and in the outlier sites, is characterized by nucleated communities that show evidence of tight social control and ritual specialization. Almost all outlier pit structures with vault features were deliberately burned at abandonment, thus continuing a trend to destroy community structures purposefully.

As with all archaeological data, there are some contradictions. There is a clear-cut example of a simple sipapu in Kiva A at Village of the Great Kivas, a kiva which also has an excellent example of a floor vault (Roberts 1932). Unfortunately, Roberts does not tell us whether this floor vault was still functional (i.e., roofed and not filled in) at the time of the structure's abandonment. The presence of more than one type of sipapu in a structure suggests that it was possible to change the role a kiva might play in a community's ritual.

Even after the collapse of the Chacoan system, vaults continued to occur in pit structures in the northern Southwest through the thirteenth century (Beals et al. 1945:49-52; Cattanach 1980:95,112; Harmon 1979:14; Hayes and Lancaster 1975:87-93; Thompson et al. 1988:23; Wilson 1974:80,112-113). Certain patterns, such as the fiery abandonment of structures with vaults, also persisted. The structures with vaults at Long House (Cattanach 1980) serve as a good example of the complexity we must confront when using these features as possible markers of community-wide ritual. One must not only infer the sequence of sipapus within a single structure, but thereafter unravel the sequence of vault feature use in two pit structures and a Great Kiva.

Roofed sipapus, central vaults, floor drums—whatever one calls them— continue to be found in pit structures usually seen in large villages throughout the late prehistoric periods (Smiley 1952:39; Kidder 1958:191,203,251; Wetherington 1968:41-42; Smith 1972:121) and historic periods (Mindeleff 1891:121-122,130; White 1932:31,41). Certainly many late prehistoric and historic pueblos are much larger than the largest of Pueblo I villages. However, these differences in scale have more to do with regional economic and political control and integration and less to do with individual community organization. I think the pattern of community organization in the Western Pueblos that combines corporate and community kivas is evident in the earliest pueblos (i.e., Pueblo I).

Summary

Most of our classifications of kivas have so far been based on the assumptions that kivas only appeared on the archaeological scene after hundreds of years of development. The shift from pit house to kiva was delimited by early field workers as having occurred between A.D. 750 and 1100. The search for kivas was further confined by the assumption that all kivas have equal rank in the performance of community rituals. As a consequence we now have a classification of pit structure change which is very informative on architectural changes, but focuses very little on what occurred in kivas and on differences between contemporary kivas.

In an attempt to clarify the present classification, I have defined two general kiva types: corporate and community. I have also used particular interior features to help define potential differences in contemporaneous kivas. I have assumed that kivas are a key means of organizing pueblos and, therefore, that kivas occur in the earliest pueblos. I hope to have demonstrated that, if kivas are defined as community ritual structures, then kivas first appear in the large Pueblo I villages.

References

Ahlstrom, R. V. N.
1985 *The Interpretation of Archaeological Tree-Ring Dates*. Ph.D. dissertation, University of Arizona. University Microfilms, Ann Arbor.

Beals, R. L., G. W. Brainerd, W. Smith
1945 *Archaeological Studies in Northeast Arizona*. University of California Publications in American Archaeology and Ethnology No. 44(1). Berkeley.

Blinman, Eric
1988 *The Interpretation of Ceramic Variability: A Case Study from the Dolores Anasazi*. Unpublished Ph.D. dissertation, Department of Anthropology, Washington State University, Pullman.

Bluhm, E. A.
1957 *The Sawmill Site: A Reserve Phase Village, Pine Lawn Valley, Western New Mexico*. Fieldiana: Anthropology, vol. 47(1). Field Museum of Natural History, Chicago.

Breternitz, D. A., C. K. Robinson, and G. T. Gross, compilers
1986 *Dolores Archaeological Program: Final Synthetic Report*. Bureau of Reclamation, Engineering and Research Center, Denver.

Breternitz, D. A.
1959 *Excavations at Nantack Village, Point of Pines, Arizona*. Anthropological Papers of the University of Arizona No. 1. Tucson.

Brew, J. O.
1946 *Archaeology of Alkali Ridge, Southeastern Utah, with a Review of the Prehistory of the Mesa Verde Division of the San Juan and Some Observations on Archaeological Systematics*. Papers of the Peabody Museum of American Archaeology and Ethnology No. 21. Harvard University, Cambridge.

Brisbin, J. M.
1986 Excavations at Poco Tiempo Hamlet (Site 5MT2378), a Basketmaker III Habitation. In *Dolores Archaeological Program: Anasazi Communities at Dolores: Early Small Settlements in the Dolores River Canyon and Western Sagehen Flats Area*, compiled by T. A. Kohler et al., pp. 837-906. Bureau of Reclamation, Engineering and Research Center, Denver.

Brisbin, J. M., A. E. Kane, and J. N. Morris
1988 Excavations at McPhee Pueblo (Site 5MT4475), a Pueblo I and Early Pueblo II Multicomponent Village. In *Dolores Archaeological Program: Anasazi Communities at Dolores: McPhee Village*, compiled by A. E. Kane and C. K. Robinson, pp. 61-403. Bureau of Reclamation, Engineering and Research Center, Denver.

Brisbin, J. M., and M. Varien
1986 Excavations at Tres Bobos Hamlet (Site 4545) a Basketmaker III Habitation. In *Dolores Archaeological Program: Anasazi Communities at Dolores: Early Anasazi Sites in the Sagehen Flats Area*, compiled by A. E. Kane and G. T. Gross, pp. 117-210. Bureau of Reclamation, Engineering and Research Center, Denver.

Bullard, W. R.
1962 *The Cerro Colorado Site and Pithouse Architecture in the Southwestern United States Prior to A.D. 900*. Papers of the Peabody Museum of Archaeology and Ethnology No. 44. Harvard University, Cambridge.

Buol, S. W., F. D. Hole, and R. J. McCraken
1973 *Soil Genesis and Classification*. Iowa State University Press, Ames.

Cassells, E. S.
1983 *The Archaeology of Colorado*. Johnson Books, Boulder, Colorado.

Cattanach, G. S., Jr.
1980 *Long House, Mesa Verde National Park, Colorado*. National Park Service Publications in Archeology No. 7H. Washington, D.C.

Cordell, L. S.
1984 *Prehistory of the Southwest*. Academic Press, Orlando.

Cushing, F. H.
1888 Preliminary Notes on the Origin, Working Hypothesis and Preliminary Researches of the Hemenway Southwestern Archaeological Expedition. *Proceedings: Congres International des Americanistes* 7:151-194. Berlin.

Daifuku, Hiroshi
1961 *Jeddito 264: A Report on the Excavation of a Basketmaker III – Pueblo I Site in Northeastern Arizona with a Review of Some Current Theories in Southwestern Archaeology*. Papers of the Pea-

body Museum of American Archaeology and Ethnology No. 33. Harvard University, Cambridge.

Donaldson, Thomas
1893 *Moqui Pueblo Indians of Arizona and Pueblo Indians of New Mexico: Extra Census Bulletin.* U.S. Census Printing Office, Washington, D.C.

Dozier, E. P.
1965 Southwestern Social Units and Archaeology. *American Antiquity* 31:38-47.

Eddy, F. W.
1977 *Archaeological Investigations at Chimney Rock Mesa: 1970-1972.* Memoirs of the Colorado Archaeological Society No. 1. Boulder.

Eggan, Fred
1950 *Social Organization of the Western Pueblos.* University of Chicago Press, Chicago.

1983 Comparative Social Organization. In *Southwest,* edited by Alfonso Ortiz, pp. 723-742. Handbook of North American Indians, vol. 9, William G. Sturtevant, general editor. Smithsonian Institution, Washington, D.C.

Fewkes, J. W.
1898 Archaeological Expedition into Arizona in 1895. In *17th Annual Report of the Bureau of American Ethnology for the Years 1895-1896,* Pt. 2, pp. 519-742. Washington, D.C.

1908 Ventilators in Ceremonial Rooms of Prehistoric Cliff Dwellings. *American Anthropologist* 10:387-398.

1909 *Antiquities of Mesa Verde National Park: Spruce Tree House.* Bureau of American Ethnology Bulletin 41. Washington, D.C.

1911 *Antiquities of Mesa Verde National Park: Cliff Palace.* Bureau of American Ethnology Bulletin 51. Washington, D.C.

1919 *Prehistoric Villages, Castles, and Towers of Southwestern Colorado.* Bureau of American Ethnology Bulletin 70. Washington, D.C.

Ford, R. I.
1972 An Ecological Perspective on the Eastern Pueblos. In *New Perspectives on the Pueblos,* edited by Alfonso Ortiz, pp. 1-18. University of New Mexico Press, Albuquerque.

Garcia-Mason, Velma
1979 Acoma Pueblo. In *Southwest,* edited by Alfonso Ortiz, pp. 450-466. Handbook of North American Indians, vol. 9, William G. Sturtevant, general editor. Smithsonian Institution, Washington, D.C.

Gillespie, W. B.
1975 *Preliminary Report of Excavations at the Ute Canyon Site, 5MTUMR2347, Ute Mountain Homelands, Colorado.* Report submitted to the Bureau of Indian Affairs, Albuquerque, in compliance with Contract No. MOOC14201498.

1976 *Culture Change at the Ute Canyon Site: A Study of the Pithouse-Kiva Transition in the Mesa Verde Region.* Unpublished Master's thesis, Department of Anthropology, University of Colorado, Boulder.

Gilman, P. A.
1987 Architecture as Artifact: Pit Structures and Pueblos in the American Southwest. *American Antiquity* 52:538-564.

Gladwin, H. S.
1957 *A History of the Ancient Southwest.* Bond Wheelwright Co., Portland, Maine.

Gross, D. R.
1979 A New Approach to Central Brazilian Social Organization. In *Brazil: Anthropological Perspectives: Essays in Honor of Charles Wagley,* edited by M. L. Margolis and W. E. Carter, pp. 321-343. Columbia University Press, New York.

Harmon, C. B.
1979 *Cave Canyon Village: The Early Components.* Brigham Young University Publications in Archaeology, n.s., No. 5. Provo, Utah.

Hayes, A. C. and J. A. Lancaster
1975 *Badger House Community, Mesa Verde National Park, Colorado.* National Park Service Publications in Archeology No. 7E. Washington, D.C.

Haviland, J. B.
1987 The Politics of Ritual and the Ritual of Politics: Holy Week in Nabenchauk, Mexico. *National Geographic Research* 3:164-183.

Hayden, Brian and Aubrey Cannon
1982 The Corporate Group as an Archaeological Unit. *Journal of Anthropological Archaeology* 1:132-158.

Hewett, E. L.
   1930   *Ancient Life in the American Southwest.* Bobbs-Merrill, Indianapolis.

Hodge, F. W.
   1923   *Circular Kivas near Hawikuh, New Mexico.* Contributions from the Museum of the American Indian No. 7(1). New York.

Hough, Walter
   1920   Explorations of a Pit House Village at Luna, New Mexico. *Proceedings of the U.S. National Museum* 55:409-431. Washington, D.C.

Johnson, G. A.
   1982   Organizational Structure and Scalar Stress. In *Theory and Explanation in Archaeology,* edited by Colin Renfrew, M. J. Rowlands, and B. A. Segraves, pp. 389-422. Academic Press, New York.

Judd, N. M.
   1922   Archaeological Investigations at Pueblo Bonito, New Mexico. *Smithsonian Miscellaneous Collections* No. 72(15):106-117. Washington, D.C.

   1959   Pueblo del Arroyo, Chaco Canyon, New Mexico. *Smithsonian Miscellaneous Collections* No. 38(1). Washington, D.C.

Kane, A. E.
   1986   Social Organization and Cultural Process in Dolores Anasazi Communities, A.D. 600–900. In *Dolores Archaeological Program: Final Synthetic Report,* compiled by D. A. Breternitz et al., pp. 633-661. Bureau of Reclamation, Engineering and Research Center, Denver.

   1988   McPhee Community Cluster Introduction. In *Dolores Archaeological Program: Anasazi Communities at Dolores: McPhee Village,* compiled by A. E. Kane and C. K. Robinson, pp. 1-59. Bureau of Reclamation, Engineering and Research Center, Denver.

   1989   Did the Sheep Look Up?: Sociopolitical Complexity in Ninth Century Dolores Society. In *The Sociopolitical Structure of Prehistoric Southwestern Societies,* edited by Steadman Upham, K. G. Lightfoot, and R. A. Jewett. Westview Press, Boulder, in press.

Kane, A. E. and C. K. Robinson, compilers
   1988   *Dolores Archaeological Program: Anasazi Communities at Dolores: McPhee Village.* Bureau of Reclamation, Engineering and Research Center, Denver.

Kent, K. P.
   1957   The Cultivation and Weaving of Cotton in the Prehistoric Southwestern United States. *Transactions of the American Philosophical Society No. 47(3).* Philadelphia.

Kessell, J. L.
   1987   *Kiva, Cross, and Crown: The Pecos Indians and New Mexico 1540-1840.* University of New Mexico Press, Albuquerque.

Kidder, A. V.
   1927   Southwestern Archaeological Conference. *Science* 66:489-491.

   1958   *Pecos, New Mexico: Archaeological Notes.* Papers of the Robert S. Peabody Foundation for Archaeology No. 5. Andover, Massachusetts.

   1962   *An Introduction to the Study of Southwestern Archaeology with a Preliminary Account of the Excavations at Pecos.* Rev. ed., Yale University Press, New Haven. Originally published 1924, Yale University Press.

Kidder, A. V. and S. J. Guernsey
   1919   *Archaeological Explorations in Northeastern Arizona.* Bureau of American Ethnology Bulletin 65. Washington, D.C.

Kleidon, J. H.
   1988   Excavations at Aldea Alfareros (Site 5MT4479), a Pueblo I Habitation Site. In *Dolores Archaeological Program: Anasazi Communities at Dolores: McPhee Village,* compiled by A. E. Kane and C. K. Robinson, pp. 557-661. Bureau of Reclamation, Engineering and Research Center, Denver.

Kubiena, W. L.
   1948   *Entwicklungslehre des Bodens.* Springer-Verlag, Wien.

Kuckelman, K. A.
   1988   Excavations at Dos Bobos Hamlet (Site 5MT8837), a Late Basketmaker III Habitation. In *Archaeological Investigations on South Canal, Four Corners Archaeological Project 11,* compiled by K. A. Kuckelman and J. N. Morris, pp. 231-297. Final report submitted to the U.S. Bureau of Reclamation, Upper Colo. Region, Salt Lake City, in compliance with Contract No. 4-CS-40-01650.

Lancaster, J. A. and J. M. Pinkley
  1954 Excavations at Site 16 of Three Pueblo II Mesa Top Ruins. In *Archeological Excavations in Mesa Verde National Park, Colorado, 1950,* edited by J. A. Lancaster, J. M. Pinkley, P. F. Van Cleave, and Don Watson, pp. 23-86. National Park Service Archeological Research Series No. 2. Washington, D.C.

Lekson, S. H.
  1984 *Great Pueblo Architecture of Chaco Canyon, New Mexico.* National Park Service Publications in Archeology No. 18B. Washington, D.C.

  1988 The Idea of the Kiva in Anasazi Archaeology. *The Kiva* 53:213-234.

Lekson, S. H., T. C. Windes, J. R. Stein, and W. J. Judge
  1988 The Chaco Canyon Community. *Scientific American* 249(7):100-109.

Lightfoot, K. G.
  1984 *Prehistoric Political Dynamics.* Northern Illinois University Press, DeKalb.

Lightfoot, R. R.
  1988 Roofing an Early Anasazi Great Kiva: Analysis of an Architectural Model. *The Kiva* 53:253-272.

Lightfoot, R. R., A. M. Emerson, and Eric Blinman
  1988 Excavations in Area 5, Grass Mesa Village (Site 5MT23). In *Dolores Archaeological Program: Anasazi Communities at Dolores: Grass Mesa Village,* compiled by W. D. Lipe, J. N. Morris, and T. A. Kohler, pp. 561-766. Bureau of Reclamation, Engineering and Research Center, Denver.

Lipe, W. D., J. N. Morris, and T. A. Kohler, compilers
  1988 *Dolores Archaeological Program: Anasazi Communities at Dolores: Grass Mesa Village.* Bureau of Reclamation, Engineering and Research Center, Denver.

McGregor, J. C.
  1965 *Southwestern Archaeology* 2d ed. University of Illinois Press, Urbana.

McKenna, P. J. and M. L. Truell
  1986 *Small Site Architecture, Chaco Canyon, New Mexico.* National Park Service Publications in Archeology No. 18D.

McLellan, G. E.
  1969 *The Origin, Development, and Typology of Anasazi Kivas and Great Kivas.* Unpublished Ph.D. dissertation, Department of Anthropology, University of Colorado, Boulder.

Martin, P. S., Lawrence Roys, and Gerhart von Bonin
  1936 *Lowry Ruin in Southwestern Colorado.* Field Museum of Natural History, Anthropological Series, vol. 23(1). Chicago.

Martin, P. S. and J. B. Rinaldo
  1939 *Modified Basket Maker Sites, Ackmen-Lowry Area, Southwestern Colorado, 1938.* Field Museum of Natural History, Anthropological Series, vol. 23(3). Chicago.

Mindeleff, Victor
  1891 A Study of Pueblo Architecture: Tusayan and Cibola. In *8th Annual Report of the Bureau of Ethnology for the Years 1886-1887,* pp. 13-228. Washington, D.C.

Morley, S. G.
  1908 The Excavation of the Cannonball Ruins in Southwestern Colorado. *American Anthropologist* 10:596-610.

Morris, E. A.
  1980 *Basketmaker Caves in the Prayer Rock District, Northeastern Arizona.* Anthropological Papers of the University of Arizona No. 35. Tucson.

Morris, E. H.
  1919 Preliminary Account of the Antiquities of the Region Between the Mancos and La Plata Rivers in Southwestern Colorado. In *33rd Annual Report of the Bureau of American Ethnology,* pp. 155-206. Washington, D.C.

  1921 *The House of the Great Kiva at the Aztec Ruin.* Anthropological Papers of the American Museum of Natural History No. 26(2). New York.

  1939 *Archaeological Studies in the La Plata District, Southwestern Colorado and Northwestern New Mexico.* Carnegie Institution of Washington Publication 519. Washington, D.C

Morris, E. H., and R. F. Burgh
  1954 *Basketmaker II Sites near Durango, Colorado.* Carnegie Institution of Washington Publication 604. Washington, D.C.

Nordenskiold, G. E. A.
[1893] *The Cliff Dwellers of the Mesa Verde, Southwest Colorado: Their Pottery and Their Implements.* Translated by D. L. Morgan. P. A. Norstedt and Soner, Stockholm and Chicago. Reprinted by Rio Grande Press, Glorieta, New Mexico, 1979.

O'Bryan, Deric
1950 *Excavations in Mesa Verde National Park 1947-1948.* Gila Pueblo Medallion Papers No. 39. Globe, Arizona.

Olson, A. P.
1971 *Archaeology of the Arizona Public Service Company 345KV Line.* Museum of Northern Arizona Bulletin No. 46. Flagstaff.

Orcutt, J. D. and Eric Blinman
1987 Leadership and the Development of Social Complexity: A Case Study from the Dolores Area of the American Southwest. Ms. in possession of authors, Santa Fe, New Mexico.

Orcutt, J. D., Eric Blinman, and T. A. Kohler
1988 Explanations of Population Aggregation in the Mesa Verde Region Prior to A.D. 900. Paper presented at the Southwest Symposium, Tempe.

Ortiz, Alfonso
1972 Ritual Drama and the Pueblo World View. In *New Perspectives on the Pueblos,* edited by Alfonso Ortiz, pp. 135-161. University of New Mexico Press, Albuquerque.

Parsons, E. C.
1939 *Pueblo Indian Religion.* University of Chicago Press, Chicago.

Pepper, G. H.
1920 *Pueblo Bonito.* Papers of the American Museum of Natural History No. 27. New York.

Plog, Fred
1974 *The Study of Prehistoric Change.* Academic Press, New York.

Prudden, T. M.
1914 The Circular Kivas of Small Ruins in the San Juan Watershed. *American Anthropologist* 16:33-58.

Rappaport, R. A.
1968 *Pigs for the Ancestors.* Yale University Press, New Haven.

1971 The Sacred in Human Evolution. *Annual Review of Ecology and Systematics* 2:23-44.

Reed, A. D., W. K. Howell, P. R. Nickens, and Jonathan Horn
1985 *Archaeological Investigations on the Johnson Canyon Road Project, Ute Mountain Tribal Lands, Colorado.* Report submitted to Bureau of Indian Affairs, Albuquerque, New Mexico in compliance with Contract No. MOOC14204255.

Roberts, F. H. H., Jr.
1929 *Shabik'eshchee Village: A Late Basket Maker Site in Chaco Canyon, New Mexico.* Bureau of American Ethnology Bulletin 92. Washington, D.C.

1931 *The Ruins at Kiatuthlanna, Eastern Arizona.* Bureau of American Ethnology Bulletin 100. Washington, D.C.

1932 *The Village of the Great Kivas on the Zuni Reservation, New Mexico.* Bureau of American Ethnology Bulletin 111. Washington, D.C.

1939 *Archaeological Remains in the Whitewater District, Eastern New Mexico. Pt. 1: House Types.* Bureau of American Ethnology Bulletin 121. Washington, D.C.

Schiffer, M. B.
1976 *Behavioral Archeology.* Academic Press, New York.

Schlanger, S. H.
1985 *Prehistoric Population Dynamics in the Dolores Area, Southwestern Colorado.* Unpublished Ph.D. dissertation, Department of Anthropology, Washington State University, Pullman.

Schroeder, A. H.
1955 *Archeology of Zion Park.* University of Utah Anthropological Paper No. 22. Salt Lake City.

Siegel, Sidney
1956 *Nonparametric Statistics for the Behavioral Sciences.* McGraw-Hill, New York.

Smiley, T. L.
1952 *Four Late Prehistoric Kivas at Point of Pines, Arizona.* University of Arizona Bulletin No. 23(3). Social Science Bulletin No. 21. Tucson.

Smith, Watson
1952 *Excavations in Big Hawk Valley, Wupatki National Monument, Arizona.* Museum of Northern Arizona Bulletin No. 24. Flagstaff.

1972 *Prehistoric Kivas of Antelope Mesa, Northeastern Arizona*. Papers of the Peabody Museum of Archaeology and Ethnology No. 39(1). Harvard University, Cambridge.

Stephen, A. M.
1936 *Hopi Journal of Alexander M. Stephen*, edited by E. C. Parsons. Columbia University Contributions to Anthropology 23. New York.

Stevenson, M. C.
1894 The Sia. In *11th Annual Report of the Bureau of American Ethnology for the Years 1889-1890*, pp. 3-157. Washington, D.C.

Steward, J. H.
1937 Ecological Aspects of Southwestern Society. *Anthropos* 32:87-104.

Thompson, Charmaine, J. R. Allison, S. A. Baker, J. C. Janetski, Byron Loosle, and J. D. Wilde
1988 *The Nancy Patterson Village Archaeological Research Project—Field Year 1986*. Brigham Young University Museum of Peoples and Cultures Technical Series No. 87-24. Provo, Utah.

Toll, H. W., III
1985 *Pottery, Production, Public Architecture, and the Chaco Anasazi System*. Unpublished Ph.D. dissertation, Department of Anthropology, University of Colorado, Boulder.

Varien, M. D.
1984 *Honky House: The Replication of Three Anasazi Surface Structures*. Unpublished M.A. report, Department of Anthropology, University of Texas, Austin.

Vivian, R. G., D. N. Dodgen, and G. H. Hartmann
1978 *Wooden Ritual Artifacts from Chaco Canyon, New Mexico, the Chetro Ketl Collection*. Anthropological Papers of the University of Arizona No. 32. Tucson.

Vivian, Gordon and Paul Reiter
1960 *The Great Kivas of Chaco Canyon and Their Relationships*. School of American Research and the Museum of New Mexico Monograph No. 22. Santa Fe.

Wetherington, R. K.
1968 *Excavations at Pot Creek Pueblo*. Fort Burgwin Research Center Publication No. 6. Southern Methodist University, Dallas.

Wheat, J. B.
1955 *Mogollon Culture Prior to A.D. 1000*. Society for American Archaeology Memoir No. 10.

White, L. A.
1932 The Acoma Indians. In *47th Annual Report of the Bureau of American Ethnology for the Years 1929-1930*, pp. 17-192. Washington, D.C.

Whiteley, P. M.
1987 *Deliberate Acts: Changing Hopi Culture Through the Oraibi Split*. University of Arizona Press, Tucson.

Wilshusen, R. H.
1986a The Relationship Between Abandonment Mode and Ritual Use in Pueblo I Anasazi Protokivas. *Journal of Field Archaeology* 13:245-254.

1986b Excavations at Rio Vista Village (5MT2182), a Multicomponent Pueblo I Village. In *Dolores Archaeological Program: Anasazi Communities at Dolores: Middle Canyon Area,* compiled by A. E. Kane and C. K. Robinson, pp. 209-658. Bureau of Reclamation, Engineering and Research Center, Denver.

1988a Sipapus, Ceremonial Vaults, and Foot Drums (Or a Resounding Argument for Protokivas). In *Dolores Archaeological Program: Supporting Studies: Additive and Reductive Technologies,* compiled by Eric Blinman, C. T. Phagan, and R. H. Wilshusen, pp. 649-671. Bureau of Reclamation, Engineering and Research Center, Denver.

1988b The Abandonment of Structures. In *Dolores Archaeological Program: Supporting Studies: Additive and Reductive Technologies,* compiled by Eric Blinman, C. T. Phagan, and R. H. Wilshusen, pp. 673-702. Bureau of Reclamation, Engineering and Research Center, Denver.

Wilson, C. J. (editor)
1974 *Highway U-95 Archeology: Comb Wash to Grand Flat,* vol. 2. Special report, Department of Anthropology, University of Utah, Salt Lake City.

8
Potluck in the Protokiva: Ceramics and Ceremonialism in Pueblo I Villages

Eric Blinman

Richard Wilshusen has described a range of ritual features that occur in Anasazi pit structures and has argued that different combinations of these features define a hierarchy of ritual activity within villages (such as corporate and community kivas). This architectural hierarchy is evident at McPhee Village, a Pueblo I community in the Dolores area of southwestern Colorado. One of the implications of the hierarchy is that the intensity and elaboration of associated rituals should be detectable in material culture through differential participation in exchange or through subtle differences in site function related to hosting gatherings. Nonlocal red ware sherds are relatively more abundant, the ratio of cooking jar sherds to decorated bowl sherds is lower, and cooking jars are generally smaller at the roomblocks highest in the hierarchy. The jar:bowl ratio and the differential distribution of cooking jar sizes suggests that potluck-style gatherings occurred most frequently at the ritually most complex roomblocks of the village. The concentration of exchanged red ware sherds is partly an epiphenomenon of the potluck gatherings, but it is likely that the more intense ritual activity at the highest-ranking roomblocks did confer on their residents some degree of preferential access to exchanged goods.

Introduction

Ritual activities have been attributed to Pueblo I pit structures based on the presence of features ranging from possible prayer stick holes in structure floors to floor vaults with wooden roofs (possible foot drums; see Wilshusen, this volume). These features lack any demonstrable domestic function, and they are assigned ritual functions by analogies to features and practices of Pueblo Indian cultures during the past century. Although analogy alone is a relatively weak form of archaeological argument, it is supported in the case of Pueblo I pit structures in the Dolores area of southwestern Colorado by circumstantial evidence from settlement organization and abandonment context (Wilshusen 1986). These observations provide a credible argument for the existence of ritual activities within pit structures, and for a ranking of ritual activity in Pueblo I villages by scale of participation and elaboration of activity.

Material culture associations have been used as independent evidence to support reconstructions of ritual (or leadership) activity within Anasazi communities. Many of these arguments have involved ceramic data by interpreting differential distributions of particular wares, or through evidence of exchange. Differentially high frequencies of decorated sherds in association with a kiva were detected by statistical analyses of Carter Ranch pottery assemblages (Freeman and Brown 1964), and a walled plaza within the Glen Canyon region had an unusually high proportion of decorated ceramics compared to assemblages found at habitation sites (Lipe 1966:299-301; 1970:116,118). The latter case was explicitly interpreted as a group assembly site, with the implication that food consumption rather than preparation was a significant activity. More recent Southwestern archaeological studies that explore ceremonial or political activity tend to emphasize models of centralization or monopolization of exchange (Lightfoot 1984; Lightfoot and Feinman 1982; S. Plog 1986; Upham 1982; Upham et al. 1981). They demonstrate a coincidence of exchange goods with kivas or large kivas and use that observation to support particular models of social organization or interaction.

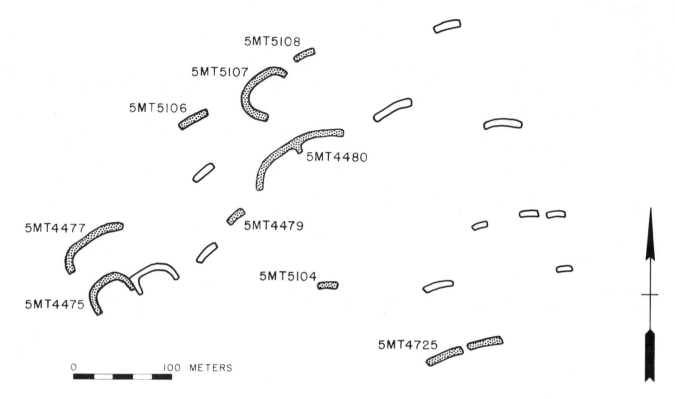

Figure 1: Plan of the roomblocks of McPhee Village. The excavated roomblocks used in this report are labeled with their site numbers.

These studies suggest that both functional and exchange aspects of material culture, and pottery in particular, can be used to examine the nature of ceremonial or political activity inferred from other archaeological observations. In this paper ceramic data are compared with a ranking of pit structures at McPhee Village, a Pueblo I village in the Dolores area of southwestern Colorado. The pit structures are ranked on the basis of ritual feature size and complexity (Wilshusen 1985), floor area, and associated roomblock shape. If Wilshusen (this volume) is correct, and this ranking reflects differential participation in village ritual activity, comparable rankings should be evident in the functional or exchange characteristics of the associated ceramic assemblages.

McPhee Village

McPhee Village was excavated as part of the Dolores Archaeological Program (Breternitz et al. 1986). The village is the largest of four excavated late ninth-century villages in the Dolores area and was composed of 21 contemporary roomblocks (Figure 1), ranging in size from 15 to 126 m in length (Kane 1988:Table 1.9). One of these roomblocks (5MT4654 [Hewitt and Harriman 1984]) was too disturbed to provide meaningful data, and it is excluded from these discussions. Portions of the village appear to have been established as early as A.D. 829 (Brisbin 1988:Table 6.8), and the population peaked at approximately 200 households within the A.D. 860–880 period (Kane 1988:Figure 1.10).

Portions of nine roomblocks and associated pit structures were excavated, and the pit structures encountered contain a range of ritual features: lateral vaults, central vaults, and complex and simple sipapus. Wilshusen (1985, this volume) argues that this series is associated with a decreasing scale of ritual integration. Although the scale is defined by individual pit structure characteristics, it is assumed that they served the domestic and ritual needs of those who lived in the associated roomblock as a social and corporate unit. The highest scale represented by any of the associated pit structures is assumed to reflect the level at which the roomblock as a whole was involved in community integration.

A single pit structure at each of four of these roomblocks (5MT4475, 5TM4477, 5MT5106, and 5MT5107) contained rectangular central vaults or lateral vaults. Pit Structure 3 at 5MT4475 (Brisbin et al. 1988) was originally constructed in the late A.D. 850s or early 860s with a large central vault. In A.D. 875, it was extensively remodeled, the central vault was decommissioned, and two lateral vaults were con-

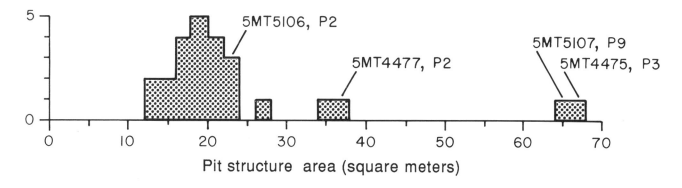

Figure 2: Histogram of pit structure areas for the excavated pit structures of McPhee Village (after Kane 1988:Figure 1.15).

structed. The other excavated pit structures at the roomblock contained complex sipapus rather than vaults. Pit Structure 9 at roomblock 5MT5107 was constructed and remodeled at least once within the A.D. 840–870 period (Brisbin 1988). It contained a central vault that had been filled (decommissioned) prior to abandonment, a lateral vault that was functional at the time of abandonment, and another decommissioned lateral vault. Pit Structure 2 at roomblock 5MT4477 was probably constructed in the A.D. 850s or 860s, and it contained two lateral vaults during this period (Kuckelman 1988). It was extensively remodeled in A.D. 871, and the lateral vaults were replaced by a central vault. Pit Structure 2 at roomblock 5MT5106 was occupied in the A.D. 860s and 870s and was equipped with a central vault, but had no evidence of lateral vaults (Morris 1988). The roofed areas of these four pit structures were 67, 64, 37, and about 24 m^2, respectively; this compares with a median size of about 20 m^2 for all excavated pit structures within McPhee Village (Figure 2).

Although not all other pit structures within these four roomblocks were excavated, those that were excavated contained either simple or complex sipapus rather than floor vaults. Pit structures associated with three other roomblocks where all pit structures were excavated (5MT4479, 5MT5104, and 5MT5108) contained only simple or complex sipapus (Kleidon 1988; G. Nelson 1985; Kuckelman 1988). Pit structures at the remaining roomblocks (5MT4480 and 5MT4725) contained only simple or complex sipapus, but feature characteristics are known only for a subset of the pit structures that were present (Kuckelman and Harriman 1988; Chenault 1983). (Pit Structure 4 at roomblock 5MT4725 may have had a central vault [Kane 1988:Table 1.12], but the description indicates that the feature conforms poorly with the other central vaults in size, shape, and placement [Chenault 1983:46-51]; it is interpreted as a complex sipapu here.)

These architectural patterns can be used to define contexts for comparative studies of material culture. Utilizing ritual features and pit structure size, roomblocks can be categorized or ranked into four levels of possible ritual or ceremonial intensity.

(1) The extremely large pit structures at roomblocks 5MT4475 and 5MT5107 began with central vaults that were remodeled in the A.D. 870s (at the height of village population) into lateral vaults. Based largely on their size and the rarity of lateral vaults in all Dolores villages (see Wilshusen, this volume), these structures are interpreted as the locations of the most intense ritual activity within McPhee Village. In addition to their size and feature content, these structures are associated with roomblocks that curve relatively sharply around the pit structure or plaza area, forming a U-shape not associated with the other ceremonial ranks.

(2) The large pit structure at 5MT4477 was altered from a lateral-vault structure to a central-vault structure in the A.D. 870s; it is assumed that slightly less intense ritual activity occurred there, especially during and after the population peak.

(3) The normal-sized structure at 5MT5106 contained only a central vault throughout its use history, and probably was the site of slightly less intense ritual activity than the structure at 5MT4477.

(4) Finally, the other roomblocks whose pit structure characteristics are known (5MT4479, 5MT5104, and 5MT5108) are normal-sized or small and contain only complex sipapus. These roomblocks form the lowest rank of expected ritual intensity.

Pit structures at the remaining roomblocks (5MT4480, 5MT4725) have only simple or complex sipapus, though some structures were not investigated. The roomblocks could fall into any one of the lower three levels if U-shaped roomblocks are a necessary defining characteristic of the highest level (Kane 1986). However, if roomblock shape is irrelevant to ritual rank, then these partially-investigated roomblocks could belong to any of the four levels.

Pottery as a Measure of Ritual Activity

Exchange and function are two dimensions of pottery that can be influenced by, and therefore can reflect, ritual or political activity. However, both exchange and function are influenced by other aspects of cultural systems as well. This ambiguity results in a potentially confounding situation in which the background assumptions and interpretive models related to each dimension are extremely important to the interpretation.

Exchange

Exchange of a commodity is partially dependent on its production pattern. During the A.D. 840–900 period, production of gray ware pottery appears to have been a household activity within the Dolores area and probably within the Mesa Verde region as a whole (Blinman 1988; Blinman and Wilson 1988). It is likely that contemporary white ware production was specialized to the extent that not all households regularly produced these vessels, but there is no evidence for large-scale or geographically specialized production within the Mesa Verde region (Blinman 1988). In contrast with the low-level specialization and dispersed sources of white ware vessels, red ware production *does* appear to be geographically specialized within the western portion of the Mesa Verde region. Most, if not all, San Juan Red Ware vessels were produced in southeastern Utah and exchanged eastward across the remainder of the region.

Decorated wares are presumed to be valuable in both an energetic and aesthetic sense (Feinman et al. 1981), and red ware vessels in particular have been implicated in linkages between ceremonial organization and exchange in the northern Southwest (see S. Plog 1986 and this volume). Red ware production patterns in the region require exchange for vessel distribution, and red ware exchange is the best candidate for assimilation into larger patterns of ritual or political organization. If patterns of ritual activity influenced the distribution of red wares in the Dolores area, then higher exchange frequencies should coincide with the architectural and feature indices of ritual intensity.

Function

Independent of exchange patterns, the principal roles of pottery in Dolores Anasazi culture were as cooking and serving containers (Blinman 1985, 1988). It could be argued that some vessel forms (such as effigies) played a role in ceremonialism, but they are too rare to allow an independent assessment of that interpretation, or to allow their use in inter-roomblock comparisons. However, the lack of distinctly "ritual" pottery does not preclude the evaluation of food preparation and consumption patterns, which may imply ceremonial gatherings.

A consequence of food preparation and consumption is the breakage and eventual discard of vessels. People presumably prepared and ate food within rooms, pit structures, or plazas, and broken vessels were eventually discarded in the formal midden or refuse dumps of the roomblock where breakage occurred. (There are no refuse deposits in the Dolores area at this time period that can be linked to individual households, and the practical resolution of refuse-based studies is limited to the architectural and social unit of the roomblock.) Cooking jars should have shorter life-spans than serving bowls, and jar sherds should accumulate at a faster rate in middens. However, breakage of both forms should be stochastic phenomena, and in the context of large samples (many households cooking and consuming food over the course of a generation) there should be a consistent ratio of cooking jar to bowl sherds.

If all cooking and eating occurred in domestic contexts, this ratio should be identical between roomblocks. However, if food consumption played a significant role in social gatherings, there is a possibility for differential accumulations of cooking jar and bowl sherds, depending upon the specific spatial pattern of food preparation and consumption. Food consumption plays a significant role in modern Pueblo Indian ceremonialism (Toll 1985:369-406) and is a general characteristic of most gatherings throughout the world; one can safely assume a linkage between feasting and ceremonial gatherings at Dolores.

Size is a second aspect of vessel function. Vessels are manufactured for specific needs, which result in size classification of vessels within specific forms. The distribution of Dolores area cooking jar sizes is bimodal, with a long tail that includes the largest jars (Blinman 1988:Figure 4.4). This pattern appears to reflect a common need for small jars of about 1 liter and medium jars of about 4 liters' effective capacity; the long tail of the distribution reflects an occasional need for large jars that range up to 11 liters in effective volume. Large cooking jars have been described as "fiesta pots" in ethnographic contexts (B. Nelson 1981), based on their occasional use in preparing large quantities of food for social gatherings.

Two basic patterns of food preparation and consumption are possible, termed here the "potlatch" and the "potluck" models of hosting. In the former model, the host roomblock group is responsible for provisioning the ceremony by preparing food drawn from its own stores or contributed by others. In this model both cooking and eating occur at the host roomblock, breakage locations of the two forms coincide, and cooking jar and bowl ratios in the host roomblock refuse should not differ significantly from ratios at others. However, larger cooking jars would likely be used for ceremonial gatherings, and their presence should make a detectable difference between refuse of the host roomblock and at other roomblocks.

The potluck model assumes that food is prepared elsewhere and brought to the site of the ceremony for consumption. In this model the different locations of use and breakage would result in a surplus of cooking jar sherds at the roomblocks where food was prepared and a surplus of bowl sherds in the refuse of the host roomblock. Again, large cooking jars would have been used for food preparation, and they should be more abundant in the refuse at the supporting roomblocks than at the host roomblock.

In either model, if hosting and provisioning responsibilities were rotated evenly through the village, no material differences would be detectable. Also, if ceremonial gatherings were rare, the differential accumulations of vessel sherds would not be significantly different than those of a purely domestic pattern. However, if hosting responsibilities were differentially distributed, the potlatch model should result in a concentration of sherds from larger cooking jars in refuse at the host roomblocks; the potluck model should be detectable as a concentration of cooking jar sherds and sherds from larger jars away from the host roomblock, and a concentration of bowl sherds in refuse at the host roomblock. If the ritual feature hierarchy reflects a ceremonial hosting hierarchy, roomblock refuse comparisons should reveal some evidence of one of these two models.

Red Ware Exchange and Ceremonial Activity

Importation of red wares from the western Mesa Verde region to the Dolores area began in the mid-eighth century. The peak of exchange volume was reached in the early ninth century (a supply accounting for 8.5 percent of sherds in Dolores area refuse), with a decline in availability (to 6.3 and then to 4.0 percent) during the height of the village period in the mid-ninth century (Blinman 1988:Table 5.2).

Red ware frequencies in A.D. 860–900 refuse from McPhee Village roomblocks are presented in Table 1. The red ware frequency from roomblock 5MT5104 can be discounted due to the small sample of well-dated refuse, and the sample from 5MT4475 is so small its relevance could be arguable. Red ware sherds are relatively more abundant in the refuse from the three roomblocks with the highest-ranking ritual pit structures. Those roomblocks with pit structures whose lateral vaults were in use during this period (5MT4475 and 5MT5107) are associated with the most red ware

sherds. Two other pit structures had central vaults that were active late in their use-life. Only the roomblock associated with the larger of these (5MT4477) has a high red ware frequency. There are few red ware sherds in the roomblock which has the normal-sized central-vault pit structure (5MT5106), and in those roomblocks where pit structures contain only simple or complex sipapus. Although the sample size is too small for confident interpretation, relative red ware abundance appears to correspond strongly with pit structure size and, to a lesser extent, with the type of ritual feature.

Based on this evidence, an argument can be made that the distribution of exchanged vessels at McPhee Village was influenced by both ritual space and ritual features, and the direction and magnitude of the influence supports the architectural model of different scales of pit structure ceremonialism. This differential distribution of exchanged vessels is similar to that interpreted as centralization of exchange for Great Kivas (Upham et al. 1981) and sites with kivas (S. Plog 1986, this volume) elsewhere in the Southwest. However, although a correspondence between ritual activity and nonlocal pottery at McPhee Village is apparent, the concentrations of nonlocal sherds can be interpreted as a centralization of exchange only if we can assume that the location of vessel use, breakage, and discard (and archaeological recovery) is the same as the location of exchange. This assumption cannot be supported for McPhee Village, and a relationship (detailed in the following sections) between red ware sherd frequency, bowl use and breakage, and ritual rank complicates the interpretation of the nonlocal sherd concentrations.

Feasting Evidence and Ceremonial Activity

Although the principles behind functional interpretations of vessel-form data are simple, their practical application in the Dolores area can be complex. Ratios of vessel forms in refuse deposits are affected by several variables. There were different degrees of dependence on agriculture, both through time and between contemporary villages in the Dolores area, and this may affect cooking practices, and hence, the relative frequency of some vessel forms. The ability to assign sherds accurately to particular vessel-form classes also varies between wares, and changing styles of cooking jar shapes affect measures of vessel size (Blinman 1988:188-226). When comparisons are restricted to roomblocks within a single village, some of these confounding sources of variation are minimized; but temporal variation still remains a problem with some vessel-form data.

Valid comparisons between sherd frequencies from different vessel forms (bowls and cooking jars, in this

Table 1: Red ware frequencies in A.D. 860–900 refuse from McPhee Village.

Ceremonial ranking	Roomblock (5MT)	Highest ranking pit structure characteristics	Red ware sherd frequency (%)	Sample size
1	4475	Very large floor area, central and lateral vaults, U-shaped roomblock	4.9	288
1	5107	Very large floor area, central and lateral vaults, U-shaped roomblock	6.5	19,137
2	4477	Large floor area, lateral and central vaults	3.5	9,362
3	5106	Normal floor area, central vault	1.7	778
4	4479	Normal floor area, complex sipapu	2.1	3,113
4	5108	Normal floor area, complex sipapu	1.1	1,162
4	5104	Small floor area, complex sipapu	4.1	49
?	4480	Unknown	3.4	5,819
?	4725	Unknown	3.3	4,988

NOTE: The "refuse" data set includes all well-dated and relatively uncontaminated proveniences identified as containing secondary refuse types; proveniences interpreted as containing use-association or de facto refuse materials are excluded. Refuse occurs both in pit and structure fills as well as in formal middens. Ceramic data in this table are taken from Blinman (1988:Tables 5.6 and 5.8).

case) require two corrections. Counts of gray ware jar sherds must be transformed into estimates of cooking jar sherds by deleting sherds that probably derive from other gray ware jar forms (Blinman 1988:161-167). We can confidently identify undecorated gray ware bowl sherds only if they have rims, so comparisons in this paper are limited to decorated bowls (white-, red-, and smudged-ware vessels), whose sherds can be reliably identified.

Cooking-jar size estimates are based on measurements of rim-sherd radii (rim radius and the log of effective cooking jar capacity are strongly correlated throughout the A.D. 840–900 period [Blinman 1988:170-174]). Although this relationship is constant, there is a slight increase in the sizes of cooking jars used and broken prior to as opposed to after A.D. 880. This apparent increase requires that separate vessel-size comparisons be carried out for the A.D. 840–880 and 880–900 periods to avoid confusing temporal differences between refuse collections with the synchronic functional variation in cooking jar size that is of interest in this paper. Although the temporal change in cooking jar size preferences will also affect the stability of the bowl:jar sherd ratio (larger cooking jars yield more sherds per breakage), the implications of this effect are less since its magnitude is smaller. (The observed 0.45 cm increase in median cooking jar rim radius at A.D. 880 translates into an increase of about 20 percent in effective volume, but only an estimated increase of about 10 percent in sherd production.)

Vessel-form data for the roomblocks of McPhee Village are presented in Table 2. A lower ratio implies a relative excess of decorated bowl breakage (food consumption), whereas a higher ratio implies a relative excess of cooking-jar breakage (food preparation). Again, the sample size from roomblock 5MT5104 is too small for the ratio to be valid, and the sample size from roomblock 5MT4475 is small enough that the relevance

Table 2: Cooking jar and decorated bowl frequencies in A.D. 840–900 refuse from McPhee Village.

Ceremonial ranking	Roomblock (5MT)	Cooking jar sherds	Decorated bowl sherds	Jar:bowl ratio
1	4475	242	26	9.31
1	5107	15,911	1,622	9.81
2	4477	8,131	649	12.53
3	5106	658	45	14.62
4	4479	2,775	219	12.67
4	5108	955	81	11.79
4	5104	37	6	6.17
?	4480	4,979	390	12.77
?	4725	4,199	379	11.08

NOTE: Cooking jar sherd counts have been corrected (decreased in number) to compensate for the presence of sherds derived from other gray ware jar forms.

of its ratio is arguable. Given these *caveats*, the smallest ratios coincide with the roomblocks associated with the highest-ranking ritual structures: those very large pit structures with central and lateral vaults. This suggests an excess of food *consumption* at these two roomblocks. The other levels of possible ceremonial participation are associated with higher ratios, regardless of position within the lower levels of the ritual hierarchy. This suggests both a relatively greater participation in food *preparation* than at the highest-ranking roomblocks and a lack of clear differentiation between the lower ranks.

The distinctiveness of the roomblocks with highest-ranking pit structures is also reflected in the cooking jar size data from the village (Figure 3). The refuse data sets for the jar size comparison have been augmented for some roomblocks by the addition of refuse that was not included in the ratio or exchange comparisons because it contains a small amount of contamination from

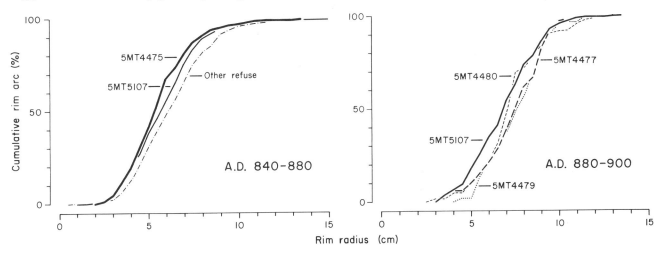

Figure 3: Cumulative frequency curves of cooking jar sherd rim radii for A.D. 840–880 and A.D. 880–900 refuse from selected roomblocks of McPhee Village. Sample sizes for the A.D. 840–880 period are 271 sherds subsuming 7,465 degrees of arc for 5MT4475, 641 sherds subsuming 16,910 degrees of arc for 5MT5107, and 681 sherds subsuming 17,590 degrees of arc for the collections from other villages in the Dolores area. Sample sizes for the A.D. 880–900 period are 232 sherds subsuming 8,260 degrees of arc for 5MT5107, 160 sherds subsuming 4,260 degrees of arc for 5MT4477, 48 sherds subsuming 1,500 degrees of arc for 5MT4479, and 64 sherds subsuming 1,845 degrees of arc for 5MT4480.

earlier and later occupations at the village. This contamination (from corrugated and plain gray cooking jars) has been isolated and removed from the jar size data set by limiting the comparison to data from neckbanded cooking jars. No rim radius measurements are available for refuse from the 5MT5108 roomblock, and cooking jar size data from occupations at other villages in the Dolores area are used for the A.D. 840–880 comparison, due to limited data from McPhee Village. The jar-size data are expressed as cumulative degrees of rim arc for each rim radius increment (0.5 cm). Cumulative degrees of rim arc can be interpreted as an estimate of the number of vessels present in the refuse (360 degrees of rim arc are equivalent to a whole vessel). Cumulative curves to the left of the figure indicate the breakage of relatively more vessels with smaller rims, whereas curves to the right indicate the breakage of relatively more vessels with larger rims. Since rim radii increase linearly, while cooking jar volumes increase geometrically, slight differences in median rim radius imply considerable increases in potential food preparation volume.

Within the A.D. 840–880 period, refuse associated with the two highest-ranking pit structures contains relatively smaller cooking jars. The implications of this are weakened, since the comparison is with cooking jars from other villages in the Dolores area rather than with other McPhee Village roomblocks; it is conceivable that dietary variation or even stylistic variation between villages could account for the differences. However, the direction of the difference is the same as that within McPhee Village in the post–A.D. 880 period, and the difference could easily reflect the same intravillage trend described below.

Within the A.D. 880–900 period, cooking jar size data are available for four McPhee Village roomblocks (see Figure 3), but only two of the collections (5MT5107 and 5MT4477) have satisfactorily large sample sizes. Median cooking jar rim radii are smallest for 5MT5107, the highest level of the ceremonial ranking. The 5MT4480 collection includes a slightly larger median, but its rank is unknown; the other two roomblocks are similar, with larger median jar sizes. The latter includes refuse from the 5MT4477 roomblock, which is associated with a second-rank pit structure.

Although conclusions are weakened somewhat by the scarcity of data for comparisons, the cooking jar size curves imply that smaller batches of food were prepared at the two roomblocks at the top of the ceremonial hierarchy and that larger batches were prepared at the others, regardless of position within the pit structure ranking. The difference in sizes could conceivably account for a 10 percent difference in number of cooking jar sherds generated per incident of breakage at the supporting roomblocks, and this difference contributes to the perceived vessel-form ratio differences between the highest-ranking and other roomblocks, making the apparent increase in bowl breakage at the highest-ranking room blocks questionable. However, even if the cooking jar sherd counts are inflated by 10 percent for the 5MT4475 and 5MT5107 collections in Table 2, the bowl:jar ratios remain lower than those of the other roomblocks.

These patterns conform to the model of potluck ceremonialism, with differential participation in hosting focused on the highest level of the ritual hierarchy. Larger batches of food were prepared at the lower ranking roomblocks than at the highest ranking roomblocks of McPhee Village, and there is evidence that some of this food was eaten at the roomblocks with pit structures of the highest ceremonial rank.

Discussion

Ceramic data from McPhee Village provide some support for the model of a hierarchy of ritual rank and intensity, as derived from Wilshusen's analysis of ritual feature elaboration, pit structure size, and roomblock plan. There are higher relative frequencies of exchanged red ware vessels at roomblocks with central or lateral vaults (ranks 1 and 2), and especially at those with inordinately large pit structures (rank 1). Decorated bowls are relatively more abundant in refuse associated with roomblocks having the largest ritual pit structures (rank 1), but bowl abundance does not differentiate within the other levels of the hierarchy. Cooking jar size is also differentially distributed, but the smallest cooking volumes coincide with the highest level of the ritual hierarchy, and the largest cooking jar volumes with the lower levels of the hierarchy.

These results generally correspond with previous observations in the Southwest that there are differential associations of types of material culture with kivas or types of kivas, but there is one potentially misleading aspect to the observations: the abundance of exchanged red ware sherds at the highest-ranking roomblocks of McPhee Village may only reflect the tendency for decorated bowls to be more frequently broken at those roomblocks. The potluck model of hosting and the functional movement of vessels between roomblocks raises the possibility that the presence of nonlocal sherds in the highest-ranking middens could have little to do with the process of exchange.

About 70 percent of red ware sherds are from bowls, and red wares comprise 57 percent of decorated bowl sherds during the A.D. 840–880 period, and 41 percent during the A.D. 880–900 period. Any increase in bowl breakage should result in an increase in red ware sherd deposition. This relationship suggests that the apparent concentration of exchanged red wares at the highest-

Table 3: Bowl sherd frequencies in A.D. 880–900 refuse from McPhee Village.

Ceremonial ranking	Roomblock (5MT)	Red ware sherds (%)	Other decorated ware sherds (%)	Total decorated (N)
1	4475	38.5	61.5	26
1	5107	48.5	51.5	359
2	4477	36.4	63.6	649
3	5106	13.3	86.7	45
4	4479	23.3	76.7	219
4	5108	9.9	90.1	81
4	5104	33.3	66.7	6
?	4480	33.3	66.7	390
?	4725	37.1	62.9	367

NOTE: Except for a single smudged ware sherd from refuse at Site 5MT4480, all of the "other decorated" ware sherds are from white ware vessels.

ranking roomblocks is simply an epiphenomenon of an increased breakage of bowls used in ceremonial food consumption. Residents of supporting roomblocks would bring food to the gathering in decorated bowls, some of these bowls would break, and the sherds would be discarded with the refuse of the host roomblock, thereby inflating the numbers of nonlocal sherds at the most ceremonially active roomblocks.

Insufficient data are available to investigate this possibility for the A.D. 840–880 period, but some refuse collections are large enough to support an examination of the ware composition of bowl sherds at the various McPhee Village roomblocks in the A.D. 880–900 period. (Refuse data from the two periods cannot be combined for this comparison, due to a strong temporal decline in red ware sherds that would add a potentially confounding dimension of variability.) If increased bowl breakage alone were responsible for the apparent increase in exchanged red ware sherd frequency, then a consistent proportion of red ware bowl sherds should be present in all collections.

The red ware contributions to the decorated bowl sherds in roomblock refuse are presented in Table 3. The greatest relative frequencies of red ware bowl sherds are in the refuse from the highest-ranking roomblocks, although the sample size from the 5MT4475 collection is too small to interpret the frequency as a reliable estimate. The next highest reliable frequencies are associated with the second- ranked and two unranked roomblocks. The lowest reliable red ware percentage occurs in the collection from the lowest-ranked roomblock (5MT4479). Deleting the small and unranked examples, the relative contribution of red ware vessels to the bowl category increases with the increasing rank of pit structure ceremonialism. This pattern implies a strong preference for the use (and breakage) of red ware rather than other decorated bowls for ceremonial food consumption, but the pattern does not in itself confirm a relationship between the ceremonial hierarchy and centralization of exchange.

The only suggestion that some centralization of red ware exchange may correspond with ceremonial ranking comes from the vessel forms in the red ware category. If the serving function alone accounts for the increased red ware sherds at the highest-ranking roomblocks, then the proportion of bowl sherds within the red ware category should be higher in those collections than in collections from the lower-ranked roomblocks.

Adequate comparative data are available only for the A.D. 880–900 period and are presented in Table 4. Small samples limit the comparison somewhat, but there are relatively fewer rather than more bowl sherds within the red wares from the highest-ranking roomblocks. This observation suggests either that other red ware forms played important roles in pit structure ceremonialism at McPhee Village (were being brought to and broken at the roomblock) or that at least some preferential access to red ware vessel exchange was enjoyed by residents of the highest roomblock ranks.

Table 4: Red ware vessel form frequencies in A.D. 880–900 refuse from McPhee Village.

Ceremonial ranking	Roomblock (5MT)	Bowl sherds (%)	Other vessel forms (%)	Total (N)
1	4475	71.4	28.6	14
1	5107	66.9	33.1	260
2	4477	72.3	27.7	326
3	5106	46.1	53.9	13
4	4479	79.6	20.4	64
4	5108	61.5	38.5	13
4	5104	100.0	0.0	2
?	4480	64.1	35.9	201
?	4725	84.4	15.6	161

Conclusion

Even without the exchange interpretation, ceramic data from McPhee Village provide support for Wilshusen's suggestion that pit structures can be categorized as corporate and community kivas as early as Pueblo I. This conclusion is based on a strong pattern of potluck-style hosting centered on the roomblocks having the two highest-ranking pit structures in terms of ritual feature elaboration, floor area, and roomblock shape (5MT4475 and 5MT5107). The roomblock with a second-ranked ceremonial pit structure (5MT4477) is associated with intermediate characteristics for red ware sherd frequencies, but cooking jar volume and jar:bowl ratio do not support a comparable role in hosting intravillage gatherings. The lack of strong patterns at the second ranked structure or within the other lower ranks does not preclude their participation in ceremonial hosting, but it does suggest that either their participation was at a lower magnitude than the highest rank, or that the responsibilities of participation were evenly distributed.

The strong differentiation of the highest rank, even though ritual features were shared with the second rank, suggests that Wilshusen's caveat about his kiva typology is also correct: although Anasazi ceremonial hierarchies existed and included ritual features in their definition, other factors (such as pit structure size) must be considered as part of a polythetic approach to understanding the scale of prehistoric ceremonialism. Associating the highest-ranking pit structures with U-shaped roomblocks is an ancillary issue: the sample size (two cases from one village) is too small for confident extrapolation, but if the relationship is valid, U-shaped roomblocks can be used to infer the presence of community kivas from surface observations of sites (Kane 1986).

The relationship between ceremonialism and exchange in McPhee Village is complex and unresolved. Some, and perhaps most, of the concentration of red-ware sherds in the highest-ranking roomblocks can be explained as an epiphenomenon of the functional concentration of bowl sherds at those roomblocks. Red ware vessels were apparently preferred for ceremonial gatherings, but that clearly does not exclude their use in domestic contexts or more corporate ceremonialism. However, the abundance of red ware forms other than bowls in these refuse collections does suggest an enhanced access to red ware vessels by residents at the three highest-ranking roomblocks. The mechanism of this access remains unknown, and no confident discrimination can be made between possible factors that range from overt political control of a valued commodity to simple exploitation of the large gatherings for trade by entrepreneurs, without implying any control of exchange by roomblock residents.

Acknowledgments

Some of the data used in this paper were generated by the Dolores Archaeological Program, funded by the U.S. Bureau of Reclamation (Contract No. 8-07-40-S0562). Many of the ideas have benefited from the discussions and advice of my colleagues on the Dolores Archaeological Program and from my dissertation committee at Washington State University. William D. Lipe, Ricky Lightfoot, and Janet Orcutt provided valuable comments on an earlier draft of this paper.

References

Blinman, Eric
    1985   Ceramic Vessels and Vessel Assemblages in Dolores Archaeological Program Collections. *Dolores Archaeological Program Technical Reports* DAP-269. Final report submitted to the U.S. Bureau of Reclamation, Upper Colorado Region, Salt Lake City, in compliance with Contract No. 8-07-40-S0562.

    1988   *The Interpretation of Ceramic Variability: A Case Study from the Dolores Anasazi.* Unpublished Ph.D. dissertation, Department of Anthropology, Washington State University, Pullman.

Blinman, Eric, and C. Dean Wilson
    1988   Ceramic Data and Interpretations: the McPhee Community Cluster. In *Dolores Archaeological Program: Anasazi Communities at Dolores: McPhee Village,* compiled by A.E. Kane and C.K. Robinson, pp. 1293-1341. Bureau of Reclamation, Engineering and Research Center, Denver.

Breternitz, David A., Christine K. Robinson, and G. Timothy Gross, compilers
    1986   *Dolores Archaeological Program: Final Synthetic Report.* Bureau of Reclamation, Engineering and Research Center, Denver.

Brisbin, Joel M.
    1988   Excavations at Pueblo de las Golondrinas (Site 5MT5107), a Multiple-Occupation Pueblo I Site. In *Dolores Archaeological Program: Anasazi Communities at Dolores: McPhee Village,* compiled by A.E. Kane and C.K. Robinson, pp. 789-903. Bureau of Reclamation, Engineering and Research Center, Denver.

Brisbin, Joel M., Allen E. Kane, and James N. Morris
    1988   Excavations at McPhee Pueblo (Site 5MT4475), a Pueblo I and Early Pueblo II Multicomponent Village. In *Dolores Archaeological Program: Anasazi Communities at Dolores: McPhee Village,* compiled by A.E. Kane and C.K. Robinson, pp. 61-401. Bureau of Reclamation, Engineering and Research Center, Denver.

Chenault, Mark L.
    1983   Excavations at Tres Chapulines Hamlet (Site 5MT4725), a Pueblo I Habitation Site. *Dolores Archaeological Program Technical Reports* DAP-102. Final report submitted to the Bureau of Reclamation, Upper Colorado Region, Salt Lake City, in compliance with Contract No. 8-07-40-S0562.

Feinman, Gary M., Steadman Upham, and Kent G. Lightfoot
    1981   The Production Step Measure: an Ordinal Index of Labor Input in Ceramic Manufacture. *American Antiquity* 46:871-884.

Freeman, Leslie G., Jr., and James A. Brown
    1964   Statistical Analysis of Carter Ranch Pottery. In Chapters in the Prehistory of Eastern Arizona, II, by Paul S. Martin et al., pp. 126-154. *Fieldiana: Anthropology* 55. Chicago.

Hewitt, Nancy J., and Raymond G. Harriman
    1984   Excavations at Beaver Trap Shelter (Site 5MT4654), a Multiple-Occupation Site. *Dolores Archaeological Program Technical Reports* DAP-168. Final report submitted to the Bureau of Reclamation, Upper Colorado Region, Salt Lake City, in compliance with Contract No. 8-07-40-S0562.

Kane, Allen E.
    1986   Social Organization and Cultural Process in Dolores Anasazi Communities, A.D. 600–980. In *Dolores Archaeological Program: Final Synthetic Report,* compiled by David A. Breternitz et al., pp. 633-661. Bureau of Reclamation, Engineering and Research Center, Denver.

    1988   McPhee Community Cluster Introduction. In *Dolores Archaeological Program: Anasazi Communities at Dolores: McPhee Village,* compiled by A.E. Kane and C.K. Robinson, pp. 1-59. Bureau of Reclamation, Engineering and Research Center, Denver.

Kleidon, James H.
    1988   Excavations at Aldea Alfareros (Site 5MT4479), a Pueblo I Habitation Site. In *Dolores Archaeological Program: Anasazi Communities at Dolores: McPhee Village,* compiled by A.E. Kane and C.K. Robinson, pp. 557-661. Bureau of Reclamation, Engineering and Research Center, Denver.

Kuckelman, Kristin A.
    1988   Excavations at Masa Negra Pueblo (Site 5MT4477), a Pueblo I/Pueblo II Habitation. In *Dolores Archaeological Program: Anasazi Communities at Dolores: McPhee Village,* compiled by A.E. Kane and C.K. Robinson, pp. 405-555. Bureau of Reclamation, Engineering and Research Center, Denver.

Kuckelman, Kristin A., and Raymond G. Harriman
1988 Excavations at Rabbitbrush Pueblo (Site 5MT4480), a Pueblo I Habitation. In *Dolores Archaeological Program: Anasazi Communities at Dolores: McPhee Village,* compiled by A.E. Kane and C.K. Robinson, pp. 987-1057. Bureau of Reclamation, Engineering and Research Center, Denver.

Lightfoot, Kent G.
1984 *Prehistoric Political Dynamics: A Case Study from the American Southwest.* Northern Illinois University Press, DeKalb.

Lightfoot, Kent G., and Gary M. Feinman
1982 Social Differentiation and Leadership Development in Early Pithouse Villages in the Mogollon Region of the American Southwest. *American Antiquity* 47:64-86.

Lipe, William D.
1966 *Anasazi Culture and its Relationship to the Environment in the Red Rock Plateau Region, Southeastern Utah.* Ph.D. dissertation, Yale University. University Microfilms, Inc., Ann Arbor.

1970 Anasazi Communities in the Red Rock Plateau, Southeastern Utah. In *Reconstructing Prehistoric Pueblo Societies,* edited by William A. Longacre, pp. 84-139. University of New Mexico Press, Albuquerque.

Morris, James N.
1988 Excavations at Weasel Pueblo (Site 5MT5106), a Pueblo I–Pueblo III Multiple-Occupation Site. In *Dolores Archaeological Program: Anasazi Communities at Dolores: McPhee Village,* compiled by A.E. Kane and C.K. Robinson, pp. 663-787. Bureau of Reclamation, Engineering and Research Center, Denver.

Nelson, Ben A.
1981 Ethnoarchaeology and Paleodemography: A Test of Turner and Lofgren's Hypothesis. *Journal of Anthropological Research* 37:107-129.

Nelson, G. Charles
1985 Excavations at Willow Flat Pueblo (Site 5MT5104), a Pueblo I Habitation. *Dolores Archaeological Program Technical Reports* DAP-136. Final report submitted to the Bureau of Reclamation, Upper Colorado Region, Salt Lake City, in compliance with Contract No. 8-07-40-S0562.

Plog, Stephen
1986 Change in Regional Trade Networks. In *Spatial Organization and Exchange: Archaeological Survey on Northern Black Mesa,* edited by Stephen Plog, pp. 282-309. Southern Illinois University Press, Carbondale.

Toll, Henry Wolcott, III
1985 *Pottery, Production, Public Architecture, and the Chaco Anasazi System.* Ph.D. dissertation, Department of Anthropology, University of Colorado, Boulder. University Microfilms International, Ann Arbor.

Upham, Steadman
1982 *Polities and Power: an Economic and Political History of the Western Pueblo.* Academic Press, New York.

Upham, Steadman, Kent G. Lightfoot, and Gary M. Feinman
1981 Explaining Socially Determined Ceramic Distributions in the Prehistoric Plateau Southwest. *American Antiquity* 46:822-833.

Wilshusen, Richard H.
1985 Sipapus, Ceremonial Vaults, and Foot Drums (or a Resounding Argument for Protokivas). *Dolores Archaeological Program Technical Reports* DAP-278. Final report submitted to the Bureau of Reclamation, Upper Colorado Region, Salt Lake City, in compliance with Contract No. 8-07-40-S0562.

1986 The Relationship Between Abandonment Mode and Ritual Use in Pueblo I Anasazi Protokivas. *Journal of Field Archaeology* 13:245-254.

9
The Styles of Integration: Ceramic Style and Pueblo I Integrative Architecture in Southwestern Colorado

Michelle Hegmon

The relationship between ceramic style and type of integrative structure is examined. Comparisons are made between (1) pit structures used primarily as habitations with no integrative function above the household level, (2) pit structures shared by several households, and (3) pit structures used for larger scale integrative activities. The potential for ceramic style to convey information—measured as design diversity—is found to be high in association with pit structures used for large-scale integrative activities and also in structures used in times of upheaval. The stylistic information is argued to be important in relations with socially distant persons. The formality of style, argued to be related to ritual, is greatest in association with shared structures of any size. The analysis involves black-on-white ceramics from the late Pueblo I period (A.D. 840–920) in southwestern Colorado.

Architecture creates places where people live and work, and some architecture creates special places where people come together for ritual and other activities that help to integrate communities and other social groups. Here I focus on activities that took place in certain architectural contexts and on their artifactual remains. More specifically, I am interested in the style of ceramics associated with structures that are argued to have served various integrative functions. My goal is to explore the potential of using data on stylistic variation as an indicator of integrative activities and possibly as a measure of social integration. This research deals with black-on-white ceramics from the late Pueblo I period (ca. A.D. 840–920) in a portion of southwestern Colorado.

Integrative architecture provides space that is shared or used by a number of households or other social units and thereby helps to integrate them. By this definition, a small pit structure shared by several households and a Great Kiva where people from across a region gather for periodic rituals are both examples of integrative architecture. Thus, integrative structures are places where socially distant persons come together. Various activities can be housed by integrative structures, but ritual has a particularly important role. Ritual, and religion in general, have long been recognized as important means of promoting community solidarity (Durkheim 1965; Wallace 1966). Ritual is also an important means of increasing cooperation between social units, because ritual sanctifies communication and makes the actions of the ritual's participants more predictable (Rappaport 1971).

Food plays an important role in many integrative activities. Food—for human participants and for the gods—is an essential component in many rituals, and the centerpiece for many social gatherings. Ethnographic accounts of Pueblo ceremonials demonstrate the importance of food exchange, even—or especially— in times of scarcity (Ford 1972). Ceramics are used in preparing, storing, serving, and eating the food, and thus necessarily have a role in integrative activities. In prehistoric pueblos the locations of large gatherings—for example, at Pueblo Alto in Chaco Canyon—are often marked by large deposits of ceramics (Toll 1985).

The basic premise of this research is that ceramics used in integrative activities will differ in some way from those used in other contexts. A wide range of ethnographic and archaeological examples support the general association of distinctive ceramics with special (i.e., ritual, elite, etc.) contexts. Among the Azande of the Sudan, ceramics used in ritually charged male-female encounters are highly decorated (Braithwaite 1982). In recent Anglo-American society, china used in special or ceremonial occasions tends to be finely made, imported, or otherwise expensive (see Deetz 1972:57). "Well made, carefully decorated and delicately finished" Hopewell ceramics (from the eastern United States, a millennium before the Pueblo I period) are contrasted to local wares and are suggested to have had ceremonial significance (Prufer 1965:39; see also Sears 1973). In later periods in the Southwest, certain ceramic styles, wares, and vessel forms tend to be associated with special contexts. Labor-intensive black-on-white fine-line hachure may be associated with the Chaco system (Neitzel 1985; Toll 1985:215; Windes 1984:109) and appears more commonly on sites with kivas (Plog, Chapter 10, this volume). Upham et al. (1981) claim that imports and wares requiring extra production steps are associated with elite contexts in the Chavez Pass area. Pueblo III kiva jars are assumed to have had a special function because of their distinctive shape, though they are not always found in kivas (Rohn 1971:181). Zuni stepped bowls, painted with naturalistic designs of water animals, have a particular ritual function (Bunzel 1972:23; Hardin 1983), and modern Zia vessels prepared for use in ritual contexts are distinctive in shape but not decoration (B. Bradley, personal communication).

These many examples support the basic premise that special ceramics are used in special contexts; these ceramics display easily recognized formal differences from "everyday" ceramics and hence may mark the occasions when they are used. Although they share a common general role, these examples do not provide a single clear-cut set of criteria that can be used to identify special ceramics. The ceramics may be (1) decorated in contrast to plainwares; (2) more finely made; (3) specially shaped; (4) decorated with distinctive elements; (5) more labor-intensive to produce; (6) imported; or (7) a combination of the above. These properties may carry a variety of information about ritual meanings and social relations. Therefore, I examine a number of criteria, derived from the theoretical and ethnographic literature, to study the possible association of ceramic style with integrative architecture.

The Pueblo I period is an important starting point for the study of integrative architecture and ceramic style in the Anasazi cultural tradition. Pit structures during this period commonly have both domestic and ritual features and are argued to have served some integrative functions; hence, they are often called protokivas. However, a number of criteria, including size, site structure, and features, suggest that Pueblo I pit structures are not all equal in terms of the integrative activities they shelter or the number of households that use them (Wilshusen, Chapter 7, this volume). Similarly, Pueblo I white wares appear be fairly homogeneous; the types are relatively clear-cut, and there are no obviously fancy forms or wares. However, there may be subtle but significant patterns of variation within the types. In this paper I examine patterns of ceramic stylistic variation associated with various kinds of pit structures.

Setting the Problem

The ceramics used in this analysis are from eight Pueblo I sites in Montezuma County, southwestern Colorado (Chapter 1, Figure 2). Seven were excavated as part of the Dolores Archaeological Program's (DAP) work in the Dolores River Valley between 1978 and 1983. Four DAP sites are part of the large McPhee community in the southern portion of the Dolores area; these are Aldea Alfareros (5MT4479) (Kleidon 1988), Weasel Pueblo (5MT5106) (Morris 1988), Pueblo de las Golondrinas (5MT5107) (Brisbin 1988) and Golondrinas Oriental (5MT5108) (Kuckelman 1988). House Creek Village (5MT2320) is a smaller site across the river from the McPhee community (Robinson and Brisbin 1986). Grass Mesa Village (5MT0023) is a large site in the northern part of the Dolores area (Lipe et al. 1988) and Prince Hamlet (5MT2161) is a small site near Grass Mesa Village (Sebastian 1986). The eighth is the Duckfoot Site (5MT3868), located approximately 15 miles southwest of the Dolores area, and excavated by the Crow Canyon Archaeological Center from 1983 to 1987 (Adams 1984; Lightfoot 1985, 1987; Lightfoot and Van West 1986; Lightfoot and Varien 1988; Varien and Lightfoot, Chapter 6, this volume).

The ninth century A.D. was a period of population growth and flux in the Dolores River Valley. People moved into the area until the population peaked in the A.D. 860s or 870s. Then, after A.D. 880, a time when the agricultural potential declined, people moved out of the valley (Schlanger 1986). The area was mostly abandoned by A.D. 910, and very few securely dated tenth century sites are known from the Dolores River Valley or surrounding area. (See Kane [1986a] for a general overview of Dolores area prehistory.) The settlement history of the area immediately surrounding the Duckfoot Site is known in less detail, but it seems to conform generally to the Dolores model. Duckfoot was part of a late ninth century community that includes at least one site with a probable oversized pit structure (identified in surface survey). It was occupied in the late ninth century A.D. and abandoned by the 880s (the latest tree-ring dates are in the A.D. 870s [R. Lightfoot, personal communication]).

The Dolores area, especially after A.D. 850, was primarily inhabited by aggregated communities, but with various sizes and forms of settlement organization. The basic unit of occupation was an interhousehold cluster consisting of several surface roomsuites and a pit structure. Several interhousehold clusters made up a roomblock, and one or more roomblocks constituted a village (Kane 1986a:356-358; see Figure 2 in Varien and Lightfoot, this volume). Aggregated settlements with interhousehold clusters and roomblocks were characteristic of the Periman subphase (A.D. 840–910) in DAP systematics (Kane 1986a). However, after A.D. 880 at a few sites in the northern portion of the Dolores area, small pit structures became the primary units of habitation. Occupations characterized by small pit structures are classified as part of the Grass Mesa Subphase (Kane 1986a:370-377). These habitations are often not associated with any surface rooms and may evidence an increased household mobility and less rigid community organization in the period just prior to abandonment of the area (Lipe et al. 1988).

Different sizes and forms of pit structures, possibly with a variety of integrative functions, are present in the late Pueblo I sites. Much of the analysis undertaken in this paper compares ceramics associated with different kinds of pit structures; as a basis for this comparison, three categories of pit structures are developed. The ceramic assemblages associated with each category are listed in Table 1, and details of the ceramic contexts are discussed in the Analysis section below.

Category I consists of *household pit structures,* or pit houses, that are argued to have served little or no integrative function above the household level. Many Grass Mesa Subphase pit structures are included in this category because they lack ritual features and appear to have been occupied by single households (Lipe et al. 1988:1245, 1259). Category I ceramic assemblages used in this analysis are those associated with selected Grass Mesa Subphase pit structures at Grass Mesa Village (i.e., excepting the large Pit Structure 32 and some Grass Mesa Subphase pit structures associated with Periman Subphase roomblocks).

Category II consists of pit structures that were part of interhousehold clusters, including most Periman Subphase pit structures. They would have been shared by several households and thereby would have served to integrate them. These Category II *interhousehold pit structures* fit the classic Prudden Unit model (Prudden 1903) and are basically synonymous with Wilshusen's (this volume) definition of corporate kivas. Interhousehold pit structures typically have both domestic and ritual features, including regular and sometimes complex sipapus (Wilshusen 1985 and this volume). Ceramic assemblages associated with interhousehold pit structures and used in this analysis are from the Periman Subphase occupations at Prince Hamlet, House Creek Pueblo, Aldea Alfareros, Golondrinas Oriental, Duckfoot, and from selected contexts at Grass Mesa Village (i.e., the post–A.D. 880 Periman Subphase occupation as well as Grass Mesa Subphase pit structures associated with Periman roomblocks).

Category III includes a limited number of pit structures that may have been used by community groups larger than interhousehold units and thus may have had larger scale integrative functions. These are called *community pit structures,* though they may also have had a role in regional relationships as a place where members of a number of communities gathered (see Plog, this volume). Community pit structures can be recognized on the basis of several characteristics, including size, position in the site layout, and ritual features. Different researchers emphasize various characteristics. Wilshusen (this volume, see also 1985) argues that the presence of central or lateral floor vaults are good indicators of what he calls *community kivas.* According to Lipe et al. (1988:1233) "... there is somewhat equivocal evidence ... [that at least some of the Grass Mesa

---

Table 1: Ceramic assemblages used in the analysis.

Category I: Household pit structures
1) Grass Mesa Village (5MT0023), portions of the Modeling Period (MP) 5* occupation (Grass Mesa Subphase)**

Category II: Interhousehold pit structures
1) Grass Mesa Village (5MT0023), portions of MP 5 occupation (Periman and Grass Mesa Subphases)**
2) Prince Hamlet (5MT2161), MP 4* occupation
3) Prince Hamlet (5MT2161), MP 5 occupation
4) House Creek Pueblo (5MT2320), MP 4 occupation
5) Aldea Alfareros (5MT4479), MP 5 occupation
6) Golondrinas Oriental (5MT5108), MP 5 occupation
7) Duckfoot Site (5MT3868), MP 4

Category III: Community pit structures
1) Grass Mesa Village (5MT0023), MP 4 occupation
2) Weasel Pueblo (5MT5106), MP 5 occupation
3) Pueblo de las Golondrinas (5MT5107), MP 4 occupation
4) Pueblo de las Golondrinas (5MT5107), MP 5 occupation

---

* Modeling Period 4 = A.D. 840–880; Modeling Period 5 = A.D. 880–910/920
** Ceramics from Modeling Period 5 at Grass Mesa Village are divided between categories I and II. Category I includes Grass Mesa Subphase elements not associated with any integrative structure (Element/Episode Numbers [EEN] 2, 3, 4, 6, 8, 11, 12, 19, 25, 26, 27, 31, 33, 36, 37, 38, 39, 42, 44, 45, 46, 48, 59, 60, 61, 87, 93, 94, 95, 96, 98, 99). Category II includes all Periman Subphase elements (EENs 73, 83, 84) and those Grass Mesa Subphase elements that are associated with Periman roomblocks (EENs 7, 74, 76).

Village] oversized pitstructures [sic] are associated with unusually large interhousehold groups." On the basis of a survey from the whole DAP area for the Periman Subphase, Kane (1986b, 1988) argues that certain pit structures had special "managerial-ritual functions." This inference is based on the presence of floor vaults and also on the structures' size and association with large roomblocks (though not all the structures included in Kane's classification are exceptionally large).[1] Kane identifies pit structures with managerial-ritual functions at a number of sites, including Weasel Pueblo, Pueblo de las Golondrinas, and the pre–A.D. 880 occupation at Grass Mesa Village. Another classification of pit structures would include only those that are clearly oversized (greater than 60 m^2), have rectangular vaults and other ritual features but few obvious domestic features, and are found in larger settlements in U-shaped roomblocks that partially enclosed plazas (Kane 1986a:415). Pit Structure 9 at Pueblo de las Golondrinas fits these criteria. Blinman (Chapter 8, this volume) investigates the integrative functions of both these U-shaped roomblocks and the associated oversized pit structures. In this analysis, pit structures that are relatively large (though not necessarily greater than 60 m^2) and/or have floor vaults are considered to be community pit structures; they are included in my Category III, following Kane's classification. Community pit structure ceramic assemblages used here are from Weasel Pueblo and Pueblo de las Golondrinas and from the pre–A.D. 880 occupation at Grass Mesa Village.

Previous analyses of ceramics and their distribution—using criteria other than design style—support these classifications of pit structures based on size and ritual features. In the McPhee community, roomblocks that have pit structures with floor vaults (including Weasel Pueblo and Pueblo de las Golondrinas) have larger percentages of imported red wares than other roomblocks (Blinman and Wilson 1988). This could indicate control of imports at these locations and/or use of imports in special activities. U-shaped roomblocks with very large pit structures also stand out in terms of their ceramic assemblages (Blinman 1988 and this volume). U-shaped roomblocks have higher percentages of imported vessels—primarily bowls—including both red wares and white wares. Also, these sites have relatively few cooking jars and low jar-to-bowl ratios, and in some cases they have smaller jars than other sites. Thus Blinman concludes that food was being prepared at various locations and brought to the U-shaped roomblocks for consumption, a form of ceremonial hosting possibly resembling modern "potlucks."

Great Kivas are much larger than even the largest oversized pit structures and could constitute a fourth category of pit structures. However, because of a lack of adequate well-dated ceramic samples, Great Kivas are not included here. A Great Kiva was excavated at Grass Mesa Village, but it was constructed between A.D. 760 and 800 (Lightfoot 1988:253) and thus predates the period of interest here. An extremely large (769 m^2 floor area) unroofed Great Kiva was located in Singing Shelter (5MT4683) (Nelson and Kane 1986), near House Creek Village. Nelson and Kane (1986:923) argue that the Great Kiva was used during the Periman subphase (A.D. 840–910), but Kane (1988:415) says the "use of the structure could only be assigned an A.D. 800–900 bracket date." Other DAP researchers argue that the Singing Shelter Great Kiva was used prior to A.D. 840 (Orcutt and Blinman 1987). Few ceramics (including only four white ware sherds) were found in clear association with this Great Kiva.

In summary, in this paper I examine patterns of ceramic stylistic variation associated with different kinds of pit structures. I have divided the pit structures and associated ceramic assemblages into three categories (Table 1). Category I consists of household pit structures not associated with surface roomblocks, with no apparent integrative function above the household level. Category II includes interhousehold pit structures that served to integrate a small group of households. Category III consists of community pit structures that are relatively large and/or have floor vaults. These community pit structures were used by groups larger than interhousehold clusters and thus had larger-scale integrative functions.

Style

Southwestern archaeologists have long sought to relate style to prehistoric social organization. In a florescence of analyses since the 1960s they have focused on different aspects of style, including elements and combinations of elements (Longacre 1970), a hierarchy of attributes (Plog 1980), symmetry (Washburn 1977), and design schema (Jernigan 1986). One important development in recent work on style has been a reduction in the debate about *which* aspect is most important, and some agreement about the value of multivariate interpretations (see the exchange between Sackett [1985,1986]

---

[1] Kane (1986b:636) defines pit structures with floor areas greater than 34 m^2 as oversized. In all cases where their floor features were excavated, those oversized pit structures contained floor vaults. However, Kane notes that several smaller pit structures also have floor vaults, and based on Wilshusen's (1985) model, Kane (1986b:637) adopts floor vaults as the distinguishing characteristic of pit structures with managerial-ritual functions. The mean floor area of the McPhee Community pit structures that Kane (1988:46) classifies as having a managerial-ritual function is 41.5 m^2 and the smallest of these (Pit Structure 2 at Weasel Pueblo) is 24.3 m^2. The mean floor area for the Dolores and Duckfoot Pueblo I pit structures (not including Great Kivas) is 24.9 m^2 (Lipe, Chapter 5, this volume).

and Wiessner [1983,1984,1985]; also Kintigh [1985]; Plog [1987]). Thus, design attributes may provide information relevant to some problems, while design symmetry and structure or typological designations provide different kinds of information.

The Meaning of Style

A recent statement by Hodder (1987) emphasizes different levels not only of style, but of the meaning of an object. Hodder identifies three levels of meaning: use or function, structure, and historical content. I explore the first two levels here. The third would be important in understanding the presence of a 100-year-old heirloom pot in a modern pueblo.

The first level of meaning—use and function—has broad application. Ceramics containers are used—in integrative structures and elsewhere—to store various materials and to prepare, serve, and eat food. Ceramic style may also have a function in that it can carry information, such as information about social roles (Plog 1980, 1983; Wobst 1977). Such stylistic information can carry various meanings at different levels of specificity; thus, stylistic information is sometimes similar and sometimes quite dissimilar to information conveyed by human language. For example, the !Kung San use beadwork in part to establish their personal identities. The beadwork may imply that someone is innovative or conservative, but, unlike language, the designs convey few specific meanings (Wiessner 1984). In the now classic study that established the "information exchange" theory of stylistic variation, Wobst (1977) noted that Yugoslavian hat styles carried specific information about ethnic group affiliation. Finally, some designs carry very specific, often highly symbolic meanings; for example, the feather-like patterns on Zuni vessels serve as a sort of painted version of prayer sticks (Bunzel 1972:70).

Stylistic information is expected to be particularly important when there is a need to establish one's intentions or identity prior to, or in the absence of, verbal communication. Thus, stylistic information plays an important role in interactions with socially distant persons (Wobst 1977). Such interactions are fraught with potential uncertainty. As social distance increases, the persons interacting are closer to being strangers and increasingly do not know what to expect in a meeting. Stylistic information can reduce this uncertainty by establishing, for example, that a person is a prestigious and conservative member of a certain clan. The importance of style in reducing the uncertainty of socially distant persons' interactions is supported by various studies. Stylistic expression of group identities and ethnic boundaries increases at times of increased social tension (Hodder 1979; Wobst 1977). Self-decoration by New Guinea big men is most elaborate (varying among three dimensions) during the large gatherings that take place at major exchanges (Strathern and Strathern 1971). Layton (1981:101) argues that the self-decoration gives "tangible expression to the particular form of current relationships between groups."

The second level of meaning identified by Hodder involves structure. An "object has meaning because it is part of a code, set or structure" (1987:1); thus the object's meaning derives from its relationship with other objects. The structural meaning of style plays an important role in social relationships, since they are often structured in terms of comparisons and oppositions (Wiessner 1984). So, for example, !Kung beadwork both carries information about personal identity and helps to establish individual identity in relation to other individuals and their beadwork. Similarly, ethnic styles mark a person as a member of one group rather than another.

The structural meaning of style is also an important means of marking distinctions between different contexts, such as public vs. private or secular vs. ritual. Style can be used to mark the special nature of integrative activities, including religious ceremonies or other gatherings of socially distant persons. These activities tend to be distinctive in that they are formal and rule-bound. Religious ritual involves invariant and formal actions (Rappaport 1979:175). Furthermore, etiquette (a sort of ritualized social behavior) also demands increased formality in interactions with socially distant persons (Brown and Levinson 1978).

Measuring the Meaning

An object's two levels of meaning—the use and function, and the structural meaning—relate to different dimensions of stylistic variation that are expected to be associated with integrative activities. First, the function of style as a medium of information is argued to be particularly important in interactions with socially distant persons. Thus, stylistic information should be particularly important in integrative activities. One way of measuring the information content of style is with the information statistic, or H, which measures the amount of information that can be conveyed by a code (Shannon 1949). The H-statistic was developed for the technical study of communication channels; it measures how accurately symbols of communication can be transmitted and whether or not the symbols convey culturally meaningful information (Weaver 1949). The analyst must determine whether the measured quantity actually relates to meaningful information. Archaeologists have found the information statistic to be useful in studies of ceramic style (Braun 1985; Hegmon 1986; Pollock 1983) as well as studies of mortuary practices (e.g.,

Tainter 1978) and the nature of archaeological data (Justeson 1973).

The H-statistic is a measure of diversity, such as the diversity of states of a given attribute. H measures diversity as a function of the number of categories or states into which a sample is divided and the evenness of the distribution (Pielou 1969).

$$H = -\sum_{i=1}^{n} p_i \log p_i$$

where p_i is the fraction of observances of the ith state.

Thus, if there are four states of a given attribute, and the states occur with equal frequencies ($p_i = 0.25$), then $H = 0.60$. Somewhat paradoxically, the information statistic is also a measure of entropy and uncertainty; the greater the uncertainty, the more information is provided by the occurrence of a given state. That is, if only one state is possible, then the occurrence of that state provides no information; only if there is some uncertainty about which state will occur (e.g., if 10 states are possible) will the occurrence of a state provide information. Thus H measures the information that can be conveyed by a single occurrence.

Integrative activities, which involve ritual and interactions of socially distant persons, are structurally different from other activities; specifically, integrative activities tend to be more formal. Therefore, the style of material items associated with these activities should convey the formality of the occasion. Unfortunately, there is no convenient "formality statistic" archaeologists can use, but aspects of formality can be measured. First, increased formality should involve greater care in the execution of designs; thus, well-painted designs may indicate increased formality. Second, formality should involve careful adherence to the rules of design. Thus, if a design grammar can be developed or rules of design structure determined, the rules should be followed more strictly in formal contexts. A proxy measure of adherence to design rules can be developed by analyzing the states of stylistic attributes and the covariation of attributes (Plog 1987). That is, attributes may be simple or elaborate, but limited variation in the attribute states that are used and high covariation between attributes indicates strong adherence to rules and increased formality.

Now, let us return to Pueblo I pit structures. The second half of the ninth century was increasingly fraught with upheaval and uncertainty due to population migration, aggregation, and climatic changes. As the population moved in and out, there would have been a great deal of contact between socially distant persons and a need for integrative activities to reduce the social distances. Pit structures provided an important context for integrative activities, and the three categories of structures would have been associated with increasingly large-scale integrative activities involving increasing social distance between the participants. Category I household pit structures had no integrative function above the household level. Category II interhousehold pit structures integrated interhousehold clusters, and Category III community pit structures were associated with community or other larger scale integrative activities. The meaning of style and the measurable dimensions of that meaning—formality and information—can be related to the integrative activities and to social distance. More specific archaeological expectations for ceramic style can be developed, assuming that the frequency of ceramic breakage and discard in and around the pit structures is roughly proportional to the frequency of use.

First, if socially distant persons gathered—for ritual or other integrative activities—in certain pit structures, the ceramics used in those structures should have conveyed information that would help reduce the uncertainty inherent in such gatherings. These ceramics should exhibit increasing stylistic diversity as the social distance between the participants increased. Thus, stylistic information and design diversity should be greatest in ceramics associated with community pit structures, intermediate with interhousehold pit structures, and least with household pit structures. Second, if integrative activities took place in certain pit structures, the ceramics used in those structures would have been structurally distinctive, reflecting the distinctive nature of those activities. Integrative activities—involving a few households or people from across the region—might involve different degrees of formality in the occasions themselves and in the associated ceramics. Thus, the formality of design execution and rules should be greatest in ceramics associated with community pit structures, intermediate with interhousehold pit structures, and least with household pit structures.

The Analysis

The basic thrust of the analysis consists of comparisons of ceramic style associated with the three pit structure categories. Unfortunately, but not unexpectedly, few ceramics were found conveniently smashed on floors or otherwise unambiguously associated with the use of any particular structure. Therefore, the unit for most comparisons is the ceramic assemblage from an entire site—or, in the case of Grass Mesa Village, from a relatively well-defined portion of a site—that can be associated with a certain temporal period (modeling period in DAP terminology). For example, the sample from Weasel Pueblo, a site with a community pit structure, includes ceramics recovered from the pit structure itself as well as from midden deposits and surface rooms. The entire Weasel Pueblo sample is included as a Category III (community pit structure) assemblage.

More specifically, the data base consists of black-on-white ceramics—including sherds and more or less whole vessels—from seven DAP habitation sites and the Duckfoot Site (Table 1). The contextual interpretations of the DAP investigators were accepted, and samples from the DAP sites include all ceramics from relatively unmixed deposits (element integrity = 3 or 4) that could be assigned to a modelling period with a relatively high degree of confidence (modelling period confidence = 3 or 4). The samples from Grass Mesa Village were associated with specific occupational episodes (EENs, see Table 1); for the other DAP sites, whole site assemblages were used. The sample from the Duckfoot Site—which was almost completely excavated and had a much larger collection of black-on-white ceramics than any of the DAP sites—included all black-on-white ceramics associated with the pit structures and roomblock, and a random sample of the ceramics from the midden.

The analysis covers the time period from A.D. 840 to (at latest) 920, and the sample is divided into pre- and post–A.D. 880 spans (i.e., into DAP modeling periods 4 and 5). Chronological control is based on multiple criteria, including absolute dates, architectural style, and ceramic assemblages. Ceramic dating relies most heavily on the presence of certain gray ware types and on relative percentages of wares and tempers, rather than on black-on-white design styles; however, the presence of Cortez Black-on-White is one of the criteria used to determine post–A.D. 880 contexts (Blinman 1984). Therefore, in order to avoid circularity, ceramic style is not compared between time periods. Temporal breakdowns are retained to provide some control of contemporaneity for the ceramics that are grouped together in assemblages.

Most ceramics were probably produced locally, but non-local ceramics were not excluded from the analysis. This is because focus is on what people had, and on what they brought to or used in certain structures, regardless of where the ceramics were made.

As a basis for analysis, ceramic assemblages were grouped into three categories corresponding to the three categories of pit structures (Table 1). The ceramic sample from Grass Mesa Village is divided among all three categories, while the samples from other sites are placed exclusively in one. Ceramics associated with the household pit structures at Grass Mesa Village constitute the Category I sample. Ceramics associated with interhousehold pit structures from the post–A.D. 880 occupation at Grass Mesa Village and from the Duckfoot Site, Prince Hamlet, House Creek Pueblo, Aldea Alfareros, and Golondrinas Oriental (all of which have interhousehold pit structures but no community pit structures) are included in the Category II sample. The Category III sample includes ceramics from sites or occupations that have community pit structures, including the MP 4 occupation at Grass Mesa Village and the occupations at Weasel Pueblo and Pueblo de las Golondrinas.

Coding

The analysis is based on a system of coding designed to take advantage of information on both sherds and vessels.[2] In addition to vessel form and technological variables such as paint type and surface finish, the coding system includes variables of design neatness, primary and secondary forms, composition, and line state; these are described below. In addition to these four sets of variables, aspects of overall design structure and symmetry were recorded, but the small number of large fragments and whole vessels was insufficient to permit further analysis of structure and symmetry.

(1) The neatness of design execution was coded by analyzing the straightness of edges and the quality of fill in solid areas. Five categorical states of neatness were developed, ranging from designs that had gaps in solid areas and edges with frequent deviations greater than 1 mm (score = 1) to fully solid designs with ruler-straight edges (score = 5) (Figure 1).

(2) Primary and secondary forms such as primary triangles and lines or secondary ticks on a line were analyzed, using a modified version of the system developed for analysis of Black Mesa ceramics (Plog and Hantman 1986) (Figure 2).

(3) Composition refers to how areas are filled, for example with solids or hachure (Figure 2).

(4) The state of primary lines includes measurements of median line widths to the nearest millimeter (or to the nearest 0.5 mm for lines less than 3 mm in width) and categorical variables describing whether the lines are straight, curved, bent at right angles, or bent diagonally (Figure 2).

The unit of coding was the vessel, though many vessels were represented by only single sherds. Prior to coding, the collections were analyzed for refits, and sherds that were obviously part of the same vessel were grouped together as a single case.

---

[2] The coding system was developed for the ceramics from the DAP sites, which were discussed in the version of this paper presented in the symposium at the 1988 Society for American Archaeology meetings. The sample from the Duckfoot Site was subsequently added to the analysis, using an abbreviated coding system that included only those variables that had provided useful information on the DAP ceramics.

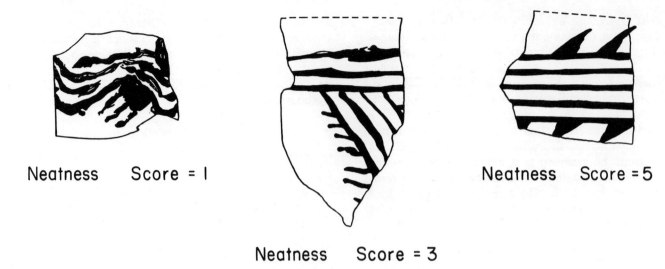

Figure 1: Design neatness examples. Scores are judged on the basis of gaps in solid areas and straightness of lines. Scores range from 1 to 5: the neatest is 5.

Attributes	Attribute States			
Primary Forms	Single/double lines	Multiple lines	Checks	4-sided figures
	Terraces	Scrolls	Dots	Triangles
Secondary Forms	Ticks	RR tracks	V's	Hooks
	T's	Triangles		
Composition	Single/double lines	Multiple lines	Solid	Hachure
	Dots/dashes	Z's		

Figure 2: Attributes used in information statistics.

Information

Ceramics used in activities that involve socially distant persons are expected to convey information that can help to reduce the uncertainty of those relationships. The amount of information that can be conveyed by designs on ceramics is quantified with the information statistic (Shannon 1949), which provides a measure of design diversity. Focus here is on the diversity of states of a given attribute—for example, a primary form could be a single line, triangle, terrace, scroll, etc.—rather than on how the attribute is used in the overall design.

Designs on bowls and jars cannot be assumed to be the same, if only because the decorative fields are different (Plog 1980). Therefore, the designs on these different vessel forms should be separated in analysis. Because the sample of painted white wares included many more bowls than jars, and because Blinman's (1988 and this volume) work suggests that bowls might be particularly important in integrative activities, only bowls were included in this portion of the analysis.

The information statistic was used to measure the diversity of three kinds of attributes: (1) primary forms, (2) secondary forms, and (3) composition (Figure 2).[3] The statistics were calculated to determine the potential information content of assemblages, that is, the ceramics from a temporal period on a site or a portion of a site. The sample sizes and information statistics are given in Table 2.

Assemblage sizes from the various contexts differ, and not every variable could be coded for each vessel or sherd. As a result, the sample sizes (N) for the H-statistics differ between assemblages and between the various forms of the statistic. The H-statistic is a measure of the amount of information that can be conveyed by a *single* occurrence (i.e., a design on one vessel), and the statistic is calculated using percentages rather than raw frequencies. Therefore, H-statistic measures of diversity should be independent of sample size, at least with the ideal case of very large samples. However, in less than ideal cases sample size may affect the H-statistic. To examine the relationship, the correlation between H-values and sample size were examined for the three versions of the H-statistics. The correlation coefficients range from -0.29 to 0.58, and none are statistically significant at an 0.05 confidence level (Table 2).

Information statistics from assemblages associated with different kinds of integrative structures can be compared across the three categories of pit structures using two techniques of comparison. First, comparisons can be based on the mean value for each category (Table 3a). Unfortunately, given the small numbers of samples from each category, statistical significance cannot be demonstrated for the differences between categories. The second comparative technique provides some control for possible temporal differences in the information statistic, differences that might be caused by a general increase in stylistic elaboration over time. Information statistics are first averaged across all the assemblages in each time period (A.D. 840–880 and A.D. 880–910/920, Table 3b). Then the H-values for each assemblage are compared to the average value for the given time period (Table 3c).

When information statistics from Category II and III assemblages are compared, there is a small but consistent difference (Figure 3). Assemblages associated with community pit structures and larger-scale integration (Category III) have larger average H values for all three forms of the information statistic (Table 3c). Also, Category III assemblages tend to have H values above the period means (eight above, two below), and Category II assemblages tend to have H values below the period means (ten below, four above, Table 3c). The trend is consistent across all three measures: Category III assemblages exhibit more stylistic diversity. Thus, I argue that more information was conveyed by ceramic style in contexts associated with larger-scale integrative architecture.

Information statistics from the Category I assemblage (household pit structures) do not fit the picture as neatly. Category I H values are greater than the average values of both other categories and than the average values for the post–A.D. 880 period. Category I includes assemblages from the Grass Mesa Subphase, a time of probable increased mobility just prior to abandonment of the area. Lipe et al. (1988) suggest that the household pit structures may have been occupied by settlers from other sites moving into the Grass Mesa community. The trend toward increased information in the ceramic designs of this period may indicate that there was a great deal of uncertainty and contact with socially distant persons, even in contexts with no clear-cut integrative structures.[4]

Formality

Integrative activities that involve ritual and/or socially distant persons are expected to be more formal than other activities. Ceramics used in these contexts are

---

[3] Information statistics were also calculated using several sets of categorical states of the line width measurements. The H-statistics for line widths showed no consistent differences between the different kinds of assemblages, so they are not included in subsequent analyses.

[4] No patterned differences were noted in the stylistic attributes that were present on different sites. Therefore, it is unlikely that the increase in design diversity during this period of increased mobility is a result of the mixing of local traditions.

Table 2: Information statistics and sample sizes.

Category	Site (Context)	MP	Primary forms N	Primary forms H	Secondary forms N	Secondary forms H	Composition N	Composition H
I	Grass Mesa Village (GM Subphase)	5	14	0.54	3	-	17	0.52
II	Grass Mesa Village (Periman Subphase)	5	21	0.50	6	0.38	27	0.49
II	Prince Hamlet	4	2	-	1	-	5	0.46
II	Prince Hamlet	5	3	-	1	-	4	0.45
II	House Creek Village	4	6	0.44	1	-	13	0.40
II	Aldea Alfareros	4	55	0.40	21	0.69	71	0.53
II	Golondrinas Orient.	5	18	0.41	7	0.26	21	0.44
II	Duckfoot	4	110	0.43	19	0.56	185	0.51
III	Grass Mesa	4	18	0.47	7	0.67	36	0.51
III	Weasel Pueblo	5	30	0.48	10	0.52	36	0.52
III	Pueblo de las Golondrinas	4	6	0.44	2	-	10	0.45
III	Pueblo de las Golondrinas	5	37	0.51	10	0.41	42	0.50
	H–N correlation		-0.29		0.58		0.46	
	R@ 0.05 probability		0.63		0.75		0.58	

also expected to be more formal. One aspect of formality is expressed in the way painted designs are executed, and the neatness of the designs is here used as a proxy measure of overall execution. Neatness was judged on the straightness of edges and on gaps in painted solids (Figure 1).[5]

The analysis of neatness included all vessel forms. The frequencies of scores for the ceramics associated with the three categories of pit structures are shown in Table 4. Both categories II and III (interhousehold and community pit structures) include a full range of neatness scores, and the distribution of neatness scores is not significantly different between the two categories ($x^2 = 1.1$, df = 4). However, the Category I ceramics (household pit structures) tend to be less neat than ceramics from other contexts (Table 5), and a Chi-squared test (although not technically valid because of the small expected frequencies[6]) suggests that the difference is significant. Perhaps more importantly, there are no very neat ceramics in the Category I assemblage. These results must be seen as tentative, given the small size of the Category I assemblage. However, they suggest that highly formalized (very neat) ceramics are associated with all kinds of integrative structures (interhousehold and community pit structures), but that the very neat ceramics are absent when these structures are also absent.

---

[5] Organic paint generally creates less crisp ceramic designs than mineral paint, because more of the organic paint is absorbed into the clay. However, in the sample of DAP ceramics, only three percent had exclusively organic paint, and the neatness scores associated with organic paint were not significantly different from scores associated with mineral paint in an organic binder ($x^2 = 3.28$, df=4).

[6] According to Siegel (1956:110), the Chi-squared test should be used with contingency tables larger than two-by-two only if fewer than 20 percent of the cells have expected frequencies of less than 5. Other nonparametric tests (including the Mann-Whitney U and the Kolmogorov-Smirnov tests) could technically be used with these samples, but these tests compare the overall distributions of scores (based on ranks or cumulative frequency curves). Therefore, these tests would not be highly sensitive to the absence of certain scores in a category, a very important factor in this analysis.

Table 3: Information statistics compared across categories.

Table 3a: Average values of information statistics by category.

Category	Primary forms N	Primary forms Mean H	Secondary forms N	Secondary forms Mean H	Composition N	Composition Mean H
I	1	0.54	1	–	1	0.52
II	5	0.44	4	0.47	7	0.47
III	4	0.48	3	0.53	4	0.50

Table 3b: Average values of information statistics by time period.

Period	Primary forms N	Primary forms Mean H	Secondary forms N	Secondary forms Mean H	Composition N	Composition Mean H
A.D. 840—880 (MP4)	5	0.44	3	0.64	6	0.48
A.D. 880—910/920 (MP5)	5	0.49	4	0.39	6	0.49

Table 3c: Assemblage information statistics in relation to period means.

Category	Site Assemblage	MP	Primary forms	Secondary forms	Composition
I	Grass Mesa Village (GM Subphase)	5	>	–	>
II	Grass Mesa Village (Periman Subphase)	5	>	<	=
II	Prince Hamlet	4	–	–	<
II	Prince Hamlet	5	–	–	<
II	House Creek Village	4	=	–	<
II	Aldea Alfareros	4	<	>	>
II	Golondrinas Oriental	5	<	<	<
II	Duckfoot	4	<	<	>
III	Grass Mesa Village	4	>	>	>
III	Weasel Pueblo	5	<	>	>
III	Pueblo de las Golondrinas	4	=	–	<
III	Pueblo de las Golondrinas	5	>	>	>

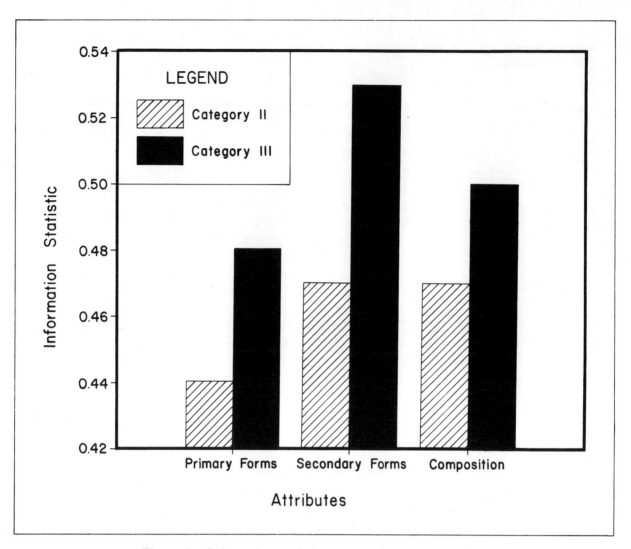

Figure 3: Information statistics compared across categories.

Table 4: Neatness scores by category.

	Neatness Scores				
	← least neat				neatest →
Category	1	2	3	4	5
I	1	3	0	11	0
II	15	29	65	167	37
III	9	10	27	66	13

A second aspect of formality involves the rules of design. Adherence to rules is stricter in more formal situations. Probably the best way to study the rules of design would be with an analysis of overall design structure. However, such an analysis was not possible in this study because of the small sample of large sherds and whole vessels.

An alternative means of examining the rules of design is through an analysis of the covariation of attributes (Plog 1987). Such an analysis was attempted,

Table 5: Comparison of neatness scores.

	Neatness Scores				
	← least neat				neatest →
Category	1	2	3	4	5
I	1	3	0	11	0
(expected)	(1)	(1)	(3)	(8)	(2)
II & III	24	39	92	233	50
(expected)	(24)	(41)	(89)	(236)	(48)

$x^2 = 10.44$, df = 4

significant at between 0.05 and 0.025 (see footnote 6)

again using only bowl designs. However, Pueblo I types are so homogeneous that many attributes covaried almost perfectly, and there were no differences in covariation that could be interpreted. For example, the dominant type —Piedra Black-on-white— is characterized by series of triangles arranged on series of multiple parallel lines. Thus, no differences in the formality of design rules associated with integrative activities could be evaluated.

Summary and Conclusions

The goal of this research has been to explore the relationship between ceramic style and the integrative activities that took place in association with integrative architecture—specifically, various kinds of pit structures. The study covered the late Pueblo I period in Southwestern Colorado and focused on the style of painted designs on black-on-white ceramics.

As a basis for comparison, ceramic assemblages were grouped into three categories, associated with categories of pit structures argued to have had different integrative functions. Category I included household pit structures that had no integrative function above the household level. Category II included pit structures that were shared by several households and thus integrated an interhousehold group. Category III community pit structures were larger and/or had special ritual features and thus are argued to have had larger-scale integrative functions.

Integrative activities that took place in these pit structures involved at least two components relevant to an understanding of ceramic style. That is, these activities brought together socially distant persons and included ritual. These components can be related to the use and the structure of style. First, style can be used to convey information, and such information will be particularly important in interactions among socially distant persons. Second, religious ritual and also general social etiquette among socially distant persons both involve formalized behavior. Style used in these contexts should also be more formal than—and thus structurally different from—style used in other settings.

The potential use of style to convey information was determined with the information or H-statistic, which measures the diversity of design attributes. Category III (community pit structures) assemblages had larger information statistics than Category II (interhousehold pit structures) assemblages, as would be expected if more socially distant persons gathered at the larger scale integrative activities. However, Category I (household pit structures) assemblages had the largest values for the information statistic. The results for Category I suggest that there was a large role for information during the occupation of these pit structures—a period of increased mobility and possible upheaval just prior to the abandonment of the area.

The analysis of the H-statistic indicates that stylistic information does not vary directly with the scale of integrative architecture. Instead, stylistic information was greatest in situations that involved a great deal of uncertainty, including both large-scale integrative activities (Category III) and times of upheaval when there is little evidence of integrative architecture (Category I). A similar analysis of stylistic information on Pueblo II ceramics from Black Mesa suggested that an increase in stylistic information several decades prior to the abandonment of the area was related to an increase in social integration at that time, perhaps involving more tightly knit social networks that drew together socially distant persons (Hegmon 1986).

Stylistic information is argued to provide a means of establishing one's individual identity, social status, and/or ethnic affiliation. Such information plays an important role in social relationships, particularly relationships between socially distant persons. Relationships between socially distant persons—and thus stylistic information—will be important in a variety of social situations, including general increases in integration, large-scale integrative activities, and times of upheaval.

The formality of style should be expressed in both the manner of design execution and in adherence to the rules of design. Because of the relative homogeneity of Pueblo I ceramics and the small sample of large sherds and vessels available for study, analysis of the formality of rules yielded no meaningful conclusions. However, the neatness of the painted designs was analyzed as a measure of design execution and an aspect of formality. Category II and III ceramics were not significantly different in terms of neatness. However, Category I ceramics were less neat than ceramics from the other categories, and Category I included no very neat (i.e., highly formalized) ceramics. These results indicate that formalized ceramics are associated with formal activities (ritual and etiquette) in integrative structures, and that the formality does not vary with the scale of the activities. Formalized ceramics are not used in contexts that lack these architectural indicators of formalized integrative activities.

To conclude, the results of this study indicate that patterns of variation in ceramic style are associated with different kinds of integrative structures. The study was an exploratory effort, and the results should be viewed as preliminary, but they do offer some promise. Studies of stylistic variation in ceramics associated with various architectural contexts can provide a better understanding of the role of style in the activities that occurred in those contexts. Conversely, style can be used in functional interpretation of certain contexts.

The method may be especially promising when large samples of whole vessels are available and in later periods when differences between contexts (e.g., "ceremonial center" vs. small habitation sites) are more pronounced.

Acknowledgment

I never worked on the Dolores Archaeological Program and saw only a few short weeks of excavation at the Duckfoot Site, but working with the material from these projects has been a real pleasure, thanks to the well-organized collections and to many extraordinarily helpful people. The Anasazi Heritage Center (which houses the DAP material) and the Crow Canyon Archaeological Center allowed me generous use of their facilities and access to the material. Victoria Atkins, Shela McFarlin, Steve Harmon and Margo Surovik-Bohnert at the AHC and Mary Etzkorn, Ricky Lightfoot, and Angela Schwab at Crow Canyon provided a tremendous amount of help in working with the collections, far beyond the call of duty. Many Crow Canyon and former DAP staff members—Eric Blinman, Tim Kohler, Ricky Lightfoot, Bill Lipe, Mark Varien, Richard Wilshusen—gave generously of their time, ideas, books, and manuscripts.

Bill Lipe, Steve Plog and Richard Wilshusen helped me develop the stylistic analysis and some of the ideas that are examined in this paper. Mike Adler, David Breternitz, Tim Kohler, Karin Jones, Bill Lipe and Carla Sinopoli contributed ideas and comments on drafts of this paper. Teryl Lynn prepared Figure 1.

This research was supported by grants from the Rackham School of Graduate Studies and the Museum of Anthropology's James B. Griffin Fund, both of the University of Michigan.

References

Adams, E. Charles
    1984 *Preliminary Report of Work Accomplished During 1983 Under State Permit Nos. 83-8 and 83-9.* Ms. on file, State Archaeologist's Office, Colorado Historical Society, Denver.

Blinman, Eric
    1984 *Dolores Archaeological Program Ceramic Dating: Justification and Procedures.* Technical Reports DAP-144. Dolores Archaeological Program, Dolores, Colorado. Final draft submitted to the Bureau of Reclamation, Upper Colorado Region, Salt Lake City, Contract No. 8-07-40-S0562.

    1988 *The Interpretation of Ceramic Variability: A Case Study from the Dolores Anasazi.* Unpublished Ph.D. dissertation, Department of Anthropology, Washington State University, Pullman.

Blinman, Eric and C. Dean Wilson
    1988 Ceramic Data and Interpretations: The McPhee Community Cluster. In *Dolores Archaeological Program: Anasazi Communities at Dolores: McPhee Village,* compiled by A. E. Kane and C. K. Robinson, pp. 1295-1344. Bureau of Reclamation, Engineering and Research Center, Denver.

Braithwaite, Mary
    1982 Decoration as Ritual Symbol: A Theoretical Proposal and an Ethnographic Study in Southern Sudan. In *Symbolic and Structural Archaeology,* edited by I. Hodder, pp. 80-88. Cambridge University Press, Cambridge.

Braun, David P.
    1985 Ceramic Decorative Diversity and Illinois Woodland Regional Integration. In *Decoding Prehistoric Ceramics,* edited by Ben A. Nelson, pp. 128-153. Southern Illinois University Press, Carbondale.

Brisbin, Joel M.
    1988 Excavations at Pueblo de las Golondrinas (Site 5MT5107), a Multiple-Occupation Pueblo I Site. In *Dolores Archaeological Program: Anasazi Communities at Dolores: McPhee Village,* compiled by A. E. Kane and C. K. Robinson, pp. 791-908. Bureau of Reclamation, Engineering and Research Center, Denver.

Brown, Penelope and Stephen Levinson
    1978 Universals in Language Usage: Politeness Phenomena. In *Questions and Politeness: Strategies in Social Interaction,* edited by E. N. Goody, pp. 56-289. Cambridge University Press, Cambridge.

Bunzel, Ruth
    1972 *The Pueblo Potter: A Study of Creative Imagination in Primitive Art.* Reprinted by Dover Publications, New York. Originally published 1929, Columbia University Press, New York.

Deetz, James
    1972 *In Small Things Forgotten.* Anchor Books, Garden City, New Jersey.

Durkheim, Emile
    1965 *The Elementary Forms of the Religious Life.* Translated by J. W. Swain. Collier Books, New York. Originally published 1915, George Allen and Unwin, Ltd., New York. Originally published 1912.

Ford, Richard I.
1972 An Ecological Perspective on the Eastern Pueblos. In *New Perspectives on the Pueblos,* edited by A. Ortiz, pp. 1-17. University of New Mexico Press, Albuquerque.

Hardin, Margaret Ann
1983 *Gifts of Mother Earth: Ceramics in the Zuni Tradition.* Heard Museum, Phoenix.

Hegmon, Michelle
1986 Information Exchange and Integration on Black Mesa, Arizona, A.D. 931–1150. In *Spatial Organization and Exchange: Archaeological Survey on Northern Black Mesa,* edited by S. Plog, pp. 256-281. Southern Illinois University Press, Carbondale.

Hodder, Ian
1987 The Contextual Analysis of Symbolic Meanings. In *The Archaeology of Contextual Meanings,* edited by I. Hodder, pp. 1-10. Cambridge University Press, Cambridge.

1979 Economic and Social Stress and Material Culture Patterning. *American Antiquity* 44:446-454.

Jernigan, E. Wesley
1986 A Non-Hierarchical Approach to Ceramic Decoration Analysis: A Southwestern Example. *American Antiquity* 51:3-20.

Justeson, John S.
1973 Limitations of Archaeological Inference: An Information-Theoretic Approach with Applications in Methodology. *American Antiquity* 38:131-149.

Kane, Allen E.
1988 McPhee Community Cluster Introduction. In *Dolores Archaeological Program: Anasazi Communities at Dolores: McPhee Village,* compiled by A. E. Kane and C. K. Robinson, pp. 4-62. Bureau of Reclamation, Engineering and Research Center, Denver.

1986a Prehistory of the Dolores River Valley. In *Dolores Archaeological Program: Final Synthetic Report,* compiled by D. A. Breternitz et al., pp. 353-435. Bureau of Reclamation, Engineering and Research Center, Denver.

1986b Social Organization and Cultural Process in Dolores Anasazi Communities, A.D. 600–900. In *Dolores Archaeological Program: Final Synthetic Report,* compiled by D. A. Breternitz et al., pp. 634-662. Bureau of Reclamation, Engineering and Research Center, Denver.

Kintigh, Keith W.
1985 Social Structure, the Structure of Style, and Stylistic Patterns in Cibola Pottery. In *Decoding Prehistoric Ceramics,* edited by Ben A. Nelson, pp. 35-74. Southern Illinois University Press, Carbondale.

Kleidon, James H.
1988 Excavations at Aldea Alfareros (Site 5MT4479), a Pueblo I Habitation Site. In *Dolores Archaeological Program: Anasazi Communities at Dolores: McPhee Village,* compiled by A. E. Kane and C. K. Robinson, pp. 559-664. Bureau of Reclamation, Engineering and Research Center, Denver.

Kuckelman, Kristin A.
1988 Excavations at Golondrinas Oriental (Site 5MT5108), a Pueblo I Hamlet. In *Dolores Archaeological Program: Anasazi Communities at Dolores: McPhee Village,* compiled by A. E. Kane and C. K. Robinson, pp. 909-988. Bureau of Reclamation, Engineering and Research Center, Denver.

Layton, Robert
1981 *The Anthropology of Art.* Columbia University Press, New York.

Lightfoot, Ricky R.
1988 Roofing an Early Anasazi Great Kiva: Analysis of an Architectural Model. *The Kiva* 53:253-272.

1987 *Annual Report of Investigations at the Duckfoot Site (5MT3868), Montezuma County, Colorado.* Crow Canyon Archaeological Center, Cortez, Colorado. Report submitted to Office of the State Archaeologist, Colorado Historical Society, Denver.

1985 *Report of 1984 Investigations Conducted Under State Permit 84-15.* Crow Canyon Archaeological Center, Cortez, Colorado. Report submitted to the Office of the State Archaeologist, Colorado Historical Society, Denver.

Lightfoot, Ricky R. and Carla Van West
1986 *Excavation and Testing Conducted on Private Land Under State Permit 85-22.* Crow Canyon Archaeological Center, Cortez, Colorado. Report submitted to the Office of the State Archaeologist, Colorado Historical Society, Denver.

Lightfoot, Ricky R. and Mark D. Varien
   1988   Report of 1987 Archaeological Investigations at the Duckfoot Site (5MT3868), Montezuma County, Colorado. Ms. on file, Crow Canyon Archaeological Center, Cortez, Colorado.

Lipe, William D., James N. Morris and Timothy A. Kohler, compilers
   1988   *Dolores Archaeological Program: Anasazi Communities at Dolores: Grass Mesa Village (Site 5MT0023)*. Bureau of Reclamation, Engineering and Research Center, Denver.

Longacre, William A.
   1970   *Archaeology as Anthropology: A Case Study*. Anthropological Papers of the University of Arizona No. 17. Tucson.

Morris, James N.
   1988   Excavations at Weasel Pueblo (Site 5MT5106), a Pueblo I– Pueblo III Multiple-Occupation Site. In *Dolores Archaeological Program: Anasazi Communities at Dolores: McPhee Village,* compiled by A. E. Kane and C. K. Robinson, pp. 909-988. Bureau of Reclamation, Engineering and Research Center, Denver.

Nelson, G. Charles and Allen E. Kane
   1986   Excavations at Singing Shelter (5MT4683), a Multicomponent Site. In *Dolores Archaeological Program: Anasazi Communities at Dolores: Middle Canyon Area,* compiled by A. E. Kane and C. K. Robinson, pp. 859-1050. Bureau of Reclamation, Engineering and Research Center, Denver.

Neitzel, Jill
   1985   Regional Styles and Organizational Hierarchies: The View from Chaco Canyon. Paper presented at the 50th Annual Meeting of the Society for American Archaeology, Denver.

Orcutt, Janet D. and Eric Blinman
   1987   Leadership and the Development of Social Complexity: A Case Study from the Dolores Area of the American Southwest. Ms. in possession of authors, Santa Fe, New Mexico.

Pielou, E. C.
   1969   *An Introduction to Mathematical Ecology*. John Wiley, New York.

Plog, Stephen
   1987   Sociopolitical Implications of Southwestern Stylistic Variation. In *The Use of Style in Archaeology,* edited by M. Conkey and C. Hastorf. Cambridge University Press, Cambridge, in press.

   1983   Analysis of Style in Artifacts. *Annual Review of Anthropology* 12:125-142.

   1980   *Stylistic Variation in Prehistoric Ceramics*. Cambridge University Press, Cambridge.

Plog, Stephen and Jeffrey L. Hantman
   1986   Multiple Regression Analysis as a Dating Method in the American Southwest. In *Spatial Organization and Exchange: Archaeological Survey on Northern Black Mesa,* edited by S. Plog, pp. 87-113. Southern Illinois University Press, Carbondale.

Pollock, Susan
   1983   Style and Information: An Analysis of Susiana Ceramics. *Journal of Anthropological Archaeology* 2:354-390.

Prudden, T. Mitchell
   1903   The Prehistoric Ruins of the San Juan Watershed in Utah, Arizona, Colorado and New Mexico. *American Anthropologist,* n.s., 5:224-288.

Prufer, Olaf H.
   1965   *The McGraw Site: A Study in Hopewellian Dynamics*. Cleveland Museum of Natural History, Cleveland, Ohio.

Rappaport, Roy A.
   1979   *Ecology, Meaning and Religion*. North Atlantic Books, Richmond, California.

   1971   Ritual, Sanctity and Cybernetics. *American Anthropologist* 73:59-76.

Robinson, Christine K. and Joel M. Brisbin
   1986   Excavations at House Creek Village (Site 5MT2320), a Pueblo I Habitation. In *Dolores Archaeological Program: Anasazi Communities at Dolores: Middle Canyon Area,* compiled by A. E. Kane and C. K. Robinson, pp. 661-858. Bureau of Reclamation, Engineering and Research Center, Denver.

Rohn, Arthur
   1971   *Mug House, Mesa Verde National Park, Colorado*. National Park Service Archeological Series No. 7-D. Washington, D.C.

Sackett, James R.
   1985   Style and Ethnicity in the Kalahari: A Reply to Wiessner. *American Antiquity* 50(1):154-159.

   1986   Isochrestism and Style: A Clarification. *Journal of Anthropological Archaeology* 5:266-277.

Schlanger, Sarah H.
    1986   Population Studies. In *Dolores Archaeological Program: Final Synthetic Report,* compiled by D. A. Breternitz et al., pp. 493-524. Bureau of Reclamation, Engineering and Research Center, Denver.

Sears, William
    1973   The Sacred and Secular in Prehistoric Ceramics. In *Variations in Anthropology: Essays in Honor of John McGregor,* edited by D. Lathrap and J. Douglas, pp. 31–42. Illinois Archaeological Survey, Urbana.

Sebastian, Lynne
    1986   Excavations at Prince Hamlet (Site 5MT2161), a Pueblo I Habitation Site. In *Dolores Archaeological Program: Anasazi Communities at Dolores: Early Small Settlements in the Dolores River Canyon and Western Sagehen Flats Area,* compiled by T. A. Kohler et al. Bureau of Reclamation, Engineering and Research Center, Denver.

Shannon, Claude E.
    1949   The Mathematical Theory of Communication. In *The Mathematical Theory of Communication,* by C. E. Shannon and W. E. Weaver, pp. 1-91. University of Illinois Press, Urbana.

Siegel, Sidney
    1956   *Nonparametric Statistics for the Behavioral Scientist.* McGraw-Hill Book Co., New York.

Strathern, Andrew and Marilyn Strathern
    1971   *Self-decoration in Mount Hagen.* Duckworth, London.

Tainter, Joseph A.
    1978   Mortuary Practices and the Study of Prehistoric Social Systems. *Advances in Archaeological Method and Theory,* vol. 1, edited by Michael B. Schiffer, pp. 241-295. Academic Press, New York.

Toll, H. Wolcott, III
    1985   *Pottery, Production, Public Architecture and the Chaco Anasazi System.* Ph.D. dissertation, University of Colorado, Boulder. University Microfilms, Ann Arbor.

Upham, Steadman, Kent G. Lightfoot and Gary M. Feinman
    1981   Explaining Socially Determined Ceramic Distributions in the Prehistoric Plateau Southwest. *American Antiquity* 46(4):822-832.

Wallace, Anthony F. C.
    1966   *Religion: An Anthropological View.* Random House, New York.

Washburn, Dorothy K.
    1977   *A Symmetry Analysis of Upper Gila Area Ceramic Design.* Papers of the Peabody Museum of Archaeology and Ethnology, vol. 68. Harvard University, Cambridge, Massachusetts.

Weaver, Warren E.
    1949   Recent Contributions to the Mathematical Theory of Communication. In *The Mathematical Theory of Communication,* by C. E. Shannon and W. E. Weaver, pp. 93-117. University of Illinois Press, Urbana.

Wiessner, Polly
    1983   Style and Social Information in Kalahari San Projectile Points. *American Antiquity* 48:253-276.

    1984   Reconsidering the Behavioral Basis for Style: A Case Study Among the Kalahari San. *Journal of Anthropological Archaeology* 3(3):190-234.

    1985   Style or Isochrestic Variation? A Reply to Sackett. *American Antiquity* 50(1):160-166.

Wilshusen, Richard
    1985   *Sipapus, Ceremonial Vaults, and Foot Drums (or a Resounding Argument for Protokivas).* Technical Reports DAP-278. Final draft submitted to Bureau of Reclamation, Upper Colorado Region, Salt Lake City, Contract No. 8-07-40-S0562.

Windes, Thomas C.
    1984   A View of the Cibola Whiteware from Chaco Canyon. In *Regional Analysis of Prehistoric Ceramic Variation: Contemporary Studies of the Cibola Whitewares,* edited by Alan P. Sullivan and Jeffrey L. Hantman, pp. 94-119. Anthropological Research Papers No. 31. Arizona State University, Tempe.

Wobst, H. Martin
    1977   Stylistic Behavior and Information Exchange. In *Papers for the Director: Research Essays in Honor of James B. Griffin,* edited by C. E. Cleland, pp. 317-342. Anthropological Papers No. 61. Museum of Anthropology, University of Michigan, Ann Arbor.

10
Ritual, Exchange, and the Development of Regional Systems

Stephen Plog

The importance of ritual in integrating Southwestern societies has long been recognized. From Steward's study of room-to-kiva ratios to more recent analyses, archaeologists have examined the frequency of ceremonial or ritual structures to infer aspects of community organization. The importance of ritual in the initial development of larger regional networks of exchange and alliance has been less frequently addressed. Theoretical and empirical studies are summarized which suggest that an association between ritual and regional networks was an important component of the development of agricultural villages. This association is then tested, using archaeological information from a large survey area on northern Black Mesa in northeastern Arizona.

The importance of ritual structures in understanding the nature of community organization in the prehistoric American Southwest has been clear for several decades. Beginning at least as early as Julian Steward's (1937) study of room-to-kiva ratios as a means of inferring the development of lineage and clan organization, Southwestern archaeologists have continued to examine information on the frequency and location of ritual structures. While the kinds of conclusions reached from such analyses have varied, a common goal has been to draw inferences about the nature of organizational units, whether within communities—following Steward's analysis—or among a limited set of communities in a locality, as in Longacre's (1964:167) discussion of Great Kiva distributions in the Hay Hollow Valley. Assessments of the degree of "integration" within and among communities has been another common goal of such studies.

Although many questions still remain about the accuracy of some of these inferences, few would disagree that an understanding of ritual—and therefore structures built for ritual activities—is a key aspect of understanding local organization. It is much less common, however, to study ritual structures as a way to understand relationships on a regional scale. The excellent analysis of Hohokam ballcourts by Wilcox and Sternberg (1983) is one noteworthy exception. Research on the distribution of Great Kivas, outliers, and roads in the Chaco region (e.g., Powers et al. 1983; Marshall et al. 1979) could be considered another, depending on whether one accepts interpretations of these features as ritual phenomena. Such regional studies are, however, almost exclusively confined to areas comparable to Chaco, Casas Grandes, and the Hohokam core, where most would agree that social patterns and relationships were more complex than in the typical Southwestern region. The importance of relationships among rituals, ritual structures, and regional social ties in more typical areas, where population densities and aggregates never reached the levels of a Chaco Canyon, has received much less attention. In the remainder of this paper, I will argue that such relationships are important to understanding the nature of prehistoric societies throughout the Southwest, even in regions often characterized as marginal or peripheral. I will first consider this issue from a more general, theoretical perspective, and will then present a summary of data from one section of the northern Southwest.

Villages, Sedentism, and Social Relationships

The following discussion will concentrate on social relationships during and after the evolution of villages in which domesticated plants are an important component—and often the most important component—of the diet. Villages, sedentism, and significant dependence on agriculture are clearly independent when one considers cross-cultural evidence (Flannery 1972:24), but in the northern Southwest they appear to be strongly interdependent. The term "village" is used as a shortened version of Flannery's (1972:38-39) "village of rectangular houses"—settlements also characterized by dwellings "designed to accommodate families rather than individuals," storage facilities associated with each dwelling, rectangular ground plans that allow rooms to be added or subtracted easily, and social institutions that crosscut kinship (see also Braun and Plog 1982).

I have argued that in the northern Southwest a variety of processes involving the "coevolution" (Braun 1987; O'Brien 1987) of technology (e.g., increased use of ceramic containers), ritual, ideology, and socioeconomic ties were necessary for the evolution of villages (S. Plog 1988b; see also LeBlanc 1982). These processes explain the gap of several centuries between the initial use of cultigens by groups in the northern Southwest and the common appearance of villages. Some of these processes will be discussed below. Although there are differences of opinion concerning when villages developed, current evidence suggests that in most areas they appeared between approximately A.D. 500 and 1050. It is always somewhat arbitrary, however, to identify beginning or ending points for what was clearly a set of long-term processes.

Given my focus on village life, it is important to emphasize a fundamental point often neglected in such discussions. Although we have considerably less evidence of ritual behavior prior to the establishment of sedentary villages of agriculturalists, ethnographic studies (e.g., Meggitt 1962; Munn 1973) show that ritual was an important component of behavior during these earlier periods as well. The key transition—both in behavior and for the archaeologist attempting to monitor changes in that behavior—may not have been an increase in the amount of ritual behavior as much as a change in the scheduling of rituals and the increasing construction of permanent, formal, ritual structures or public buildings (Flannery 1972; Adler, Chapter 4, this volume).

As I will argue below, such changes may have been part of a general trend, during the development of villages, toward the formalization of several aspects of settlements. This ranged from the increasing association of storage features with habitation structures to the presence of well-defined cemeteries within settlements. The earliest examples of such settlements in the northern Southwest are often referred to as unit pueblos or "Prudden units" (Prudden 1903; Gorman and Childs 1981). Moreover, these trends are not limited to the Southwest, as is demonstrated by studies ranging from Chang's (1958) descriptions of the planned nature of Neolithic villages to Flannery's (1972) discussion of evolving community structure in the Near East and Mesoamerica.

These changes seem to be part of a movement toward better-defined, more discrete social units at a variety of scales as the highly flexible nature of the social relationships of more mobile hunters and gatherers was transformed (Braun and S. Plog 1982). Phrased in another way, as groups became less mobile and more restricted to particular areas, patterns of widespread resource-sharing evolved toward more restricted networks of obligations. These more localized networks did not have boundaries or formal divisions comparable to modern political demarcations. Rather, they more likely were part of a larger, regional network of communication and exchange that encompassed the entire Southwest (as well as areas beyond), but were defined by areas where information and material exchange was much more frequent than similar exchanges with other surrounding groups. Such differences potentially can produce spatial discontinuities in absolute or relative frequencies of materials or stylistic symbols (Braun and S. Plog 1982; S. Plog 1988a). Isaac (1972) has illustrated the extreme cases of complete interconnection versus strongly discrete networks (Figure 1). Real cases undoubtedly fall between these extremes. Thus, networks as conceived here are marked by degrees of discontinuity in information or material flow and have

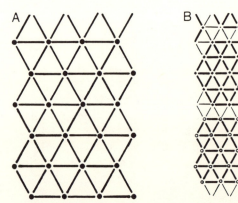

Figure 1: Representations of two different systems of interaction, with line thicknesses denoting frequencies of communication and exchange: (A) a system in which there are no differences in interaction among centers or nodes and (B) a higher density system in which there are barriers to interaction, leading to the development of "cultural isolates" or a tendency toward "bounded" networks within the overall system (after Isaac 1972).

"boundaries" that may be characterized as less or more permeable (Hantman 1983). Moreover, from the perspective of any particular individual, there may be several relevant social boundaries. It is likely that the frequency of such boundaries increased and hierarchical relationships among boundaries became more complex during the period in question. In addition, it is important to recognize that rates of personal interaction do not necessarily coincide with rates of exchange, information flow or shared material symbols (Hodder 1977). It is the latter characteristics on which the following discussion will concentrate.

Dwellings, Storage, and Sharing

At least three settlement characteristics suggest a trend toward more formalized social boundaries in the northern Southwest. First, on the average, early sedentary villages appear to have been smaller than settlements of prior periods. The range of variation in settlement size also became more restricted (e.g., F. Plog 1974:119-121), a phenomenon with ethnographic parallels (Hitchcock 1982:251). Perhaps more important were the increasingly strong patterns of association between household units and storage facilities (e.g., Varien and Lightfoot, Chapter 6, this volume; Gilman 1987:557; Wills and Windes 1989). These patterns, along with the consistent room-to-kiva ratio of 6:1, led Steward (1937:163-164) to argue that "it is difficult to reconcile the division of the early villages into small house clusters with any other social unit than a unilateral lineage or band."

Such patterns of association are consistent with predictions concerning social relationships generated by a recent simulation study by Hegmon (1988). Based on Hopi environmental, demographic, and agricultural information, the simulation supported the likelihood that some type of formal, well-defined social unit of limited size would evolve as dependence on agriculture increased. Hegmon (1988:Tables 1-3) found that if agricultural surplus is not shared among all households in a simulated community with 20 families, only 44 percent would survive after 20 years, largely because households often could not recover from a bad year or a series of bad years that depleted their storage reserves. Surprisingly, the survival rate was worse with complete sharing among households in which all agricultural resources are averaged out among families; only 22.5 percent of the families survived after 20 years. In contrast, a form of restricted sharing in which households only shared surplus production with a limited number of other groups increased the survival rate to an average of 97 percent. The survival rate improved as the number of households sharing resources increased to between six and eight, but minimal change occurred with further increases (Hegmon 1988:21; see also Winterhalder 1986).

In short, the sharing ideology so characteristic of hunting and gathering groups is likely inconsistent with an agricultural strategy requiring reduced mobility, individual accumulation of resources, and restricted sharing (Lee 1979:117, 156, 412-413; Vierich 1982:218). In addition to the problems with resource-sharing noted above, other social problems also develop with increased sedentism. Group tensions, for example, may no longer be relieved by groups leaving camps, by groups voting "with their feet" (Lee 1979:367). An initial result of such trends in the Southwest appears to have been restricted settlement size and increased associations between dwelling and storage units, a pattern that suggests more formal definition of social units smaller than those recognized during earlier periods.

Cemeteries and Group Ideology

A second noteworthy characteristic of early villages was well-defined cemetery areas. Though less frequent during earlier periods, they became increasingly common during the period in question. Ethnographic studies suggest that mobile hunting and gathering groups tend to lack cemeteries; they either bury their dead away from settlements in shallow, unmarked graves or actually move settlements away from burial locations, often to avoid the ghost of the deceased (e.g., Hamilton 1982:101; Howell 1979:51; Meggitt 1962:318-322; Woodburn 1982). Such behavior appears to have characterized the more mobile, early historic Native American groups in the Southwest, including the Navajo, Apache, and Yavapai (Khera and Mariella 1983:48; Opler 1983a:377, 1983b:415-16; 1983c:436-37; Reichard 1928:142-43). With the Apache, for example,

> The deceased was placed on his favorite horse with as many of his personal possessions as could be carried and taken far from the habitations of the people, into hilly or mountainous country, if possible. Because of the risk of contamination, the burial party was small. It proceeded silently, and tribesmen it encountered turned away. A crevice in the rocks that could be covered with earth, brush, and stones was sought as a grave (Opler 1983a:377).

Such practices contrast with those of historic Pueblo groups, who bury their dead in well-defined cemeteries or under house floors (e.g., Brown 1979:273; Schroeder 1979:251; Stanislawski 1979:599). Kaut (1959:100-01, personal communication 1988) notes variation in Apache practices that similarly correlates with economy, population distribution, and sedentism.

With the transition from mobility to sedentism, we thus see a transformation from burials as "negative space" to be avoided, to cemeteries as "positive space," intimately associated with day-to-day activities. Flannery (1972:29) has argued that

> The placing of permanent, nucleated communities on or near localized areas of strategic resources probably changed group ideology from one of weak territoriality to the pattern of a small, defended core area versus a large, undefended periphery, further emphasized in concepts of descent. In this regard, we should perhaps not be surprised to find burials under house floors or in adjacent courtyards, as in Early Formative Mesoamerica; repositories for multiple secondary burials, as in both regions; or the saving of ancestor's skulls, as in the Near East.

From this point of view, the increasing association of cemeteries with the other characteristics of village sites noted above is indicative of more bounded social units attempting to mark and legitimate their claim to particular resources or parcels of land. Such groups stand in sharp contrast to the flexible organization of hunting and gathering groups described by Richard Lee (1979:457, emphases in original; see also Silberbauer 1982:24):

> ... [it] is clear that the maintenance of *flexibility* to adapt to changing ecological circumstances is far more important to hunter-gatherer group structure than is the maintenance of exclusive rights to land. Flexibility favors a social policy of *bringing in* more personnel rather than keeping them out, hence the emphasis on the social principle of *recruitment* rather than *exclusion*.

Among more sedentary groups, however, the flexible hunting and gathering organization is often transformed, through increased emphasis on lineality and locality, into a more structured society in which individual rights to resources are more clearly defined and can be limited when necessary. One result may be that the more restricted form of sharing produces a smaller, more formalized social group composed of a limited number of households with associated storage units; this limits risk while increasing the probability of group survival. One way to reinforce those genealogical and territorial ties is to possess formal cemeteries containing one's ancestors. Thus, greater sedentism leads to an increasing congruence of social space and resource space, promotes an associated transformation of burial locations from negative to positive space, and changes the emphasis from recruiting new group members to restricting access.

Ritual and Ritual Structures

A final characteristic of villages is the common construction of ritual structures. Although such structures also are known from the periods preceding sedentary villages, they were built at a small proportion of settlements (e.g., the Great Kiva at Juniper Cove [Dean 1970:148], or the large structures at the SU Site and Shabik'eschee, which many regard as ritual structures [Wills and Windes 1989]). These early ritual structures or "public buildings" (Flannery and Marcus 1976) were modified versions of habitation structures, located in portions of the sites where they would be visible and accessible, and relatively standardized when compared with other types of structures.

Archaeologists working in the Southwest and elsewhere often have suggested that the observed increase in specialized ritual structures in sedentary villages is related to sharing goods or information within individual settlements or among a limited set of villages (e.g., Hegmon, Chapter 9, this volume). As suggested above, however, the evolution of ritual behavior should not be examined just from a perspective of the individual community or locality immediately proximate to the ritual structures. More well-defined social boundaries of the type described above may have had certain selective advantages, but they also created potential disadvantages. Greater restrictions on access to resources, for example, increased the potential for intergroup conflict. Moreover, individual villages or groups of villages were not viable social units in the long run, given such additional considerations as the minimum size of mating networks (S. Plog 1980) or the risks involved in limiting the range and flexibility of external linkages (Cashdan 1985, Hantman 1983, Madden 1984). For these reasons, it can be expected that social alliances crosscutting the increasingly formalized local units also would have been maintained, while other extensive economic and political linkages may have developed. Hantman (1983:179), for example, argues that while local social boundaries may become more formalized, exchange alliances will still link spatially more distant groups residing in environmentally distinct zones.

Furthermore, it is likely that these regional ties would have been maintained in association with ritual activity. Although many have emphasized that exchange relationships build social ties, whether within or between groups, Brian Foster (1977:3) has suggested that exchange (in particular, exchange involving utilitarian items) "does not in itself promote social solidarity or stability, but rather is fundamentally a dissociative, conflict relation which must be carefully regulated." Foster (1977:12-16) suggests that exchange activity, therefore, may be regulated by embedding it in larger ritual context, as "ritualization gives trading behavior an affective dimension and in many cases provides supernatural sanctions" that may reduce conflicts and obscure the many inequalities that can develop through exchange activities. This may explain why archaeological data from the northern Southwest, as well as such areas as highland Mesoamerica (Flannery et al. 1981:65-68; S. Plog 1986a; Stark 1981; Toll 1985), suggest a strong association between the frequency of public buildings and the growth of regional exchange systems during periods when sedentary villages developed.

A Case Study

The relationship between ritual and regional ties is difficult to document more specifically because of the few studies of associations between ritual structures and various types of artifacts, features, or other structures. We can, however, examine it more closely for one part of the northern Southwest by analyzing data relevant to both information and material exchange from a section of the Kayenta Anasazi region in northeastern Arizona (S. Plog 1986a, 1988a). Using data from a survey of a 120.4 km^2 area on northern Black Mesa, I have measured the association between ceremonial rooms and both material and information exchange. Before discussing that study, however, I should comment on issues recently raised about the identification of ritual structures in the northern Southwest.

Interpretations of Subterranean Structures

The Black Mesa ritual structures are round, subterranean rooms, centrally located within a settlement. In addition to the subterranean structures, those settlements have several other characteristics that typify villages as defined above. Masonry storage structures, usually one to three in number, are often located east or northeast of the central, subterranean structure. Attached to each end of the masonry rooms at roughly perpendicular angles are jacal rooms that served as dwellings. Numbers vary considerably, but usually are less than 10. Middens also are common on the west or southwest side of the central structure, and most burials were placed in those areas. Although other subterranean structures are occasionally present on the perimeter of these sites, each occupation appears to have been characterized by only one of the central, subterranean structures. The first occurrence of villages with these characteristics in the study area dates to approximately A.D. 850 to 900.

I agree with Lekson (1988) that use of the term "kiva" for prehistoric ceremonial structures implies a degree of similarity with historic societies that is difficult to support. In addition, use of the term has probably served to obscure considerable variation among such structures. At the same time, however, Lekson's argument that these structures served only habitation rather than ceremonial purposes is unconvincing for several reasons. First, he cites evidence supporting the use of pit houses as dwellings after the supposed transition from subterranean to surface dwellings suggested by the Pecos Classification. Although many recent studies have shown the persistence of pit houses after A.D. 700–900, as Lekson suggests, that conclusion in no way demonstrates that a large percentage of subterranean structures have been misclassified. On northern Black Mesa, for example, subterranean structures used for grinding, storage, or habitation after A.D. 900 are not unusual, but are markedly different from the contemporaneous, central, subterranean structures that have been classified as ceremonial. Not only are the centrally located subterranean structures found in a consistent location relative to other structures, but they also are more homogeneous in size, shape, depth, and feature content. Subterranean structures found in other locations are much more variable in depth, location, shape, and internal features. Thus, those structures typically regarded as ceremonial in nature are much more formalized, in the sense referred to above, than other structures.

Second, Lekson (1988:228-229) concludes that frequencies of above- and below-ground structures indicate that the latter, and not the former, were habitation structures until the Pueblo III period. This conclusion is based on the constant rate of increase in below-ground structures in contrast to the irregular rate of change in frequencies of above-ground structures. The constant rate of increase for below-ground structures matches his expectation of a steady rate of population increase through time. He provides, however, no justification for his belief that such a Malthusian pattern of steady population growth should be the expected pattern. Both theoretical considerations (e.g., S. Plog 1986b) and empirical evidence suggest that not only was steady growth unlikely, but also that irregular rates of growth were typical throughout the northern Southwest (e.g., Zubrow 1971; F. Plog 1975; S. Plog 1986b). Population growth is a complex process, determined by a wide variety of factors ranging from the availability of adequate resources to social organization and intergroup competition. It is improbable that all these factors would remain constant or interact in such a manner that they would produce constant rates of population growth for the length of time considered by Lekson. Unless Lekson's expectation of constant population growth can be justified, the irregular rates of changes in frequencies of above-ground structures provide no reason to reject current belief that many above-ground structures served as dwellings.

Finally, given the low room-to-kiva ratios in some areas, Lekson argues that the interpretation of kivas as integrative structures must be questioned because

> ... it is difficult to envisage what was being integrated. Ten rooms are not a village, at least in the San Juan area. Indeed, as Rohn (1977) has persuasively argued, clusters of small, 8-room to 10-room sites often made up a

community. Each 10-room unit is more realistically viewed as an individual house within a larger village (Lekson 1988:225).

No support, however, is provided for the suggestion that a single household occupied 10 rooms, and many previous studies contradict that proposal (e.g., Hill 1970:75-76). Moreover, Rohn's proposal that small sites were grouped into larger communities says nothing about the nature of the social units that occupied the small sites (and other statements [1977:83] suggest that he believes multiple households occupied 8- to 10-room sites). It simply indicates that there was another level of integration or interaction beyond the smaller settlements.

Lekson's statement also implicitly assumes that the individuals or groups integrated by kivas were those who lived closest to the structure. That assumption is inconsistent with what is known about the integrative nature of historic kiva societies—the analogical basis for interpretating prehistoric kivas as integrative. If we avoid that specific analogy, his implicit assumption also is inconsistent with the general relationship between ritual behavior and external alliances outlined above. Even in simpler hunting and gathering societies, social and ritual ties often connect groups that are spatially not proximate (e.g., Wiessner 1977:350-351). Local ratios of rooms to kivas may therefore indicate little about the integrative function of the latter structures.

In short, although Lekson's study provides ample reason for us to be cautious in our interpretations of structures traditionally referred to as "kivas," his suggestion that subterranean structures were only for habitation, not ritual activities, before A.D. 1300 (1988:229) is not well-supported. I therefore continue to regard the Black Mesa subterranean structures with distinctive architectural and locational characteristics as ceremonial buildings. Whether the types of behavior typical in historic kivas were always comparable to those in the Black Mesa structures is not critical to the following analysis. Moreover, if problems exist in our understanding of subterranean structures, they will not be corrected by changing our terminology, but by adopting theoretical perspectives that place greater emphasis on ritual behavior and on a more careful examination of contextual information from those structures.

Ritual Structures and Exchange

Returning to analysis of the Black Mesa data, two tests were conducted to assess the relationship between regional exchange and ritual. These tests were run independently as part of different studies and are described in greater detail elsewhere (S. Plog 1986b, 1988a). As a result, they employ somewhat different groups of sites. Nevertheless, both consider the relationship between some aspect of exchange and the presence of ceremonial structures. The first involved analysis of San Juan Red Ware and Tsegi Orange Ware ceramics. Petrographic and stylistic analyses have demonstrated that both were manufactured outside the study area, most likely in the northern San Juan region of southern Utah and Colorado (for red wares) or in other parts of northeastern Arizona (for orange wares) (Garrett 1986). Absolute artifact frequencies had to be adjusted for the estimated population of the site in order that differences in per capita utilization, and thus differential site populations, would not affect the results. Thus, the relevant artifact frequencies were first divided by the estimated number of rooms at each settlement to derive an estimate of exchange intensity (S. Plog 1986a:297). Use of this index assumes that lengths of occupations were similar at all sites, an assumption that seems reasonable given the brief occupations that appear to be typical at settlements in the study area (Hantman 1983).

Several comparisons of red and orange ware frequencies at various types of sites have been made (S. Plog 1988a:303-305), but only a few will be highlighted here. These tests attempt to control for temporal variation by dividing sites into those that predate A.D. 1050 and those that postdate A.D. 1050. That division is relevant for two reasons: (a) A.D. 1050 is roughly the beginning of a major period of culture change in the study area, including significant increases in population density, and (b) the division separates an earlier period characterized by higher frequencies of San Juan Red Wares from a later period characterized by higher frequencies of Tsegi Orange Wares (S. Plog 1980:140, 142; 1986b:317). In addition, only sites considered to be habitation sites were included in the analysis. Variation in red and orange ware frequencies therefore should not reflect functional variation among settlements.

Employing two-way analysis of variance, with the two time periods as the dependent variable, demonstrates that settlements with ceremonial structures have almost three times as many red or orange wares per room than sites that lack such structures (Table 1). This difference characterizes both the pre- and post–A.D. 1050 periods and is statistically significant ($F = 6.07$, $p = 0.02$, $n = 140$). There is thus a strong association between (a) the occurrence of ceremonial structures and (b) unusually high frequencies of red or orange ware ceramics manufactured outside the study area.

The second test examined proportional frequencies (and therefore did not need to be corrected by an estimate of village or assemblage size) of a particular stylistic characteristic—hatching or "Dogoszhi-style" designs—on the black-on-white pottery. This design style is a characteristic Chacoan feature that some scholars have suggested may have been associated with

Table 1: Average frquencies of red and orange wares per room and of Dogoszhi-style white wares on habitation sites with and without ceremonial structures.

	Red and Orange Wares Per Room		Dogoszhi-style White Wares (%)	
	A.D. 850–1050	A.D. 1051–1150	A.D. 1051–1075	A.D. 1076–1100
Ceremonial Structure Present	14.6	20.4	16.5	15.0
Ceremonial Structure Absent	5.0	7.1	16.9	8.7

participation in the Chacoan regional system (Toll 1985; Neitzel 1985). An examination of several aspects of decorative styles from the northern Southwest supports this idea. In contrast to both earlier and contemporaneous decorative patterns, the Dogoszhi style has several of the characteristics that Wiessner (1985) has suggested should typify active, symbolic styles, including high rates of change and strong associations among characteristic attributes (S. Plog 1988a). Although there is no evidence of direct relationship between Chaco Canyon and the northern Black Mesa study area, a variety of evidence suggests the possibility of indirect ties and information exchange that could have caused patterned distributions of particular ceramic styles (LeBlanc 1986; S. Plog 1986a, 1988a). It is therefore possible that distributions of Dogoszhi style ceramics may be related to information exchange as a result of participation in a broad regional social network.

Focusing on the period from approximately A.D. 1050 to 1100, when Dogoszhi style ceramics were common in the study area, the tests demonstrate a changing pattern over time for habitation sites. From A.D. 1050 to 1075 there is no significant difference in the frequency of such ceramics on settlements with or without ceremonial structures ($t = -0.09, p > 0.10, n = 21$). Between A.D. 1076 and 1100, however, Dogoszhi-style ceramics are proportionally almost twice as abundant on sites with ceremonial structures (15.0% of all black-on-white ceramics) than on sites that lack such structures (8.7% of all black-on-white ceramics)(Table 1), and the difference is statistically significant ($t = 2.87, p < 0.01, n = 36$). In contrast, stylistic characteristics regarded as diagnostic of other contemporaneous black-on-white styles are equally abundant on northern Black Mesa sites with and without ceremonial structures (S. Plog 1988a).

This change in the distribution of Dogoszhi-style ceramics between A.D. 1050–1075 and A.D. 1076–1100 corresponds with two other aspects of culture change in the study area and the northern Southwest. First, there is evidence for increasing centralization of exchange activity on northern Black Mesa between approximately A.D. 1060 and 1110. More detailed analyses of red and orange ware frequencies have shown that settlements with kivas, roomblocks, and more than ten rooms had over six times as many red and orange ware sherds per room (43.8 sherds per room, $n = 7$) as contemporaneous habitation sites with only roomblocks (7.1 sherds per room, $n = 35$), and twice as many as smaller sites with ceremonial structures (17.8 sherds per room, $n = 63$). In addition, fewer habitation sites had ceremonial structures between A.D. 1076–1100 than during earlier or later time periods (S. Plog 1986a:306). It is thus possible that ritual activity—and associated exchange activity—was becoming concentrated at fewer settlements during the last part of the eleventh century and the first part of the twelfth.

The A.D. 1076–1100 period is also notable because it approximates the period of greatest construction activity in Chaco Canyon (Lekson 1984:259; Sebastian 1988:154), when most of the Chacoan road system was created (Nials et al. 1983:11-3; Nials et al. 1987:25), and the greatest number of settlements were involved in the Chaco system (Toll 1985:482). Although there is no sign of direct ties between the study area and Chaco Canyon, as noted above, I agree with LeBlanc (1986) that there is increasing evidence of a social network or interaction sphere over a broad area of the northern Southwest. The suggested trend toward centralization of ritual and exchange activity and, in particular, its association with higher frequencies of a typical Chacoan symbolic motif, may be tied to an involvement of northern Black Mesa groups in just such a broad regional network.

Both the above tests thus suggest a strong pattern of association between (a) ceremonial structures and (b) material remains likely to have been deposited as a result of participation in large regional networks. Such variation among sites cannot be explained by differences in occupation lengths or typical functional dichotomies. To argue that the greater absolute frequencies of red or orange wares are simply a product of larger assemblage sizes begs the questions of why those assemblages occur; it is not an answer, but a different version of the original question. Similarly, temporal control is not an issue. Site dates are based on independent criteria, and assessments of the dating method have documented both its accuracy and precision (Plog and Hantman 1986).

Conclusions

It therefore appears that exchange patterns of material (red and orange wares) and information (stylistic symbols) are consistent in suggesting important changes in regional social networks in the northern Southwest. In particular, ritual sanctions of trade may have been one way to maintain social relationships and control the social tensions that accompanied the increasing exchanges of regional information and commodities during the evolution of sedentary villages. That is, exchange became more embedded in a ritual context as the village formation process unfolded. This view contrasts with discussions of Anasazi prehistory that often separate exchange from ritual, as illustrated by the current debate over whether Chaco Canyon was an exchange center or a ritual center. The data presented above, as well as more general theoretical proposals (e.g., Sahlins 1972), suggest that dividing Southwestern societies into independent economic, ritual, or social components is unlikely to be either accurate descriptively, or productive from an explanatory point of view.

The increases in regional exchange could also have been associated with change in several other aspects of group organization and ideology. As Wiessner (1977:369) has argued, sedentary groups need to be organized differently than more mobile groups who cope with environmental variation by moving. I have suggested that the establishment of villages was associated with trends toward (1) decreased mobility and (2) increased storage as a means of buffering environmental variation. A third associated trend was a change in group ideology from one that emphasized sharing and recruitment to one that allowed individual control of resources and land, with restricted access by others. These trends are suggested by increases in numbers of sites and areas settled, the development of regional style zones, the strong spatial association of habitation and storage rooms (e.g., Prudden units), the appearance of more formal and more frequent cemetery areas, and an initial reduction in average settlement size (S. Plog 1988b). With increased dependence on agricultural resources at the expense of hunted or gathered foods, for example, an individual must

. . . build up a surplus to tide him through hard times . . . [and] some items must be taken out of the realm of those to be shared and put into the realm of private property or property of a community—particularly items critical to food production, seed, livestocks, tools, etc. (Wiessner 1977:369-70).

While Wiessner (1977:373-74) argues that these trends may also lead to a reduction in the widespread nature of social ties and obligations that characterize hunters and gatherers, she also suggests that ties to outside groups will still likely be necessary, though "relationships of mutual obligations between groups" may be "redefined from one of generalized reciprocity to one where terms are more fixed" (see also Braun and S. Plog 1982). As perceived social distance increased with the change in mutual obligations away from generalized reciprocity (Sahlins 1972), exchange may have become more ritualized to control increased social tensions that arose during various transactions.

Given this early association of ritual and exchange, it would not be surprising if further integration or centralization of exchange networks also occurred in a ritual context, as many have proposed (e.g., Windes 1987) for other areas of the Southwest, where socioeconomic complexity appears to have been greater than in the Black Mesa area. Such relationships also are consistent with the ritual basis of leadership and social differentiation among some historic Pueblos (e.g., Whiteley 1988). Thus, these patterns highlight the importance of the studies presented in this volume and the need to give more attention to ritual behavior in prehistoric Southwestern societies.

References

Braun, David P.
1987 Coevolution of Sedentism, Pottery Technology, and Horticulture in the Central Midwest, 200 B.C.–A.D. 600. In *Emergent Horticultural Economies of the Eastern Woodlands,* edited by W. Keegan, pp. 155-184. Center for Archaeological Investigations Occasional Paper No. 7. Southern Illinois University, Carbondale.

Braun, David P., and Stephen Plog
1982 Evolution of "Tribal" Social Networks: Theory and Prehistoric North American Evidence. *American Antiquity* 47:504-525.

Brown, Donald N.
1979 Picuris Pueblo. In *Southwest*, edited by Alfonso Ortiz, pp. 268-277. Handbook of North American Indians vol. 9, William G. Sturtevant, general editor. Smithsonian Institution, Washington, D.C.

Cashdan, Elizabeth A.
1985 Coping With Risk: Reciprocity Among the Basarwa of Northern Botswana. *Man* 20:454-474.

Chang, Kwang-Chih
1958 Study of the Neolithic Social Grouping: Examples From the New World. *American Anthropologist* 60:298-334.

Dean, Jeffrey S.
1970 Aspects of Tsegi Phase Social Organization: A Trial Reconstruction. In *Reconstructing Prehistoric Pueblo Societies,* edited by W. A. Longacre, pp. 140-174. University of New Mexico Press, Albuquerque.

Flannery, Kent V.
1972 The Origins of the Village As a Settlement Type in Mesoamerica and the Near East: A Comparative Study. In *Man, Settlement, and Urbanism,* edited by P. J. Ucko et al., pp. 23-53. Gerald Duckworth and Co. Ltd., London.

Flannery, Kent V., and Joyce Marcus
1976 Evolution of the Public Building in Formative Oaxaca. In *Cultural Continuity and Change, Essays in Honor of James B. Griffin,* edited by C. E. Cleland, pp. 205-221. Academic Press, New York.

Flannery, Kent V., Joyce Marcus, and Stephen A. Kowalewski
1981 The Preceramic and Formative of the Valley of Oaxaca. In *Supplement to the Handbook of Middle American Indians,* vol. 1, edited by J. A. Sabloff, pp. 48-93. University of Texas Press, Austin.

Foster, Brian L.
1977 Trade, Social Conflict, and Social Integration: Rethinking Some Old Ideas on Exchange. In *Economic Exchange and Social Interaction in Southeast Asia,* edited by K. Hutterer, pp. 3-22. Michigan Papers on South and Southeast Asia No. 13. University of Michigan, Ann Arbor.

Garrett, Elizabeth M.
1986 A Petrographic Analysis of Black Mesa Ceramics. In *Spatial Organization and Exchange: Archaeological Survey on Northern Black Mesa,* edited by S. Plog, pp. 114-142. Southern Illinois University Press, Carbondale.

Gilman, Patricia A.
1987 Architecture as Artifact: Pit Structures and Pueblos in the American Southwest. *American Antiquity* 52:538-564.

Gorman, Frederick J. E., and S. Terry Childs
1981 Is Prudden's Unit Type of Anasazi Settlement Valid and Reliable? *North American Archaeologist* 2:153-192.

Hamilton, Annette
1982 Descended from Father, Belonging to Country: Rights to Land in the Australian Western Desert. In *Politics and History in Band Societies,* edited by E. Leacock and R. Lee, pp. 85-108. Cambridge University Press, Cambridge.

Hantman, Jeffrey L.
1983 *Stylistic Distributions and Social Networks in the Prehistoric Plateau Southwest.* Ph.D. dissertation, Department of Anthropology, Arizona State University. University Microfilms, Ann Arbor.

Hegmon, Michelle
1988 The Risks of Sharing and Sharing as Risk Reduction: Inter-Household Food Sharing in Egalitarian Societies. In *Between Bands and States: Sedentism, Subsistence, and Interaction in Small Scale Societies,* edited by Susan A. Gregg, in press.

Hill, James N.
1970 *Broken K Pueblo: Prehistoric Social Organization in the American Southwest.* Anthropological Papers of the University of Arizona No. 18. Tucson.

Hitchcock, Robert K.
1982 Patterns of Sedentism Among the Basarwa of Eastern Botswana. In *Politics and History in Band Societies,* edited by E. Leacock and R. Lee, pp. 223-267. Cambridge University Press, Cambridge.

Hodder, Ian
1977 The Distribution of Material Culture Items in the Baringo District, Western Kenya. *Man* 12:239-269.

Howell, Nancy
1979 *Demography of the Dobe !Kung.* Academic Press, New York.

Isaac, Glyn
1972 Early Phases of Human Behavior: Models in Lower Paleolithic Archaeology. In *Models in Archaeology,* edited by D. L. Clarke, pp. 167-199. Methuen, London.

Kaut, Charles R.
1959 Notes on Western Apache Religious and Social Organization. *American Anthropologist* 61:99-102.

Khera, Sigrid and Patricia S. Mariella
    1983   Yavapai. In *Southwest,* edited by Alfonso Ortiz, pp. 38-54. Handbook of North American Indians vol. 10, William G. Sturtevant, general editor. Smithsonian Institution, Washington, D.C.

LeBlanc, Steven A.
    1982   The Advent of Pottery in the Southwest. In *Southwestern Ceramics: A Comparative Review,* edited by Albert H. Schroeder, pp. 27-51. Arizona Archaeologist No. 15. The Arizona Archaeological Society, Phoenix.

    1986   Aspects of Southwestern Prehistory: A.D. 900-1400. In *Ripples in the Chichimec Sea,* edited by F. J. Mathien and R. H. McGuire, pp. 105-134. Southern Illinois University Press, Carbondale.

Lee, Richard Borshay
    1979   *The !Kung San.* Cambridge University Press, Cambridge.

Lekson, Stephen H.
    1984   *Great Pueblo Architecture of Chaco Canyon, New Mexico.* Publications in Archeology No. 18B, Chaco Canyon Studies. National Park Service, Albuquerque, N.M.

    1988   The Idea of the Kiva in Anasazi Archaeology. *The Kiva* 53:213-234.

Longacre, William A.
    1964   Sociological Implications of the Ceramic Analysis. In Chapters in the Prehistory of Eastern Arizona II, by P. S. Martin et al., pp. 155-167. *Fieldiana:Anthropology* 53. Chicago.

Madden, Marcie
    1984   Social Network Systems Amongst Hunter-Gatherers Considered Within Southern Norway. In *Ideology, Power, and Prehistory,* edited by D. Miller and C. Tilley, pp. 191-200. Cambridge University Press, Cambridge.

Marshall, Michael P., John R. Stein, Richard W. Loose, and Judith E. Novotny
    1979   *Anasazi Communities of the San Juan Basin.* Public Service Company of New Mexico and New Mexico State Planning Division, Albuquerque and Santa Fe.

Meggitt, M. J.
    1962   *Desert People.* University of Chicago Press, Chicago.

Munn, Nancy D.
    1973   *Walbiri Iconography.* University of Chicago Press, Chicago.

Neitzel, Jill E.
    1985   Regional Styles and Organizational Hierarchies: The View from Chaco Canyon. Paper presented at the 50th annual meeting of the Society for American Archaeology, Denver, Colorado.

Nials, Fred L., Chris Kincaid and John R. Stein
    1983   Summary and Conclusions. In *Chaco Roads Project Phase I: A Reappraisal of Prehistoric Roads in the San Juan Basin 1983,* edited by Chris Kincaid, pp. 11-1 to 11-4. Bureau of Land Management, Albuquerque, N.M.

Nials, Fred, John Stein and John Roney
    1987   *Chacoan Roads in the Southern Periphery: Results of Phase II of the BLM Chaco Roads Project.* Cultural Resources Series No. 1. Bureau of Land Management, Albuquerque, New Mexico.

O'Brien, Michael J.
    1987   Sedentism, Population Growth, and Resource Selection in the Woodland Midwest: A Review of Coevolutionary Developments. *Current Anthropology* 28:177-197.

Opler, Morris E.
    1983a   The Apachean Culture Pattern and Its Origin. In *Southwest,* edited by Alfonso Ortiz, pp. 368-392. Handbook of North American Indians, vol. 10, William G. Sturtevant, general editor. Smithsonian Institution, Washington, D.C.

    1983b   Chiricahua Apache. In *Southwest,* edited by Alfonso Ortiz, pp. 401-418. Handbook of North American Indians, vol. 10, William G. Sturtevant, general editor. Smithsonian Institution, Washington, D.C.

    1983c   Mescalero Apache. In *Southwest,* edited by Alfonso Ortiz, pp. 419-439. Handbook of North American Indians, vol. 10, William G. Sturtevant, general editor. Smithsonian Institution, Washington, D.C.

Plog, Fred
    1974   *The Study of Prehistoric Change.* Academic Press, New York.

    1975   Demographic Studies in Southwestern Prehistory. In *Population Studies in Archaeology and Biological Anthropology: A Symposium,* edited by

A.C Swedlund, pp. 94-102. Memoirs of the Society for American Archaeology No. 30.

Plog, Stephen
1980 Village Autonomy in the American Southwest: An Evaluation of the Evidence. In *Models and Methods in Regional Exchange,* edited by R. E. Fry, pp. 135-146. SAA Papers No. 1. Society for American Archaeology, Washington, D.C.

1986a Change in Regional Trade Networks. In *Spatial Organization and Exchange: Archaeological Survey on Northern Black Mesa,* edited by S. Plog, pp. 282-309. Southern Illinois University Press, Carbondale.

1986b Understanding Culture Change in the Northern Southwest. In *Spatial Organization and Exchange: Archaeological Survey on Northern Black Mesa,* edited by S. Plog, pp. 310-336. Southern Illinois University Press, Carbondale.

1988a Agriculture, Sedentism, and Environment in the Evolution of Political Systems. In *The Evolution of Political Systems: Sociopolitics in Small-Scale Sedentary Societies,* edited by S. Upham. Cambridge University Press, Cambridge, in press.

1988b Sociopolitical Implications of Southwestern Stylistic Variation. In *The Use of Style in Archaeology,* edited by M. Conkey and C. Hastorf. Cambridge University Press, Cambridge, in press.

Plog, Stephen and Jeffrey H. Hantman
1986 Multiple Regression Analysis as a Dating Method in the American Southwest. In *Spatial Organization and Exchange: Archaeological Survey on Northern Black Mesa,* edited by S. Plog, pp. 87-113. Southern Illinois University Press, Carbondale.

Powers, Robert P., William B. Gillespie, and Stephen H. Lekson
1983 *The Outlier Survey: A Regional View of Settlement in the San Juan Basin.* Reports of the Chaco Center No. 3. Division of Cultural Research, National Park Service, Albuquerque.

Prudden, T. Mitchell
1903 The Prehistoric Ruins of the San Juan Watershed of Utah, Arizona, Colorado and New Mexico. *American Anthropologist* 5:224-288.

Reichard, Gladys A.
1928 *Social Life of the Navajo Indians.* Columbia University Contributions to Anthropology, vol. 7. Columbia University, New York.

Rohn, Arthur H.
1977 *Cultural Change and Continuity on Chapin Mesa.* The Regents Press of Kansas, Lawrence, Kansas.

Sahlins, Marshall
1972 *Stone Age Economics.* Aldine-Atherton, Chicago.

Schroeder, Albert H.
1979 Pueblos Abandoned in Historic Times. In *Southwest,* edited by Alfonso Ortiz, pp. 236-254. Handbook of North American Indians, vol. 10, William G. Sturtevant, general editor. Smithsonian Institution, Washington, D.C.

Sebastian, Lynne
1988 *Leadership, Power, and Productive Potential: A Political Model of the Chaco System.* Ph.D. dissertation, Department of Anthropology, University of New Mexico. University Microfilms, Ann Arbor.

Silberbauer, George
1982 Political Process in G/wi Bands. In *Politics and History in Band Societies,* edited by E. Leacock and R. Lee, pp. 23-35. Cambridge University Press, Cambridge.

Stanislawski, Michael B.
1979 Hopi-Tewa. In *Southwest,* edited by Alfonso Ortiz, pp. 587-603. Handbook of North American Indians, vol. 10, William G. Sturtevant, general editor. Smithsonian Institution, Washington, D.C.

Stark, Barbara L.
1981 The Rise of Sedentary Life. In *Supplement to the Handbook of Middle American Indians,* edited by J. A. Sabloff, pp. 345-72. University of Texas Press, Austin.

Steward, Julian H.
1937 Ecological Aspects of Southwestern Society. *Anthropos* 32:87-104.

Toll, H. Wolcott III
1985 *Pottery, Production, Public Architecture, and the Chaco Anasazi System.* Ph.D. dissertation, Department of Anthropology, University of Colorado. University Microfilms, Ann Arbor.

Vierich, Helga I. D.
   1982   Adaptive Flexibility in a Multi-Ethnic Setting: The Basarwa of the Southern Kalahari. In *Politics and History in Band Societies*, edited by E. Leacock and R. Lee, pp. 189-222. Cambridge University Press, Cambridge.

Whiteley, Peter M.
   1988   *Deliberate Acts*. University of Arizona Press, Tucson.

Wiessner, Polly
   1977   *Hxaro: A Regional System of Reciprocity for Reducing Risk Among the !Kung San*. Ph.D. dissertation, Department of Anthropology, University of Michigan. University Microfilms, Ann Arbor.

   1985   Style or Isochrestic Variation? A Reply to Sackett. *American Antiquity* 50:160-166.

Wilcox, David R., and Charles Sternberg
   1983   *Hohokam Ballcourts and Their Interpretation*. Arizona State Museum Archaeological Series No. 160. University of Arizona, Tucson.

Wills, Wirt H., and Thomas C. Windes
   1989   Evidence for Population Aggregation and Dispersal During the Basketmaker III Period in Chaco Canyon, New Mexico. *American Antiquity*, 54(2):347-369.

Windes, Thomas C.
   1987   *Investigations at the Pueblo Alto Complex, Chaco Canyon*, vol. 1. Publications in Archeology No. 18F, Chaco Canyon Studies. National Park Service, Santa Fe, New Mexico.

Winterhalder, Bruce
   1986   Diet Choice, Risk, and Food Sharing in a Stochastic Environment. *Journal of Anthropological Archaeology* 5:369-392.

Woodburn, James
   1982   Social Dimensions of Death in Four African Hunting and Gathering Societies. In *Death and the Regeneration of Life*, edited by Maurice Bloch and Jonathan Parry, pp. 187-210. Cambridge University Press, Cambridge.

Zubrow, Ezra B. W.
   1971   Carrying Capacity and Dynamic Equilibrium in the Prehistoric Southwest. *American Antiquity* 36:127-138.

11
Changing Form and Function in Western Pueblo Ceremonial Architecture from A.D. 1000 to A.D. 1500

E. Charles Adams

The goals of this paper are to analyze and interpret changes in kiva form and village layout at sites occupied by prehistoric people in northeastern Arizona. Between A.D. 1000 and 1500, kivas changed from circular to D-shaped or rectangular forms. Developments that correspond with the appearance of the rectangular kiva include a drastic increase in village size, a change in village layout, the development of the enclosed plaza, and the appearance of iconography associated with the katsina cult. Relationships among these changes are examined.

At the junction of the Colorado Plateau and the Mogollon Rim, an active interplay of ideas flourished between the plateau's Anasazi occupants and the occupants of the Mogollon Rim. The mingling of these two cultural traditions, relatively distinct away from their frontiers, has led to a confusing array of terms for the people who lived there (Reed 1948; Johnson 1965; Speth 1988). The tradition that developed after A.D. 1000, of white decorated wares and brown utility wares associated with small pueblos, and numerous other traits, has been defined by Reed (1948) as the Western Pueblo. This term will be retained for the discussion that follows.

This paper will consider the proposition that between A.D. 1000 and 1500 the role of ritual in pueblo society changed in the upper Little Colorado River valley. It changed primarily because the size of settlements increased. Although this process of aggregation was slow until the mid–A.D. 1200s, it accelerated during the late thirteenth and fourteenth centuries. Manifestations of change in ritual include a new kiva form, the replacement of Great Kivas by enclosed plazas (cf. Longacre 1964), and the appearance of katsina cult iconography (Adams and Hull 1980).

Aggregation and Immigration

The late 1200s witnessed a magnitude of changes in settlement location and structure, previously unequaled in formative cultures of the Colorado Plateau. Depopulation of all the Four Corners region was accompanied by immigration into refugia, including well-watered drainages such as the upper and central Little Colorado River valley north of the Mogollon Rim. Haury (1958) documented a Kayenta Anasazi migration into the Point of Pines region in east central Arizona in the late 1200s, and Di Peso (1958) documented Anasazi further south in the San Pedro River valley of southeastern Arizona. Carlson (1970, 1982) argues that extensive Anasazi influence, caused by their immigration into the upper Little Colorado River region, produced Pinedale Polychrome, which developed about A.D. 1275. The triggering mechanism for movements into refuge areas is usually attributed to the major environmental transformation termed "the Great Drought," which is dated A.D. 1276-1299. The complex relations between environment and culture obviously changed during this period, contributing to widespread depopulation of northern Anasazi areas and to the southerly movement of these people. In this paper I will emphasize the effects of this population movement rather than the causes.

The communities which began to develop in the refuge areas around A.D. 1275 seemingly incorporated populations of both immigrant Anasazi and indigenous Western Pueblo, who were descendants of southern Anasazi and Mogollon people. The villages these people built and occupied were remarkably different from their pre–A.D. 1275 counterparts. First and foremost, average site size for year-round habitations increased over 500 percent (Adams et al., 1987; Kintigh 1985, 1988). Second, the layout or village plan became formalized into plaza-oriented villages. Third, the kiva form became rectangular.

It is not fortuitous that these formal changes in architecture and use of space occurred together with population movement and resettlement. The processes underlying the changes in form and space-use, however, are social rather than environmental or subsistence-caused. They reflect the need to develop mechanisms within the new village units to encourage cooperation rather than competition between formerly autonomous social units. An analysis of the architectural changes and how they came to be will provide the opportunity for a better explanation of their development.

The Plaza—Rectangular Kiva Ritual System

Researchers have documented variability in western Anasazi kiva forms for the past 80 years (cf. Gumerman and Dean 1989). After A.D. 1000 forms are known that can be characterized as circular, square, and D-shaped, with intermediate forms as well. The transition from circular to D-shaped and rectangular kivas in the western Anasazi area is strongly related to changes in pit house form. Unlike regions to the east, Anasazi continued to live in pit structures in many areas of the west for at least part of the year (Ambler and Olson 1977; Gumerman and Skinner 1968; Gumerman and Dean 1989). These pit structures changed from circular to square by A.D. 1100. A semicircular or rectangular "bench" was simply attached to one end of the rectangular pit structure to construct the forms we recognize as either D-shaped or rectangular kivas. It is interesting that none of these forms seem directly related to the rectangular kivas which developed in the aggregated villages from the Hopi Mesas southward to the Mogollon Rim after A.D. 1275. The Mogollon kivas apparently developed out of square or rectangular rooms, with a bench or raised platform covering the floor at one end of the room.

Therefore, the Western Pueblo rectangular kiva seems to have developed in the Mogollon cultural tradition. Details of the rectangular kiva form's transition lie in the sequence of sites dug by Paul Martin and his colleagues and students in the Pine Lawn and Tularosa River valleys of west central New Mexico, in the upper Little Colorado River valley between Springerville and Saint Johns, and in the Hay Hollow Valley region of the upper Little Colorado River. I suggest the following sequence from the perusal of these various works. From about A.D. 1000–1250 the Great Kiva was the dominant ceremonial structure in all the above-listed areas, and probably also in the Grasshopper/Forestdale areas south to Point of Pines. Although initially built of pole roof supports and wattle-and-daub sides, it eventually became a structure mostly walled with masonry. Initially, the Great Kiva was built several meters away from the pueblo and accessed through a southern or eastern ramp entry. Excellent examples of the early part of the sequence occur in the Pine Lawn area in the Reserve Phase (A.D. 1000-1150) Sawmill site (Bluhm 1957). Thirteenth century examples of these Great Kivas were found at the Mineral Creek and Hooper Ranch sites along the upper Little Colorado River (Martin et al. 1961).

Martin et al. (1962:219-220) note that there were no kivas apparent at the Rim Valley Pueblo along the upper Little Colorado River, dating about A.D. 1225; but there *were* rectangular ceremonial rooms within the pueblo. Later, more formalized examples of rectangular ceremonial rooms appeared, usually with raised platforms on the south or east ends. With the addition of raised platforms, the ceremonial rooms have all the characteristics of kivas, except that they are not physically separated from the room block. The Field Museum researchers referred to both the structures with raised platforms and to the small rectangular structures physically separated from the room block, whether the raised platform was present or not, as kivas. It is logical to equate the platforms with a modification of the ramp entries of the separate Great Kivas. Kivas with platforms within the room block occur at Hooper Ranch Pueblo (Martin et al. 1962), Carter Ranch Pueblo (Martin et al. 1964; Longacre 1970), and at Broken K (Martin et al. 1967; Hill 1970). Those at Hooper Ranch date about A.D. 1200-1250, at Carter Ranch about A.D. 1200-1225, and at Broken K about A.D. 1180-1250. Both Hooper Ranch and Carter Ranch also have isolated Great Kivas.

The next development was the elimination of the Great Kiva and its replacement by the enclosed plaza area as a pan-village ceremonial structure. This process is earliest seen at Broken K, dating about A.D. 1250; it has no Great Kiva, but instead has an enclosed plaza (Hill 1970). Carter Ranch has a wall on the east side of the room block that could be considered as a plaza enclosure. Within these plazas are some of the small kivas with platforms, formerly located in the room block. Some, however, are still abutted by rooms. (Even in modern pueblos, kivas can be incorporated into the room block.) After A.D. 1275, the rectangular kiva with the platform on the south or east side appeared in villages over a broad area, usually with enclosed plazas.

Village Form and Cooperation

Archaeologists have long maintained that Great Kivas functioned to integrate larger segments of the local population. After all, one way to make ritual more integrative is to make aspects of it more accessible, or public (cf. Drennan 1976: 353-356). As villages increased in size in the late 1200s, they may have outgrown the ability of the Great Kiva to accomplish its integrative function. (See Adler, Chapter 4, this volume, for a cross-cultural analysis of integrative structures.) Thus, new mechanisms had to be developed to first reduce conflict between indigenous villages and their new immigrant neighbors, and ultimately to incorporate all into single, integrated communities. If a suitable social structure could not be developed, the community was in danger of collapse and dispersal due to scalar stress. The new structure must have involved the development of formalized leadership roles to identify and perhaps supervise cooperative enterprises and to mediate disputes.

Individuals must feel they are an essential element in the success of a group if leaders are to effect cooperative behavior. Public rituals meet those needs in societies at nearly all cultural levels throughout the world (Adler, this volume). A public ritual is one that can be viewed by most or all segments of the population, and whose purpose it is to entertain, instruct, and involve the viewing public. If individuals are served by the ritual and made to believe that their participation (or cooperation) is essential to its success, then the ritual will be effective in integrating the village populace. The historic Pueblo people made such use of public ritual, and it is reasonable to assume that their prehistoric counterparts did also.

When the Great Kiva disappeared as the integrative structure in Western Pueblo society, the plaza was the only logical replacement in the layout of the new aggregated villages. Thus, in its enclosed, rectangular form of the thirteenth and fourteenth centuries, the plaza continued the pan-village ceremonial function of the Great Kiva, but satisfied a much larger populace. The enclosed plaza was first a ceremonial place used to conduct public ritual, and second, a place for secular activities, much like Pueblo kivas and plazas are today.

Katsina Iconography

The katsina cult is the most public of modern Western Pueblo ceremonialism. Public performances of katsinas occur in the plazas from April through July among the Hopi. The katsina cult is also the only social institution having nearly universal membership among the Western Pueblos. In Acoma and Hopi society all individuals are expected to be initiated, whereas at Zuni all males and some females are expected to join. Thus, the katsina cult is the most socially integrative institution in modern Western Pueblo society.

Prehistoric examples of icons bearing strong resemblances to modern Pueblo katsinas, particularly the better-known Hopi and Zuni katsinas, have been noted in rock art (Schaafsma and Schaafsma 1974), in ceramics (Ferg 1982), and in kiva murals (Smith 1952; Dutton 1963). The origin of katsina iconography is not clear, although the Schaafsmas (1974) believe it originally derived from Mexico.

Recent research (Adams 1988) points to the development of the katsina cult at the same time and place as the rectangular kiva-plaza ritual complex: that is, in the upper Little Colorado River region during the late A.D. 1200s or early 1300s. The development of the katsina cult in a region which endured considerable stress from immigration supports the model that cooperative systems were developed in response to this stress.

If the roots of the katsina cult bear any resemblance to its modern form, the cult seems to have evolved as a visual means of integrating divergent groups of individuals into cooperative wholes in large, aggregated villages. The parallel development of the enclosed plaza would have provided a perfect architectural form for displaying the public aspects of such a visual religious system.

Thus, the development of enclosed plazas with village aggregation in the late A.D. 1200s seems most likely tied to the ritual needs of the community rather than to defense, more efficient energy use, or other needs. The evolution of ritual within the community is almost certainly tied to the need to integrate large groups of people into cooperative communities.

Conclusions

Although probably more complex than the relations outlined above, there is a clear association between immigration into the upper and middle Little Colorado River region and radical changes in architecture and village plan. In refuge areas such as the Little Colorado River valley, immigration caused a strain on fixed resources that required a solution. Given the existing technology and new intervillage relations, one solution could have been conflict—or even warfare—which would have reduced the population to carrying capacity. The other solution was cooperation. This option suggests that new immigrants were absorbed into existing villages and that those villages combined or aggregated. The aggregation process should increase productivity due to a larger labor force and a broader spectrum of resources from which to draw (cf. Boserup 1965). Widespread warfare and conflict are not suggested in the archaeological record to date, implying the cooperative solution was selected.

When the stresses of overpopulation were first being felt, the rectangular Great Kiva was the structure used in the Little Colorado River region to integrate multiple households—and in some cases, multiple hamlets. The enclosed-space village plan, or plaza, was in use to the south in Hohokam compounds and many Salado sites by the mid–A.D. 1200s. Adobe architecture and abundant Salado ceramics in upper Little Colorado River hamlets indicate extensive contact and borrowing between the two groups. The result was that the upper Little Colorado groups seemingly combined the ritual aspects of the Great Kiva with the enclosed village space of the southern groups to create enclosed plazas. The enclosed plazas combined the integrative functions of the Great Kiva with the public aspects of the plaza. The ritual use of open space may have introduced a new concept of public ritual to pueblo culture, or it may have expanded upon the earlier, more restrictive public ritual role of the Great Kiva. Therefore, the enclosed plaza is considered to be a conscious response by Western Pueblo people to the overpopulation problem and stress on existing resources caused by immigrants from the north. The enclosed plaza expanded the integrative role of the Great Kiva by making aspects of ritual accessible to many or all village members, much as they are today in modern Pueblos.

Though the public aspects of village ritual may facilitate intravillage cooperation, it is still imperative in unstratified societies, such as the modern Pueblos, and probably those of their ancestors, that aspects of ritual be kept secret. As noted by Adler (this volume), ritual specialization, or secrecy, is essential for the successful use of integrative facilities in larger groups, such as the post–A.D. 1300 Western Pueblo villages. Those with access to restricted ritual knowledge are the decision-makers or village leaders. This private or restrictive aspect of pueblo ritual is served by the small rectangular kivas. It may even be that the relocation of rectangular ceremonial structures to enclosed plazas was a symbolic means of sanctifying the plaza spaces.

The best-understood aspect of historic Hopi and Zuni ceremonialism is the katsina cult. The cult uses the kivas to plan and practice the katsina ritual. Only a restricted group of individuals has the knowledge, power, and authority to plan a katsina ceremony. The public performances of the katsina dance can involve any male initiate and are held in the plaza for all to see, and for most to actively join in through interaction with the performers or katsinas. Is it merely coincidence, then, that the katsina cult also apparently developed in the upper Little Colorado River area between A.D. 1275 and 1325? The integrative role of the cult, still paramount in modern Hopi and Zuni society, may have been the key to its development in the upper Little Colorado region, where so much change and aggregation were taking place.

The study of settlement change and reorganization of village layouts in late thirteenth- and fourteenth-century pueblos of the Little Colorado River valley has suggested that, at least for this period, pueblo ritual did not take place just in the kiva; in fact, it may not even have been *centered* there. In effect, ritual required the use of many features and structures around the village, as well as the kiva. By realizing that ritual is adaptive and may have required a changing complex of architectural and nonarchitectural characteristics in and around the village, we provide ourselves a chance to broaden our understanding of the evolution of prehistoric ritual on the Colorado Plateau.

References

Adams, E. Charles
    1987   Spatial Organization in the Hopi Mesas-Hopi Buttes-Middle Little Colorado River Valley, A.D. 1300-1600. Ms. on file, Arizona State Museum Library, Tucson.

    1988   The Appearance, Evolution, and Meaning of the Katsina Cult to the Pre-Hispanic Pueblo World of the Southwestern United States. Ms. on file, Arizona State Museum Library, Tucson.

Adams, E. Charles and Deborah Hull
    1980   The Prehistoric and Historic Occupation of the Hopi Mesas. In *Hopi Kachina: Spirit of Life*, edited by Dorothy K. Washburn, pp. 10-27. California Academy of Sciences, San Francisco.

Ambler, J. Richard and Alan P. Olson
    1977   *Salvage Archaeology in the Cow Springs Area*. Museum of Northern Arizona Technical Series No. 15. Flagstaff.

Bluhm, Elaine A.
    1957   *The Sawmill Site: A Reserve Phase Village, Pine Lawn Valley, Western New Mexico*. Fieldiana: Anthropology, vol. 47, No. 1. Field Museum of Natu-

Boserup, Esther
1965 *The Conditions of Agricultural Growth*. Aldine, Chicago.

Carlson, Roy L.
1970 *White Mountain Redware: A Pottery Tradition of East-Central Arizona and Western New Mexico*. Anthropological Papers No. 19. University of Arizona Press, Tucson.

1982 The Polychrome Complexes. In *Southwestern Ceramics: A Comparative Review*, edited by Albert H. Schroeder, pp. 201-234. The Arizona Archaeologist No. 15. The Arizona Archaeological Society, Phoenix.

Di Peso, Charles C.
1958 *The Reeve Ruin of Southeastern Arizona*. Amerind Foundation Publication No. 8. Dragoon, Arizona.

Drennan, Robert D.
1976 Religion and Social Evolution in Formative Mesoamerica. In *The Early Mesoamerican Village*, edited by Kent V. Flannery, pp. 345-368. Academic Press, New York.

Dutton, Bertha
1963 *Sun Father's Way: The Kiva Murals of Kuaua*. University of New Mexico Press, Albuquerque.

Ferg, Alan
1982 14th Century Kachina Depiction on Ceramics. In *Collected Papers in Honor of John W. Runyon*, edited by Gerald X. Fitzgerald, pp. 13-29. Papers of the Archaeological Society of New Mexico No. 7. Albuquerque.

Gumerman, George J. and Jeffrey S. Dean
1989 Prehistoric Cooperation and Competition in the Western Anasazi Area. In *Dynamics of Southwestern Prehistory*, edited by George J. Gumerman and Linda S. Cordell. Smithsonian Institution Press, Washington, in press.

Gumerman, George J. and S. Alan Skinner
1968 A Synthesis of the Prehistory of the Central Little Colorado Valley, Arizona. *American Antiquity* 33:185-199.

Haury, Emil W.
1958 Evidence at Point of Pines for a Prehistoric Migration from Northern Arizona. In *Migrations in New World Culture History*, edited by Raymond H. Thompson, pp. 1-8. University of Arizona Bulletin No. 29(2), Social Science Bulletin No. 27. Tucson.

Hill, James N.
1970 *Broken K Pueblo: Prehistoric Social Organization in the American Southwest*. Anthropological Papers No. 18. University of Arizona, Tucson.

Johnson, Alfred E.
1965 *The Development of Western Pueblo Culture*. Unpublished Ph.D. dissertation, Department of Anthropology, University of Arizona, Tucson.

Kintigh, Keith
1985 *Settlement, Subsistence, and Society in late Zuni Prehistory*. Anthropological Papers No. 44. University of Arizona, Tucson.

1988 Protohistoric Transitions in the Western Pueblo Area. Ms. on file, Arizona State University, Tempe.

Longacre, William
1964 A Synthesis of Upper Little Colorado Prehistory, Eastern Arizona. In Chapters in the Prehistory of Eastern Arizona II, by P. S. Martin et al., pp. 201-215. *Fieldiana: Anthropology* 55. Chicago.

1970 *Archaeology as Anthropology: A Case Study*. Anthropological Papers No. 17. University of Arizona Press, Tucson.

Martin, Paul S., John B. Rinaldo, and William A. Longacre
1961 Mineral Creek Site and Hooper Ranch Pueblo, Eastern Arizona. *Fieldiana: Anthropology* 52. Chicago.

Martin, Paul S., William A. Longacre, Constance Cronin, Leslie G. Freeman, Jr., and James Schoenwetter
1962 Chapters in the Prehistory of Eastern Arizona I. *Fieldiana: Anthropology* 53. Chicago.

Martin, Paul S., William A. Longacre, Leslie G. Freeman, Jr., James A. Brown, Richard H. Hevly, and Maurice E. Cooley
1964 Chapters in the Prehistory of Eastern Arizona II. *Fieldiana: Anthropology* 55. Chicago.

Martin, Paul S., William A. Longacre, and James N. Hill
1967 Chapters in the Prehistory of Eastern Arizona III. *Fieldiana: Anthropology* 57. Chicago.

Reed, Erik K.
1948 The Western Pueblo Archaeological Complex. *El Palacio* 55(1):9-15.

Schaafsma, Polly and Curtis F. Schaafsma
 1974 Evidence for the Origin of the Pueblo Kachina Cult as Suggested by Southwestern Rock Art. *American Antiquity* 39:535-545.

Smith, Watson
 1952 *Kiva Mural Decorations at Awatovi and Kawaika-a, with a Survey of other Wall Paintings in the Pueblo Southwest*. Papers of the Peabody Museum of American Archaeology and Ethnology, vol. 37. Harvard University, Cambridge.

Speth, John D.
 1988 Do We Need Concepts Like "Mogollon", "Anasazi", and "Hohokam" Today? A Cultural Anthropological Perspective. *The Kiva* 53: 201-204.

12
Kivas?

Stephen H. Lekson

I am the bad guy in this book, because I don't believe in kivas—at least, I doubt that the things we call "kivas" at Pueblo II and Pueblo III sites were very much like the things we call kivas at modern Pueblos (Lekson 1988). I have difficulties with Pueblo II and Pueblo III sites like Pueblo Bonito, Yellow Jacket, and Sand Canyon that had been called ceremonial centers because they had lots of so-called kivas. These places were apparently the Çatal Hüyüks of the Southwest, where every third room's a shrine and every home's a church.

There are simply too many "kivas" at these Pueblo II and Pueblo III sites for them all to be kivas. I've got no problem with Great Kivas, but I did wonder about those hundreds of smaller "clan" kivas. Modern kivas (and the ceremonial organizations they house) integrate the Pueblo, or large chunks of big villages. In Pueblo II and Pueblo III, there is a small "kiva" for every six or seven rooms, and it's hard to understand exactly what was being integrated—an extended family? As Joe Ben Wheat asked at the 1988 Pecos Conference, why did they need all those little kivas at Yellow Jacket? (I don't think Dr. Wheat doubted that they were kivas, but he was slightly alarmed at their numbers.)

Pueblo Bonito, with many more rooms per kiva, is a slightly (but only slightly) different story. I have argued elsewhere (Lekson 1984) that the "kivas" of Pueblo Bonito were associated with a limited number of Prudden unit-like room suites, and that excess rooms (that is, rooms lacking associated "kivas") were nondomestic in function. If they were associated with only a limited number of the many rooms at Pueblo Bonito, then the smaller "kivas" are probably not real kivas either, but rather a round room in the suite of rooms that made up a Chacoan house. (Chaco will be revisited below.)

If Pueblo II and Pueblo III round rooms aren't kivas, then what are they? I suggested that they are a lot like pit houses, which is what kivas were before the meter clicked over from Pueblo I to Pueblo II. Dress up that dingy old pit house with a little stone masonry, remove a few unsightly pits, custom fit a couple of ritual doodads, and *voilà*: a spiffy new Pueblo II kiva/pit house. There's much more to the argument, of course; I refer the interested reader to the original paper (Lekson 1988).

I thought this and I wrote it. Was mine a rash act? It was, and I worried about the how my ideas might be received. In my terrified imagination I saw myself before a grim tribunal of real Southwestern archaeologists, judging my heresy: Guilty, of an unpardonable reformation process. They drag me to the stake, atop a smoldering pile of old site reports. Peering through the smoke, I see a hooded figure holding up a brass-bound copy of Hewett's *Indians of the Rio Grande*, but the smudge of burning paper blacks out the view. . . .

I needn't have worried. My arguments have not been received with wild enthusiasm, but the papers in this symposium and my invited participation prove to me (and I hope, to the reader) that Southwestern archaeologists are a fair-minded and tolerant lot. One or two of the papers here even suggest that I am not entirely alone in my thinking, and other heretics are nailing like-minded theses to other doors (Cater and Chenault 1988). I appreciate the fine spirit of scholarship that provides a soapbox for the loyal opposition by including my comments on these very interesting papers.

If, as I contend, the things that Jesse Fewkes and Edgar Hewett called "kivas" weren't really kivas, then what were they? I say they're pit houses, but I've been wrong before. There are a lot of them out there, and it would be good to know what they might really be. I think the papers in this volume take several long steps towards answering that question.

Adler's cross-cultural approach puts the question into long-needed perspective, removed from the entanglements of Southwestern cultural history and Southwestern humanities. I agree with Adler's assessment: "one major benefit of this approach is that it will allow archaeologists to break out of the present cycle of interpreting kivas based solely upon Southwestern ethnography and archaeological data." Adler makes the problem of kiva origins less a regional, particularistic issue and more a general, anthropological concern; this is a great foundation for future "K" word studies.

Adler's interest in community scale is, to my mind, pivotal. Community size is the point of reference around which our inquiry should turn. Sedentary communities face size thresholds that correspond to (and, I think, cause) the development of various social mechanisms. For example, I have argued from cross-cultural data that a sedentary community cannot exceed about 2,500 people without developing some form of social or political complexity, perhaps to prevent fission (Lekson 1985). Significantly, Rohn notes an upper limit of about 2,500 to 3,000 for both the modern Pueblos and the large Pueblo III towns of the Montezuma Valley (Rohn 1985). Twenty-five hundred may be the upper limit of an egalitarian town; but even egalitarian towns need integrating, and Adler is very productively pursuing the thresholds for various forms of integration that leave particular types of architectural evidence behind.

If types of integrative structures could be calibrated to population thresholds, we may then be able to estimate population size from the number of such structures. Chacoan Great Kivas (which, along with most authors in this volume, I have no difficulty in recognizing as "integrative structures") may correspond to regular increments in population size (Lekson 1984:51). Calibrating population and integrative structures—if that is indeed possible—remains to be done, but Adler makes a start, although this was not the main goal of his study.

Lipe's paper is a fine synthesis of the large body of data on the northern Anasazi. Disregarding, for the moment, problematic Chacoan "outliers," the number of rooms to kivas remains nearly constant from Pueblo I through Pueblo III, ranging from about seven to nine; but in Pueblo IV this ratio jumps to at least 30 (western Pueblo) and 60 (eastern Pueblo). The shift in room/kiva ratio at about A.D. 1300 is very dramatic, and is telling us something about the little round rooms if we care to listen. I will return to this unheard message in my comments on Adams' paper.

The shift seems less dramatic than it might because of the Chacoan sites, with an intermediate room/kiva ratio. Chaco is always fouling things up. The Chacoan anomaly (in both Lipe's and Steward's classic tables) requires a brief digression addressing the function of these sites. I suggested above that large parts of Pueblo Bonito were not residential; that is, the place was not solely a habitation (like a Prudden Unit) or a village (like a big cliff dwelling). What was it, then? We don't really know. Chaco scholars, when pressed, refer to this archaeological phenomenon by the technical term "weirdness." I think that the quality of "Chacoan weirdness"—non-residential but otherwise inexplicable architecture—can be extended to almost all Great Houses.

None of the Great Houses in Chaco were simply (or even mostly) residential structures, although sections of each may have been habitations (Lekson 1984; Windes 1988); I think this is also true of "outliers" (Lekson et al. 1988). The nonresidential character is, in part, what marks the architectural shell as a recognizable "outlier": If it's weird, it probably is one. There is little that is tidy or neat about that argument, but its logical loops reflect the discouraging fact that—even after a century of work—we still don't know what most of these things are, much less what "outliers" represent in regional terms (what does "Chacoan" mean?). But we should realize that room/kiva ratios from these buildings are almost certainly not comparable to room/kiva ratios at other Anasazi residential sites.

Many of the Great House characteristics that contribute to "Chacoan weirdness" continued in some of the larger Pueblo III structures (Flower et al. 1987). Thus the lack of association between rooms and kivas that Lipe notes at Sand Canyon may indeed reflect a nonresidential (even ceremonial) function, but from my point of view, it is the kiva-less rooms that are of interest, not the room-less kivas. If "kivas" are, as I suggest, indicators of habitation, and if they are clustered in one part of a settlement, as at Penasco Blanco or Sand Canyon, that clustering might be telling us more about non-domestic functions of the "kiva"-less part of the settlement than defining a ceremonial precinct of clustered "kivas."

According to Lipe, clusters of kivas at Sand Canyon without associated rooms suggests "some of the kivas may not have been part of standard habitation units used by a few households. In other words, it seems possible that some of these kivas may have been used by groups that did not reside in the immediately adjacent rooms." In Lipe's formulation, the *kivas* are the controlling variable. They are always assumed to be kivas, and variation in the number of associated rooms can only be explained in relation to their kivaness: kivas are kivas, rooms are pueblos, and never the twain shall meet. The converse logical possibility, that variation in numbers of rooms is telling us something *about the function of rooms* is never considered. Why is that so unthinkable? It is not only thinkable, it is demonstrable at Chacoan sites (e.g., Windes 1988).

Lipe (and Plog) objects to my polemic suggestion of a solely or exclusively domestic function for Pueblo II and Pueblo III "kivas." He doubts that "domestic activities in a kiva or protokiva precluded their use for integrative religious or social rituals." Agreed; most societies do not separate church and state, and many do not separate church and house. If Basketmakers had indoor rituals (and we can assume they did, when Junior turned 13 or Grandma's lumbago flared up or the rain didn't fall) they must have done them in the pit house, since that was the only available indoor venue. But does the presence of ritual make a Basketmaker pit structure a ceremonial building? Not in any meaningful sense. A temple, a church, or a modern kiva is a ceremonial structure; a hogan or a split-level ranch house, in which periodic or episodic ritual takes place, is not. I can hang a crucifix on my wall and say my prayers every night, but that doesn't make my house a church.

Varien and Lightfoot offer a careful analysis of pit structures and above-ground rooms at the Pueblo I Duckfoot site. Pit structures at Duckfoot had ample evidence of use as habitations. They also had sipapus and other archaeological flags for ritual, and above-ground rooms did not.

Would most archaeologists recognize a simple "sipapu" in an above-ground room? I do not ask this as a criticism of Varien and Lightfoot, since they obviously thought about it; but I suspect that the simple unlined pit, which we would call a sipapu in a pit structure, might be called something else in above ground rooms or plazas. We wouldn't consider calling a pit a sipapu unless it was in the appropriate sipapu context. This problem does not, of course, affect Wilshusen's very elaborate roofed sipapus. Those would be odd anywhere.

From the evidence at this well-preserved, well-excavated site, Varien and Lightfoot conclude that things in the real world are not as cut-and-dried as we would like them to be. As I read their paper, there is no smoking-gun evidence for either purely ritual or purely habitation use of any pit structure at Duckfoot. This is unfortunate for testing our simple models of pit houses and kivas. But simple models are doomed from the start, since life—alas—is seldom simple. Since I tend to be a bit simple on this subject, I will file this paper away as a corrective, to use if I find myself itching to write something else silly about kivas. R_x: read Duckfoot twice and go to bed.

Wilshusen's, Blinman's, and Hegmon's papers use different tactics, but a very similar strategy that assumes kivas are both real and really early. Wilshusen defines early ritual architecture through a set of unusual features, and then Blinman and Hegmon examine evidence (in this case, ceramics) that may be consistent with that ritual function.

Wilshusen argues that kivas began even earlier than the traditional Pueblo II tee-time by noting the near identity of prayer stick impressions, altars and (especially) sipapus found in Pueblo I pit structures and those found in modern kivas. By his criteria, which are carefully defined and consistently applied, these things are kivas—in fact, the earliest kivas (so far, and discounting Great Kivas). Searching for origins is an overarching concern of archaeology, and follows from the pragmatic operation of the field. Operationally, we stand in the present and study the past; thus, it seems reasonable to pursue origins of present phenomena back into that past. But our operational limits need not proscribe how the past actually worked.

Rather than chase origins back into antiquity, finding "earliests" and "firsts," could we instead assume that early forms will perpetuate or continue, all things being equal, and ask how far *forward* in time can we follow earlier forms and phenomena? Without slipping too far into organic fallacies, can we see the conservatism inherent in evolutionary processes? This is what I have tried to do by making pit houses last into Pueblo III. Please note that Wilshusen's perspective is not inimical to evolutionary conservatism; indeed, he argues for a much *longer* history for Pueblo ceremonial structures than they currently enjoy. But looking for the origins of things will almost unfailingly reveal something that can be interpreted as the original; it is simply a matter of rationalizing elements common to the final phenomenon and its presumed predecessor. Origin-hunting arguments are usually judged as either more or less plausible, and I admit that Wilshusen's argument is certainly plausible.

Blinman accepts Wilshusen's identifications of ritual structures, and then marshals ceramic evidence that may support those identifications. Following earlier studies by Plog, the distribution of red wares is thought to identify ritual *loci*. Since red wares were not locally made, red wares are "the best candidate for assimilation into larger patterns of ritual or political organization." Therefore, higher percentages of red wares should mean higher degrees of ritual intensity. This formula is not easy for me to accept; I need some of the links in the argument spelled out for me in nice, short words.

And is it red wares *per se* that are important? Red wares had to come from somewhere; what did red ware-making people do to mark their kivas for archaeologists? At the site discussed, the total number of red ware sherds is comparable to the total number of white ware sherds. The distribution of the two wares is almost perfectly complementary; that is, in some contexts (such as the designated ritual structures), red wares are high and white wares are low, while at others (the designated nonritual structures), exactly the reverse is the case (Blinman and Wilson 1988). But why are red wares more significant than white wares? Simply because they are found in putatively ritual structures?

I asked Blinman (whose paper was added to this collection after the SAA seminar) about this. He argued that white wares are mostly locally made and include (by definition) *any* polished sherd, with or without decoration; technologically and stylistically, white wares as a group are measurably inferior to red wares (Blinman, personal communication, 1989; "inferior" is my word, not his). Apparently there are reasons, independent of their context, to value red wares analytically above white wares. I am not very familiar with either the red or white wares of this time period, but because of the complementary distribution I do have some problems with this part of Blinman's argument — along with a whole series of recent studies of trade and exchange in Southwestern ceramics that go far beyond the limits of my comments here.

Blinman's second line of analysis looks at vessel forms as an indication of ritual function (in particular, ritual feasting). I applaud this approach; it sidesteps or avoids many of the ambiguities inherent in typological and tradeware analyses, and speaks directly to vessel functions. However, in seeking evidence for ritual, the most commonly accepted ritual form is eliminated from consideration: "some vessel forms (such as effigies) could be argued to have played a role in ceremonialism, but they are too rare ... to allow their use in inter-roomblock comparisons."

Eliminating rare forms, simply because they are rare, only makes sense if you assume that Pueblo I ritual was *not* rare. Blinman (following Wilshusen's arguments) evidently assumes that Pueblo I ritual was wide-spread, nearly omnipresent. And if it's not? If formal ritual were much more limited than Wilshusen's Pueblo I "kivas" would suggest, might this not account for the "lack of distinctly 'ritual' pottery" — not a lack, but a much lower intensity of ritual than Blinman and Wilshusen were expecting? Perhaps the rarity of figurines *is* telling us something.

I asked Blinman about this, too. He replied that the only real evidence for a ritual function of effigies is their rarity (Blinman, personal communication 1989); and I agree that effigies could have had any number of non-ritual functions. They could have been cream jugs or salt shakers. But I cannot help but think the analytical deck is being stacked, if ever so slightly, by *assuming* that ritual is so extensive and so formalized that its archaeological calling card should be sought in abundant, rather than rare, artifact classes. Like red wares, this seems a little bit like selecting evidence that supports, rather than tests, the *a priori* model.

Hegmon also studies the relationship of ceramics and ceremonial structures, but she focuses on white wares. Looking at white wares seems to contradict Blinman's argument that white ware are junk (for this purpose), but on closer reading the two papers do seem to be pulling in the same traces. They both present evidence that might identify Pueblo I ritual.

According to Hegmon, white ware sherds found in ritual structures can be used to measure integrative functions. Yet by far the largest ceremonial structure in the Dolores area (Singing Shelter Great Kiva) contained only four white ware sherds — and, of course, the structures analyzed by Blinman contain relatively few white wares. Odd, but not necessarily fatal. Hegmon makes her case for white wares as an appropriate ritual measure, but to obtain a sufficient sample the sherds must come, not from the putative setting of integrative ritual (the pit structures identified as early kivas), but from entire roomblocks and sites. That might be fatal. Hegmon, of course, realizes that this is a big problem; but acknowledging a problem does not solve it or render it a non-problem.

In setting measures of ceremony in sherds, Hegmon equates formality (which she sees as a necessary quality of integrative ritual) with neatness in ceramic painting. This seems to me to be a tenuous linkage. I've known little kids who are very neat, but not very formal, and not the least bit ritual. I assume that this argument is more fully presented in the study which the paper summarizes.

Despite these quibbles, I follow Hegmon's analyses so far; but I run into real problems with the scale that frames the argument. Most of Hegmon's ideas about ceramic design hinge on the integration of socially distant people. I know that social distance does not equal physical distance, but how "socially distant" could people be in an area as small as the Dolores project? Please do not mistake me: the Dolores archaeological project was not a tiny endeavor: much sweat, heavy toil, many tears, and a great deal of money went into one of the largest projects (along with Black Mesa) in the Anasazi area. But we shouldn't judge prehistoric social scales by modern archaeological budgets. In my opinion, the social scale of the Dolores area, like Black Mesa, is small. Since almost every archaeologist I know would disagree with that perception of the Dolores Project area, Hegmon should not take my criticism too seriously.

But I have trouble envisioning any paralyzing social distances within the little Dolores valley. Everybody probably knew (and had firm opinions about) everyone else; did they need to flash a pot to identify themselves to somebody from across the hill? Perhaps, but I suspect that Hegmon's assumptions about pottery design will work better on the larger scales she is currently addressing.

Plog aims at this larger scale. I agree fully with Plog that regional relationships — such as those marked by ball courts and Chacoan roads — "are important to our understanding of the nature of prehistoric societies throughout the Southwest, even in regions often characterized as marginal or peripheral," adding only that as our knowledge grows, more and more of the "peripheral" appears to be incorporated, on some level, with these core centers. Plog evidently considers Black Mesa a sufficiently large research domain, but I see Black Mesa as the edge of something much larger. I fear that patterns evident at Black Mesa may be no more appropriate for characterizing Anasazi regional systems, writ large, than Montana constitutes a valid sample of the United States. (Would that it did.)

For example, Plog suggests that the earliest villages or village-like settlements in the northern Southwest were Prudden Units or Unit Pueblos; Unit Pueblos, according to the textbooks, are little mini-villages scattered all over the landscape. The traditional view of Pueblo II "dispersion" may describe conditions on Black Mesa, but for most of the Anasazi area, multiple Unit Pueblos are usually found clustered in "communities" (Rohn 1977), many of which also incorporated a Great Kiva and a Great House (Lekson et al. 1988). If this community form was absent in the Kayenta area, this absence is a matter of interest and a possible point-of-entry in understanding Anasazi settlement structure.

Plog's discussion of cemeteries in sedentary village life is very interesting. I know of no formal, village-wide cemeteries until Pueblo IV (discounting household cemeteries in the midden of every Unit Pueblo). As Plog (personal communication 1989) points out, the absence of village-wide cemeteries at Pueblo II "communities" is something to ponder. Perhaps the archeaological clustering we have called "communities" is still something short of a real village—possibly a locus periodically used and reused by a series of Unit Pueblos? Great Kivas and Great Houses could serve to mark territory and maintain use rights at a favored locale between reoccupations. These are simply ideas—ideas arising from the combination of Plog's ideas about cemeteries with our notions about "communities."

None of my observations negate Plog's conclusions for Black Mesa, but simply serve to warn the reader that in my opinion those conclusions may be more relevant to Black Mesa than the larger scale which Plog addresses. However, I've been wrong before.

Plog aims several criticisms at my anti-kiva paper (Lekson 1988). They are fair and productive criticisms, and I welcome the chance to back off from some points and shore up some others.

First, he questions my assertion that Pueblo II–Pueblo III pit structures were purely domestic. *Mea culpa*. I overstated my case and I agree with Plog (and Lipe) that ritual must have taken place in these things. I see this as a failure of my rhetoric, but I think my basic premise escapes more or less unscathed.

Second, Plog notes that I offer no reasons to *assume* that population growth was relatively steady in the Southwest, when I contrasted the surprisingly regular doubling of the numbers of kiva-pit houses every 200 years to the very irregular trajectory of above-ground rooms over the same time span. I suggested that kiva-pit houses "act like population indices while above-ground rooms march to the beat of a very different drummer" (I ask the interested reader to please refer to Lekson 1988 for all the caveats and conditions omitted here). Plog objects: ". . . empirical evidence suggests that not only was steady growth unlikely, but also that irregular rates of growth were typical throughout the northern Southwest."

That is certainly true; the references Plog provides (and many others) are nearly unanimous in concluding that Anasazi population rocketed up and down like a roller-coaster. But almost all of those population estimates were based on *room counts*, and this was precisely the point I was trying to make. Room counts offer one estimate of Anasazi population growth, and it is a very wavy curve. Kiva-pit house counts give you a second estimate, and it is a surprisingly regular, almost linear curve. For reasons touched on above and discussed at more length in the anti-kiva tract (Lekson 1988) I argue that the kiva-pit house index might be the more accurate of the two; Plog prefers the room counts. But Plog (personal communication 1989) and I both agree that the difference in room and kiva-pit house curves is telling us *something* neat, and the race is now on to find out what that something really is.

Finally, Plog argues that 8 to 10 rooms represent a social group needing formal integration and that rooms closest to kivas need not be associated with the proximate kivas. Therefore room-kiva ratios at unit pueblos may not accurately reflect the integrative functions of early kivas. For his first point, that 8 to 10 rooms equal a group large enough to require a formal integrative facility, I can only register doubt and look forward to more cross-cultural or perhaps small group studies. Kivas need not be associated with nearby rooms; but if this were generally true, it would defeat analyses like Hegmon's and (to a lesser extent) Blinman's. But I admit the possibility. There are unit pueblos without kivas and kivas without unit pueblos; and the unit pueblo itself is no cookie-cutter (Gorman and Childs 1981). In preference to seeking elaborate ritual networks that cross-cut unit pueblos, I would suggest first exploring family cycle, functional, or even seasonal causes to explain these variations in Anasazi Pueblo II architecture.

Plog concludes: ". . . if problems exist in our understanding of subterranean structures, those problems will not be corrected by changing our terminology, but by adopting theoretical perspectives that place greater emphasis on ritual behavior and on a more careful examination of contextual information from subterranean structures." I agree with about one-third of that statement: "changing our terminology" may seem minor and cosmetic, but ridding ourselves of the "K" word would be a good idea, because, in my opinion, our current terminology leads to excessive "emphasis on ritual behavior" to the detriment of "careful examination of contextual information"—which, I agree, is what we need. Plog's criticisms of my anti-kiva arguments are certainly valid and focus our thinking on context, and I welcome them.

Adams' paper deals with kivas in the upper Little Colorado from Pueblo II through Pueblo IV. He notes the replacement of Great Kivas by plazas in the late A.D. 1200s. Anyon and LeBlanc (1984) see a very similar shift from Great Kivas to plazas in the Mimbres area, two centuries earlier than Adams' reconstruction for the upper Little Colorado. We may have a neat pair of very interesting parallel cases, with all the possibilities for learning that comparative situations allow—or perhaps both reconstructions were inspired by the same source, Haury's (1950) "Sequence of Great Kivas in the Forestdale Valley." Diffusion, or the psychic unity of mankind?

It is the span from Pueblo III to Pueblo IV, which Adams examines in more depth than any other paper, that interests me strangely. The shift from Pueblo III to Pueblo IV is of enormous significance to the theme of this volume. As Adams (and Lipe) points out, A.D. 1300 is a watershed in Anasazi prehistory. (Adams says 1275, but why quibble over 25 years?) Thirteen hundred (or 1275) marks a spectacular threshold of major dislocation, aggregation, and re-adaptation, when everyone and his dog bailed out of the Four Corners and moved to the Mogollon uplands, to Zuni, to Hopi, and to the Rio Grande. This was change on a scale seldom seen in the Anasazi record: a real, major wrinkle.

As Lipe noted in his analysis of room:kiva ratios, the big change in room:kiva ratios comes between Pueblo III and Pueblo IV. The remarkable increase from seven to nine rooms per "kiva" to 30 to 50 rooms per kiva is telling us something, and what I hear is this: The things we have called kivas in Pueblo I, Pueblo II and Pueblo III are not kivas, but when the Pueblo IV ratios hit the 30s and 50s, "kiva" starts to be a meaningful and useful term.

In many ways, A.D. 1300 marks the real boundary between prehistory and protohistory. Chasing continuities across that gap, from post- to pre-1300, is a dangerous business. That is why looking for kivas, a post-1300 institution, in pre-1300s sites is truly unwise. Lipe looks for integrative structures, and that's dandy, since Adler tells us that almost everybody has integrative structures. But we must allow ourselves to be surprised by how pre–A.D. 1300 integrative structures look and work, and not force these things to be kivas before they are ready. We shouldn't stack the deck by looking for protokivas, or protokivas are all we'll see—and perhaps undervalue Great Kivas, the clearest candidates for integrative structures that I know of in Pueblo II and Pueblo III. We probably need to rethink "Great Kivas," too; but one icon at a time, please.

References

Anyon, Roger and Steven A. LeBlanc
1980 The Architectural Evolution of Mogollon-Mimbres Communal Structures. *The Kiva* 45(3): 253-277.

Blinman, Eric and C. Dean Wilson
1988 Ceramic Data and Interpretations: The McPhee Community Cluster. In *Dolores Archaeological Program: Anasazi Communities at Dolores: McPhee Village*, edited by A. E. Kane and C. K. Robinson, pp. 1295-1341. Bureau of Reclamation, Denver.

Cater, John D. and Mark L. Chenault
1988 Kiva Use Reinterpreted. *Southwestern Lore* 54(3):19-32.

Fowler, Andrew P., John R. Stein, and Roger Anyon
1987 *An Archaeological Reconnaissance of West-Central New Mexico: The Anasazi Monuments Project*. State Historic Preservation Division, Santa Fe.

Gorman, Frederick J. E. and S. Terry Childs
1981 Is Prudden's Unit Type of Anasazi Settlement Valid and Reliable? *North American Archaeologist* 2(3):153-192.

Haury, Emil W.
1950 A Sequence of Great Kivas in the Forestdale Valley, Arizona. In *For The Dean*, edited by Erik K. Reed and Dale S. King, pp. 29-39. Southwest Parks and Monuments Association, Santa Fe.

Lekson, Stephen H.
1984 *Great Pueblo Architecture of Chaco Canyon, New Mexico*. Publications in Archeology 18B. National Park Service, Albuquerque.

1985 Largest Settlement Size and the Interpretation of Socio-Political Complexity at Chaco Canyon, New Mexico. *Haliksa'i* 4: 68-75.

1988 The Idea of the Kiva in Anasazi Archaeology. *The Kiva* 53(3):213-234.

Lekson, Stephen H., Thomas C. Windes, John R. Stein, and W. James Judge
    1988   The Chaco Canyon Community. *Scientific American* 259(1): 100-109.

Rohn, Arthur H.
    1977   *Cultural Change and Continuity on Chapin Mesa.* Regents Press of Kansas, Lawrence.

    1985   Prehistoric Developments in the Mesa Verde Region. In *Understanding the Anasazi of Mesa Verde and Hovenweep*, edited by David Grant Noble, pp. 3-10. School of American Research, Santa Fe.

Windes, Thomas C.
    1987   *Investigations at the Pueblo Alto Complex, Chaco Canyon.* Publications in Archeology 18F. National Park Service, Santa Fe.

13
Comment on Social Integration and Anasazi Architecture

T. J. Ferguson

Introduction

Our knowledge that ritual behavior plays an important role in the integration of ethnographically known societies presents a scientific challenge to find the material correlates of similar social processes in the archaeological record. The eight substantive papers in this volume seek to find those correlates in the architecture used for ritual activities. Individually, each of the papers advances Southwestern archaeology by addressing problems of identification, measurement, or explanation of ritual behavior and social integration. As a collection, the papers raise important issues about how archaeologists conceptualize social groups and the evolution of prehistoric social structure in the Southwest.

In my comment I examine the integrative role kivas play in Pueblo social structure and how archaeologists think this social structure has changed through time. I begin with Kroeber's ethnographic investigation of how kivas functioned to integrate Zuni society in 1916, since I think this is pertinent to the intellectual history of how archaeologists have conceptualized Puebloan social organization.

The Integrative Role of Zuni Kivas

In his classic study of Zuni kin and clan, Kroeber (1917:47-50) found that the foundation of Zuni society was the family. An individual's first and most important social ties were to kin and household groups, and these were the fundamental groups that ramified Zuni society. The kin and household groups were integrated into a tightly knit community of 1600 people through the social ties of their members to an intricate system of other social groups. These other social groups included 16 clans, 6 kivas, 12 medicine societies or fraternities, and 17 priesthoods (Ladd 1979:485-487). As Kroeber (1917:183) noted,

> Four or five different planes of systematization cross cut each other and thus preserve for the whole society an integrity that would be speedily lost if the planes merged and thereby inclined to encourage segregation and fission. The clans, the fraternities, the priesthoods, the kivas, in a measure the gaming parties, are all dividing agencies. If they coincided, the rifts in the social structure would be deep; by countering each other, they cause segmentations which produce an almost marvelous complexity, but can never break the national entity apart.

Kroeber's investigation showed that Zuni kivas integrated society through the process of dividing that society along non-residential lines. Macrosocial integration was achieved through structural differentiation. Kroeber schematically modeled Zuni social structure as a field of kinship cross-cut by other social groups, as depicted in Figure 1. It is significant that kivas provided only one of the social groups that integrated Zuni society.

Kroeber opposed the actual scheme of Zuni social structure with an alternative type of social organization that he thought was often ascribed to Pueblo Indians or implicitly assumed for them. In this hypothetical Puebloan social structure there was a spatial congruence between residential and other social groups, as depicted in Figure 2. As Kroeber (1917:184-186) noted, this social structure predicated that a group of kinsmen from locality "A" constitute clan "A" of their tribe, as well as compose the membership of secret society "A", of priesthood "A", and of kiva "A". The same situation holds for kin "B" and so forth, such that the social structure comprises parallel and coinciding units.

Kroeber found that the actual structure of Zuni society differed greatly from the hypothetical social struc-

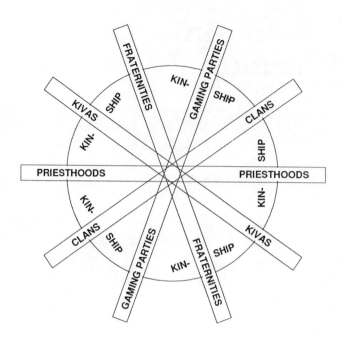

Figure 1: Kroeber's schematic model of Zuni social structure. Adapted from Kroeber (1917:185).

KIN A	LOCAL GROUP A	CLAN A	SOCIETY A	KIVA A	PRIESTHOOD A

KIN B	LOCAL GROUP B	CLAN B	SOCIETY B	KIVA B	PRIESTHOOD B

KIN C	LOCAL GROUP C	CLAN C	SOCIETY C	KIVA C	PRIESTHOOD C

KIN D	LOCAL GROUP D	CLAN D	SOCIETY D	KIVA D	PRIESTHOOD D

Figure 2: Kroeber's hypothetical scheme of Puebloan social structure. Adapted from Kroeber (1917:185).

ture. He found no evidence that members of a clan came from a separate locality. Every clan comprised a number of different kin and residential groups, and each furnished members to different fraternities, priesthoods, and kivas. Thus, as Kroeber (1917:186) describes,

> ... a given individual of clan A may be of kin group b, father's clan C, fraternity D, priesthood E, and kiva F; his next clan mate that we encounter, will perhaps be of blood group d, father's clan E, fraternity F, priesthood A, kiva B. By the time the tribe has been gone through, every clan, society, priesthood, and kiva is thus likely to be connected, in the person of one or several individuals, with every other, and each with each in about equal degree; but— and this is the significant point—the connections are almost wholly through individuals as individuals, and with reference to the national organization as a solitary scheme. Connection between group and group as such is always faint; often lacking; the plan of the fabric throughout seems calculated to avoid it.

Kroeber (1917:188) recognized that the size of Zuni Pueblo and its reduction in the historic period to a single, permanently occupied village may have caused Zuni social structure to be more intricate than that of other pueblos. Nonetheless, he thought that the main features of Zuni society also occurred in other Pueblos, as well as among other tribes in the Southwest. Kroeber concluded that, however different the elements of various Southwestern societies, the interrelations of those elements must be in some measure analogous to the interrelations he found in the elements of Zuni society.

Puebloan Social Structure and Room : Kiva Ratios

Kroeber's "hypothetical" scheme of Puebloan social structure represented the conventional view of kiva organization in early twentieth century anthropology. This conceptualization of social structure is implicit in the interpretation of "Prudden Units" as co-residential households with an associated kiva, and thus underlies the conventional interpretation of the changes in room: kiva ratios found by Steward (1937) and Lipe (Chapter 5). Whereas Kroeber discarded the "hypothetical" model of kiva organization and social structure, archaeologists have projected it into the past by incorporating it in an evolutionary model of social organization.

In the archaeological interpretation, kivas prior to A.D. 1300 are thought to have integrated a small group of co-residential households, resulting in a low room : kiva ratio. After A.D. 1300, with the aggregation and nucleation of settlement into large, plaza-oriented pueblos, a smaller number of kivas are thought to have functioned as sodalities to integrate larger scale groups, yielding a higher room : kiva ratio. The change in room : kiva ratios thus seems to represent a change through time in both the size and composition of the ritual groups thought to have integrated society.

Room : kiva ratios thus seem to signal a change from the hypothetical social structure characterized by Kroeber as having parallel and spatially coinciding social units to the more differentiated social structure actually found by Kroeber at Zuni. There are several problems with this interpretation, however, that suggest it is too simple an explanation for the variability we find in the archaeological record.

Several people in this volume persuasively argue that some kivas served larger groups of people than co-residential households. Various terms are used to describe two basic types of kivas, e.g., low and high level integrative structures (Adler, Chapter 4), corporate and community kivas (Wilshusen, Chapter 7), kivas and Great Kivas (Adams, Chapter 11). The basic idea is that some kivas integrated discrete, co-residential units, while other kivas integrated larger communities or regions. As Plog (Chapter 10) points out, the Prudden Unit pueblos of the pre–A.D. 1300 period had to have been organized at a regional level for purposes of maintaining marriage and exchange networks, and some kivas probably served to integrate social networks at this regional scale.

If all kivas are not equal, however, then the meaning of room:kiva ratios is not as straightforward as it seems, because the terms are not the same on each side of the comparative equation. Before A.D. 1300 we either have a substantially different kind of kiva or more kinds of kivas than we do after A.D. 1300. To call the earlier organizations or the buildings they use "kivas" when their organization is fundamentally different obscures the very thing we are trying to study.

As the papers in this volume demonstrate, the identification of exactly which buildings were used by kivas prior to A.D. 1300 is problematical. At one time many archaeologists assumed that all Anasazi pit structures that were associated with surface roomblocks were kiva buildings. Yet Varien and Lightfoot (Chapter 6) and Wilshusen (Chapter 7) clearly show that some were used for domestic activities, some were used for ritual activities, and some pit structures were used for both domestic and ritual activities. Since all pit structures are not "kivas," conventional room:kiva ratios are less meaningful. A fundamental archaeological problem is the methodological reduction of kivas as social groups to kivas as buildings. We make an equation between contemporary kivas and the buildings they use, then through analogy we equate prehistoric buildings with similar organizations. The fact that prehistoric kiva buildings are not isomorphic with historic kiva buildings interjects considerable confusion into the argument, as does the fact that kiva groups use plazas and other areas in addition to their kiva buildings (Adams, Chapter 10). Ultimately the interpretation of room : kiva ratios rests on weak morphological arguments, or on controversial functional classifications.

Theoretical Considerations

As Kroeber (1917:187) pointed out, the social structure hypothesized prior to A.D. 1300 would segregate rather than integrate social groups, and work to break communities apart. Since each of the basic social units performed all the functions of all the other basic social units, there would have been little cohesion forming a community. The integration of society had to have functioned through some other mechanism than the intense social interaction and differentiation that characterized historic Zuni society.

One alternative mechanism for social integration is the structural repetition of basic social elements. With this mechanism, the common structure shared by all interacting groups provides the basis for social solidarity. The strong "unit pueblo" settlement pattern reported for the period prior to A.D. 1300 is seemingly related to this type of social integration. If this is the case, however, it is the whole architectural complex that is integrative, not just the buildings identified as kivas.

The idea that there are two basic types of social integration, one based on structural repetition and the other on structural differentiation, derives from the work of Durkheim (1933[1893]). Durkheim, of course, did not think these two forms of social integration were mutually exclusive. Although Durkheim thought there was evidence of evolution in social structure towards the development of increased social differentiation, he recognized that both forms of social integration co-occur in all societies. Southwestern archaeologists, in contrast, have developed a theory that treats the two types of integration as sequential and separate developments.

Like many archaeologists today, Durkheim thought that evolution of social structure was related to changes in the size and density of population. Adler's cross-cultural research building on Johnson's scalar stress theory is relevant here, as it shows that in small communities (less than 175 people) it is to be expected that structures are used for both domestic and ritual activities. Larger communities often have structures dedicated to religious use, and these structures often have restricted access. I think the functional specialization and restriction of access in space used for religious activities is related to the structural differentiation of social groups.

Archaeology and Integrative Architecture

Durkheim's theory of social structure has a strong spatial component in that social integration based on structural repetition requires a segregated and dispersed space, while social integration based on differentiation requires an integrated and dense space (Hillier and Hanson 1984). While the theoretical linkage between the structure of architecture and the structure of society is clear, we still need to build a methodology that can generate inferences about social structure from the types of architectural space that are found in the archaeological record.

As the papers in this volume demonstrate, many Southwestern archaeologists are still seeking to understand the archaeological record in ethnographic terms, i.e., through the concept of the kiva. In the methodological reduction of the kiva as a social group to the kiva as a building, however, architecture is analytically reduced to a container of other things that are thought to have actually integrated society, e.g., ritual activities or symbolic meaning. Analyses of artifacts associated with buildings identified as kivas show that these assemblages are often significantly different from those associated with other buildings in a settlement. While this approach produces interesting and useful results, such as the papers by Blinman, Hegmon, and Plog in this volume, it does not deal with the intrinsic nature of architecture as a social artifact.

An important clue to understanding the social dimensions of architecture is provided by Lipe when he recognizes that "spatial propinquity counts for something in social interaction." Architects building theory that departs from this premise conceptualize social relations as restrictions on random encounter patterns (Hillier and Hanson 1984). Since architecture also restricts encounter patterns, these architects are seeking a direct and measurable link between architectural and social structures.

Walls and doors (or roof entryways) function to control access within buildings, while open areas, streets, and plazas structure the movement of people into and through the settlement as a whole. Architecture establishes patterns of spatial relationships composed of boundaries that restrict access. These boundaries are embedded in an open space structure that permits various kinds of permeability. By structuring the ways that people encounter one another within a settlement, architecture also directly structures social interaction by creating and maintaining communication networks. Architecture can and does have other meanings, but it is the communication network created by architecture that provides its most immediate sociological referent (Ankerl 1981).

Architectural theory that explains how buildings structure social interaction by controlling encounters is closely related to the theory that Plog develops in this volume that explains the development of social structure in terms of increasingly restricted social networks. Placed in an evolutionary perspective, the development of restrictive networks co-occurs with the development of agricultural economies and sedentary village settlement. As Plog points out, the process of restricting social networks works towards the development of a land use system that has a well-defined core where families have use rights to individual parcels of land, surrounded by a larger peripheral area where use rights are held by the community in common. I think this social process explains much of the settlement change that occurred in the late prehistoric period, when there was a shift to the occupation of a smaller number of much larger settlements than in earlier periods, each surrounded by large tracts of open space used for resource procurement.

Conclusion

I think that the current focus on kivas as the mechanism that integrated Anasazi society is too narrow a theoretical concept to explain the relationship between architecture and social integration. To fully investigate how architecture integrates society, we need to analyze both buildings and their open space structure, as Adams does in this volume when he examines the development of the kiva-plaza complex of the prehistoric and historic Western Pueblos. At the same time, we need to pay attention to how the elemental groups of society are spatially segregated, as well as to the spatial and social mechanisms that integrated these groups.

The papers in this volume provide important elements of the method and theory we need to construct a unified theory capable of explaining the underlying structural links between architecture and society. They also serve to point out additional elements that we still need to develop. In so doing, the volume serves to stimulate the additional research that is needed if we are to fully explain how architecture served to integrate Anasazi society.

References

Ankerl, Guy
    1981   *Experimental Sociology of Architecture, A Guide to Theory, Research, and Literature.* Mouton Publishers, The Hague.

Durkheim, Emile
    1933   *The Division of Labor in Society,* translated by George Simpson. The Free Press, New York. Originally published 1893 as *De la Division du Travail Social: Etude sur l'organisation des Societes Superieures.* Paris: Alcan.

Hillier, Bill and Julienne Hanson
    1984   *The Social Logic of Space.* Cambridge University Press, London.

Kroeber, Alfred
    1917   *Zuni Kin and Clan.* Anthropological Papers of the American Museum of Natural History, vol 18, Part II, pp. 41-204. New York.

Ladd, Edmund J.
    1979   Zuni Social and Political Organization. In *Southwest,* edited by A. Ortiz, pp 482-491. Handbook of North American Indians, vol. 9, W. C. Sturtevant, general editor. Smithsonian Institution, Washington, D.C.

Steward, Julian
    1937   Ecological Aspects of Southwestern Society. *Anthropos* 32:87-104.

List of Contributors

E. Charles Adams (Ph.D., University of Colorado, 1975) is an Associate Curator of Archaeology and the Director of the Homolovi Archaeological Research Project at the Arizona State Museum. Address: Arizona State Museum, University of Arizona, Tucson, Arizona 85721.

Michael A. Adler is a Ph.D. candidate in anthropology at the University of Michigan, and a Research Affiliate of the Crow Canyon Archaeological Center. Address: Museum of Anthropology, Ruthven Museums Building, University of Michigan, Ann Arbor, Michigan 48109.

Eric Blinman (Ph.D., Washington State University, 1988) is Laboratory Supervisor in the Research Section of the Museum of New Mexico. Address: Research Section, Laboratory of Anthropology, Museum of New Mexico, P.O. Box 2087, Santa Fe, New Mexico 87504.

T. J. Ferguson (MCRP, University of New Mexico, 1986) is a Ph.D. candidate in anthropology at the University of New Mexico and the Director of the Southwest Program of the Institute of the NorthAmerican West. Address: 6246 Willow Loop, Flagstaff, Arizona 86004.

Michelle Hegmon is a Ph.D. candidate in anthropology at the University of Michigan, and a Research Affiliate of the Crow Canyon Archaeological Center. Address: Museum of Anthropology, Ruthven Museums Building, University of Michigan, Ann Arbor, Michigan 48109.

Stephen H. Lekson (Ph.D., University of New Mexico, 1988) is a Research Associate at the Arizona State Museum. Address: Arizona State Museum, University of Arizona, Tucson, Arizona 85721.

Ricky R. Lightfoot is a Research Archaeologist at the Crow Canyon Archaeological Center and a Ph.D. candidate in anthropology at Washington State University. Address: Crow Canyon Archaeological Center, 23390 County Road K, Cortez, Colorado 81321.

William D. Lipe (Ph.D., Yale University, 1966) is a Professor of Anthropology at Washington State University and the Director of Research at the Crow Canyon Archaeological Center. Address: Department of Anthropology, Washington State University, Pullman, Washington 99164-4910.

Stephen Plog (Ph.D., University of Michigan, 1977) is an Associate Professor of Anthropology at the University of Virginia. Address: Department of Anthropology, University of Virginia, Charlottesville, Virginia 22903.

Mark D. Varien (M.A., University of Texas at Austin, 1984) is a Research Archaeologist at the Crow Canyon Archaeological Center. Address: Crow Canyon Archaeological Center, 23390 County Road K, Cortez, Colorado 81321.

Richard H. Wilshusen is a Ph.D. candidate in anthropology at the University of Colorado and a Research Affiliate of the Crow Canyon Archaeological Center. Address: Department of Anthropology, Campus Box 233, University of Colorado, Boulder, Colorado 80309.